STAFFORDSHIRE PARISH REGISTERS S(

President

Col. I.S. Swinnerton

Chairman

Dr. P.D. Bloore

Hon. Secretary

Mr. I. Wallbank,
82 Hillport Avenue,
Newcastle-under-Lyme,
Staffs.,
ST5 8QT

The Society has pleasure in placing in the hands of members a further volume of printed Staffordshire Parish Registers consisting of the registers of the parish of Tipton.

Enquiries concerning copies of registers already printed and still available for sale should be addressed to the Hon. Secretary.

ISBN: 978-0-9565117-5-1

British Library Cataloguing in Publication Data
A catalogue record for this book is available from the British Library

Acknowledgements

Part 1 of the Parish Registers of Tipton covering the period 1573 to 1736 was published by the Society in 1923. Although the later registers to 1812 were transcribed some eighty years ago, it was not until 2011 that the Society published Part 2 covering the Baptisms and Burials from 1736 to 1770 and Marriages from 1736 to 1812. This, Part 3, primarily covers the registers containing Baptisms and Burials from 1770 to 1812. However, included in this Register are many of the Marriages performed at the Church during that period.

The basic transcription of the Registers contained herein was again made by Mr. & Mrs Brown of Tipton for the Staffordshire Parish Registers Society but has remained in manuscript format from the 1940's in the William Salt Library until the current publication. The original transcription has been checked by Dr. Peter D. Bloore against the original registers but has not been checked against the Bishop's Transcripts.

The Society would express it's thanks to:
- The Rev. J. Dunn, Vicar of St. Martins and St. Paul, Tipton, for permission to publish this current volume
- The William Salt Library for the custodianship of the original manuscript transcription.

Please note that in certain places the original registers used for this publication are faded and whilst every effort has been made to produce as accurate as possible publication, complete accuracy can not be guaranteed. Notes within square brackets thus: [....] indicate illegible entries, variations in entries or comments made by the transcribers.

TIPTON PARISH

The original name for the parish was Tibbington and as will be seen in this transcription, the parish is often described as the "Parish of Tipton alias Tibberton". The ancient parish church was dedicated to St. Martin. The original settlement was around the site of the village church but by the time of the start of these registers the development had moved to some distance from the church.

When Thomas Shaw took over as Minister, the church was in a very poor condition. In 1762 he wrote to John Wyrley, Esq., the Lord of the Manor, seeking his assistance. He describes: *"the Parish Church of Tipton is in so old and ruinous state as no longer to be a decent, or even safe place of Divine Worship. Not only the Roof is decayed, admitting the rain and the Snow, but the walls also are so cracked and bulged, as to require taking down and re-building. In this unhappy situation, having no proper place of Divine Worship and utterly unable to assist themselves, being entirely Tenants at rack-rents and Carriers of Coal, or Nailors, or Colliers, they most humbly and earnestly entreat the generous consideration of the Friends to Virtue and Religion....."*. Despite an appeal, insufficient funds were raised at that time to enable any rebuilding.

In November 1793 the ever worsening state of the old church led to a further attempt to repair or rebuild. This time it was successful and the original church ceased to serve its original function around 1797 when a new replacement church was built and opened in Lower Church Lane nearer to the centre of population. The new Church retained the name of St. Martin's.

The population in the Parish of Tipton increased dramatically during this period in the early 19th Century. Whilst the population of the parish in 1801 was 4,288, by 1831 it was 14,951, and by 1851 had increased to 24,858. Thus, after lying derelict for a number of years, the body of the old church was rebuilt to meet the growing needs of the population. It was dedicated on the 25th April 1854 and became the centre of the new Ecclesiastical Parish of St. John's with its own set of Parish Registers.

TIPTON PARISH REGISTERS

In 1923, the Staffordshire Parish Registers Society published the early registers of St. Martin's, Tipton, from 1573 to 1736. There had been speculation that the Tipton Parish Registers had commenced in 1513 which, if indeed fact, would have made them the earliest Parish registers in the country. The date 1513 is argued very forcibly by John Parkes in "A History of Tipton, Staffordshire" published in 1915. However, it has been subsequently concluded that the start date was 1573.

This Part 3 of the Parish Registers of Tipton includes the Register for Baptisms and Burials from 1770 to 1812. However, it would appear that in general, the names of the parties who married in the Church were also noted in this Register despite the full details being entered into the separate Marriage Register. These marriage entries are not complete and the practice appears in general to have stopped around 1783. A number of marriages are then included from 1795 to 1797 but inserted at the time of providing the triennial transcript for the Bishop in 1798 is the note: *"List of Marriages not registered from this time here them being Kept in a separate book used only for that purpose."* However, some later incumbent obviously didn't agree with this and that comment is crossed out and it is obvious from the fact that the entries are squeezed in, that someone went back through the register and entered the marriages

REFERENCES

1. "Old St. Martin's Church (now St. John's) Tipton A Short History" by J.S. Allen, (1971)
2. "History of Tipton" By F.W. Hackwood (1891) reprinted 2001 ISBN 1 85858 195 8
3. "Parkes's History of Tipton", (1915)

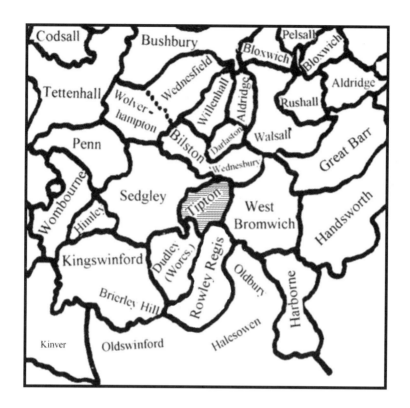

Tipton
and the Parishes of South Staffordshire

1770

Apr 3	William MILLS	bur
Apr 3	Samuel MALLIN	bur
Apr 3	Sarah ELWELL	bur
— Apr 8	Hannah, d of Thos & M Sarah RUDGE of Sedgley Parish	bap
Apr 8	John TUBBS took to wife to Mary JONES by Banns	mar
Apr 15	Abraham, s of Joseph & Ann GEORGE	bap
← Apr 15	Samuel, s of John & Elisabeth INGRAM	bap
Apr 15	Ellner, d of John & Phebe RABEL	bap
Apr 15	Sarah, d of Daniel & Sarah WHITEHOUSE	bap
⤳ Apr 18	Hannah, wife of Joseph PARKES	bur
Apr 22	John, s of Richard & Mary JEWKES	bap
Apr 29	Samuel DARBY took to wife to Hannah WINCHURCH by Lycence	mar
Apr 29	Ann, d of William & Ann SHELDON	bap
Apr 29	Isbell, a base begot Child of Elisabeth WHITEHOUSE	bap
May 6	Isbell, d of Charles & Sarah LORD, born April 9	bap
⁓ May 9	Thomas PARKES	bur
✝ May 13	Mary, d of James & Elisabeth HILL	bap
May 20	John WHITEHOUSE took to wife to Jane DARBY by Banns	mar
May 27	Willm RICHARDS & Hannah WEATLEY	mar
May 27	Joseph HIPKISS took to wife to Hannah LAWD by Banns	mar
Jun 3	Jane, wife of Daniel ELWELL	bur
Jun 3	Jno, s of Joseph & Mary WHITEHOUSE	bap
⤳ Jun 3	Han^h, d of John[crossed out] Jno & Han^h WILLDEY	bap
Jun 3	Mary, d of James & Elisabeth WILLIAMS	bap
Jun 3	Sobey, d of Thos & Mary WHEALE	bap
Jun 10	A Child of Jane FISHER, Widow	bur
Jun 13	Jno, a Child of Jo: & Mary WHITEHOUSE (soaker)	bur
Jun 3[sic]	Mary, d of James & Eliz: WILLIAMS	bap
Jun 13	Jinney, d of James & Jane TRUMAN	bap
Jun 15	Jno:, s of Saml & Mary WHITEHOUSE (Moses)	bur
Jun 17	Jno, s of Eutychus & Eliz: FISHER	bap
Jun 20	Mary, d of Jos: & Mary GREYER	bur
Jun 20	Abra:, s of Benjamin & Mary WHESTON	bap
Jun 24	Phebe, d of Daniel & Mary MILLS, Born May 29	bap
Jun 24	Saml, s of Jo^s & Mary BIRD, Bap: Sutton Colefield	bap
Jul 1	James WHITEHOUSE (Parrott)	bur
Jul 3	Phebe, d of Danl & Mary MILLS	bap
✝ Jul 8	Mary, d of Thomas & Phebe COOK	bap
Jul 15	John WILLIAMS	bur
Jul 15	James, s of William & Rachel WHITEHOUSE	bap
⤳ Jul 15	George, s of John & Phebe HORTON	bap
Jul 17	Elisabeth WHITEHOUSE	bur
Jul 29	Elisabeth, d of William & Elisabeth FEREDAY	bap
+ Jul 29	Samuel, s of Isaac & Sarah GUTTRIDGE, born 20 Day of May 1770	bap

1770

Jul 30   William SMITH took to wife to Elisabeth TALBOTT by Banns   mar
Aug 4   John BLACKHAM took to wife to Shusanna BISSELL by Banns mar
        [*The next entry has been squeezed in*]
† Aug 5   Ann, d of Joseph & Phebe STANLEY   bap
Aug 12   William, s of Joseph & Mary WHESSON   bap
Aug 13   Isaac MOSLEY   bur
Aug 21   Elisabeth, wife of John WHITEHOUSE   bur
Aug 21   William, s of William & Sarah GRISE   bap
Aug 21   Thomas, s of Edward & Phebe BATE   bap
Aug 26   Sarah, d of W^m & Hannah HIPKISS   bap
Sep 8   Henry, s of W^m & Hannah SMITH   bur
~ Sep 9   Joseph, s of Joseph & Jane PEASOLL[?]   bap
Sep 16   Edward DUDLEY took to wife to Elizabeth DANKS by Banns   mar
Sep 16   Jeremiah, s of Jeremiah & Mary HARRISS   bap
~ Sep 16   Hannah, d of Joseph & Phebe STANLEY   bap
Sep 16   Hannah, d of Thomas Mallin ELLWELL & [blank] his wife   bap
Sep 23   John, s of William & Phebe ROUND   bap
Sep 23   Rich^d, s of Rich^d & Ann NIGHTINGALE   bap
† Sep 25   Joseph, s of Joseph & Jane PEARSELL   bur
~ Sep 30   Benjamin PARTRIDGE took to wife to Hannah PERSEHOUSE,
        by Lycence   mar
Oct 7   Daniel, s of Daniel & Sarah WARR   bap
Oct 5 [sic] James RICHARDS & Ann WHITEHOUSE by Banns   mar
Oct 8   A Child of William LAWD   bur
Oct 8   John, s of John & Jane WHITEHOUSE   bap
⅃ Oct 8   Tabatha, d of Richard & Sarah TIMMINS   bap
Oct 11   Sarah, wife of Ambrass BLACKHAM   bur
Oct 11   Richard, a base begot Child of Hannah CARTWRIGHT or MASII,
        NICOLDS   bap
Oct 11   Edwd, s of James & Ann WHITEHOUSE   bap
~ Oct 24   Zaccariah PARKES took to wife to Ann WHEATLEY by Banns   mar
Nov 3   Ann, a base begot Child of Hannah CALLOW'S   bap
Nov 11   Joseph HORTON took to wife to Mary PANE by Banns   mar
Nov 25   Mary, d of John & Constant SHELDON   bap
† Nov 25   James, s of John & Elizabeth HILL, of Sedgley Parish   bap
⅃ Nov 25   Aaron, s of Moses & Elizabeth HILL, of Sedgley Parish   bap
~ Nov 25   Hannah NICKOLDS, d of Zekel & Shusannah TURNER of
        Sedgley   bap
Nov 25   Lydia, d of John & Elizabeth CALLOW   bap
Nov 27   Samuel FIELD from Toll End   bur
Dec 3   Jane, wife of Peter FISHER   bur
Dec 3   George, s of Abraham & Sarah FISHER   bap
Dec 3   Elisabeth SMITH, a base begot Child of Elisabeth YARDLEY   bap
Dec 9   Joseph, s of Richard & Elizabeth WHITEHOUSE   bap
~ Dec 9   Joshua, s of Joshua & Elizabeth PARTRIDGE   bap
Dec 11   Samuel Hargrove TAYLOR, from Tipton Green   bur
Dec 11   Edward, s of Richard & Elizabeth GRIFFITH   bap
Dec 11   Sarah, d of Joseph & Elizabeth GRIFFITH   bap
Dec 13   Edwd, s of Joseph & Ann NICKOLDS   bap

1770

Dec 13	Sarah, d of John & Joice PARKES	bur
ꞌ Dec 16	Joseph WRIGHT took to wife to Hannah HIDE by Banns	mar
Dec 21	Hannah, wife of William HATTWOOD	bur
Dec 31	James, s of Isaac & Rebekah ASTON	bap
Dec 31	William WHEAL took to wife to Ann ROWLASON of Dudley by Banns	mar

1771

Jan 4	William WHITEHOUSE took to wife to Mary SMITH by Banns	mar
Jan 5	Joseph BLACKHAM took to wife to Sarah BISSEL by Banns	mar
Jan 6	Catharine, d of Abraham & Catharine SHELDON	bap
Jan 13	Edwd SMITH	bur
Jan 16	Nancy, a base begot Child of Hannah HOWEN, of Tipton Green	bap
Jan 16	Elizabeth, d of James & Elisabeth FISHER, of Tipton Green	bap
Jan 16	Elisabeth, d of Joseph NICKLIN, Tipton Green	bur
Jan 20	James, s of James & Sarah WHITEHOUSE	bap
Jan 27	Mary, d of George & Hannah WHITEHOUSE	bap
Jan 27	Elizabeth, d of Joseph & Mary PASKIN	bap
Jan 27	Edwd STOCKWIN took to wife to Mary BIRD by Banns	mar
– Jan 29	A Child of Benjamin HUNTS, from Prise Thos Forge	bur
ꞇ Feb 7	John PERESHOUSE took to wife to Sarah SUTTON by Lycence	mar
Feb 10	Yalse, d of James & Sarah FEREDAY, of Sedgley P.	bap
Feb 17	Mary, d of Daniel & Sarah WARR	bur
Feb 17	Isaac, s of Abraham & Sarah WALTERS, of Sedgley	bap
⁻ Feb 19	William SMITH took to wife to Elizabeth HALL of West Bromwich	mar
ꝉ Feb 24	John, s of William & Susannah HORTON, Born 27th Jan 1771	bap
– Feb 24	Sarah, d of James & Ann FELOWS	bap
ꞇ Feb 24	Mary, d of Jo^s & Sarah WALTON	bap
Mar 3	Abel, s of Abraham & Sarah MALLIN from Coasly	bap
Mar 3	Abraham DUDLEY took to wife to Hannah SMITH by Banns	mar
Mar 6	Thomas WOODHOUSE took to wife to Susanna FULLWOOD by Banns	mar
Mar 10	Sarah, d of William & Elisabeth SMITH	bap
Mar 10	Sarah, d of John & Ann FLETCHER, Princes End	bap
ꝉ Mar 10	Benjamin FISHER took to wife to Joice GUTTRIDGE by Banns	mar
Mar 14	Thomas, s of James & Ann RICHARDS	bap
Mar 14	Bettey, d of Jo^s & Elisabeth SMITH	bap
Mar 12[sic]	Nancy, d of Daniel & Sarah GRIFFITH	bap
Mar 14	Mr Muskhamp JEVON	bur
Mar 17	Mary, d of Thomas & Mary BADGER	bap
Mar 17	Henry, s of William & Hannah SMITH	bap
Mar 19	Richard WHITEHOUSE from Tipton Green	bur
ꝉ Mar 19	Mary GUTTRIDGE	bur
Mar 19	Isaac, s of Jo^s & Mary BATE, born Jan 24	bap
Mar 19	Judeth, d of Jo^s & Mary DUDLEY, born Feb 17 1766	bap
Mar 19	Stephen, s of George & Ann WHITEHOUSE	bap
Mar 21	Sarah, d of John & Ann DREW	bap

1771

Mar 21	Mary, wife of Thos HODGYETS	bur
Mar 24	Elizabeth, d of W^m & Mary NAILER	bap
Mar 24	William, s of Thomas & Sarah SATCHILL	bap
Mar 31	Daniel, s of Benjamin & Hannah JEVON	bap
Mar 31	Abraham, s of Joseph & Martha HICKMANS	bap
Mar 31	Nancy, d of Samuel & Hannah PASKIN	bap
Mar 31	Phebe, d of Willm & Sarah PITEWAY	bap
Apr 4	James DARBY took to wife to Margaret WOOLEY by Banns	mar
Apr 7	Moses, a base begot Child of Rachel WHITEHOUSE, Twit	bap
Apr 9	A Child of Thomas SCRIBENS	bur
Apr 14	Joseph, s of Daniel & Sarah FISHER	bap
Apr 15	Edward WACKLAM	bur
Apr 17	Sarah WARREN	bur
Apr 26	A daughter of Thomas FISHER from Hust Lane	bur
Apr 28	William, s of William & Hannah RICHARDS	bap
Apr 28	William, s of John & Mary TATE	bap
May 5	Joseph FISHER took to wife to Eleanor DARBY by Banns	mar
May 5	John, s of James & Mary NOCK	bap
May 5	James, s of Thomas & Sarah PARTRIDGE	bap
May 5	Sarah, d of Joseph & Sarah GREYER	bap
May 12	Ann, d of John & Shusanna BLACKHAM was born March 20	bap
May 12	M^r. John JEVON, Attorney at Law	bur
May 19	Richard, s of Thomas & Ann FOSTER	bap
May 19	William, s of Thomas & Sarah SMITH	bap
May 19	Abraham, s of Jo^s & Martha HICKMANS	bur
May 20	Richard FISHER took to wife to Mary CARTWRIGHT by Banns	mar
May 26	Henry, s of James & Hannah HORTON	bap
Jun 2	Sarah, d of William & Mary PARRISH of Rowley Parish, was born the 17th May	bap
Jun 5	Samuel MARTIN, Tipton Green	bur
Jun 5	Joseph, s of Thomas & Esther NICKOLDS	bap
	Frances, s of Frances & [blank]	bap
Jun 9	Timothy, s of Bayley & Sarah SAUNDERS	bap
Jun 9	Hannah, d of Abraham & Elizabeth WANDWRIGHT	bap
Jun 9	Elisabeth, d of Joseph & Elisabeth HORTON	bap
Jun 9	Sarah, d of John & Elisabeth SMITH	bap

A Transcript of the Register of Tipton alis Tibbington was Exhibited into the Deans Visitation held at is Court at Lichfield being in June the 17th 1771

Jun 23	Peter ROUND took to wife to Mary WHEAL	mar
Jun 23	Thomas, a base begot Child of Hannah WHITEHOUSE	bap
Jun 23	George, s of Joseph & Mary CALLOW	bap
Jun 23	Elisabeth, d of John & Sarah DARBY	bap
Jun 23	Mary, d of Benjamin & Hannah PARTRIDGE	bap
Jun 30	A Child of Thomas Mallin ELLWELL	bur
Jul 7	Mary, d of Edwd & Hannah WHITEHOUSE	bap
Jul 7	William, s of Joseph & Sarah WHITEHOUSE, Soker	bap
Jul 14	Phebe, d of John & Jane HUGHES, of Sedgley	bap
Jul 19	Joseph, s of Richard & Ann FULLWOOD	bur
Jul 21	A Child of Daniel WHITEHOUSE, Butcher from Tipton Green	bur

1771

⤙ Jul 21	Aamos, s of Thomas & Esther RUDGE from Sedgley	bap
Jul 24	Sarah, d of John & Elizabeth SMITH	bur
Jul 28	John, s of John & Margret WILSON	bap
Jul 28	Sarah, d of Daniel & Sarah WHITEHOUSE	bur
Aug 4	John, s of Benjamin & Sarah GRIFFITH	bap
Aug 11	Thomas, s of Thomas & Hannah BOTT	bap
Aug 11	Sarah, d of Samuel & Sarah WHEAL	bap
Aug 25	Richard PRATT took to wife to Jane DAVENALL by Banns	mar
Aug 29	A Boy of William GRISE's from Tipton Green	bur
⤙ Sep 1	Abraham TIMMINS took to wife to Sarah GUTTRIDGE by Banns	mar
⤙ Sep 1	Elisabeth, d of Joseph Mary HORTON was Born Aug 29th and	bap
⤙ Sep 22	Catharine, d of Richard & Catharine INGRAM	bap
Sep 25	Charles BAKER, Younger from Tipton	bur
Sep 29	William BARNET took to wife to Sarah ELLWELL by Banns	mar
Sep 29	Mary, d of Edwd & Ann FEREDAY	bap
⤙ Oct 2	William ELWELL took to wife to Sarah FOSTER by Banns	mar
Oct 7	William CALLINGTON took to wife to Ann JEVON by Banns	mar
⤙ Oct 13	Daniel WHITEHOUSE took to wife to Sarah NOCK by Banns	mar
Oct 15	Mary, wife of Thomas WHITEHOUSE	bur
⤙ Nov 3	Samuel TART took to wife to June ROWLEY by Banns	mar
⤙ Nov 10	Thomas, s of Zacariah & Ann PARKS	bap
Nov 10	Henry, s of Henry & Esther FISHER	bap
Nov 17	Mary, d of James & Elizabeth FISHER	bap
Nov 17	Esther, d of Zacariah & Ellnor WANDWRIGHT	bap
Nov 24	James, s of Phebe BATE being a base begot Child	bap
Nov 24	John, s of Edwd & Elizabeth DUDLEY	bap
Dec 1	Joseph SHELDON took to wife to Sarah ABEL by Banns	mar
Dec 1	William, s of Richard & Elizabeth TITLEY[?]	bap
Dec 1	Joseph, s of Abraham & Sarah WHITEHOUSE	bap
Dec 1	Mary, d of James & Jane FEREDY	bap
Dec 8	Richard FISHER	bur
Dec 19	Nancy, d of Elizabeth & Thomas SHORTHOUSE	bap
Dec 22	Daniel, s of Daniel & Sarah SHELDON	bap
Dec 22	Elisha, s of Elisha & Phebe WHITEHOUSE	bap
⤙ Dec 22	Job, s of Job & Esther HILL	bap
Dec 22	Mary, d of Abraham & Hannah DUDLEY	bap
Dec 23	Benjamin, s of Peter & Mary ROUND	bap
Dec 29	A Child of Samuel LAWD	bur

1772

Jan 5	Mary, d of Abraham & Hannah DUDLEY	bur
[*Written between the above and next entry:*] "at three quarters old"		
Jan 5	James, s of Thomas & Mary COLLINS, of Coasly, bap	
Jan 5	Daniel, s of Richard & Catharine WHITEHOUSE	bap
Jan 12	James, s of John & Esther WHITEHOUSE	bap
⤙ Jan 13	A Child of Sarah HICKMANS buried not Crisoned	bur
Jan 19	Lucy, d of John & Ann SMITH	bap
⤙ Jan 19	Tamor, d of William & Phebe HUGHES	bap

1772

Jan 26	Lucy, d of John & Ann SMITH	bur
Feb 1	Joseph WHITEHOUSE took to wife to Mary BROWN, by Lycence	mar
Feb 3	Joseph WILLEYS took to wife to Mary HICKMANS by Banns	mar
Feb 3	Mary WHITEHOUSE, widow, from Huss Lane	bur
Feb 3	Hannah, d of William & Hannah COTTRIL	bur
Feb 3	Mary, d of Daniel & Sarah WARR	bap
Feb 8	Jane, wife of John STOKES	bur
Feb 11	Henry, s of James & Hannah HORTON	bur
Feb 13	Thomas HODGKINS took to wife to Judith RICHARDS, by Lycence	mar
Feb 23	Moses, s of John & Jane LAWD	bap
Feb 23	John, s of William & Sarah ELWELL	bap
Feb 23	Catharine, d of Daniel & Elizabeth GRANGER, Born Aug 1769	bap
Feb 23	Mary, d of Daniel & Elizabeth GRANGER	bap
Feb 23	Thomas DARBY from Princes End	bur
Feb 23	A Child of Peeter SMITH & Mary his wife	bur
Mar 8	Joseph, s of Joseph & Jeys WHITEHOUSE	bap
Mar 8	Sarah, d of William & Sarah HARPIN	bap
Mar 8	Sarah, d of Thomas & Phebe INCHER	bap
Mar 10	John, s of John & Mary FOWNES	bap
Mar 10	William Jones, s of John & Mary TUBBS	bap
Mar 22	William Jones, s of John & Mary TUBBS	bur
Mar 22	The Wid: FISHER from Hust Lane	bur
Mar 22	Mary, d of Daniel & Sarah WHITEHOUSE	bap
Mar 25	A Child of Benjamin WHESSON & Mary his wife	bur
Mar 29	Joseph, s of William & Elizabeth SMITH	bap
Mar 29	Phebe, d of William & Jane WHITEHOUSE	bap
Mar 29	Jane, d of Joseph & Jane JEVON from Coasly	bap
Mar 29	Rebekah, wife of Joseph BARTLEY	bur
Apr 6	A Child of Ezekel & Shusannah TURNER	bur
Apr 6	William MILLS took to wife to Elisabeth WHITEHOUSE by Banns	mar
Apr 15	Joseph HINTON took to wife to Phebe BIRTON by Banns	mar
Apr 19	Sarah WHITEHOUSE from Hocker Hill	bur
Apr 19	Sarah, d of Richard & Mary FISHER	bap
Apr 19	John, s of Joseph & Catharine JOHNSON, Born Nov 1 1771	bap
Apr 26	Edd:, a base begot Child of Mary BLOXWICH	bap
Apr 26	Samuel, s of William & Margaret SAUNDERS	bap
Apr 26	Ann, d of James & Ann BUFF	bap
Apr 26	Sarah, d of Joshua & Ellner CALLOW	bap
Apr 28	Mary, d of Samuel & Sarah WHEAL	bur
Apr 28	Sarah, d of Benjamin & Jeys FISHER, was Born Oct 31 1771	bap
Apr 28	Isaiah, s of Thomas & Susana WOODHOUSE	born & bap
May 4	Elizabeth, wife of Samuel INGRAM	bur
May 10	Zabie, d of Thomas & Jane WOTHEIT from Sedgley	bap
May 14	Sarah, d of Edd. PERRENS	bur
May 17	Aaron, s of Moses & Elizabeth HILL	bap
May 17	Sarah, d of Abraham & Sarah MILLS	bap

1772

May 17	Hannah, d of William & Hannah FISHER	bap
May 17	Squire DUNN took to wife to Sarah MILLS by Banns	mar
May 17	James WHITEHOUSE took to wife to Mary PAGE by Banns	mar
May 24	Elizabeth, d of William & Elizabeth SMITH	bap
May 24	Abraham, s of Jonas & Mary WARR	bur
May 24	John, s of Jamass & Elizabeth HATTWOOD	bur
May 26	Elizabeth, wife of Charles FISHER	bur
May 27	Elizabeth, wife of John GIBBINS	bur
May 27	Elizabeth, d of John & Elizabeth GIBBINS	bap
Jun 7	Nancy, d of John & Mary WILKINSON	bap
Jun 7	Phebe, d of Isaac & Lydia WINNINGTON	bap
Jun 7	Ellnor, d of Isaac & Ellner HILL	bap
Jun 7	Jane, d of William & Rachel WHITEHOUSE	bap
Jun 7	Rachel, d of Abraham & Phebe WHITEHOUSE	bap
Jun 7	Richard, s of Richard & Mary WHITEHOUSE	bap
Jun 7	Richard, s of John & Mary FEREDY	bap
Jun 18	John HILL took to wife to Elizabeth BLOXWICH by Lycence	mar
Jun 18	A Child of William FISHER from Hust lane	bur
Jun 19	Charles FISHER, from Toal End	bur
Jun 19	William, s of William & Mary MILLS	bap
Jun 21	John FISHER from Dudley was buried that was Drownded	bur
Jun 25	Edwd & Charles, two Twins of William & Ann EDGE	bap
Jul 5	Edwd & Charles, two twins of William & Ann EDGE	bur
Jul 5	Solomon, s of James & Ellner PEASEFALL	bap
Jul 5	William, s of William & Elizabeth GRISE	bap
Jul 19	A Child from John HUBBEL's, from Hocker Hill	bur
Jul 26	A Child of James & Elizabeth WILLIAMS	bur
Jul 26	Samuel PARTRIDGE	bur
Aug 9	Nathaniel HEELEY took to wife to Elizabeth SAUNDERS by Banns	mar
Aug 9	Hannah, d of John & Jeys MILLS	bap
Aug 16	Samuel, s of William & Phebe ROUND	bap
Aug 23	Sarah, d of Thomas & Mary WHEAL	bap
Aug 23	Ann, d of John & Rebekah COAL	bap
Aug 23	A Child of John WILKINSON's from Tipton Green	bur
Aug 30	John, s of John & Elizabeth INGRAM	bap
Sep 6	James, s of Joseph & Ann MALLIN	bap
Sep 14	Francis GARROTT took to wife to Catharine PERSHOUSE by Lycence	mar
Sep 17	Ann, wife of Joseph SMITH	bur
Sep 17	Elizabeth, d of Joseph & Ann SMITH	bap
Sep 20	Mary, d of Abraham & Catharine SHELDON	bap
Sep 20	Jane, a base begot Child of Sarah HICKMANS was Bap^d being 6 years old or there abouts	bap
Sep 20	Isaac, a base begot Child of Sarah HICKMANS, was Bap^d being 16 weeks Old or there abouts	bap
Sep 20	A Child of John STOKES	bur
Oct 4	Abraham, s of Edward & Ann BATE	bap
Oct 7	Esther, wife of Moses WHITEHOUSE	bur

1772

Oct 7	Sarah, d of John & Jane WHITEHOUSE, at 17 weeks old	bap
Oct 7	John, s of Daniel & Mary WARR, one year old	bap
Oct 7	Thomas, s of William & Sarah BARNET	bap
Oct 11	Samuel STEPHENS took to wife to Elizabeth SHAW	mar
Oct 11	William, s of Samuel & Elizabeth STEPHENS	bap
Oct 11	Richard, s of Richard & Mary JEWKES	bap
✝ Oct 18	John, s of James & Mary NOCK	bur
Oct 18	John, s of Joseph & Sarah DUDLEY, was born Sep^t 17	bap
— Oct 25	Edw:, s of Abraham & Sarah TIMMINS	bap
Oct 25	Thomas, s of Stephen & Mary HIPKISS	bap
Nov 1	Mary, d of Abraham & Hannah DUDLEY	bap
Nov 1	Elizabeth, d of John & Catharine FISHER	bap
✝ Nov 30	John STOKES took to wife to Mary NOCK by Banns	mar
Nov 30	John JEVON took to wife to Mary WHITEHOUSE by Banns	mar
Nov 30	Richard, s of John & Elizabeth SMITH	bap
Nov 30	Thos, s of John & Constant SHELDON	bap
— Nov 30	Mary, d of William & Sarah MASON	bap
✝ Nov 30	Mary, d of John & Sarah NOCK	bap
Dec 6	John HUBBILL	bur
Dec 6	Sarah, wife of John ELWELL	bur
Dec 8	Elizabeth, d of Joseph & Elizabeth SMITH	bur
Dec 20	Josiah, s of Thomas & Susannah WOODHOUSE, was Born Apr 28 1772	bap
— Dec 20	Edward TURNER took to wife to Mary ROUND	mar
Dec 23	Thomas FARMER	bur
Dec 25	Mary, wife of Thomas WHITEHOUSE, Headmond	bur
Dec 25	Betty, d of William & Mary WHITEHOUSE	bap
Dec 25	John, s of Thomas & Sarah SATCHEL	bap
— Dec 25	Samuel, s of Samuel & Esther PARTRIDGE	bap
⌐ Dec 27	Joseph HUGHES	bur
Dec 27	Thomas SHELDON	bur
Dec 27	John WHITEHOUSE	bur
Dec 27	Sarah, d of Thomas & Mary WHEAL	bap

1773

⌐ Jan 12	Samuel, s of John & Elizabeth INGRAM	bur
⌐ Jan 24	John JOHNSON took to wife to Mary MARSON by Banns	mar
Jan 24	Edward SMITH took to wife to Elizabeth YARDLEY by Banns	mar
Jan 24	Hanry, s of James & Hannah HORTON	bap
Jan 24	Benjamin, s of Benjamin & Esther WHITEHOUSE	bap
✝ Jan 24	Ellnor, d of Isaac & Lydia HILL	bap
✝ Jan 31	John BUNN took to wife to Sarah HORTON by Banns	mar
— Feb 3	A small Child of Joshua PARTRIDGES	bur
Feb 7	A Child of Joseph GRIFFITHES	bur
Feb 7	Thomas, s of Thomas & Mary BAGER	bap
Feb 7	Hannah, d of Thomas & Mary COLLINS, of Brierley	bap
Feb 7	Ann, d of Henry & Esther FISHER	bap
Feb 7	Mary, d of Abraham & Hannah WALTERS of Brierley	bap
✝ Feb 14	Judith, wife of Thomas HODSKINS	bur

1773

Feb 14	Phebe, d of Abraham & Mary FISHER	bap
Feb 21	Phebe, d of Abraham & Mary FISHER	bur
Feb 21	Chathrine KEAN	bur
Feb 21	Elizabeth, d of William & Hannah RICHARDS	bap
Feb 21	Ellner, d of William & Sarah PITEWAY	bap
Feb 21	Benjamin, s of John & Elizabeth CALLOW	bap
⌐ Feb 21	Samuel NOCK took to wife to Sarah WEBB	mar
Feb 23	Stephen WHITEHOUSE took to wife to Mary SMITH	mar
Feb 23	William WHITEHOUSE took to wife to Mary DARBY	mar
Mar 7	Michael DUFFIELD took to wife to Elizabeth DARBY	mar
Mar 14	Mary GREENEWAY	bur
Mar 14	Elizabeth, d of Benjamin & Mary WHESSON	bap
Mar 14	John, s of John & Shukey BLACKHAM	bap
Mar 21	Widow DARBY from the Workhouse	bur
⊥ Mar 21	Joseph, s of Joseph & Phebe STANDLEY	bap
Mar 21	Mary, d of John & Ann FLETCHER	bap
Mar 23	Robert GEATHAM took to wife to Mary GORTON by Banns	mar
Mar 28	John, s of William & Phebe CALLINGTON	bap
Apr 1	William MILLARD	bur
Apr 1	Mary, d of Daniel & Sarah WARR	bap
― Apr 1	Henry, s of Zachariah & Yalse PARKES	bap
Apr 8	A Child of John DUDLEY's, from Hocker Hill	bur
Apr 8	Rachel, d of William & Elizabeth FEREDY	bap
Apr 11	Mary, Housekeeper of George FISHER	bur
Apr 11	Benjamin, s of Richard & Sarah TIMMINS	bap
Apr 11	William, s of John & Mary DREW	bap
Apr 11	William, s of Edwd & Elizabeth SMITH	bap
Apr 11	Joseph, s of William & Elizabeth MILLS	bap
Apr 11	Joseph, s of Noah & Nancy FISHER	bap
Apr 11	Edwd, s of Isaac & Rebekah ASTON	bap
Apr 11	Edwd, s of John & Mary [blank]	bap
Apr 11	Samuel, s of William & Martha SHORT was born Feb 15 1772	bap
Apr 20	Mary, d of William & Ann FISHER	bap
Apr 20	Thomas BLISSET took to wife to Martha WHITEHOUSE by Banns	mar
Apr 20	Abraham FISHER took to wife to Hannah ROUND by Banns	mar
Apr 20	Richard, s of John & Sarah BUNN	bap
+ May 2	Hannah, d of James & Elizabeth HILL	bap
May 2	A Child of Daniel WARR's, from Tipton Green	bur
May 9	William, s of John & Francis SANDERS	bap
May 23	Henry, s of Richard & Elizabeth WANDWRIGHT	bap
May 23	Mary, d of John & Sarah WITTLE	bap
May 30	Joseph, s of Joseph & Mary PASKIN	bap
May 30	Joseph, s of John & Elizabeth EDWARDS	bap
May 30	William, s of Joseph & Catharine JOHNSON	bap
May 30	Abel, s of Joseph & Elizabeth FLETCHER	bap
May 31	Richard, s of Richard & Sarah GRIFFITH	bap
May 31	A Child of Benjamin MILLARDS	bur
⊥ May 30[sic]	A Child of Thomas HODGSKINS	bur

1773

Jun 13	Sarah, d of Daniel & Sarah WARR	bap
✝ Jun 15	Thomas NOCK from Great Bridge	bur
✝ Jun 15	David, s of William & Shusannah HORTON	bap
Jun 15	Mary, d of Joseph & Phebe NICKOLDS	bap
Jun 17	Sarah, d of M[r]. Ambrose & Ellnor JEVON, Gent	bap
Jun 27	Sarah, d of James & Elizabeth FISHER	bap
Jul 4	John, s of John & Ann SMITH, was Born the 1st June	bap
Jul 4	Mary, d of Thomas & Elizabeth HALE	bap
Jul 4	Hannah, d of James & Jane TRUMAN	bap
Jul 5	A Child of Thomas WOTHERT	bur
⤙ Jul 11	Richard BRADLEY, s & Base begott Child of Sarah GRANGER	bap
Jul 11	Mary, d of Daniel & Sarah FISHER	bap
⤚ Jul 14	John PARTRIDGE, Miller	bur
Jul 14	Joseph, s of Joseph & Sarah BLACKHAM, Born 11th May 1771	bap
Jul 14	William, s of Joseph & Sarah BLACKHAM, Born 19th Apl 1773	bap
Jul 14	Hannah, d of Joseph & Mary BATES, Born 26th Feb	bap
⊣ Aug 2	John, s of James & Mary NOCK	bap
Aug 2	Ann, d of [blank]	bap
Aug 3	Samuel BECK took to wife to Phebe SMITH by Banns	mar
┼ Aug 8	Elizabeth, d of William & Elizabeth WALTON	bap
Aug 8	Nelly, d of Eutychus & Elizabeth FISHER	bap
✝ Aug 9	James BRINTON took to wife to Mary GUTTRIDGE,	
	by Licence	mar
Aug 15	A Child of Joseph CALLOW	bur
Aug 22	James, s & Base begot Child of Sarah SANDERS	bap
Aug 22	Elizabeth, d of Andrew & Prissillah ROWLASON	bap
[Inserted between the above and below entry:]	Joshua	
Aug 22	Hannah, d of James & Sarah WHITEHOUSE	bap
Aug 30	Nancey, d of John & Mary WILKINSON	bap
✝ Aug 30	Sarah, d of Joseph & Mary HORTON	bap
Sep 31[sic]	James, s of Joseph & Elizabeth GLASSHARD, Born Jul 22nd	
	and Bap[d] the 31 1773	
Sep 6	Henry WILLIAMS took to wife to Sarah FISHER by Banns	mar
Sep 12	Hannah, d of Benjamin & Hannah JEVON	bap
Sep 12	Joseph, s of Joseph & Sarah GRIFFITH	bap
Sep 15	Jane, d of James & Mary BRINTON	bap
Sep 15	Thomas BATE	bur
Sep 19	Sarah, d of Joseph & Sarah WHITEHOUSE	bap
Sep 19	Hannah, d of Andrew & Hannah PEPLAR	bap
Sep 22	A Child of Sarah SHELDONs, from the Workhouse	bur
⤙ Sep 26	James, s of Samuel & Sarah NOCK	bap
Sep 26	Mary, d of Edward & Mary STOCKWIN	bap
Sep 26	Sarah, d of John & Mary JEVON	bap
Sep 26	Sarah, d of Joseph & Esther HOLLAND	bap
Sep 28	Rebekah WHITEHOUSE	bur
Oct 17	Jessey, s of Abraham & Hannah FISHER	bap
Oct 17	Hannah, d of Thomas & Elizabeth SHORTHOUSE	bap
⤙ Oct 17	Sarah, d of Thomas & Jane PEARSHALL	bap
Oct 17	Ellnor, d of Thomas & Ann LYON	bap

1773

Oct 18	Lucy, d of George & Ann WHITEHOUSE	bap
Oct 18	Mary, d of Joseph & Mary SMITH	bap
Oct 18	Samuel, s of Samuel & Martha WHEAL	bap
Oct 18	Ezekiel, s of John & Sarah PERSEHOUSE, Born Mar 11. 1772	bap
Oct 18	Thomas FISHER took to wife to Sarah CARTWRIGHT by Banns	mar
Oct 24	Joshua CALLOW, from Toal End	bur
Nov 1	Benjamin WHEAL took to wife to Mary NIGHTINGALE by Banns	mar
Nov 7	Elizabeth, d of Andrew & Prissaley ROWLINGSON	bur
Nov 10	M^r. Thomas BLINKHORN from London took to wife to Phebe PARKES of Tipton, by Licence	mar
Nov 14	Joseph SMITH	bur
Nov 25	A Child of William GRISE	bur
Nov 28	Daniel, s of Abel & Mary HILL	bap
Nov 28	John, s of Robert & Mary GEATHAM	bap
Nov 28	William, s of William & Mary TURNER	bap
Nov 28	Joseph, s of Joseph & Elizabeth TUNKS	bap
Nov 28	Joseph, s of Joseph & Ann GREENAWAY	bap
Nov 28	Hannah, d of Daniel & Sarah SHELDON	bap
Nov 28	Mary, d of Daniel & Elisabeth GRANGER	bap
Nov 28	Rachel, d of Humphery & Mary ALLEN	bap
Nov 28	Mary, d of Joseph & Sarah GRIFFITH	bap
Dec 5	A Child of William ELWELL	bur
Dec 5	Phebe Foye, d of M^r. John & Mary FOWNES	bap
Dec 5	William, s of Joseph & Elisabeth HORTON, Born Sep 6	bap
Dec 5	Mary, d of Thomas & Elisabeth EVINS was Born Sep 17	bap
Dec 8	A Child of James HIPKISSes	bur
Dec 14	A Child of Joseph SMITHs	bur
Dec 17	Joseph WINNINGTON	bur
Dec 25	Daniel WARR took to wife to Phebe FLETCHER	mar

1774

Jan 2	Jane CALLOWAY	bur
Jan 2	A Child of Joseph WHITEHOUSE Fellow	bur
Jan 2	Hannah, d of William & Sarah ROBISON	bap
Jan 2	Sarah, d of Daniel & Leah PARKES	bap
Jan 2	Sarah, d of Abraham & Phebe WHITEHOUSE	bap
Jan 9	Sarah, d of William & Ann HEDGE	bap
Jan 4[sic]	A Child of Joseph WHITEHOUSE Fellow	bur
	[The edge of the next page is mutilated and some of the dates are lost]	
	James HILL took to wife to Mary HUGHES by Banns	mar
	William COLTRILL Wife, from Tipton Green	bur
	A Child of Stephen HIPKISS	bur
	A Child of John TIMMINS Daughters	bur
	A Child of Francis MILLS	bur
Jan 16	William, s of William & Elizabeth SMITH	bap
Jan 16	William, s of Francis MILLS & Rebekah his wife	bap
Jan 16	Jinney, d of Thomas & Hannah BOTT	bap
Jan 20	A Child of Edward SMITH's	bur

1774

Jan 23	A Child of Daniel GRIFFITHS	bur
Jan 23	William, s of John & Esther WHITEHOUSE	bap
Jan 26	A Child of William WHITEHOUSE, Robin	bur
Jan 26	A Child of John DUFFIELD	bur
3	Edwd, s of Joseph & Ann GEORGE	bap
	A Child of Abraham WHITEHOUSES	bur
	A Child of Joseph GRIFFITH	bur
+	A Child of Joseph WARTONS	bur
	A Child of Joseph FISHERS	bur
←	Elizabeth, wife of Thomas HUGHES	bur
3	Sarah DOVEY, Widow	bur
Feb 9	Thomas CAMM	bur
Feb 9	A Child of William WARTONS	bur
Feb 13	A Child of Richard GRIFFITHES	bur
Feb 16	A Child of Moses WHITEHOUSE	bur
Feb 20	A Child of Phebe BATES	bur
Feb 20	Thomas WHITEHOUSE	bur
Feb 23	A Child of William WHITEHOUSE	bur
Feb 27	A Child of William SHELDONS	bur
Feb 27	William MARSON took to wife to Jane BINGLEY by Banns	mar
Mar 3	A Child of Elisha WHITEHOUSE	bur
Mar 6	A Child of Joseph WARTONS	bur
Mar 13	Thomas, s of Thomas & Jane WOTHERT	bap
	William, s of Joseph & Mary GREYER	bap
Mar 20	Sarah, d of Stephen & Mary HIPKISS	bap
Mar 20	Thos HOLLINGTON took to wife to Betty SNELSON by Banns	mar
Mar 27	Widow WHITEHOUSE, Jonas	bur
Mar 27	Hannah, d of Abraham & Mary FISHER	bap
Mar 27	Esther, d of Elisha & Phebe WHITEHOUSE	bap
Apr 3	A Child of Benjamin WHESSONS	bur
Apr 3	George, s of Benjamin & Mary GORTON	bap
Apr 3	Shusannah, d of John & Mary TUBBS	bap
Apr 3	Jinney, d of William & Mary HUGHES	bap
Apr 3	Edwd, s of Edwd & Ann FEREDAY, Born Jan 21	bap
Apr 3	Richard, s of Thos & Mary PARTRIDGE	bap
Apr 3	Hannah, d of Benjamin & Mary HORTON	bap
	Thomas, s of Thomas & Shusannah WOODHOUSE was born Feb 4. 1774	bap
Apr 10	Elias, s of James & Elizabeth BENNET	bap
Apr 18	James HORTON, Clark	bur
Apr 18	Ezekiel, s of Ezekiel & Shusannah TURNER	bap
Apr 18	Ruth, d of Benjamin & Joice FISHER	bap
Apr 18	Daniel HICKMANS took to wife to Hannah CALLOW by Banns	mar
May 15	Joseph, s of John & Rebekah COAL	bap
May 22	Benjamin HORTON & Sarah JOHNSON both of this Parish	mar
May 22	Joseph, s of John & Martha PARTRIDGE	bap
May 29	Martha, d of & base begot Child of Hannah WHITEHOUSE	bap
May 29	Jessey, s & base begot Child of Sarah NICKLIN	bap
Jun 5	Mary, d of Joseph & Sarah BECK	bap

1774

Jun 5   Wid: MALLIN from Coasley   bur
Jun 5   Wid: MILLARD   bur

A Transcript of the Register Book of Tipton Alis Tipington was Exibeted into the Deans Visetation held in the Court at Lichfield being in June the 7th 1774

[Note: At some stage it would appear that this Register was rebound with the entries from May 1774 to December 1780 being misplaced. Thus the next entry in the register is actually dated 4th December 1780 with a comment in the original register in a different hand: "go to page 230". However, the entries here are presented in consecutive date order.]

Jun 13	Henry, s of Richard & Elisabeth TITLEY	bap
Jun 16	A Child of Job SMITH's	bur
Jun 19	Mary, wife of John WESSON	bur
Jun 19	Thomas, s of Benjamin & Mary WEAL	bap
Jun 26	David, s of Abraham & Catharine SHELDON	bap
Jul 10	Mary, d of James & Phebe WHITEHOUSE	bap
Jul 17	Samuel, s of John & Mary TATE	bap
Jul 17	John FOSTER took to wife to Lydia ONIONS	mar
Jul 24	Richard NIGHTINGALE	bur
Aug 3	Joseph COWLEY	bur
Aug 3	Elizabeth, d of Zacariah & Ann PARKES	bap
Aug 10	Thomas SANDERS	bur
Aug 10	A Child from the Workhouse	bur
Aug 21	Isbell, d of William & Elizabeth SMITH	bap
Sep 13	M[rs]. DUDLEY, from Birmingham	bur
Sep 14	John NOCK	bur
Sep 15	Samuel GUTTRIDGE	bur
Sep 15	Mary ATTWOOD	bur
Sep 22	Daniel GUTTRIDGE	bur
Sep 28	Ephariam SKIDMORE & Johanna RUSSON by Banns	mar
Oct 2	William ROUND	bur
Oct 2	David HIPKISS & Ann PASKIN	mar
Oct 2	George, s of Joseph & Mary CALLOWAY	bap
Oct 16	Susanna, d of Richard & Mary GRANGER	bap
Oct 20	Daniel WHITEHOUSE (Biter)	bur
Oct 28	Benjamin, s of Benjamin & Elisabeth GRIFFITH	bap
Oct 29	Samuel, s of William & Rachel WHITEHOUSE Elisha	bap
Oct 29	John GIBBONS married Catharine JUKES by Licence	mar
Oct 30	Martha, d of William & Phebe HUGHES	bap
Oct 30	Thomas, s of Abraham & Sarah TIMMINS	bap
Oct 30	Elizabeth, d of Daniel & Ann TIMMINS	bap
Oct 30	William, s of William & Hannah WHITEHOUSE, Born Sep 7	bap
Nov 6	James, s of James & Mary HILL	bap
Nov 6	Jane, d of Obadiah & Catherine ASSTON from Brierly	bap
Nov 7	John ASTON married Phebe SMITH by Banns	mar
Nov 7	John, s of John & Jane WHITEHOUSE at 31 weeks old	bap
Nov 7	Sarah, d of William & Elizabeth GRISE, Born 11th March	bap
Nov 7	Sarah, d of Samuel & Phebe BECK	bap

1774

Nov 7	William, s of William & Mary WHITEHOUSE	bap
Nov 10	A Child of Richard INGRAM	bur
Nov 20	Widow SMITH from Tipton Green	bur
Nov 27	William JONES married Elizabeth BEARNS	mar
Nov 27	Thomas, s of Rich[d] & Mary WHITEHOUSE	bap
Nov 27	Bayley HILL, a Bas begott Child of Sarah HUGHES	bap
Dec 4	An old Woman from Hust lane	bur
Dec 11	A Child of Mary BLOXWICHES	bur
Dec 18	Joseph, s of Daniel & Hannah HICKMANS	bap
Dec 13[sic]	William WRIGHT married Mary JONES by Licence	mar
Dec 25	James WARTON	bur
Dec 25	Hannah, d of Richard & Ann NIGHTINGALE	bap
Dec 25	Sarah, d of Edw[d] & Ann BATE	bap
Dec 25	William, s of William & Sarah ELLWELL	bap
Dec 25	Daniel, s of Abraham & Hannah WALTERS	bap
Dec 25	John, s of William & Elizabeth MILLS	bap
Dec 28	Mary MASH	bur
Dec 28	Susannah, d of John & Susannah BLACKHAM, Born 7th	bap
Dec 28	Nancy, d of Thomas & Esther NICOLD, born Mar 15th	bap

1775

Jan 1	James LEWISS married Elizabeth WHITEHOUSE	mar
Jan 5	A Child of Benjamin MILLARD	bur
Jan 5	Elizabeth, d of Benjamin & Sarah HORTON	bap
Jan 10	John GUTTRIDGE	bur
Jan 10	Hannah, d of Charles & Sarah LAWDS	bap
Jan 10	Ruth, d of Abraham & Catharine MILLS	bap
Jan 15	A Child of Daniel WARRS	bur
Jan 15	Mary, d of Joseph & Mary WHITEHOUSE	bap
	William, s of Richard & Sarah TIMMINS, Bap Nov[r] 28. 1774	bap
Jan 22	Esther, d of James & Hannah HORTON	bur
Jan 22	Thomas SKIDMORE married Mary BOND	mar
Jan 22	Thomas FELLOWS married Nancy FISHER	mar
Jan 23	A Boy of William GUTTRIDGES	bur
Jan 23	Francis, s of William & Hannah MILLS	bap
Jan 29	Joseph, s of Joseph & Ellnor[crossed out] Eleanor[added above] FISHER	bap
Feb 5	Henry, s of Moses & Esther HILL	bap
Feb 6	John FISHER married Sarah ROUND	mar
Feb 7	Elizabeth, d of M[r]. Ambrose & Eleanor JEVON, Born Nov 5 1774	bap
Feb 9	Joseph, s of Joseph & Mary HORTON	bap
Feb 9	Hannah, wife of Jo[s] HIPKISS	bur
Feb 9	A Boy of Samuel HERRING	bur
Feb 12	Elizabeth, d of Andrew & Priscilla ROLINSON	bap
Feb 12	Samuel, s of John & Elizabeth EDWARDS	bap
Feb 19	Joseph, s of Peter & Mary SMITH	bap
Feb 19	Sarah, d of John & Phebe ASTON	bap
Feb 22	A Child of Abraham FELLOW[crossed out] WHITEHOUSE	bur

1775

Feb 26	James, s of James & Nancy FELLOWS	bap
Feb 26	Thomas ROUND married Mary BROOKS	mar
Mar 12	James, s of Abraham & Hannah DUDLEY	bap
Mar 26	John, s of Thomas & Sarah FISHER, 5 weeks old	bap
Mar 26	Joseph, s of John & Lydia FOSTER	bap
Jan 26	Joseph, s of William & Hannah RICHARDS	bap
Apr 2	James BUSHEL	bur
Apr 9	Catharine, d of Richard INGRAM	bur
Apr 16	William NICKLIN married Rachel CADDICK	mar
Apr 16	James, s of William & Elizabeth WARTON	bap
Apr 16	Mary, d of Abraham & Hannah FISHER	bap
Apr 16	Sarah, d of William & Ann FISHER	bap
Apr 23	Moses, s of John & Elizabeth CALLOW	bap
May 7	Daniel, s of John & Constant SHELDON	bap
May 7	Rachel, d of William & Elizabeth FEREDAY	bur
May 13	Mary, wife of Charles BAKER	bur
May 13	Daniel, s of Daniel & Hannah WHITEHOUSE Elisha	bap
May 14	Mary, d of Joseph & Mary WARTON	bap
May 28	Richard, s of Richard & Mary WHITEHOUSE	bur
May 28	Martha, a bas begot Child of Hannah WHITEHOUSE	bur
May 28	Edwd, s of James & Elizabeth FISHER	bap
May 28	Maria, d of Richard & Elizabeth MIDLEMORE	bap
Jun 4	Stephen FISHER married Mary WARTON	mar
Jun 4	Edwd SMITH married Esther DUDLEY	mar
Jun 4	Joseph, s of Thomas & Mary WHEAL	bap
Jun 4	Joseph, s of Richard & Mary JEWKS	bap
Jun 4	David, s of John & Jane LAWD	bap
Jun 4	Joseph, s of James & Hannah WHITEHOUSE, 14 weeks old	bap
Jun 4	Nancy, d of Thomas & Elizabeth HILL	bap
Jun 4	Elizabeth, d of Benjamin & Esther WHITEHOUSE	bap
Jun 4	Sarah, d of Joseph & Sarah GRIFFITH	bap
Jun 4	Sarah, d of William & Mary WRIGHT	bap
Jun 11	Sarah WHITEHOUSE, a base begot Child of Ann HILL	bap
Jun 13	Elizabeth, d of Martha ABEL	bur
Jul 2	Elizabeth, d of Richard & Rachel GUTTRIDGE	bap
Jul 9	Joseph CADROCK married Martha GREENAWAY	mar
Jul 9	John GUTTRIDGE	bur
Jul 19	Jeremiah GUTTRIDGE	bur
Jul 23	Nancy, d of Paul & Lydia GRIFFITH	bap
Aug 6	Nancy, d of Abel & Mary HILL	bap
Aug 6	Samuel NOCK wife	bur
Aug 18	Richard HIPKISS	bur
Aug 24	Samuel NOCK	bur
Sep 3	James, s of James & Mary BRINTON, 25 weeks old	bap
Sep 3	Mary, d of Edward & Elizabeth MILLS	bap
Sep 3	Daniel CALLOWAY & Sarah ATTWOOD	mar
Sep 24	John GEALEY married Hannah WHITEHOUSE	mar
Oct 1[sic]	Ann, wife of William & Elizabeth FEREDAY	bap

1775

[The next entry has been inserted]

Sep 30	Samuel, s of Daniel & Sarah SHELDON	bap
Oct 8	Mary WHITEHOUSE	bur
Oct 8	Jonas, s of Daniel & Phebe WARR	bap
Oct 15	Daniel, s of Thomas & Mary COLLINS, of Batemans Hill	bap
Oct 15	Hugh, s of Thomas & Mary COLLINS, of Batemans Hill at a Year & half old	bap
Oct 15	William, s of Joshua & Ellnor[crossed out] Eleanor[inserted above] CALLOWAY	bap
Oct 22	Edward, s of Daniel & Sarah SHELDON	bap
Oct 22	Edward WHITEHOUSE	bur
Nov 19	Margaret, d of Thomas & Elizabeth IVINS[crossed out] EVANS [inserted above]	bap
Nov 19	Mary, d of David & Ann HIPKISS	bap
Nov 22	Sarah, wife of Henry WILLIAMS	bur
Nov 26	Samuel, s of William & Elizabeth JONES	bap
Nov 26	Samuel, s of Joseph & Mary PASKIN	bap
Nov 26	John, s of John & Mary DREW	bap
Nov 26	Luke, s of Edward & Marty STOCKWIN	bap
Nov 26	Hannah, d of Thomas & Mary ROUND	bap
+ Dec 4	Jane WARTON	bur
Dec 4	William, s of James & Ann RICHARDS	bap
Dec 4	Ann, d of Joseph & Phebe NICKOLDS	bap
Dec 4	Mary, d of Joseph & Lydia WHITEHOUSE, at 1 year & 2 months old	bap
Dec 14	Mr. William SMITH	bur
Dec 14	Joseph GREENAWAY	bur
Dec 14	Thomas WARR	bur
Dec 14	John, s of John & Jane PASKIN, Born May 15 1775	bap
Dec 14	William, s of Noah & Ann FISHER	bap
Dec 14	Nancy, d of Daniel & Sarah GRIFFITH	bap
Dec 14	Hannah, d of John & Ann FLETCHER	bap
Dec 17	Joseph DUDLEY's wife	bur
+ Dec 18	John WEBB married Eleanor WHITTINGHAM	mar
Dec 19	Richard NICKLIN	bur
Dec 19	Joseph ONIONS	bur
└ Dec 24	John TIMMINS	bur
Dec 24	James FISHER	bur
Dec 24	David, s of Benjamin & Sarah WHITEHOUSE, 9 weeks old	bap
Dec 25	Daniel ELWELL	bur
~ Dec 25	Joseph, s of John & Elizabeth INGRAM	bap
Dec 27	A Strange Man	bur
Dec 27	Betty, d of William & Mary MILLS	bap
Dec 31	William WEATLEY	bur
~ Dec 31	Mary, d of Samuel & Sarah NOCK	bap

1776

Jan 16	Mary, wife of Abraham FISHER	bur
~ Jan 21	Nancy, d of Thomas & Nancy FELLOWS	bap

1776

Jan 21	Richard LAWD	bur
Jan 23	Joseph WHITEHOUSE's wife	bur
Jan 23	Edward, s of William & [blank] SMITH	bap
Jan 23	John, a base begot Child of Mary DREW	bap
Jan 30	John SMITH	bur
Feb 4	John DREW	bur
Feb 4	Joseph SMITH	bur
Feb 4	William WHITEHOUSE	bur
Feb 4	Jane DOMINGO	bur
Feb 4	Frances EDGE	bur
Feb 4	Hannah, d of James & Hannah HORTON	bap
Feb 11	Amoss DARBY married Ann HICKMANS	mar
Feb 18	William SAUNDERS married Mary HILL	mar
Feb 18	Mary, a bas begot Child of Elizabeth FOSTER	bap
Feb 25	A Child of Ezekiel TURNERS	bur
Feb 25	Joseph, s of James & Elizabeth HILL	bap
Feb 25	Daniel, s of Daniel & Jane HILL	bap
Feb 25	John, s of John & Mary JEVON	bap
Mar 3	Samuel MALLIN	bur
Mar 10	Joseph, s of Joseph & Mary HORTON	bur
Mar 13	Ezekiel TURNER	bur
Mar 13	Mary, wife of Jeremiah HARRIS	bur
Mar 13	John, s of Joseph & Sarah BLACKHAM, Born July 26	bap
Mar 13	Isaac, s of Richard & Elizabeth WAINRIGHT	bap
Mar 13	Daniel, s of Ezekiel & YALSE[crossed out] Allise PARKES	bap
Mar 15	Jeremiah WHITEHOUSE's wife	bur
Mar 17	William FOSTER married Hannah PERCIVAL	mar
Mar 17	A Child of William SMITHs	bur
Mar 17	Mary, d of William & Mary HUGHES	bap
Mar 17	Ann, d of James & Mary NOCK	bap
Mar 27	Thomas GOODBY	bur
Apr 7	Daniel, a bas begott Child of Elizabeth HOWL	bap
Apr 7	Joseph, s of Edward & Elizabeth SMITH	bap
Apr 7	Andrew, s of Andrew & Hannah PEPLAR	bap
Apr 7	Edward, s of William & Mary NOCK	bap
Apr 7	Sarah, d of Abraham & Phebe WHITEHOUSE	bap
Apr 7	Hannah, d of Joseph & Jane JEVON, one year old	bap
Apr 10	Shusannah, d of Ezekiel & Shusannah TURNER	bap
Apr 10	M^r. Ambrose JEVON	bur
Apr 12	John SMITH	bur
Apr 12	John, s of John & Mary WILKINSON	bap
Apr 12	Elizabeth, d of Joseph & Jane PERSIVALL	bap
Apr 21	Joseph, s of Joseph & Martha CADDRACK, Born March 23	bap
Apr 21	Edward, s of Edward & Elizabeth DUDLEY	bap
Apr 28	John, s of James & Sarah TURLEY	bap
Apr 28	John, s of Benjamin & Sarah HORTON, Born the 19th	bap
Apr 28	Isaac, s of Thomas & Mary BADGER	bap
Apr 28	Sarah, d of Daniel & Sarah WARR	bap
Apr 28	Abraham JEVON	bur

1776

May 1	James ROUND married Elizabeth BRINTON	mar
May 1	Samuel, s of Benjamin & Joice FISHER	bap
May 5	Edward WHITEHOUSE	bur
May 5	Edward, s of James & Elizabeth FISHER	bur
May 5	Henry, s of Eutychus & Elizabeth FISHER	bap
May 12	Mary, d of James & Elizabeth FISHER	bur
May 26	William, s of Stephen & Mary HIPKISS	bap
May 26	Henry, s of William & Elizabeth SMITH	bap
May 26	Joseph, s of Edward & Esther SMITH	bap
May 27	Thomas CARTWRIGHT married Alice HIPKISS	mar
– May 27	William INGRAM married Martha WEATLEY	mar
May 27	William BECK married Rachel DARBY	mar
Jun 9	Ann, d of William & Elizabeth FEREDAY	bur
Jun 9	Hannah, d of John & Elizabeth WITTALL	bap
Jun 16	Mary, d of William & Ann EDGE	bap
Jun 25	Phebe, a bas begott Child of Rachel GRIFFITH, about 4 years old	bap
Jun 25	Martha BLISSETT	bur
– Jun 27	Samuel FLETCHER married Sarah GRANGER	mar
Jun 30	Elizabeth, d of Joseph & Mary LANKSON	bap
Jul 7	Phebe, d of Daniel & Ann FLETCHER	bap
Jul 7	Hannah, d of Edward & Hannah WHITEHOUSE	bap
+ Jul 14	Abraham, s of Isaac & Sarah GUTTRIDGE	bap
Jul 14	Ann, d of Thomas & Sarah SATCHELL	bap
Jul 14	Elizabeth, d of Daniel & Sarah CALLOWAY	bap
– Jul 21	John, s of John & Martha PARTRIDGE	bap
Jul 21	William, s of William & Elizabeth BOWING	bap
Jul 21	Mary, d of John & Hannah GEALEY	bap
– Jul 28	Mary, d of William & Hannah FOSTER	bap
Aug 2	Thomas CLARKEs wife	bur
Aug 2	A Child of David WALTERS	bur
Aug 4	Ann, wife of Morriss CALLOWAY	bur
Aug 4	William, s of Daniel & Sarah FISHER	bap
Aug 4	James, s of James & Elizabeth ATTWOOD	bap
Aug 18	William, s of Joseph & Sarah BLACKHAM	bur
Aug 22	Susanna, d of John & Susanna BLACKHAM	bur
Aug 25	Benjamin, s of James & Jane TRUMAN	bap
Aug 25	Rosannah, d of Stephen & Mary FISHER	bap
+ Aug 25	Elizabeth, d of and base begott Child of Hannah WARTON	bap
Aug 29	A Child of James WJHITEHOUSE's	bur
Sep 1	Alice, d of Joseph & Mary SMITH	bap
Sep 15	A Child of William & Hannah MILLS	bur
Sep 15	Mary, d of William & Hannah MILLS	bap
Sep 15	Sarah, d of Samuel & Lydia ONIONS	bap
Sep 15	John, s of John & Lydia FURNEYFOOT	bap
Sep 24	A Child of Daniel WHITEHOUSE (Elisha)	bur
⇒ Sep 29	William, s of William & Martha INGRAM	bap
Sep 29	Priscilla, d of William & Elizabeth SMITH	bap
Sep 30	Ann, d of James & Elizabeth ROUND	bap

1776

Sep 30	William PRICE married Sarah HODGETTS	mar
Sep 30	Richard BECK married Sarah RICHARDS	mar
Oct 6	William, s of Daniel & Elizabeth GRANGER	bap
Oct 6	Phebe, d of Samuel & Sarah FLETCHER	bap
Oct 11	Ann GREENEWAY	bur
Oct 13	Phebe, d of Joseph & Phebe STANLEY	bap
Oct 13	William, s of John & Mary FISHER	bap
Oct 16	Elizabeth, d of Isaac & Mary DUTTON	bap
Oct 16	A Child of Thomas WOTHERT	bur
Oct 23	Widow JUKES	bur
Nov 3	Simeon, s of John & Elizabeth EDWARDS	bap
Nov 3	Samuel, s of Elisha & Jane WHITEHOUSE	bap
Nov 7	A Child of Edward DUDLEY	bur
Nov 10	William, s of James & Jane FEREDAY	bap
Nov 15	A Child of John FLETCHERS	bur
Nov 17	Catharine INGRAM, a base begott Child of Sarah WEATLEY	bap
Nov 20	Daniel WHEAL married Elizabeth GRIFFITH	mar
Nov 20	Solomon, s of Samuel & Martha WHEAL, Born June 12	bap
Nov 24	A Child of Richard WHITEHOUSE	bur
Nov 24	Joseph, s of Joseph & Mary GREYER, Born Oct 17	bap
Nov 24	William, s of Richard & Mary WHITEHOUSE	bap
Nov 26	William BARNET married Elizabeth CARTWRIGHT	mar
Nov 26	Samuel PASKIN married Elizabeth WINNINGTON	mar
Nov 26	Edward, s of Richard & Mary FISHER	bap
Dec 1	A Child of Joseph GRIFFISS	bur
Dec 1	John, s of Thomas & Yslce[crossed through] Alice CARTWRIGHT	bap
Dec 8	Elizabeth, wife of John JOHNSON	bur
Dec 2[sic]	Hannah, d of James & Hannah HORTON	bur
Dec 15	John, s of Joseph & Mary HORTON	bap
Dec 26	Timothy TURNER married Mary ASTON	mar
Dec 26	Enoss WHITEHOUSE married Hannah WILLEYS	mar
Dec 26	Jeremiah, s of Joseph & Sarah WHITEHOUSE	bap
Dec 26	Sarah, d of Robert & Mary GEATHANE	bap
Dec 29	Elizabeth, d of Richard BECK	bur
Dec 29	A Child of John WITTALL	bur

1777

Jan 5	William, a bas begott Child of Mary INGRAM	bap
Jan 5	Joseph, s of Joseph & Elizabeth HORTON	bap
Jan 5	Phebe, d of Joseph & Ann MALLIN	bap
Jan 5	Sarah, d of Joseph & Sarah GRIFFISS	bap
Jan 12	Elizabeth, d of Sarah WHITEHOUSE	bap
Jan 12	A Child of Thomas WOODWARD	bur
Jan 14	A Child of John ASTON	bur
Jan 14	A Child of William ELWELL	bur
Jan 14	A Child of James BRINTON	bur
Jan 14	John, s of John & Phebe ASTON	bap
Jan 14	Mary, d of John & Lydia FOSTER	bap

Jan 14	Elizabeth, d of Edward & ~~Ellner~~[crossed through] Eleanor SMITH		bap
Jan 15	Stephen TIMMINS		bur
Jan 15	A Child of Joseph SMITH		bur
Jan 26	~~Widow~~[crossed through] Elisabeth GUTTRIDGE, a Widow		bur
Jan 26	John, s of Amoss & Hannah DARBY		bap
Jan 26	Joseph, s of Joseph & Elizabeth RIDDING		bap
Feb 2	Benjamin, s of Edward & Ann FEREDAY, born July 2, 1776		bap
Feb 2	Benjamin, s of George & ~~Ellner~~[crossed through] Eleaner SMITH		bap
Feb 4	A Child of Samuel NOCK		bur
Feb 9	Joseph, s of Thomas & Sarah PARKES		bap
Feb 16	Zachariah, s of Zachariah & Ann PARKES		bap
Feb 16	Sarah, d of John & Elizabeth SMITH, 3 years old		bap
Feb 16	William, s of John & Elizabeth SMITH, Born Jun 16 1776		bap
Feb 19	Sarah, d of William & Mary WHITEHOUSE		bap
Feb 19	A Child of William WHITEHOUSE (Robin)		bur
Feb 26	A Child of James FELLOWS		bur
Feb 26	David, s of John & Fanny SANDERS		bap
Mar 2	William, s of John & Elizabeth SMITH		bur
Mar 2	Samuel HIGGINSON married Hannah WALTON		mar
Mar 2	Sophia, d of Benjamin & Sarah WHITEHOUSE		bap
Mar 2	Elizabeth, d of Daniel & Sarah WARR		bap
Mar 2	Rachel, d of Abel & Mary HILL		bap
Mar 2	Joseph, s of John & Mary HONE		bap
Mar 2	William, s of Philip & Mary RATHBONE		bap
Mar 6	William WHITEHOUSE		bur
Mar 6	Ann DARBY		bur
Mar 9	A Child of Thomas FISHER		bur
Mar 9	Isaac ASTON married Sarah FISHER		mar
Mar 9	Phebe, d of Richard & Hannah NIGHTINGALE		bap
Mar 9	William, s of Samuel & Phebe BECK		bap
Mar 9	William, s of William & Elizabeth MILLS		bap
Mar 9	Esther, d of Thomas & Esther RUDGE		bap
Mar 16	Jessey, s of John & Esther WHITEHOUSE		bap
Mar 16	Isaac DARBY married Mary RICHARDS		mar
Mar 16	William PRICHARD married Phebe PASKIN		mar
Mar 23	William JAMES married Sarah NAILOR		mar
Mar 23	Joseph, s of Daniel & Phebe WARR		bap
Mar 30	William, s of John & Mary JONES		bap
Mar 30	Ambrose, s of Abraham & Sarah TIMMINS		bap
Mar 30	Ambrose, s of Abraham & Hannah FISHER		bap
Mar 30	Phebe, d of William & Hannah WHITEHOUSE		bap
Mar 30	Frances, d of Abraham & Catharine SHELDON		bap
Mar 30	William, a bas begott Child of Margaret ELWELL, Born July 5 1772		bap
Mar 30	Daniel, s bas begott Child of Margaret ELWELL		bap
Apr 2	William, s of Thomas & Mary ROUND		bap
Apr 2	A Child of Samuel BECK		bur

Apr 17	Benjamin WHITEHOUSE	bur
Apr 17	Mary, d of John & Mary TATE	bap
Apr 19	Thomas BRINLEY married Sarah COALBOWIN	mar
✛ Apr 19	John HODGSKINS married Hannah FLETCHER	mar
Apr 20	Edward Whittingham, s of Edward & Jane PENNING[crossed out] PERRINS	bap
Apr 21	William, s of Daniel & Sarah FISHER	bur
Apr 24	Richard JONES	bur
May 4	David JEVON married Sarah TURLEY	mar
May 5	Joseph, s of William & Sarah PRICE	bap
May 8	Jeremiah WRIGHT married Elizabeth JONES	mar
May 12	James GRIFFISS married Shusanna COLE	mar
May 12	John ASHTON married Ann DORRALL	mar
May 12	Edward, s of William & Rachel WHITEHOUSE	bap
May 15	Benjamin WHITEHOUSE's Daughter	bur
May 19	Thomas FEREDAY married Mary LEECH	mar
May 19	Daniel SMITH & Ann TAYLOR	mar
Jun 1	Nancy, d of William & Hannah RICHARDS, Born May 17	bap
Jun 8	Stephen, s of Stephen & Mary BLOXWICH, Born Feby 25	bap
Jun 8	James, s of James & Elizabeth FISHER	bap
Jun 8	William, s of William & Elizabeth FEREDAY	bap
Jun 8	Joseph, s of Thomas & Elizabeth COX	bap
Jun 8	Elizabeth, d of William & Hannah SMITH	bap
Jun 15	William, s of William & Hannah HORTON, Born May 24	bap
Jun 15	Samuel, s of Edward & Ann BATE	bap
Jun 15	Sarah FISHERs Daughter	bur
Jun 15	A Child of Isaac ASTONS	bur
Jun 22	Daniel, s of Daniel & Hannah HICKMANS	bap
Jun 22	William, s of James & Hannah WHITEHOUSE	bap
Jun 29	Sarah, d of Thomas & Sarah SMITH	bap
Jul 6	John GUTTRIDGEs Wife	bur
Jul 11	John, s of William & Elizabeth SMITH	bur
Jul 11	Mary, d of Joseph & Mary CALLOWAY	bap
Jul 13	Sarah, d of William & Elizabeth BARNET	bap
Jul 13	Abraham, s of Edward & Elizabeth MILLS	bap

A Transcript of the Register Book of Tipton Alias Tibbington was Exhibited into the Deans Visitation held in the Court of Lichfield being in June 7 1777

July the 14th 1777

Jul 20	Benjamin, s of Benjamin & Mary WHEAL	bap
Jul 20	Daniel, s of William & Ann SHELDON	bap
Jul 20	Mary, d of John & Jane LAUD	bap
Jul 20	Catharine, d of Peter & Mary ROUND, born Novr 12, 1775	bap
Jul 21	Richard TUNKS married Lucy LOWE	mar
Jul 29	Abraham, s of Isaac & Sarah GUTTRIDGE	bur
Jul 29	Phebe, d of John & Mary DARBY, 4 years old	bap
Jul 29	Nancy, d of John & Mary DARBY, 1 year & 1 month old	bap
Jul 29	Ann, d of Daniel & Elizabeth WHEAL	bap
Aug 3	Ezekiel, s of Ezekiel & Alice PARKES	bap

1777

Aug 3	Isaac, s of Isaac & Sarah HILL	bap
Aug 3	Benjamin, s of Abraham & Hannah WALTERS	bap
Aug 3	Hannah, d of Daniel & Leah PARKER	bap
Aug 10	William, s of William & Mary TURNER	bap
Aug 10	Silvia, d of Daniel & Sarah SHELDON	bap
Aug 15	Isaac ASTON	bur
Aug 25	William, s of John & Fanny SANDERS	bur
Aug 31	William, s of Richard & Sarah BECK	bap
Aug 31	Peter, a base begotten C of Hannah FLETCHER	bap
Aug 31	Sarah PENNINGS, a base begotten C of Hannah SALT	bap
Sep 1	Thomas CRUMPTON & Elizabeth TONER	mar
Sep 7	Phebe, d of Benjamin & Hannah JEVON	bap
Sep 10	Ann SMITH	bur
Sep 14	Jeremiah, s of Joseph & Sarah WHITEHOUSE	bur
Sep 14	Henry, s of Thomas & Sarah COLLINS, Born Decr 26 1776	bap
Sep 21	Joseph, s of William & Sarah BARNEY, Born Novr 13, 1774	bap
Sep 21	John, s of William & Sarah BARNEY, Born Dec 27, 1776	bap
Sep 28	Henry, s of Moses & Elizabeth HILL	bap
Sep 28	Elizabeth, a base begotten Child of Ann HANDS	bap
Oct 5	David, s of James & Hannah HORTON	bap
Oct 19	Sarah, wife of Samuel PARTRIDGE	bur
Oct 26	James, s of Isaac & Sarah ASTON	bap
Oct 26	Sarah, d of Richard & Mary JUKES	bap
Oct 26	Joseph, s of Abraham & Catharine MILLS	bap
Nov 2	Benjamin BOTT & Ann HORTON were married	mar
Nov 5	William, s of William & Ann SHELDON	bur
Nov 5	Zachariah, s of Zachariah & Ann PARKES	bur
Nov 10	John THOMAS & Sarah BROOKS were married	mar
Nov 16	Nancy, d of David & Ann HIPKISS, Born Oct 7	bap
Nov 20	Henry BIRD & Ann MILLWARD were married	mar
Nov 23	Elizabeth, d of Thomas & Elizabeth SHORTHOUSE	bap
Nov 23	Joseph, s of Joseph & Mary WHITEHOUSE	bap
Nov 23	Mary, d of Thomas & Ann LION	bap
Nov 23	Benjamin, s of Benjamin & Jane MILLWARD	bur
Nov 24	Daniel, s of Samuel & Sarah PASKIN	bap
Nov 24	Thomas TAYLOR & Esther WHITEHOUSE	mar
Nov 24	William NIGHTINGALE & Prudence TURNER were married	mar
Nov 30	William BROOKS	bur
Nov 30	Zachariah, s of Job & Sarah SMITH	bur
Nov 30	Hannah, d of John & Joice MILLS	bur
Dec 7	William, s of John & Sarah WITTALL	bap
Dec 14	Jane, d of Stephen & Mary HIPKISS	bap
Dec 21	Daniel & Hannah, twins of Daniel & Hannah WHITEHOUSE	bap
Dec 21	Isaac, s of David & Sarah JEVON	bap
Dec 21	Elizabeth, a bas begotten Child of Martha SAUNDERS	bap
Dec 22	Richard, s of Richard & Sarah WHITEHOUSE	bap
Dec 22	Joseph, s of Joseph & Elizabeth HORTON	bur
Dec 25	Sarah MARTIN	bur
Dec 25	Joseph, s of John & Mary FEREDAY	bap

1777

Dec 25	Joseph, s of Paul & Lydia GRIFFIS	bap
Dec 25	William, s of William & Elizabeth JONES	bap
Dec 25	Richard, s of Richard & Sarah NIGHTINGALE	bap
Dec 25	Joseph, s of John & Ann SMITH, Born Nov 11, 1777	bap
Dec 25	Ann, d of Joseph & Lydia WHITEHOUSE	bap
Dec 25	Elizabeth, d of William & Elizabeth WALTON, Born Oct 11, 1777	bap
Dec 26	Richard WHITEHOUSE & Mary FOSTER were married by Banns	mar
Dec 26	Joseph MILLS & Elizabeth FOSTER were married by Banns	mar
Dec 28	Isaac & Rebekah, twins of John & Rebekah COLE	bap
Dec 28	Eleanor MARSON	bur

1778

Jan 11	Jane FISHER	bur
Jan 11	Thomas, s of Joseph & Martha CADDRACK, Born Dec 22, 1777	bap
Jan 11	Sarah, d of William & Mary HUGHES	bap
Jan 18	Samuel, s of Samuel & Sarah NOCK	bap
Jan 25	James WEBB	bur
Jan 28	Thomas CLARK & Lydia COOPER were married by Banns	mar
Feb 1	Elizabeth, d of Joseph & Ann SANDERS	bap
Feb 8	Ann FISHER	bur
Feb 8	Mary, d of John & Susanna BLACKHAM, Born Jan 23	bap
Feb 8	Jane, d of Thomas & Phebe JUKES	bap
Feb 8	Deborah, d of Andrew & Priscilla ROLLINSON	bap
Feb 9	Thomas TISDALL & Alice BARNES were married by Banns	mar
Feb 11	Betty SHELDON	bur
Feb 13	Rebekah, wife of Richard BECK	bur
Feb 13	Selvia, d of Benjamin & Elizabeth GRIFFIS	bap
Feb 13	Elizabeth, d of William & Phebe PRITCHET	bap
Feb 15	John, a base begotten Child of Elizabeth WILLIS, Born Jan 26 1777	bap
Feb 15	Hannah, d of Thomas & Hannah BOLT, 2 months old	bap
Feb 17	Daniel WARR	bur
Feb 17	William, s of Richard & Elizabeth WAINWRIGHT	bap
Feb 17	Phebe, d of Joseph & Phebe NICKOLDS	bap
Feb 22	Samuel PASKIN	bur
Feb 22	John, a base begotten Child of Mary MILLS	bap
Feb 22	Edward, s of Joseph & Sarah BLACKHAM	bap
Feb 27	Isaac, s of Joseph & Jane JEVON	bap
Feb 27	Daniel, s of Daniel & Elizabeth BAKER, one year old	bap
Mar 1	Luke, s of Edward & Mary STOCKWIN	bap
Mar 3	John, s of Thomas & Mary WHEAL	bap
Mar 3	Mary, d of Joseph & Eleanor FISHER	bap
Mar 15	Mary, a base begotten Child of Sarah TONKS	bap
Mar 15	Joseph TINKER	bur
Mar 15	Edward, s of Sarah FISHER, Born Novr 28, 1769	bap
Mar 22	Hannah, d of John & Ann FLETCHER	bap
Mar 22	Martha SMITH	bur
Feb 8[sic]	Thomas, s of William & Martha SHORT, Born May 5 1775	bap

1778

Feb 8[sic]	John, s of William & Martha SHORT, Born July 30 1777	bap
Mar 29	Mary, d of Isaac & Amey WALTERS	bap
Mar 29	William, s of William & Ann EDGE	bap
Mar 29	Ann, d of Joseph & Betty MILLS, Born Jan 25 1778	bap
Mar 29	John, s of John & Mary STOKES	bur
Mar 31	Hannah, d of Henry & Mary WILLIAMS	bur
Apr 5	Sarah, d of John & Sarah FISHER	bap
Apr 7	Joshua CALLOWAY	bur
+ Apr 19	Joseph, s of Bayley & Sarah HILL	bap
Apr 19	Daniel, s of John & Mary DREW	bap
‒ Apr 19	Daniel, s of John & Martha PARTRIDGE	bap
Apr 19	Ann, d of William & Hannah FOSTER	bap
Apr 19	Ann, d of Daniel & Sarah FISHER	bap
⊥ Apr 19	Hannah, a bas begotten Child of Jane GUTTRIDGE	bap
Apr 19	George FISHER	bur
Apr 26	Samuel EDGE	bur
Apr 28	William, s of William & Ann EDGE	bur
Apr 29	Jane MALLIN	bur
May 5	Sarah FISHER	bur
May 10	Betty, d of Samuel & Phebe BECK	bap
⟋ May 10	Sarah, d of Daniel & Ann TIMMINS	bap
May 13	Martha FURNEFOOT	bur
May 17	Mary, d of John & Lydia FURNEFOOT	bap
May 17	Joseph, s of Abraham & Phebe WHITEHOUSE	bap
May 28	Thomas EDGE	bur
May 28	Susanna, d of Edward & Mary FISHER	bap
May 31	Mary, d of John & Lydia FURNEFOOT	bur
May 31	Sarah WHITEHOUSE	bur
Jun 7	Samuel, s of Thomas & Sarah SATCHWELL	bap
Jun 7	Mary, d of William & Sarah PITEWAY	bap
Jun 7	Elizabeth, d of William & Prudence NIGHTINGALE	bap
⊥ Jun 7	Mary, d of James & Martha GREEN	bap
✛ Jun 7	Mary, d of Joseph & Sarah HILL	bap
Jun 8	Joseph, s of Joseph & Mary SMITH	bap
Jun 8	James, s of John & Hannah DARBY	bap
Jun 8	George COLLINS married Sophia SHELDON by Banns	mar
Jun 8	Daniel NICKLIN married Jane LEWISS by Banns	mar
Jun 8	Joseph, s of Joseph & Mary WILLEYS, 5 yrs old in Oct 1777	bap
Jun 8	Benjamin, s of Joseph & Mary WILLEYS, 3 yrs old in Dec 1777	bap
Jun 8	Phebe, d of Joseph & Mary WILLEYS, 1 yr old	bap
‒ Jun 8	Elizabeth EDWARDS, a base begotten Child of Lydia TURNER	bap
Jun 9	William HONE	bur
Jun 9	William, s of Thomas & Ester TAYLOR	bap
Jun 14	Benjamin, s of William & Elizabeth SMITH	bap
Jun 21	Samuel, s of Thomas & Mary FEREDAY, Born May 14	bap
‒ Jun 21	John, s of Richard & Sarah INGRAM	bap
Jun 24	Rachael, wife of Thomas FEREDAY	bur
Jun 28	Peter, s of James & Elizabeth ROUND	bap
Jul 5	Sarah WILLIAMS	bur

1778

Jul 5	Elizabeth, d of Jaby & Elizabeth FISHER	bap
Jul 12	Abednego, s of Benjamin & Joice FISHER	bap
Jul 12	William, s of Amos & Hannah DARBY	bap
Jul 12	Mary, d of James & Ann WHITEHOUSE	bap
Jul 26	Elizabeth, d of Daniel & Jane NICKLIN, Born June 11, 1778	bap
Jul 26	Hannah, a bas begotten Child of Sarah NICKLIN	bap
Aug 2	Edward, s of Edward & Ann FEREDAY	bur
Aug 2	Ann, d of William & Mary WHITEHOUSE	bap
Aug 3	Sarah GEATHEM	bur
Aug 9	Mary WHITEHOUSE	bur
Aug 9	John Nathaniel, s of Nathaniel & Mary THOMPSON	bap
Aug 9	Mary, d of Charles & Sarah LAW	bap
Aug 9	Mary, d of John & Elizabeth EDWARDS	bap
Aug 16	Edward GEORGE	bur
Aug 16	Richard NIGHTINGALE	bur
⚜ Aug 16	Ruth, d of Joseph & Mary WALTON	bap
⤬ Aug 16	Sarah, d of Thomas & Nancy FELLOWS	bap
Aug 18	Jinney, d of William & Elizabeth SMITH	bap
Aug 18	Thomas WHITEHOUSE	bur
Aug 20	Maria, d of James & Anna Maria BARBER	bap
Aug 18[sic]	Samuel, s of Abel & Ann WHITEHOUSE	bap
Aug 23	Joseph WHITEHOUSE	bur
Aug 23	Joseph, s of Joseph & Jenny PERCIVAL	bap
Aug 30	Edward, s of James & Jane FEREDAY	bap
Aug 30	Samuel, s of Samuel & Sarah FLETCHER	bap
✝ Aug 30	Abraham, s of Isaac & Sarah GUTTRIDGE	bap
Sep 15	Rachel, d of Jeremiah & Isabell WALTERS	bap
Sep 15	Mary, d of William & Rachel GAUNT	bap
⟶ Sep 15	Sarah MARSON	bur
Sep 16	Richard BATE	bur
— Sep 16	Mary FOSTER	bur
Sep 16	James, s of Thomas & Esther NICKOLDS, bap^d at 8 weeks old	bap
Sep 16	Lucy, d of John & Mary DUDLEY, bap^d at 9 weeks old	bap
⤴ Sep 20	Richard, s of William & Martha INGRAM	bap
✝ Oct 4	Joseph, s of James & Mary NOCK	bap
✝ Oct 11	Abel, s of Abel & Mary HILL	bap
Oct 15	Sarah SMITH	bur
Oct 25	William, s of Benjamin & Mary WESSON	bap
Nov 1	Thomas MILLS	bur
Nov 1	Abraham MILLS	bur
✝ Nov 8	Mary, d of Joseph & Mary HORTON	bap
Nov 10	Elizabeth, wife of Joseph WHITEHOUSE	bur
Nov 10	James, s of Stephen & Mary FISHER	bap
	[Entered between the lines at this point:] 1666	
⟶ Nov 15	Elizabeth PARTRIDGE	bur
Nov 18	Thomas FISHER	bur
Nov 20	John, s of Joseph & Mary NICKOLDS	bur
Nov 29	Elizabeth, d of Philip & Mary RATHBONE	bap
Nov 29	Nancy, d of Joseph & Sarah GRIFFIS	bap

1778

Dec 8	William ELWELL	bur
Dec 25	Joseph & Mary, s & d of Thomas & Alice CARTWRIGHT	bap
Dec 28	Henry, s of Thomas & Alice TISDALL, born November the 3	bap
Dec 28	William EDWARDS & Lydia TURNER were married by Banns	mar
Dec 28	Lucy FISHER	bur

1779

Jan 10	Nancy, d of William & Hannah MILLS	bap
Jan 17	James, s of Abraham & Catharine SHELDON	bap
Jan 17	Henry, s of John & Constant SHELDON	bap
Jan 24	Hannah, d of Eutychus & Elizabeth FISHER	bap
Jan 24	Isabel, d of Peter & Mary SMITH	bap
Feb 2	Catharine, wife of Richard INGRAM	bur
Feb 2	Joice, wife of John MILLS	bur
Feb 7	Edward, s of James & Elizabeth FISHER	bap
Feb 7	Sarah, d of Nathaniel & Elizabeth HEELIN	bap
Feb 14	John, s of Joseph & Elizabeth FLETCHER	bap
Feb 21	Ann, d of Richard & Jane HARTILL	bap
Feb 22	Joseph GORTON & Mary SMITH were married by Banns	mar
Feb 22	Abraham, s of Isaac & Mary DUTTON	bap
Feb 26	James BRASSINGTON & Margaret PRICE were married by Banns	mar
Feb 28	John GUTTRIDGE	bur
Feb 28	Mary, d of Edward & Elizabeth SMITH	bap
Mar 2	John, s of Peter & Rachel ROWLEY	bap
Mar 2	Benjamin, s of Thomas & Hannah RUDGE	bap
Mar 2	Phebe, d of Daniel & Elizabeth GRANGER	bap
Mar 2	Hannah, a base begotten Child of Sarah SMITH	bap
Mar 2	Mary, wife of John JEVON	bur
Mar 2	Samuel HERRING	bur
Mar 14	Isaac, s of Abraham & Hannah FISHER	bap
Mar 14	Mary, d of Daniel & Sarah WARR	bap
Mar 14	William, s of Isaac & Sarah ASTON	bap
Mar 14	Mary, d of William & Elizabeth MILLS	bap
Mar 14	Thomas, s of Benjamin & Sarah WHITEHOUSE	bap
Mar 15	Thomas ROLINSON married Mary MILLS by Banns	mar
Mar 15	Edward DARBY married Mary FELLOWS by Banns	mar
Mar 15	Richard STOKES married Hannah FOSTER by Banns	mar
Mar 21	Thomas, s of Benjamin & Sarah CRESWELL	bap
Mar 21	John, s of William & Sarah ELWELL	bap
Mar 21	Mary, d of Thomas & Sarah SMITH	bap
Mar 28	Ann, d of Edward & Ann BATE	bap
Apr 4	Isaac, s of Isaac & Mary DARBY	bap
Apr 4	John, s of Abraham & Sarah TIMMINS	bap
Apr 4	Phebe, d of Richard & Violetta PARKES	bap
Apr 4	Sarah, d of Daniel & Sarah CALLOWAY	bap
Apr 6	Joseph SHARROD & Elizabeth JEWKS were married by Banns	mar
Apr 6	James HEELIN & Hannah SAUNDERS were married by Banns	mar
Apr 6	Henry KENDRICK & Sarah OWEN were married by Banns	mar

1779

Apr 11	Thomas, s of William & Ann FISHER	bap
Apr 11	Phebe, d of Thomas & Mary COLLINS	bap
Apr 14	William HIGGS & Ruth PERRINGS were married by Banns	mar
Apr 18	Abednego, s of Benjamin & Joice FISHER	bur
Apr 18	Sarah, d of Daniel & Sarah SHELDON	bap
Apr 18	Ann, d of Abraham & Hannah DUDLEY	bap
⊹ May 2	John, s of John & Hannah HODGSKINS	bap
May 2	John, s of William & Elizabeth BARNETT	bap
May 9	Thomas, s of Edward & Jane PERRINS	bap
May 9	Mary WHITEHOUSE	bur
May 16	David, s of Benjamin & Mary SAUNDERS	bap
May 23	John, s of Edward & Esther SMITH	bap
May 23	Jeremiah, s of Edward & Elizabeth DUDLEY	bap
May 23	Eutychus, s of Benjamin & Patience FISHER	bap
May 31	Richard, s of Richard & Mary FISHER	bap
May 31	William FOSTER married Ann DUDLEY by Banns	mar
May 31	Edward SMITH married Ann CARTWRIGHT by Banns	mar
Jun 2	Ruth, d of Benjamin & Joice FISHER	bur
Jun 4	Thomas PASE	bur
+ Jun 4	Ann, wife of William GUTTRIDGE	bur
Jun 4	Elizabeth, d of Peter & Mary ROUND	bap
Jun 10	Mary PARTRIDGE	bur
Jun 13	Thomas WHITEHOUSE	bur
⌄ Jun 13	John, s of John & Lydia FOSTER	bap
Jun 20	George, s of William & Mary TURLEY	bap
Jun 20	Elizabeth, d of Joseph & Mary WHITEHOUSE	bap
Jun 20	Nancy, d of Thomas & Rachel SHAW	bap
Jun 23	David SMITH married Phebe CONSTABLE by Banns	mar
⊣ Jun 27	Nancy, d of Benjamin & Sarah HORTON	bap
Jul 4	Betty, d of William & Mary WHITEHOUSE	bap
Jul 4	Sophia, d of Daniel & Jane NICKLIN	bap
Jul 19	George, s of Richard & Alice JONES	bap
Jul 19	John, s of William & Hannah RICHARDS	bap
Jul 19	Mary, a base begotten Child of Rachel WHITEHOUSE	bap
Jul 26	Mary, d of Steven & Mary WHITEHOUSE, Born Dec 29 1773	bap
Aug 1	Moses WHITEHOUSE	bur
Aug 1	John SATCHWELL	bur
Aug 8	Mary FISHER	bur
Aug 9	Lydia, d of Edward & Hannah WHITEHOUSE, one Year & a half old	bap
Aug 9	William, s of Thomas & Sarah FISHER	bap
⊬ Aug 9	Sarah, d of Joseph & Elizabeth HORTON	bap
Aug 11	Ann, d of Joseph & Sarah GRIFFIS	bur
Aug 11	Mary, d of Henry & Sarah KENDRICK	bap
Aug 11	John SMITH & Mary HIPKISS were married by Banns	mar
⌐ Aug 11	John WARD & Charlotte ROLINSON were married by Banns	mar
⌐ Aug 15	Samuel, s of Samuel & Elizabeth HICKMANS	bap
Aug 20	Elizabeth, d of Daniel & Jane NICKLIN	bur
Aug 20	Sarah, d of John & Mary ATTWOOD	bap

1779

Aug 29	John, s of Henry & Mary WILLIAMS	bap
Sep 5	Hannah, d of Joseph & Esther SMITH	bap
Sep 11	Elizabeth, d of Richard & Mary WHITEHOUSE	bap
Sep 21	Henry HONE	bur
Sep 26	David, s of David & Sarah JEVON	bap
Sep 26	Mary, d of Thomas & Mary THOMAS	bap
Sep 28	Jonas, s of Thomas & Mary ROUND, bap one year & a Half old	bap
Sep 28	Thomas, s of Thomas & Mary ROUND	bap
Sep 28	Hannah, d of William & Hannah WHITEHOUSE	bap
Sep 28	Nancy, d of William & Mary WHITEHOUSE	bur
Sep 28	Nancy, d of Paul & Lydia GRIFFIS	bur
Oct 4	William JONES & Hannah LOCK	mar
Oct 10	Phebe, d of William & Mary ROUND	bur
Oct 12	Joseph, s of Abraham & Catharine MILLS	bur
Oct 12	Sarah, d of John & Sarah FISHER	bur
✝ Oct 17	Hannah, d of James & Martha GREEN	bap
✝ Oct 18	John NORRIS & Lydia HORTON were married by Banns	mar
Oct 24	Hannah, d of John & Mary JOHNSON	bur
Oct 24	Hannah & Mary, twins of Samuel & Hannah ONIONS	bap
Oct 31	David, s of William & Elizabeth FEREDAY	bap
✝ Oct 14 [sic]	Joseph, s of William & Elizabeth HILL	bap
✝ Nov 1	Thomas NICKOLIS & Phebe HILL were married by Banns	mar
✝ Nov 1	John, s of Daniel & Jane HILL, Born June the 14, 1778	bap
Nov 2	Samuel, s of David & Ann WHITEHOUSE	bur
Nov 2	Sarah GRIFFIS	bur
Nov 2	Nancy, d of David & Ann HIPKISS	bur
Nov 2	William, s of William & Rachel WHITEHOUSE	bap
Nov 8	Richard, s of Edward & Elizabeth MILLS	bap
Nov 8	Samuel MILLS & Elizabeth NIGHTINGALE were married by Banns	mar
− Nov 8	Thomas LOWE & Sarah TURNER were married by Banns	mar
Nov 12	John CALLOWAY	bur
Nov 14	Sargaent, s of John & Sarah THOMAS	bap
✝ Nov 14	Abraham GUTTRIDGE	bur
Nov 17	Hannah, d of Eutychus & Elizabeth FISHER	bap
Nov 17	John PERSHOUSE	bur
Nov 17	Thomas, s of Edward & Jane PERRINS	bur
Nov 17	Joseph, s of John & Mary TATE	bap
Nov 21	William, s of Isaac & Sarah ASTON	bur
Nov 21	Sarah, d of Joseph & Elizabeth HORTON	bur
Nov 24	Joseph WILLEYS	bur
Nov 28	Maria, d of William & Lydia DANGERFIELD	bap
Nov 28	Michael, s of Joseph & Ann SAUNDERS	bap
− Nov 28	Joseph, s of Isaac & Rachel FLETCHER	bap
− Nov 28	John ONION, a base begotten Child of Sarah COX	bap
Nov 28	Daniel, s of Benjamin & Mary GORTON	bap
Nov 28	James, s of William & Elizabeth JONES	bap
Nov 28	Isaac, s of William & Elizabeth SMITH	bap
Nov 28	Betty, d of Samuel & Sarah PASKIN	bap

Nov 28	Hannah, d of John & Jane LAWD	bap
Nov 28	Sarah, d of Joseph & Mary WILLEYS	bap
Dec 1	Phebe, d of Daniel & Sarah GRIFFIS	bap
Dec 1	Nancy, d of Richard & Sarah GRIFFIS	bur
Dec 5	William DREW	bur
Dec 12	Nancy, d of Daniel & Sarah WARR	bur
Dec 12	Mary, wife of John JOHNSON	bur
— Dec 19	Hannah, d of William & Hannah FOSTER	bap
Dec 19	John, s of Thomas & Mary WHEAL	bur
Dec 25	Joseph DUDLEY	bur
⟶ Dec 25	Samuel, s of Samuel & Sarah FLETCHER	bur
Dec 25	Joseph, s of Joseph & Mary GORTON	bap
Dec 25	Sarah, d of Thomas & Phebe INCHER	bap
— Dec 25	Ann, d of Thomas & Sarah LOW	bap
Dec 25	Sarah, d of George & Selvia COLLINS	bap
Dec 31	Jane, d of John & Mary WILKINSON	bap
Dec 31	Thomas, s of William & Mary FISHER	bur

⟋ Jan 2	Sarah, d of Thomas & Sarah LOW	bur
Jan 2	Joseph, s of Samuel & Ann MILLS	bap
Jan 3	William SHELDON married Ann FISHER by Banns	mar
Jan 6	Elizabeth, d of William & Lydia EDWARDS	bur
Jan 9	Jane, d of John & Sarah PERSHOUSE	bap
Jan 16	Hannah, d of Richard & Ann LEACH, Born August 20, 1779	bap
Jan 19	Nancy, d of Richard & Sarah GRIFFIS	bap
Jan 19	Thomas, a base begotten Child of Nancy WHEAL	bap
Jan 19	Nancy, d of Edward & Ann BATE	bur
Jan 23	William & Mary, twins s & d of John & Mary FEREDAY	bap
Jan 23	Thomas, a base begotten Child of Elizabeth EDGE	bap
⟋ Jan 23	Hannah, d of Daniel & Ann FLETCHER	bap
Jan 23	Mary, d of Stephen & Mary HIPKISS	bap
✝ Jan 30	Henry, s of James & Mary NOCK	bap
Feb 3	John, s of James & Hannah HEELEY	bap
Feb 4	Elizabeth, d of William & Martha SHORT, Born Nov 1, 1779	bap
Feb 4	Elizabeth, d of Joseph & Phebe NICHOLDS	bap
— Feb 6	Sarah, d of Richard & Sarah INGRAM	bap
— Feb 7	Richard TONKS & Mary INGRAM were married by Banns	mar
⇒ Feb 13	Sarah, d of John & Sarah PARKES	bur
Feb 13	Richard CARTER	bur
Feb 16	Sarah WILLEYS	bur
Feb 16	John, s of Stephen & Mary WHITEHOUSE	bap
— Feb 23	Zachariah PARKES	bur
Feb 23	Edward, s of Edward & Ann FEREDAY, Born Novr 15, 1779	bap
Feb 27	Hannah, d of John & Sarah WITTALL	bap
Feb 27	Hannah, d of Samuel & Elizabeth MILLS	bap
Feb 28	Richard FULLWOOD	bur
Mar 5	Thomas, s of Joseph & Elizabeth HEEDS, Born Jan 1 1780	bap
✝ Mar 5	William, s of Samuel & Sarah NOCK	bap

1780

Mar 5	Benjamin, s of James & Hannah HORTON	bap
~ Mar 5	John, s of James & Jane PRICE	bap
Mar 5	Sarah, d of John & Phebe ASTON	bap
Mar 5	Elizabeth, d of Richard & Sarah BECK	bap
Mar 5	Lydia, d of Edward & Mary DARBY	bap
Mar 5	Daniel ROUND	bur
Mar 5	Samuel, a bas begotten Child of Jane SMITH	bap
Mar 22	Daniel FISHER	bur
✓ Mar 22	Thomas BAILEY & Catherine SHEAREWOOD [altered to "SHERWOOD"], were married by Licence.	mar
Mar 26	James, s of James & Elizabeth ROUND	bap
Mar 26	Nancy, d of John & Elizabeth EDWARDS	bap
Mar 26	Mary, d of Thomas & Phebe NICHOLIS	bap
Mar 27	Abraham, s of Richard & Mary JEWKS	bap
Mar 27	Joseph, s of Thomas & Esther TAYLOR	bap
Mar 27	Benjamin, s of Benjamin & Joice FISHER	bap
Mar 27	Sarah, d of James & Ann RICHARD	bap
Apr 16	Henry WILLIAM	bur
Apr 17	Sarah, d of Enas & Hannah WHITEHOUSE	bap
Apr 17	Elizabeth, d of John & Frances SAUNDERS	bap
Apr 17	Richard WHITEHOUSE & Sarah SMITH were married by Banns	mar
~ Apr 23	Jesse, s of Bailey & Sarah HILL	bap
Apr 23	Nancy, d of Paul & Lydia GRIIFFIS	bap
Apr 30	Winneyfred MOSLEY	bur
— Apr 30	William, s of Joseph & Phebe STANLEY	bap
May 7	James, s of James & Elizabeth FISHER	bur
May 7	Ann, d of David & Ann HIPKISS, Born March 27th	bap
― May 7	Elizabeth, d of John & Betty HALL, Born March 6th	bap
← May 14	Phillp, s of John & Martha PARTRIDGE	bap
May 14	Phebe, d of Edward & Ann SMITH	bap
May 14	Richard, s of Richard Ann HALDEN	bap
May 15	Phebe, d of Joseph & Lydia WHITEHOUSE	bap
May 15	Abraham, s of Michel & Elizabeth DUFFIELD	bap
May 15	William SHELDON & Hannah BECK were married by Banns	mar
May 28	Phebe, d of Benjamin & Mary WHESSON	bap
May 28	Sarah, d of Joseph & Mary CALLOWAY	bap
― May 28	Joseph WHITEHOUSE & Sarah COX were married by Banns	mar
↳ Jun 4	Joseph, s of Joseph & Sarah HILL	bap
Jun 4	Lettice, d of Daniel & Betty SMITH	bap

A Transcript of the Register Book of Tipton Alias Tibbington was
Exhibited into the Deans Visitation held in the Court of Lichfield being
on June the 6th 1780

Jun 7	Aamass DARBY	bur
Jun 7	James, s of Richard & Elizabeth WAINWRIGHT	bap
Jun 7	Elizabeth, d of Richard & Sarah WHITEHOUSE	bap
Jun 11	William, s of John & Shusannah BLACKHAM	bap
Jun 11	Isaac, s of Isaac & Sarah ASTON	bap
Jun 11	Thomas, s of John & Lydia NORRIS	bap
Jun 12	Mary WHITEHOUSE	bur

1780

Jun 12	Richard, s of Joseph & Sarah GRIFFIS	bap
Jun 26	Ann, d of John & Catharine FISHER	bap
Jun 26	Mary MILLS	bur
Jun 26	Ann, d of Thomas & Hannah BOTT	bap
Jul 9	Jeremiah, s of Richard & Sarah WHITEHOUSE	bap
Jul 9	Elizabeth WHITEHOUSE	bur
Jul 9	Elizabeth SMITH	bur
Jul 16	Phebe, d of William & Martha INGRAM	bap
Jul 26	Hannah, d of William & Hannah BROWN	bap
Aug 6	Phebe, d of Abel & Mary MILLS	bap
Aug 6	Elizabeth, d of Daniel & Leah SMITH	bap
Aug 6	Judith, d of Daniel & Ann TIMMINS	bap
Aug 7	Edward TURNER & Elizabeth BLOXWICH were married by Banns	mar
Aug 20	Joseph, s of Stephen & Mary FISHER	bap
Aug 20	Mary, d of Benjamin & Hannah JEVON	bap
Aug 20	Hannah, d of James & Sarah TURLEY	bap
Sep 3	William, s of William & Sarah ELWELL	bap
Sep 8	Judith TIMMINS	bur
Sep 8	James, s of Thomas & Hannah RUDGE	bap
Sep 13	Richard MILLS & Mary FELLOWS, were married by Licence	mar
Sep 13	Edward WHITEHOUSE	bur
Sep 24	Thomas, s of Thomas & Mary FEREDAY	bap
Sep 24	Phebe, d of Daniel & Phebe WARR	bap
Sep 24	Amelia, d of William & Nancy JOHNSON	bap
Oct 1	Isaac FISHER	bur
Oct 1	Phebe COWLEY	bur
Oct 1	Hannah, d of Peter & Rachel ROWLEY	bap
Oct 1	Jimmimey, d of Henry & Catharine HOLLAND, Born April 1st 1780	bap
Oct 2	Thomas BUNCE & Phebe TALBOTT were married by Banns	mar
Oct 9	Benjamin, s of Thomas & Mary LITTLE	bap
Oct 9	Joseph & Mary, s & d of John & Lydia FURNEFOOT	bap
Oct 10	Joseph, s of Joseph & Mary SMITH	bap
Oct 10	Aron SMITH & Mary WHITEHOUSE were married by Banns	mar
Oct 13	Betty WARTON	bur
Oct 15	Hannah, d of Richard & Mary TONKS	bap
Oct 22	Mary, d of Daniel & Sarah SHELDON	bap
Oct 24	Esther HICKMANS	bur
Oct 29	Gideon, s of Gideon & Elizabeth WHITEHOUSE	bap
Oct 29	Mary, d of Joseph & Martha CADRACK	bap
Oct 29	Prudence, d of Thomas & Mary COLLINS	bap
Oct 31	Job WHITEHOUSE	bur
Nov 5	Mary, d of James & Elizabeth FISHER	bap
Nov 5	Mary, d of Ambrose & Mary BLACKHAM, Born Sep 14th	bap
Nov 5	Elizabeth, d of Thomas & Sarah SUTTON	bap
Nov 5	Samuel, s of William & Mary TURNER	bap
Nov 5	Samuel, s of John & Phebe HICKMANS	bap

1780

Nov 12	Joshua Jones, s of James & Elizabeth HILL, Born April 30th 1778	bap
Nov 12	William, s of James & Elizabeth HILL	bap
Nov 16	Amelia, d of Samuel & Sarah FLETCHER	bap
Nov 16	Phebe, d of John & Ann FLETCHER	bap
Nov 16	Edward PERRINS	bur
Nov 19	Henry, s of Thomas & Mary KENDRICK	bap
Nov 19	Mary, d of Abraham & Sarah GUTTRIDGE	bap
Nov 19	Sarah, d of Edward & Sarah WHITEHOUSE	bur
Nov 26	Henry, s of Isaac & Sarah GUTTRIDGE	bap
Nov 26	Ziprah, d of John & Mary DARBY	bap
Nov 26	Thomas, s of Thomas & Sarah PARKES	bap
Nov 26	Jane, d of James & Elizabeth BENNETT	bap
Nov 26	Sarah, d of Amass & Sarah DARBY	bap
Nov 26	Jane WHITEHOUSE	bur
Dec 3	Olivar JOHNSON	bur
Dec 4	Samuel ROBERTS & Sarah SHELDON were married by Banns	mar
Dec 4	William, s of John & Rhody DOUBTY, one year old	bap
Dec 6	Hannah TIMMINS	bur
Dec 10	James, s of Joseph & Mary HORTON	bap
Dec 10	James WEBB & Jane STRINGER were married by Banns	mar
Dec 24	Aamass, s of John & Hannah DARBY	bap
Dec 24	Rhody, d of Nathaniel & Elizabeth HEYLIR[?]	bap
Dec 24	Joseph, s of Joseph & Jane JEVON	bap
Dec 25	Joseph, s of John & Mary ATTWOOD	bap
Dec 25	Joseph, s of John & Hannah DUFFIELD	bap
Dec 25	Jane, d of John & Sarah WHITEHOUSE	bap
Dec 25	Heyley, s of Benjamin & Sarah WHITEHOUSE	bap
Dec 27	Richard STANTON & Sarah BLACKHAM were married by Banns	mar
Dec 27	David SMITH & Phebe TURNER were married by Banns	mar

1781

Jan 7	Richard LAW	bur
Jan 14	Thomas FOSTER	bur
Jan 21	Richard, s of William & Elizabeth HARRISON	bap
Feb 4	Joseph, s of Joseph & Mary WALTON	bur
Feb 4	William, s of William & Mary WHITEHOUSE	bap
Feb 4	Hannah, d of David & Ann WHITEHOUSE	bap
Feb 7	Joseph WHITEHOUSE	bur
Feb 7	Edward, s of Edward & Ann BATE	bap
Feb 7	Samuel, s of Samuel & Elizabeth HICKMANS	bap
Feb 7	Martha & Mary, bas begotten Children of Phebe WHEAL, Born November 7th 1772	bap
Feb 11	Hebrew, s of Abraham & Sarah TIMMINS	bap
Feb 11	Mary, d of Isaac & Mary DARBY	bap
Feb 11	Mary, d of Thomas & Sarah LOWE	bap
Feb 18	John, s of Thomas & Jane PERRY	bap
Feb 18	Thomas, s of John & Hannah HODGSKINS	bap

1781

Feb 18	John, a base begotten C of Elizabeth SMITH	bap
Feb 21	John, s of William & Rachel GAUNT	bap
Mar 1	Joseph, s of Abraham & Catharine MILLS	bap
Mar 1	Joice PARKES	bur
Mar 1	Benjamin, s of Benjamin & Joice FISHER	bur
Mar 4	Sarah, d of John & Sarah FISHER	bap
Mar 11	Elizabeth, d of William & Elizabeth BOWEN	bap
Mar 11	Sarah, d of Joseph & Sarah BLACKHAM	bap
Mar 18	Mary, d of Samuel & Phebe BECK	bap
Mar 25	William, s of William & Elizabeth SMITH	bap
Mar 25	John, s of Daniel & Sarah FISHER	bap
Mar 25	Elizabeth, d of David & Jane NICKLIN	bap
Mar 25	Mary, d of Thomas & Mary WHEAL, Born Sep 24, 1780	bap
Mar 25	Ann, d of Richard & Jane ARTILL	bap
Apr 2	Elias, s of John & Jimmimey PRESSON	bap
Apr 2	Elizabeth, d of William & Hannah MILLS	bap
Apr 2	Ruth, a bas begotten Child of Ann GRIFFIS, Born Mar 10, 1778	bap
Apr 2	Joseph, s of Joseph & Elizabeth HORTON	bap
Apr 2	James, s of Joseph & Mary HORTON	bur
Apr 2	Betty, wife of Joseph TONKS	bur
Apr 2	Joseph, s of Abraham & Hannah WALTERS	bap
Apr 10	Moses WARR	bur
Apr 15	Lydia WEATLEY	bur
Apr 15	Edward, s of Abraham & Phebe WHITEHOUSE	bap
Apr 15	Phebe, d of Andrew & Priscilla ROLINSON	bap
Apr 15	James, s of Thomas & Sarah SATCHWELL	bap
Apr 15	Lucretia, d of Edward & Mary STOCKWIN	bap
Apr 16	Thomas MORRIS & Elizabeth WHEAL were married by Banns	mar
Apr 17	Moses TIMMINS married Hannah FLETCHER by Banns	mar
Apr 17	James, s of Benjamin & Sarah HORTON	bap
May 4	Joseph FOSTER	bur
May 4	John, s of Richard & Mary WHITEHOUSE	bap
May 6	Thomas GREYER	bur
May 7	Joseph ROSS married Elizabeth DAVIS by Banns	mar
May 7	Benjamin, s of Isaac & Mary DUTTON	bap
May 20	Hannah, d of Thomas & Nancy FELLOWS	bap
May 23	Phebe GRIFFIS	bur
May 27	Thomas, s of John & Hannah HODGSKINS	bur
May 27	Joseph, s of Benjamin & Patience FISHER	bap
May 27	James, s of Benjamin & Sarah CRESWELL	bap
May 28	William, s of Joseph & Phebe STANLEY	bur
Jun 3	Jane, wife of William MARSON	bur
Jun 3	Jane, d of William & Jane MARSON	bap
Jun 3	Ann, d of Edward & Elizabeth SMITH	bap
Jun 17	Nanney, d of Richard & Sarah NIGHTINGALE	bap
Jun 17	Daniel, s of Daniel & Sarah CALLOWAY	bap
Jun 24	William JAMES, a bas begot Child of Ann HUGHES	bap
Jun 27	John UNITE	bur
Jul 1	William, s of William & Sarah FOSTER	bap

<u>1781</u>

Jul 8	Elizabeth, d of Thomas & Margaret BROCKHURST	bap
Jul 8	Sarah, d of Edward & Ann ROBERTS	bap
Jul 22	Thomas, s of George & Elizabeth GUTTRIDGE, Born July 14, 1778	bap
Jul 22	William, s of Thomas & Phebe BUNCE	bap
Jul 22	Elizabeth, d of George & Elizabeth GUTTRIDGE	bap
Jul 22	Hannah, d of John & Constant SHELDON	bap
Jul 24	Isaac TIMMINS married Martha DUDLEY by Banns	mar
Jul 24	Hannah, d of Joseph & Ellnor FISHER, Born July the 14, 1780	bap
Jul 24	Sarah WHITEHOUSE	bur
Jul 28	Joseph, s of Stephen & Mary FISHER	bur
Jul 29	Ann, d of Joseph & Elizabeth WHITEHOUSE, Born Jan 1, 1781	bap
Aug 19	Rebekah, d of James & Sarah WHITEHOUSE	bap
Aug 19	John Fellows, s of Edward & Mary DARBY	bap
Aug 19	Sarah, d of Samuel & Sarah PRITCHETT	bap
Aug 26	Mary, d of Joseph & Jane PERCALL	bap
Sep 2	Hannah, wife of William TAYLOR	bur
Sep 3	Hannah, d of Richard & Sarah NIGHTINGALE	bur
Sep 9	Ann, d of Joseph & Ann LESTER	bap
Sep 16	Nancy, d of Joseph & Sarah GRIFFIS	bur
Sep 16	Timothy, s of Job & Phebe SMITH	bur
Sep 16	Hannah, d of Benjamin & Elizabeth GRIFFIS	bap
Sep 17	Thomas, s of James & Ann WHITEHOUSE	bap
Sep 17	James ASTON & Jane COOPER were married by Banns	mar
Sep 23	Lucy, d of Thomas & Phebe INCHER	bap
Sep 24	James FEREDAY & Mary STANTON were married by Banns	mar
Sep 25	Benjamin STOKES & Elizabeth PITCHFORK were married by Lycence	mar
Sep 26	William SMITH	bur
Sep 30	Beneretha, d of Richard & Ann LEECH	bap
Sep 30	Thomas, s of James & Martha GREEN	bap
Oct 3	Hannah, d of Benjamin & Mary WHEAL	bap
Oct 3	Mary WHITEHOUSE	bur
Oct 3	Mary, d of William & Mary WHITEHOUSE	bap
Oct 8	Edward ALEXANDER & Mary PERSHOUSE were married by Lycence	mar
Oct 9	Sarah, d of Peter & Mary SMITH	bap
Oct 9	Ann, d of Richard & Sarah STANTON	bap
Oct 9	Samuel INGRAM	bur
Oct 14	Joseph, s of Thomas & Elizabeth SHORTHOUSE	bap
Oct 14	Lucy, d of Thomas & Sarah CORFIELD	bap
Oct 21	William, s of William & Rachael HOOLEY	bap
Oct 21	John, s of William & Sarah LAW	bap
Oct 21	Sophia, d of William & Ann FISHER	bap
Oct 22	Thomas HORTON & Elizabeth WHITEHOUSE were married by Banns	mar
Oct 24	Nancy GRIFFIS	bur
Oct 25	Phebe FLETCHER	bur
Oct 27	Jonathan, s of Benjamin & Mary SAUNDERS, Born October 19	bap

Oct 28	Sarah MILLS	bur
Oct 29	Richard REED married Margaret MILLARD by Banns	mar
Oct 31	William, s of Thomas & Dinah ALLEN	bap
Oct 31	James, s of Daniel & Sarah WARR	bap
Nov 2	William, s of William & Ann CALLINGTON, one year old	bap
Nov 2	Elizabeth, d of William & Ann CALLINGTON, three years old	bap
Nov 2	Sarah, d of Thomas & Alice CARTWRIGHT	bap
Nov 2	William, s of William & Ann FOSTER, Born Sep 1	bap
Nov 2	Mary, d of William & Lydia EDWARDS	bap
Nov 2	William, s of Joseph & Elizabeth FLETCHER	bap
Nov 2	Honour, d of Edward & Ann KERRY, Born Aug 7	bap
Nov 4	Jesse, s of Moses & Hannah TIMMINS	bap
Nov 7	Hannah, d of Thomas & Hannah TRANNTER	bap
Nov 7	John BLOOMFIELD	bur
Nov 11	Jane JOHNSON	bur
Nov 19	Jane, d of Thomas & Mary ROUND	bap
Nov 19	William, s of William & Martha INGRAM	bur
Nov 19	Ann, d of William & Hannah FOSTER	bur
Nov 25	Elizabeth, d of Joseph & Sarah WHITEHOUSE	bap
Nov 25	Sarah, d of Joseph & Jane LAWD	bap
Nov 25	Sarah, d of Joseph & Ellnor TURVEY, Born Jun 15	bap
Nov 26	Joseph FIELDHOUSE married Nancy FORREST by Banns	mar
Nov 28	Henry, s of John & Constant SHELDON	bur
Dec 9	William, s of Joseph & Mary GORTON	bap
Dec 9	David, s of Thomas & Phebe NICHOLIS	bap
Dec 9	Ann, d of Joseph & Ann PARKER	bap
Dec 18	Hannah, d of Joseph & Mary WHITEHOUSE	bap
Dec 18	Sarah LAWE	bur
Dec 18	Thomas CADDROCK	bur
Dec 20	Sarah NIGHTINGALE	bur
Dec 23	Elizabeth WHITEHOUSE	bur
Dec 23	Honour, d of George & Sophia COLLINS	bap
Dec 25	Jane WHEAL	bur
Dec 29	William, s of Joseph & Mary NICKLIN	bur
Dec 30	Jane, d of John & Sarah COOPER	bur
Dec 30	Joseph, s of Francis & Hannah WHITEHOUSE	bap

Jan 1	Joseph, s of Joseph & Elizabeth HORTON	bur
Jan 3	William, s of William & Sarah ELWELL	bur
Jan 4	Hannah, d of William & Hannah BROWN	bur
Jan 5	Amelia, d of Joseph & Elizabeth HEEDS, Born Decr 2, 1781	bap
Jan 6	Thomas, s of William & Hannah BROWN	bap
Jan 13	Hannah, d of Joseph & Mary HORTON	bap
Jan 16	James WHITEHOUSE	bur
Jan 16	William, a bas begotten Child of Elizabeth ROUND	bap
Jan 16	Moses, a bas begotten Child of Tamer RICHARDS	bap
Jan 16	Sarah, d of Samuel & Elizabeth MILLS	bap
Jan 18	Sarah, wife of Richard WHITEHOUSE	bur

1782

Jan 18	Sarah, d of Richard & Sarah WHITEHOUSE	bap
Jan 20	Stephen, s of Stephen & Mary HIPKISS	bap
Jan 22	Joseph WHITEHOUSE	bur
Jan 22	Jeremiah, s of William & Mary WHITEHOUSE	bap
Jan 22	Sophia, d of John & Mary WILKINSON	bap
Jan 25	Samuel HICKMANS	bur
Jan 28	Joseph, s of Joseph & Mary WARTON	bap
Jan 28	Rosannah, d of William & Hannah SHELDON	bur
Feb 1	Thomas WHITEHOUSE	bur
Feb 1	Benjamin, s of Thomas & Elizabeth HORTON	bap
Feb 3	Daniel SHELDON	bur
Feb 3	Jane, d of John & Sarah COOPER	bap
Feb 3	Moses, s of Aron & Mary SMITH	bap
Feb 10	Edward, s of William & Rachel WHITEHOUSE	bap
Feb 10	Joseph WINNINGTON	bur
Feb 10	Mary MILLS	bur
Feb 12	Thomas CAMM & Hannah MAULIN were married by Licence	mar
Feb 12	John WHITEHOUSE & Mary DARBY were married by Banns	mar
Feb 12	Daniel, a bas begotten Child of Phebe GUTTRIDGE	bap
Feb 17	Ann, wife of Robert LAWTON	bur
Feb 17	Joseph, s of Richard & Mary WHITEHOUSE	bur
Feb 24	Sarah, d of Samuel & Sarah NOCK	bap
Feb 24	William, s of William & Mary FISHER, Born Feb 22 1781	bap
Mar 2	James LEA married Margaret WILLINGTON by Lycence	mar
Mar 3	Mary SMITH	bur
Mar 3	Thomas, s of William & Hannah RICHARDS	bap
Mar 3	Elizabeth, d of Samuel & Sarah ROBERTS	bap
Mar 10	Nancy, d of John & Elizabeth EDWARDS	bap
Mar 10	Isaac, s of David & Sarah JEVON	bap
Mar 10	Hannah, d of Richard & Mary TONKS	bur
Mar 11	Isaac, s of Isaac & Rachel FLETCHER	bap
Mar 11	Joseph LAW married Lettice TIMMINS by Banns	mar
Mar 17	Hannah, d of John & Phebe JEVON	bap
Mar 17	Stephen, s of Daniel & Sarah SHELDON	bap
Mar 24	Samuel, a bas begotten Child of Sarah INGRAM	bap
Mar 31	William, s of Richard & Sarah INGRAM	bap
Mar 31	William, s of Isaac & Sarah ASTON	bap
Apr 7	Richard, s of William & Elizabeth HARRISON	bur
Apr 8	Thomas FEREDAY	bur
Apr 8	Edward, s of Edward & Mary ALEXANDER	bap
Apr 8	Thomas, s of William & Elizabeth FEREDAY	bap
Apr 14	Mary, d of John & Hannah HODGSKINS	bap
Apr 14	Phebe, d of Thomas & Mary LITTLE	bap
Apr 21	Thomas, s of Thomas & Sarah FISHER	bap
Apr 21	John, s of Thomas & Elizabeth MORRIS	bap
Apr 21	Mary, d of John & Lydia FURNEYFOOT	bap
Apr 21	Ann, wife of Edward BATE	bur
Apr 21	William, s of William & Hannah WHITEHOUSE	bap
Apr 23	James FOSTER & Mary MASH were married by Banns	mar

1782

Apr 28	Joseph, s of Joseph & Nancy SAUNDERS	bap
Apr 28	David, s of David & Ann HIPKISS	bap
Apr 28	James FISHER	bur
Apr 28	Elizabeth NICKLIN	bur
May 1	George FISHER	bur
May 12	John PITEWAY	bur
May 16	Sarah, d of Richard & Sarah WHITEHOUSE	bur
May 19	Thomas, s of William & Elizabeth SMITH	bap
May 19	Job, s of John & Sarah FISHER, born Mar 25, 1781	bap
May 19	Edward, s of Joseph & Ann GEORGE, Born April 26	bap
May 19	Mary, d of Michael & Elizabeth DUFFIELD	bap
May 19	Catharine, d of Gilbert & Martha OWELL	bap
May 19	William, s of William & Jane WHITEHOUSE	bap
Jun 3	Mary, d of Isaac & Martha TIMMINS	bap
Jun 3	Ezekiel CASE & Ann POWERS were married by Banns	mar
Jun 3	Joseph TRUMAN & Elizabeth JEWKS	mar
Jun 9	Thomas, s of Thomas & Sarah SMITH	bap
Jun 9	James, s of James & Mary HILL	bap
Jun 9	Leah, d of Benjamin & Patience FISHER	bap
Jun 16	Elizabeth, wife of William MILLS	bur
Jun 16	Sarah, d of Philip & Mary RATHBONE	bap
Jun 16	Richard, s of Richard & Ann SMITH	bap
Jun 20	Ann, wife of Richard ALLDEN	bap
Jun 23	Mary, d of Daniel & Betty SMITH	bap
Jun 23	Ann & Martha, d of Richard & Ann ALLDEN, born June 28, 1775	bap
Jun 23	William, s of Richard & Ann ALLDEN, Born July 20, 1778	bap
Jun 23	Richard, s of Richard & Ann ALLDEN	bap
Jun 26	Thomas PARKES	bur
Jun 26	James, s of Benjamin & Sarah LAW	bap
Jun 26	John, s of John & Mary GRICE, Born May 10	bap
Jun 26	Mary, d of William & Elizabeth WALTON, one Year & a half old	bap
Jun 30	Richard ALLDEN	bur
Jun 30	Rachel, d of James & Mary FEREDAY	bap
Jul 7	Thomas, s of James & Elizabeth FISHER, Born April 11	bap
Jul 7	William, s of Richard & Margaret REED	bap
Jul 7	Nancy, d of Samuel & Elizabeth MILLS	bap
Jul 7	Mary, a bas begotten Child of Sarah NICKLIN	bap
Jul 10	Sophia NICKLIN	bur
Jul 10	Daniel, s of Richard & Mary FISHER	bap
Jul 14	James, s of Eutychus & Elizabeth FISHER	bap
Jul 14	William ASHLEY married Elizabeth WILLIM by Lycence	mar
Jul 24	Hannah WHEAL	bur
Jul 24	Richard & Ann, s & d of Richard & Sarah GRIFFIS	bap
Jul 28	James, s of James & Jane FEREDAY	bap
Jul 28	Sophia, d of Benjamin & Mary WESSON	bap
Jul 28	Maria, d of Peter & Margaret RUDGE	bap
Jul 28	Aron, s of John & Sarah DAVIS	bap
Aug 4	Daniel, s of Daniel & Sarah WARR	bap
Aug 18	Mary, d of James & Mary NOCK	bap

1782

Aug 20	Martha TURLEY	bur
Aug 23	George KERRY	bur
Sep 1	William, s of Paul & Lydia GRIFFIS	bap
Sep 2	Hannah, d of William & Mary HUGHES	bap
Sep 2	Richard WHITEHOUSE married Hannah HIGGINSON by Banns	mar
Sep 2	James OWEN married Ann WHEAL by Banns	mar
Sep 6	John MARSON	bur
Sep 11	John JEVON	bur
Sep 11	Elizabeth, a bas begotten Child of Hannah SAULT	bap
Sep 15	Sarah IVINS	bur
Sep 15	Edward, s of Joseph & Ann GEORGE	bur
Sep 15	Daniel, s of William & Elizabeth BARNEY	bap
Sep 15	Mary, d of Richard & Sarah BECK	bap
Sep 15	Mary, d of Joseph & Mary WILLEYS	bap
Sep 15	Jeremiah, s of Enass & Hannah WHITEHOUSE	bap
Sep 16	Joseph ONIONS married Hannah ELWELL by Banns	mar
Sep 17	Thomas FISHER	mar
Sep 29	Maria, d of Daniel & Sarah FISHER	bap
Oct 3	Elizabeth GUTTRIDGE	bur
Oct 3	Joseph, s of James & Ann RICHARDS, born May 29	bap
Oct 3	Daniel, s of Daniel & Sarah GRIFFIS, born June 20	bap
Oct 3	Sarah, d of William & Elizabeth WARTON	bap
Oct 6	John, s of James & Hannah HORTON	bap
Oct 20	Hannah, d of Richard & Sarah NIGHTINGALE	bap
Oct 20	Elizabeth, d of Thomas & Phebe BUNCE	bap
Oct 20	Sarah, d of Thomas & Mary KENDRICK	bap
Oct 20	Elizabeth, a bas begotten Child of Phebe WHITEHOUSE	bap
Oct 20	Mary, d of William & Mary TURNER	bap
Oct 27	Phebe, d of John & Sarah WITTALL	bap
Oct 27	Esther, d of Richard & Jane ARTIL	bap
Oct 30	Philip, s of Bayley & Sarah HILL, born July 30	bap
Nov 3	Richard, s of Richard & Catharine WHITEHOUSE	bap
Nov 3	Isaac, s of William & Phebe TURNER	bap
Nov 3	Martha, d of Daniel & Ann FLETCHER	bap
Nov 3	Hannah, d of Benjamin & Mary NOCK, born Aug 17	bap
Nov 17	Jane WHITEHOUSE	bur
Nov 17	William, s of John & Martha PARTRIDGE	bap
Nov 17	Ann, d of Moses & Elizabeth HILL	bap
Nov 17	John, s of William & Ann JOHNSON	bap
Nov 18	James EVANS married Elizabeth EDWARDS by Banns	mar
Nov 24	John, s of James & Ann OWEN	bap
Nov 24	Francis, s of Abraham & Catharine MILLS	bap
Nov 24	Samuel, s of Henry & Sarah KENDRICK	bap
Nov 24	James, s of John & Ann WOLLERS	bap
Nov 24	Maria, d of Benjamin & Sarah WHITEHOUSE	bap
Nov 25	Hannah, d of James & Sarah WESTWOOD	bap
Nov 25	Thomas, s of William & Phebe DORRALL, born Oct 20	bap
Nov 25	Robert LAWTON married Hannah JEVON by Banns	mar
Nov 25	Elisha GRIFFIS married Mary TURNER by Banns	mar

1782

Nov 25	Thomas SHELDON married Hannah GRIFFIS by Banns	mar
Dec 8	Phebe, d of Joseph & Nancy FIELDHOUSE	bap
Dec 15	Sarah, d of William & Sarah ELWELL	bap
Dec 22	Mary KERRY	bur
Dec 22	Thomas, s of David & Mary ROUND	bap
Dec 25	Richard, s of Richard & Viletta PARKES	bap
Dec 25	James, s of William & Elizabeth HARRISON, Born Oct 9	bap
Dec 25	Elizabeth, d of William & Martha INGRAM	bap
Dec 25	Joseph, s of Thomas & Hannah RUDGE	bap
Dec 30	Edward, s of Edward & Elizabeth MILLS	bap
Dec 30	Richard TOMBLINSON married Hannah MILLS by Lycence	mar

1783

Jan 1	Richard PERCON	bur
Jan 8	John, s of Thomas & Sarah LAWE	bap
Jan 8	Peter, s of Peter & Rachael ROWLEY	bap
Jan 8	James BARBOR	bur
Jan 8	Richard EDWARDS	bur
Jan 12	Samuel, s of John & Phebe HICKMANS	bap
Jan 20	Hannah FOWNS	bur
Jan 22	Mary BECK	bur
Jan 29	Hannah FISHER	bur
Jan 29	Thomas, s of Richard & Elizabeth WAINWRIGHT	bap
Jan 29	John, s of John & Ann FLETCHER	bap
Jan 29	Rachael, d of Joseph & Phebe NICKOLDS	bap
Jan 29	Elizabeth, a bas begotten Child of Sarah GUTTRIDGE	bap
Feb 5	Hannah MILLS	bur
Feb 5	Isaac HICKMANS	bur
Feb 5	Nancy, d of Thomas & Mary WHITEHOUSE, Born Feb 3/1782	bap
Feb 16	Thomas, s of Daniel & Leah SMITH	bap
Feb 23	Mary GUTTRIDGE	bur
Feb 23	Thomas, s of James & Mary FOSTER	bap
Feb 23	William, s of John & Elizabeth GUTTRIDGE	bap
Mar 2	Thomas BROWN	bur
Mar 2	Mary WILLEYS	bur
Mar 2	Jeremiah WHITEHOUSE	bur
Mar 3	Thomas MILLARD & Elizabeth JEVON	mar
Mar 9	Benjamin, s of Daniel & Jane NICKLIN	bap
Mar 19	Joseph, s of William & Mary FOSTER	bap
Mar 19	Richard FOSTER	bur
Mar 30	Benjamin, s of John & Jane LAW	bap
Mar 30	Rachael, d of Abraham & Sarah TIMMINS	bap
Mar 30	William, s of John & Hannah DARBY	bap
Mar 30	William, s of William & Hannah SHELDON	bap
Mar 30	Benjamin HODGETTS married Martha TONKS by Banns	mar
Apr 6	Abraham, s of Isaac & Mary DARBY	bap
Apr 6	Leticia, d of Edward & Mary STOCKWIN	bap
Apr 14	John WALTERHOUSE married Sarah JEVON by Banns	mar
Apr 15	Mary, d of Ambrose & Ann HILL, born Sep 30, 1782	bap

1783

Apr 15	Silace, s of John & Esther MORRIS	bap
Apr 15	Diapa, d of Thomas & Esther TAYLOR	bap
Apr 20	Mary CARTWRIGHT	bur
Apr 20	John, s of John & Sarah GIBBENS	bap
Apr 20	Nancy, d of James & Hannah HEELEY	bap
— Apr 20	Elizabeth, a bas begotten Child of Mary INGRAM	bap
Apr 20	Mary, d of Abraham, & Phebe WHITEHOUSE	bap
Apr 21	John JAMES married Hannah TALBOTT by Banns	mar
Apr 28	Daniel, s of Richard & Sarah WHITEHOUSE	bap
Apr 28	Sarah FISHER	bur
Apr 28	James FISHER	bur
Apr 28	Maria, d of William & Sarah GAUNT	bap
— Apr 30	John, s of John & Charlotte WARD	bap
Apr 30	Mary FISHER	bur
May 4	Martha NIGHTINGALE	bur
May 12	George GUEST married Ruth ASTON by Lycence	mar
— May 18	Joseph, s of William & Hannah FOSTER	bap
May 25	Sarah, d of Benjamin & Sarah HORTON, Born May 17	bap
May 29	Sarah FISHER	bur
Jun 8	Edward, s of Edward & Ann ROBERTS	bap
— Jun 8	Thomas, s of Isaac & Mary GUTTRIDGE	bap
— Jun 8	Moses, s of Samuel & Elizabeth HILL	bap
Jun 9	Benjamin MILLS married Ann GRIFFIS by Banns	mar
Jun 9	Edward, s of Edward & Ann SMITH	bap
Jun 9	Betteris, d of Isaac & Esther BUNTING	bap
Jun 10	Mary ASPLIN	bur
Jun 10	Samuel, s of Edward & Elizabeth DUDLEY, Born May 12, 1781	bap
Jun 10	Joseph, s of Thomas & Mary ROUND	bap
Jun 24	Thomas, s of David & Mary ROUND	bur
Jun 30	John SMITH & Elizabeth EVINS were married by Banns	mar
— Jul 2	John ROWLEY married Hannah FELLOWS by Banns	mar
Jul 2	Elizabeth, d of Joseph & Martha CADDRACK, born Jan 2 1782	bap
Jul 4	Joseph CAMM	bur
Jul 6	Rebekah, d of John & Phebe ASTON, Born Feb 12	bap
Jul 6	Thomas, s of James & Hannah WHITEHOUSE	bap
✷ Jul 13	Thomas WHITEHOUSE, a bas begotten Child of Mary COOPER	bap

A Transcript of the Register Book of Tipton alias Tibbington was
exhibited into the Deans Visitation held in the Court of Lichfield
being on July 14th 1783

Jul 18	Elizabeth, wife of James FISHER	bur
Jul 18	Benini, s of James & Elizabeth FISHER	bap
Jul 20	Samuel, s of Benjamin & Sarah CRESSWELL	bap
Jul 20	Sophia, d of Benjamin & Hannah RICHARDS	bap
Jul 27	Joseph ROLINSON	bur
✷ Aug 8	Nancy, d of Thomas & Catharine BAILEYS	bur
Aug 10	Benjamin, s of Benjamin & Sarah FISHER	bap
Aug 10	James, s of James & Sarah CRISTIAN	bap
Aug 17	Ann, d of John & Sarah WHITEHOUSE	bap

1783

Aug 17	Joseph, s of Richard & Elizabeth SAUNDERS	bap
Aug 17	Silvia, d of William & Margaret SAUNDERS	bur
Aug 19	Joseph PARKES	bur
Aug 19	John, s of William & Sarah INCKER, Born Jan 3, 1783	bap
Aug 19	Thomas, s of Richard & Hannah TOMBLINSON, Born Apl 3 1783	bap
Aug 19	Phebe, d of Thomas & Elizabeth MORRIS, Born May 8 1783	bap
Aug 28	John ALEXANDER married Hannah PERSHOUSE by Licence	mar
― Sep 1	Isaac LAW married Hannah GUTTRIDGE by Banns	mar
Sep 1	William, s of John & Mary WHITEHOUSE, Born Novr 5 1782	bap
⬤ Sep 1	Samuel, s of Samuel & Sarah FLETCHER, Born June 7	bap
Sep 1	Susannah, d of John & Susannah BLACKHAM	bap
Sep 1	Maria, d of Daniel & Sarah FISHER	bur
Sep 5	John WHESSON	bur
Sep 9	James, s of Richard & Mary JEWKS, Born Apl 18	bap
Sep 9	Ann, d of Thomas & Alice CARTWRIGHT	bap
Sep 9	Sarah, d of Joseph & Sarah SHELDON	bur
Sep 9	Thomas, s of James & Elizabeth FISHER	bur
― Sep 14	Martha, d of Thomas & Elizabeth HUGHES	bap
Sep 18	James, s of Benjamin & Mary WHEAL	bap
Sep 18	Eleanor, d of Samuel & Sarah ROBERTS	bap
Sep 18	Sarah NICKLIN	bur
Sep 21	Sarah, d of David & Ann WHITEHOUSE	bap
Sep 21	John, s of Richard & Sarah STANTON	bap
Sep 22	John SHAROT married Mary WINNINGTON by Banns	mar
Sep 28	Isiah, s of William & Ann FISHER	bap
Sep 28	Sarah, d of William & Mary WHITEHOUSE	bap
― Sep 30	Benjamin LAW married Sarah TONKS by Banns	mar
Sep 30	Thomas, s of Richard & Hannah LAW, Born Dec 17, 1772	bap
Sep 30	Daniel, s of Daniel & Elizabeth WHITEHOUSE, Born July 14 1771	bap
Sep 30	Rosannah, d of Daniel & Elizabeth WHITEHOUSE, Born Jan 3 1774	bap
Sep 30	Jane, d of Isaac & Hannah LAW	bap
Sep 30	Scott Sainia, d of William & Martha SHORT, Born Dec 11, 1782	bap
Oct 5	Fanny, d of John & Fanny SAUNDERS	bap
⌐ Oct 5	Joseph, s of Richard & Sarah INGRAM	bap
Oct 19	Ann, d of Thomas & Elizabeth MORRIS	bap
Oct 19	Richard NICKLIN	bur
Oct 20	Mary, d of Richard & Hannah WHITEHOUSE, Born Aug 20	bap
Oct 22	Richard WHITEHOUSE	bur
Oct 22	Ann, d of Joseph & Ann CIVILL	bap
Oct 29	Sarah FISHER	bur
Nov 21	Ann WHITEHOUSE	bur
Nov 23	Hannah, d of John & Sarah FISHER	bap
Nov 23	Joseph, s of William & Hannah BROWN	bap
Nov 30	Sarah FULLWOOD	bur
Nov 30	Hannah SKITHERT	bur
Dec 3	Hannah FULLWOOD	bur

1783

Dec 3	Richard BIRTON	bur
Dec 3	Amelia, d of William & Hannah MILLS	bap
Dec 7	John WILLIAMS	bur
~ Dec 14	Mary, d of John & Sarah COOPER	bap
Dec 16	Ann, d of Thomas & Hannah SHELDON	bap
Dec 16	Joseph WHITEHOUSE	bur
Dec 21	Mary, d of Edward & Mary DARBY	bap
Dec 25	Sarah, d of Edward & Elizabeth SHELDON	bap
Dec 25	Priscilla, d of Richard & Margaret REED	bap
Dec 25	John, s of Joseph & Elizabeth HEEDS, Born Decr 2	bap

1784

Jan 5	James, s of Joseph & Mary HORTON	bap
~ Jan 10	Eli, s of James & Elizabeth BENNETT	bap
Jan 12	Joseph, s of John & Mary HAMBLETT	bap
Jan 12	Charles, s of John & Sophia LAW	bap
Jan 18	Daniel MILLS	bur
Jan 23	William COTTRILL	bur
~ Feb 1	Joseph, s of James & Martha GREEN	bap
Feb 1	Samuel, s of William & Lydia EDWARDS	bap
Feb 1	Elizabeth, d of Frances & Martha WHITEHOUSE	bap
Feb 6	Hannah BAKER	bur
~ Feb 8	Mary MARSON	bur
Feb 8	William, s of David & Ann HIPKISS	bap
Feb 8	Thomas, s of Thomas & Phebe BUNCE	bap
Feb 8	Solomon, s of Aron & Mary SMITH	bap
Feb 8	Elizabeth, a bas begott Child of Martha WHITEHOUSE	bap
Feb 15	John, s of Thomas & Ann MILLINGTON	bap
Feb 22	Richard, s of Richard & Hannah LEECH	bap
Mar 7	Daniel, s of Joseph & Mary GORTON	bap
Mar 7	Benjamin, s of Daniel & Sarah SHELDON	bap
Mar 7	Joseph WHITEHOUSE	bur
Mar 14	James WILLIAMS	bur
~ Mar 14	Hannah, d of John & Hannah HODGSKINS	bap
Mar 21	William, s of Joseph & Isabel SMITH	bap
Mar 21	Richard, s of Richard & Elizabeth EDWARDS	bap
Mat 21	John, s of Thomas & Elizabeth SHORTHOUSE	bap
Mar 21	Phillis, d of Edward & Elizabeth DUDLEY	bap
Mar 28	Thomas, s of Thomas & Jane PERRY	bap
Apr 7	Martha, d of John & Lydia TURNEYFOOT	bap
Apr 7	Ann GORTON	bur
Apr 8	Ann ROLINSON	bur
Apr 11	John, s of John & Jimmimey PRESSON	bap
Apr 11	Henry, s of Benjamin & Sarah WHITEHOUSE	bap
~ Apr 11	Mary, d of William & Phebe TURNER	bap
Apr 11	Mary, d of Thomas & Elizabeth HORTON	bap
Apr 14	Hannah, a bas begott Child of Ann FISHER	bap
Apr 14	John MILLS	bur
Apr 23	Thomas EDGE	bur

1784

Apr 26	Joseph, s of William & Sus Hannah HORTON	bap
May 2	John, s of John & Lydia FOSTER	bap
May 9	Job, s of William & Elizabeth SMITH	bap
May 9	Sarah, d of Benjamin & Mary NOCK	bap
May 16	Samuel, s of Joseph & Mary CALLOWAY	bap
May 16	Moses, s of James & Hannah ALLEN	bap
May 16	Sophia, d of Enass & Hannah WHITEHOUSE	bap
May 16	Daniel, s of Thomas & Elizabeth HAUGHTON	bap
May 23	William, s of William & Sarah ELWELL	bap
May 30	John, s of David & Sarah JEVON	bap
May 30	Elizabeth, d of Daniel & Elizabeth GRANGER	bap
May 30	Nancy, d of Richard & Sarah NIGHTINGALE	bap
Jun 7	Hannah, d of Benjamin & Phebe WHITEHOUSE	bap
Jun 14	Lucy, d of Daniel & Sarah WARR	bap
Jun 27	Rebekah MILLS	bur
Jun 27	Nancy GRIFFIS	bur
Jun 27	John, s of William & Jane WHITEHOUSE	bap
Jun 27	Peter, s of Daniel & Phebe MILLS	bap
Jul 4	Joseph, s of Isaac & Sarah ASTON	bap
Jul 4	James, s of Abel & Mary HILL	bap
Jul 10	William, s of John & Hannah JAMES	bap
Jul 15	Charles BAKER	bur
Jul 18	Esther TINKER	bur
Jul 18	Amelia, d of Isaac & Rachel FLETCHER	bap
Jul 18	Drydon, s of Edward & Ann KERRY	bap
Jul 18	Nancy, d of Benjamin & Ann MILLS, Born Feb 2^d 1781	bap
Jul 25	Sarah, d of Benjamin & Ann MILLS, Born March 28	bap
Jul 25	John, s of James & Hannah FELLOWS	bap
Jul 25	Elizabeth, d of Daniel & Phebe WARR	bap
Jul 29	John, s of William & Martha INGRAM	bap
Aug 1	Benjamin, s of Daniel & Betty SMITH	bap
Aug 15	Amelia, d of Joseph & Elizabeth MILLS	bap
Aug 22	Daniel, s of Thomas & Elizabeth WHITEHOUSE	bap
Aug 22	Henry, s of Henry & Sarah KENDRICK	bap
Aug 22	Mary, d of Thomas & Elizabeth HILL	bap
	[The next entry has been squeezed in]	
Aug 22	William, s of Joseph & Nancy FIELDHOUSE	bap
Aug 22	Mary, d of Stephen & Mary FISHER	bap
Aug 29	Joseph, s of Joseph & Elizabeth WHITEHOUSE	bap
Aug 29	Moses, s of James & Elizabeth ROUND	bap
Sep 5	Ambrose, s of Joseph & Sarah WALTERS	bap
Sep 5	Mary, d of Joseph & Lydia WALTERS, Born March 3^d	bap
Sep 8	Ann WHITEHOUSE	bur
Sep 15	Ann, d of William & Elizabeth ASHLEY	bap
Sep 19	Joseph, s of Joseph & Mary WHITEHOUSE	bap
Sep 19	John, s of Thomas & Sarah SUTTON	bap
Sep 23	John, s of Richard & Mary FISHER	bap
Sep 23	Mary, d of John & Ann WALLORS, Born January 1 [?7?], 1784	bap
Sep 26	John, s of Thomas & Mary WHEAL, Born Jun 14	bap

1784

Sep 26	John, s of Edward & Mary ALEXANDER, Born Aug 14	bap
Sep 26	Alice, d of Joseph & Shusannah DAVIS	bap
Sep 26	Mary, d of Benjamin & Elizabeth CLARK, Born Dec 30, 1783	bap
~ Sep 27	Sarah, d of Samuel & Elizabeth HILL	bap
	[*The remainder of this page is blank and crossed through*]	
Oct 12	Sarah, d of Edward & Elizabeth WALL	bap
Oct 14	Sarah, d of Richard & Elizabeth PARKER	bap
Oct 21	Hannah, d of Michael & Elizabeth DUFFIELD, Born Aug 16	bap
Oct 21	Edward, s of William & Elizabeth FEREDAY	bap
Oct 21	Hannah ROUND	bur
Oct 21	James MILLS	bur
Oct 28	James, s of Joseph & Mary HORTON	bur
Oct 28	Samuel, s of Samuel & Sarah PASKIN	bap
Nov 8	John, s of Joseph & Sarah HORTON	bap
Nov 8	Jane, d of Thomas & Phebe NICKOLDS	bap
Nov 8	Hannah, d of James & Hannah HORTON	bap
Nov 10	Sarah ELWELL	bur
Nov 10	Joseph MILLS	bur
Nov 10	Jane, d of Daniel & Lydia GRIFFIS	bap
Nov 14	Joseph RICHARDS	bur
Nov 14	Catharine, d of John & Mary ATTWOOD	bap
~ Dec 19	William, s of James & Mary NOCK	bap
Dec 25	John WHITEHOUSE	bur
~ Dec 25	Isarael, s of Bayley & Sarah HILL	bap
Dec 25	William, s of Richard & Jane ARTILL	bap
Dec 25	Moses, s of Thomas & Catharine HEMMINS	bap
~ Dec 26	Phebe, d of Gilbert & Martha HOWELL	bap
Dec 26	James, s of John & Hannah ALEXANDER	bap

1785

Jan 2	Sarah, d of James & Mary MEERS	bap
Jan 2	Thomas, s of Thomas & Mary LITTLE	bap
Jan 9	Widow WARR	bur
Jan 9	Richard, s of Samuel & Mary BIRTON	bap
Jan 11	Abraham LAW	bur
Jan 11	William SHELDON	bur
Jan 16	Joseph INCHER	bur
Jan 18	Joseph LAW	bur
~ Jan 18	William WORSEY	bur
Jan 23	Joseph, s of Joseph & Ann SAUNDERS, Born Jan 17, 1785	bap
Jan 23	Robert EDWARDS	bur
Jan 30	Noah FISHER	bur
~ Feb 2	Sarah HUGHES	bur
Feb 6	Joseph, s of Benjamin & Catharine ORTON	bap
Feb 9	Elizabeth, wife of Edward SHELDON	bur
Feb 9	John JAMES	bur
Feb 11	Amelia GRIFFIS	bur
~ Feb 22	Joseph GUTTRIDGE	bur
Feb 22	Edward, s of William & Mary WHITEHOUSE	bap

1785

Mar 6	Thomas David, s of Ambrose & Ann HILL	bap
Mar 6	Sarah, d of Joseph & Hannah ONIONS	bap
Mar 6	Elizabeth, d of William & Phebe DORRALL, Born Jan 18 1785	bap
Mar 7	James, s of James & Ann HOWEN	bap
Mar 8	William SMITH	bur
Mar 8	Hannah, d of James & Christiannah WARTON, Born May 18 1783	bap
Mar 10	John FISHER	bur
Mar 10	Mary, d of James & Mary FEREDAY	bap
Mar 10	Mary, d of John & Hannah ROWLEY	bap
Mar 13	Robert, s of Thomas & Sarah BLARE, Born Feby 2	bap
Mar 20	William, s of William & Mary WHITEHOUSE	bap
Mar 28	Daniel, s of William & Elizabeth WHITEHOUSE	bap
Mar 28	Joseph, s of Joseph & Betty GRISE	bap
Mar 28	Richard, s of William & Nancy WARD	bap
Apr 3	William, s of William & Elizabeth BARNETT	bap
Apr 3	John, s of Richard & Elizabeth EDWARDS	bap
Apr 10	Phebe, d of Joseph & Mary WORTON	bap
Apr 10	Hannah, d of John & Elizabeth WARTON	bap
Apr 17	Lydia, d of Stephen & Mary HIPKISS	bap
Apr 17	Ann WRIGHT	bur
May 1	Henry, s of Samuel & Sarah NOCK	bap
May 3	Elizabeth DUDLEY	bur
May 6	John GRICE	bur
May 6	Thomas, s of Thomas & Elizabeth MORRIS	bap
May 8	James, s of James & Hannah HEELEY	bap
May 15	Thomas, s of Thomas & Hannah RUDGE	bap
May 15	John, s of Thomas & Elizabeth HUGHES	bap
May 15	Elizabeth, d of John & Martha PARTRIDGE	bap
May 15	Sophia, d of William & Ellnor GRIFFIS	bap
May 15	Sarah, d of Richard & Martha LAW	bap
May 16	Abraham & Isaac, twins of Abraham & Sarah TIMMINS	bap
May 16	Jane, d of John & Ann MARTIN	bap
May 16	James BREVETT, a bas begott Child of Elizabeth JONES	bap
May 23	Joseph, s of David & Mary ROUND	bap
Jun 12	Elleanor, d of William & Phebe TURNER	bap
Jun 12	Elizabeth, d of Thomas & Nancy TILLEY	bap
Jun 12	Isaac TIMMINS	bur
Jun 19	Thomas, s of Thomas & Nancy FELLOWS	bap
Jun 19	Thomas, a bas begot Child of Mary AMASS	bap
Jun 26	Thomas FEREDAY	bur
Jul 1	Mary JOHNSON	bur
Jul 1	John, s of John & Rebekah COLE	bap
Jul 1	Mary, d of Daniel & Sarah CALLOWAY	bap
Jul 3	Elizabeth PARKES	bur
Jul 3	Elizabeth BOTT	bur
Jul 10	Ann, a bas begott Child of Sarah MARTIN	bap
Jul 10	Rebekah, d of John & Elizabeth EDWARDS	bap
Jul 17	John, s of Joseph & Elizabeth HEADES, Born Apl 2	bap

<u>1785</u>

Date	Name	Event
Jul 21	Sarah FISHER	bur
Jul 22	John FISHER	bur
Jul 24	Thomas, s of Thomas & Esther TAYLOR	bap
Jul 24	Nancy, d of Samuel & Sarah FLETCHER	bap
Jul 29	Joseph TONKS	bur
Jul 31	Moses ROUND	bur
Jul 31	Richard, s of Richard & Sarah STANTON	bap
Jul 31	Sarah, d of Joseph & Ann LESTER	bap
Aug 1	Ann, d of Isaac & Mary DARBY	bap
Aug 7	Sarah, d of Thomas & Elizabeth HOUGHTON	bap
Aug 13	Francis MILLS	bur
Aug 13	Abraham, a bas begott Child of Sarah MILLS	bap
Aug 13	Jane, d of Benjamin & Sarah CRESSWELL	bap
Aug 14	James, s of Richard & Ann SHARROTT, born March 10	bap
Aug 14	James, s of Edward & Hannah MILLINGTON	bap
Aug 21	John, s of Thomas & Phebe BUNCE	bap
Aug 21	Hannah, d of William & Phebe HODGSKINS	bap
Aug 22	Sarah, d of Joseph & Martha CADRACK	bap
Sep 4	Isaac HICKMANS	bur
Sep 7	Hannah, d of Richard & Elizabeth WAINWRIGHT	bap
Sep 7	Jane TURNER	bur
Sep 11	Silvia, d of Richard & Elizabeth SAUNDERS, Born July 10	bap
Sep 11	William, s of John & Hannah HODGSKINS	bap
Sep 11	Nathaniel, s of Nathaniel & Elizabeth HEELEY	bap
Sep 11	John, s of John & Sarah WITTALL	bap
Sep 11	Samuel, s of Samuel & Sarah ROBERTS, Born May 24	bap
Sep 11	Elizabeth, a bas begott Child of Martha BECKS	bap
Jul 18	Nancy, d of William & Ann FOSTER	bap
Jul 29	James A I I WOOD	bur

$$\begin{array}{r} 1834 \\ 40 \\ \hline 94 \end{array}$$

Date	Name	Event
Oct 3	Samuel, s of Thomas & Hannah BOTT	bap
Oct 3	Thomas, s of Joseph & Mary PASKIN	bap
Oct 9	Hannah, d of Abraham & Hannah WALTERS	bap
Oct 9	Hannah, d of Job & Phebe TURLEY	bap
Oct 9	Mary, d of John & Phebe ASTON, Born Dec 1, 1784	bap
Oct 9	William, s of John & Elizabeth SMITH	bap
Oct 9	Edward, s of Thomas & Alice CARTWRIGHT	bap
Oct 9	Ann, d of Daniel & Jane NICKLIN, Born Jan 2, 1785	bap
Oct 9	John, s of Benjamin & Hannah RICHARDS, Born Feb[y] 2, 1785	bap
Oct 11	Job MAULIN	bur
Oct 23	Richard, s of Richard & Sarah GRIFFIS	bap
Oct 23	Elizabeth, d of Edward & Ann ROBERTS	bap
Oct 24	George, s of Paul & Betty EVINS, Born Nov[r] 23, 1784	bap
Oct 30	Mary, d of John & Elizabeth ONIONS	bap
Oct 30	Sarah, d of William & Silvia JONES	bap
Oct 30	Hannah, d of John & Lydia FURNEYFOOT	bap
Nov 2	Samuel PARTRIDGE	bur
Nov 6	Ann, d of Abraham & Hannah NICKOLDS	bap

1785

Nov 13	Elizabeth, d of Daniel & Sarah SHELDON	bap
Nov 13	Benjamin ROUND	bur
Nov 15	Ann WHITEHOUSE	bur
Nov 15	Elizabeth, d of James & Elizabeth HILL	bap
Nov 15	Sarah HERRING	bur
Nov 27	Joseph, s of Richard & Hannah WHITEHOUSE, Born July 16	bap
Nov 27	Thomas, s of Thomas & Mary KENDRICK	bap
Nov 27	James TURTON, a bas begott Child of Elizabeth BOTT	bap
Dec 3	Henry, s of James & Rhody GUEST	bap
Dec 18	Edward, s of Richard & Margaret REED	bap
Dec 21	James FEREDAY	bur
Dec 25	Mary, d of William & Rachel WHITEHOUSE	bap
Dec 25	Samuel, s of William & Hannah WHITEHOUSE	bap
Dec 25	Henry, s of William & Hannah PARSONS	bap
Dec 25	Amelia, d of Daniel & Hannah ROUND	bap
Dec 25	John, s of John & Elizabeth GUTTRIDGE	bap
Dec 25	William, s of Benjamin & Hannah JEVON	bap
Dec 26	Lydia, d of Joseph & Mary HORTON	bap
Dec 26	Benjamin, s of Benjamin & Sarah HORTON	bap

1786

Jan 11	Stephen TIMMINS	bur
Jan 15	William, s of Thomas & Hannah DARBY	bap
Jan 15	James, s of Joseph & Mary BOLTON	bap
Jan 15	Sarah, d of David & Ann HIPKISS	bap
Jan 18	William, s of William & Elizabeth ROUND	bap
Jan 18	Betty, d of Daniel & Phebe MILLS	bap
Feb 5	Thomas, s of John & Elizabeth HICKMANS	bap
Feb 5	Ann, d of Thomas & Elizabeth WHITEHOUSE	bap
Feb 19	William, s of James & Sarah WALTERS	bap
Feb 19	John INGRAM INGRAM[sic]	bur
Feb 20	Edward, s of Joseph & Mary WILLEYS	bap
Feb 20	Ann, d of John & Sarah COOPER	bap
Feb 20	Sarah, d of Samuel & Elizabeth HICKMANS	bap
Feb 26	James, s of James & Martha GREEN	bap
Feb 26	Edward, s of Francis & Hannah WHITEHOUSE	bap
Feb 26	William, s of Benjamin & Hannah WHITEHOUSE	bap
Mar 3	M^{rs}. Sarah JEVON	bur
Mar 3	Thomas, a bas begott Child of Ann JEVON	bap
Mar 12	John PERSHOUSE	bur
Mar 19	Hannah HILL	bur
Mar 19	John, s of John & Sarah WHITEHOUSE	bap
Mar 20	Joseph, s of Thomas & Sarah SMITH, Born Oct 10, 1785	bap
Mar 20	Joseph, s of John & Charlotte WARD, Born Nov 5, 1785	bap
Mar 20	Hannah, d of Moses & Elizabeth HILL, Born Nov 5, 1785	bap
Mar 26	Mariah, d of Daniel & Jane ARTIL	bap
Mar 26	James, s of Samuel & Mary BIRTON	bap
Mar 26	Phebe, d of Samuel & Phebe BECK	bap
Mar 26	Ann, d of Joseph & Rachel DUFFIELD	bap

1786

Mar 26	Joseph, s of William & Elizabeth WARTON	bap
Mar 26	Hannah, d of Abraham & Phebe WHITEHOUSE	bap
Mar 29	Sarah, wife of Daniel WHITEHOUSE	bur
Mar 30	Joseph WHITEHOUSE	bur
Mar 30	Ann, d of Thomas & Sarah WINNINGTON, Born Dec 11, 1785	bap
Apr 2	John, s of James & Hannah FISHER	bur
Apr 5	Sarah, wife of Richard TIMMINS	bur
Apr 16	Benjamin, s of William & Rachel NICKLIN	bap
Apr 16	John, s of Richard & Sarah BECK	bap
Apr 16	Mary, d of Edward & Esther SMITH	bap
Apr 16	David, s of David & Ann WHITEHOUSE	bap
Apr 16	Sarah, d of Thomas & Rachael WARD	bap
Apr 20	Elizabeth WARR	bur
Apr 20	Thomas, s of Isaac & Mary DUTTON, aged ab^t 2 years old	bap
Apr 20	Mary, d of Richard & Sarah WHITEHOUSE	bap
Apr 23	Amelia, d of James & Sarah RICHARDS	bap
May 7	Samuel, s of Edward & Mary STOCKWIN	bap
May 7	John, s of John & Sarah KENDRICK	bap
May 7	Sarah, d of Richard & Betty SAUNDERS	bap
May 7	Samuel, s of Joseph & Mary CALLOWAY	bap
May 7	Henry, s of Ithiael & Mary SALLMON	bap
May 7	John, s of Mathew & Ann HART	bap
May 14	Abraham PERSHOUSE	bur
May 21	John, s of Joseph & Mary GORTON	bap
May 26	Mary, d of John & Sarah COOPER	bur
May 28	Elizabeth, d of James & Elizabeth HILL	bur
Jun 1	Elizabeth, d of Richard & Sarah INGRAM	bap
Jun 1	Silvia SAUNDERS	bur
Jun 4	Wllllam, s of Wllllam & Hannah SHELDON	bap
Jun 4	John, s of James & Ellnor MILLS	bap
Jun 4	Edward, s of John & Sarah ROWLEY	bap
Jun 4	Mary, d of Joseph & Hannah SMITH	bap
Jun 9	William SMITH	bur
Jun 9	Joseph, s of Peter & Rachael ROWLEY	bap
Jun 9	John, s of Joseph & Catharine MILLS, Born May 22	bap
Jun 18	John, s of William & Phebe ALLDRETT	bap
Jun 18	Hannah, d of John & Jane GRIFFIS	bap
Jun 18	Joseph, s of William & Sarah GREENEWAY	bap

A Transcript of the Register of Tipton Alis Tibbington was Exhibited into the Deans Visitation held in the Court of Lichfield being on June 22 1786

Jun 25	John, s of John & Sopha LAW	bap
Jun 25	Ann, d of Henry & Francis PEW	bap
Jun 25	Benjamin, s of William & Ellnor GRIFFIS	bap
Jul 17	Abraham, s of William & Mary WHITEHOUSE	bap
Jul 17	Isaac, s of Isaac & Martha TIMMINS	bap
Jul 17	Timothy, s of Benjamin & Phebe WHITEHOUSE	bap
Jul 17	Joseph, s of John & Mary WHITEHOUSE	bap
Jul 17	Abraham, s of Thomas & Mary WHITEHOUSE	bap
Jul 26	Hannah, wife of James HORTON	bur

<u>1786</u>

Jul 26	Edward, s of William & Mary SARVIER	bap
Jul 26	Ellen, d of Isaac & Mary MILLARD	bap
Jul 26	Joseph, s of David & Joice WALTERS	bap
Jul 28	Joseph NIGHTINGALE	bur
Jul 28	Ambrose, s of John & Susannah BLACKHAM	bap
Jul 30	Sidonia, d of Richard & Ann LEECH	bap
Jul 30	Ann, d of Thomas & Elizabeth MORRISS	bap
Jul 30	Joseph, s of Michael & Elizabeth DUFFIELD	bap
~ Aug 6	Mary, d of James & Mary FOSTER	bap
Aug 6	Elizabeth, d of Thomas & Elizabeth DEWSON	bap
~ Aug 9	Catharine INGRAM	bur
Aug 9	Hannah, d of Thomas & Elizabeth MILLARD	bap
Aug 13	James, s of Joseph & Sarah HORTON, Born July 26	bap
Aug 20	John, s of Joseph & Phebe CROFTS, Born July 12	bap
Aug 20	Edward, s of Isaac & Sarah ASTON	bap
~ Aug 20	Phebe, s of Bayley & Sarah HILL	bap
Aug 20	Joseph CALLOWAY	bur
~ Aug 27	John HEADES	bur
Aug 27	Ellnor, d of George & Lucy MARSHALL	bap
Sep 3	Thomas, s of Joseph & Mary ROSS	bap
~ Sep 15	Nancy, d of John & Sarah COOPER	bur
Sep 17	Phebe, d of William & Lydia EDWARDS	bap
Sep 24	Sarah, d of John & Ann WALLERS, Born Dec 6, 1785	bap
Sep 24	Sarah, d of Robert & Phebe ONIONS	bap
~ Oct 1	Hannah, d of William & Mary HUGHES, Born Dec 21 1785	bap
Oct 1	Elizabeth, d of Daniel & Phebe WARR	bap
Oct 1	Hannah, a bas begot Child of Ann WARTON	bap
Oct 1	Mary, d of Robert & Hannah SMITH	bap
Oct 6	Francis, s of Francis & Catharine MILLS, Born June 27, 1785	bap
Oct 6	Nancy MILLS	bur
Oct 8	Joseph, s of Joseph & Isabell SMITH	bap
Oct 8	Hannah, d of John & Mary ATTWOOD	bap
Oct 8	Elizabeth, a bas begotton Child of Sarah NICKLIN	bap
Oct 22	Mary, d of Joseph & Hannah ONIONS	bap
Oct 22	Thomas, s of Daniel & Sarah WARR	bap
~ Oct 25	John COOPER	bur
Oct 25	Eleanor, d of Peter & Susannah HART	bap
Nov 1	Joseph, s of Richard & Mary FISHER	bap
Nov 1	Lydia, d of Joseph & Lydia WHITEHOUSE	bap
~ Oct 1	Richard GUTTRIDGE	bur
Nov 5	Lydia, d of Thomas & Elizabeth HORTON, Born Mar 12	bap
Nov 19	James, s of Thomas & Phebe JONES	bap
~ Nov 19	Joseph, s of James & Martha NOCK	bap
Nov 19	Daniel, s of John & Ann MARTIN	bap
~ Nov 22	Isiah, s of William & Nancy WARD	bap
Nov 26	Benjamin, s of Benjamin & Ann MILLS, Born Oct 22	bap
Nov 26	Epenetus, s of John & Sarah SPINK	bap
~ Nov 26	Thomas, s of Joseph & Sarah GRANGER	bap
Nov 26	Eleanor, d of Evin & Ann TOMPSON	bap

<u>1786</u>

Nov 27	Edward, s of Edward & Elizabeth SMITH	bap
Dec 14	Elizabeth WHITEHOUSE	bur
Dec 17	Charlotte, d of Charles & Ann HOUGH	bap
Dec 17	Samuel, s of David & Sarah JEVON	bap
Dec 25	Sarah, d of Thomas & Sarah FISHER	bap
Dec 25	Phebe, d of Thomas & Phebe BUNCE	bap
Dec 26	Daniel, s of Thomas & Elizabeth MORRIS	bap
Dec 26	Hannah, d of Benjamin & Mary WHEAL	bap
Dec 30	Robert, s of Joseph & Shusannah DAVIS	bap
Dec 30	Mariah, d of Thomas & Sarah SUTTON	bap
Dec 30	Joshua, s of Samuel & Sarah FLETCHER	bap
Dec 30	Benjamin, s of Benjamin & Sarah CRESSALL	bap
Dec 30	Elizabeth, d of Thomas & Phebe NICOLDS	bap

<u>1787</u>

Jan 28	John, s of Thomas & Sarah BLARE, Born Sep 22, 1786	bap
Jan 28	James, s of James & Hannah FISHER	bap
Feb 4	Ann, d of Peter & Elnor COOK	bap
Feb 5	Hannah, d of William & Hannah JONES, Born Oct 16, 1786	bap
Feb 11	Joseph, s of John & Elizabeth SMITH	bap
Feb 18	Charles, s of John & Catharine FISHER	bap
Feb 18	Thomas, s of Peter & Mary MILLS	bap
Feb 18	Kaziah, d of Joseph & Ann SAUNDERS, Born Feb 3	bap
Feb 25	John, s of William & Mary WHITEHOUSE	bap
Feb 25	Phebe, d of John & Phebe ASTON, Born Dec[r] 27, 1786	bap
Feb 25	Sarah, d of Elisha & Mary GRIFFIS, Born Sep 23, 1785	bap
Feb 18[sic]	Sarah, d of Samuel & Mary WHITEHOUSE	bur
Mar 2	Naney, d of Thomas & Sarah WHITEHOUSE	bur
Mar 4	Joseph, s of Joseph & Ann LESTER	bap
Mar 7	William, s of Thomas & Mary WHEAL	bap
Mar 7	Hannah, d of Thomas & Mary LITTLE	bap

[A comment is entered here to draw attention to the reader that the next section of the register had been incorrectly bound out of place. The correct date sequence has been maintained here in this transcript.]

Mar 7	William, s of Daniel & Elizabeth FISHER	bap
Mar 7	Daniel FISHER	bur
Mar 11	Ellnor CALLOWAY	bur
Mar 18	Hannah, d of William & Nancy JOHNSON	bap
Mar 18	Thomas, s of Richard & Martha LOW	bap
Mar 19	Mary, d of Thomas & Sarah LOW	bap
Apr 1	Isaac & Rebekah, s & d of Daniel & Betty SMITH	bap
Apr 1	Nancy, d of John & Elizabeth ONIONS	bap
Apr 4	Thomas LESTER	bur
Apr 8	Norris, s of Thomas & Elizabeth HILL	bap
Apr 8	Samuel, s of Samuel & Elizabeth MILLS	bap
Apr 8	Hannah, d of Thomas & Elizabeth HUGHES	bap
Apr 8	Sarah, d of Luke & Nancy PHILIPS	bap
Apr 8	Nancy, d of Joseph & Mary HODGETTS	bap
Apr 9	Hannamariah, a bas begott Child of Ann BOWEN	bap

1787

Apr 9	Henry, s of Thomas & Sarah COX	bap
Apr 11	Thomas FULLWOOD	bur
Apr 15	John, s of Stephen & Mary HIPKISS, Born March 1	bap
Apr 19	Widow HICKMAN	bur
Apr 22	John, s of Samuel & Sarah NOCK	bap
Apr 22	Job, s of Samuel & Sarah PASKIN	bap
Apr 22	William TIMMINS	bur
Apr 25	Elizabeth, d of John & Rhody DOUTY, Born June 25 1786	bap
Apr 25	Mary EDGE	bur
Apr 25	Thomas COCKERIN	bur
May 6	Elizabeth, d of Joseph & Mary FISHER	bap
May 13	Nancy, d of Edward & Margaret FISHER	bap
May 15	Josiah FULLWOOD	bur
May 20	Ambrose, s of Thomas & Mary JONES	bap
May 20	Barnabass, s of Joseph & Nancy CIVATER	bap
May 21	William FISHER	bur
May 27	Elizabeth, d of Thomas & Elizabeth HAWTHON[crossed out] HORTON	bap
May 27	William, s of William & Ann FISHER	bap
May 27	Sarah, d of John & Martha PARTRIDGE	bap
May 27	Maria, d of Samuel & Mary BENNETT	bap
May 27	Ann, d of William & Elizabeth WHITEHOUSE	bap
May 28	Thomas, s of William & Hannah HOLLIOAK	bap
Jun 3	Sarah, d of John & Lydia FURNEYFOOT	bap
Jun 3	Betsy, d of Benjamin & Hannah RICHARDS, Born Sep 28 1786	bap
Jun 3	John WHITEHOUSE	bur
Jun 3	George HILL	bur
Jun 5	William, s of John & Fanny SAUNDERS, Born April 20	bap
Jun 5	Thomas HUGHS	bur
Jun 10	John, s of Edward & Elizabeth WALL	bap
Jun 10	Pamela, d of Thomas & Sarah CORFIELD	bap
Jun 17	Hannah, d of John & Hannah ALEXANDER	bap
Jun 19	Hannah, d of Joseph & Phebe SMITH	bap
Jun 19	Thomas SMITH	bur
Jul 8	Joseph, s of John & Phebe WALTERS, Born January 8th	bap
Jul 8	William, s of William & Ellnor GRIFFIS	bap
Jul 15	James, s of Samuel & Elizabeth HILL	bap
Jul 15	Sarah, d of Joseph & Nancy FIELDHOUSE	bap
Jul 22	Hannah, d of Enass & Hannah WHITEHOUSE, Born April 11	bap
Jul 22	Martha, d of George & Ann WHITEHOUSE, Born May 4	bap
Aug 5	James, s of Edward & Sarah WHITEHOUSE	bap
Aug 5	Mary, d of James & Ann OWEN	bap
Aug 5	John, s of Joseph & Mary WHITEHOUSE	bap
Aug 5	Phebe, d of William & Jane WHITEHOUSE	bap
Aug 5	Mary, d of Richard & Elizabeth EDWARDS	bap
Aug 12	John, s of John & Sarah FISHER	bap
Aug 12	Rachael, d of Benjamin & Patience FISHER	bap
Aug 12	Sarah, d of John & Sarah FISHER	bap
Aug 12	Lucy, d of Richard & Elizabeth SAUNDERS	bap

1787

Date	Name	Event
Aug 18	William BECK	bur
Aug 19	James, s of Joseph & Mary PHILIPS	bap
Aug 22	Edward, s of Edward & Elizabeth SMITH	bur
Aug 26	Samuel, s of William & Ann EDGE	bap
Sep 2	William, s of John & Elizabeth EDWARDS	bap
Sep 2	Thomas, s of William & Phebe HODGSKINS	bap
Sep 2	Isaac, s of Ann BRATT	bap
Sep 6	Mary, d of Joseph & Phebe NICHOLDS	bur
Sep 9	John, s of Abraham & Hannah NICHOLDS, born August 15th	bap
Sep 16	Hannamariah, d of David & Mary ROUND	bap
Sep 16	Sarah, d of Samuel & Mary BIRTON	bap
Sep 23	Thomas BRINLEY	bur
Sep 23	Rhody, d of Nathaniel & Elizabeth HEELEY, Born Sep 15	bap
Sep 30	Edward, s of Daniel & Sarah SHELDON	bap
Sep 30	Ann, d of Elizabeth EDGE	bap
Oct 1	Mary, d of Samuel & Sarah ROBERTS, Born April 27	bap
Oct 1	Mary, a bas begott Child of Elizabeth SHELDON	bap
Oct 12	Lydia, d of Joseph & Mary HORTON	bur
Oct 12	Sarah, d of James & Elizabeth ATTWOOD, Born Feb 11	bap
Oct 14	Hannah, d of Abel & Ann MILLS, Born July 12	bap
Oct 14	Thomas, s of John & Jane BROOKS	bap
Oct 15	Mary, d of Daniel & Phebe WARR	bur
Oct 18	Isaac GUTTRIDGE	bur
Oct 21	Elizabeth, d of Richard & Hannah WHITEHOUSE	bap
Oct 25	Mark FISHER	bur
Oct 28	Sarah NICHOLIS	bur
Nov 11	Martha, a bas begott Child of Mary PARTRIDGE	bap
Nov 13	George FISHER	bur
Nov 13	William, s of William & Martha INGRAM	bur
Nov 15	Elizabeth, d of William & Martha SHORT	bur
Nov 15	Samuel, s of John & Elizabeth BRATT	bap
Nov 18	Hannah, d of John & Jane TAYLOR	bap
Nov 18	Daniel, s of Daniel & Phebe MILLS	bur
Nov 18	Mary, d of Robert & Hannah SMITH	bur
Nov 22	Mary, d of John & Hannah ROWLEY	bur
Nov 22	Nancy, d of Richard & Hannah GRIFFIS	bap
Nov 25	George, s of Daniel & Jane NICKLIN, Born May 30	bap
Nov 25	Daniel, s of James & Elleanor MILLS, Born Oct 25 1787	bap
Nov 25	Ann, d of John & Sarah WITTALL	bap
Nov 25	James, s of Daniel & Mary FISHER	bap
Nov 26	William TAYLOR	bur
Nov 26	Mary, a base begot Child of Elizabeth SHELDON	bur
Nov 28	Fanney, d of Joseph & Catharine MILLS	bap
Nov 28	Sarah SMITH	bur
Nov 28	Hannah DUFFIELD	bur
Nov 29	Elizabeth WOOD	bur
Dec 5	Sarah, d of James & Elizabeth HILL	bap
Dec 5	Ellnor HART	bur
Dec 5	Samuel, s of Joseph & Mary CALLOWAY	bur

1787

Date	Name	Event
Dec 9	Sarah, d of Thomas & Jane PERRY	bur
Dec 9	Thomas, s of Thomas & Elizabeth DREW	bap
Dec 9	Daniel, s of William & Sarah MOOR	bap
Dec 13	Ruth, d of John & Sarah WHITEHOUSE	bur
Dec 14	Joseph, s of James & Martha NOCK	bur
Dec 16	Benjamin, s of Benjamin & Mary ROUND	bur
Dec 16	Elizabeth, d of Edward & Ann ROBERTS	bur
Dec 16	Hannah, d of Stephen & Mary FISHER	bap
Dec 16	Jeremiah, s of Daniel & Leah SMITH	bap
Dec 16	Sarah, d of James & Mary NOCK	bap
Dec 18	William, s of William & Mary WHITEHOUSE	bur
Dec 18	Charlotte, d of Thomas & Elizabeth DREW	bur
Dec 18	Mariah, d of Joseph & Phebe FLETCHER	bap
Dec 23	Michael, s of Richard & Betty SAUNDERS	bap
Dec 23	Nancy, d of Edward & Ann SMITH	bap
Dec 23	William SHELDON	bur
Dec 25	Elizabeth, d of John & Sarah HILL	bap
Dec 25	Judy, d of Daniel & Ann TIMMINS	bap

1788

Date	Name	Event
Jan 2	John SMITH	bur
Jan 3	Sarah ASPLIN	bur
Jan 6	Elizabeth, d of Isaac & Ann LAW	bap
Jan 10	Mary ONIONS	bur
Jan 10	Joseph WALTERS	bur
Jan 10	Nancy, d of John & Mary CASHMORE	bap
Jan 13	Mary, d of John & Sarah GIBBANS	bap
Jan 13	Thomas, s of Peter & Mary MILLS	bap
Jan 13	Ambrose, s of John & Susannah BLACKHAM	bur
Jan 13	William WHEAL	bur
Jan 17	Hannah, d of John & Hannah ALEXANDER	bur
Jan 17	Sarah, d of Thomas & Sarah HAUGHTON	bur
Jan 20	James, s of John & Ann SHELDON	bap
Jan 20	Solomon, s of Abraham & Sarah TIMMINS	bap
Jan 20	William, s of Joseph & Elizabeth HORTON	bap
Jan 20	William ELWELL	bur
Jan 27	Ann, d of James & Elizabeth BENNETT, Born Dec 22 1787	bap
Jan 27	Thomas, s of Eutychus & Phebe FISHER	bap
Jan 30	Elizabeth GUTTRIDGE	bur
Jan 30	Thomas, s of Eutychus & Phebe FISHER	bur
Jan 30	Mary, d of Joseph & Phebe SMITH	bur
Feb 5	William, s of Robert & Ann BETTY, Born Dec 5 1787	bap
Feb 5	Sophia, d of Daniel & Sarah CALLOWAY	bap
Feb 6	William, s of James & Mary NOCK	bur
Feb 6	Prudence, d of William & Rachael GAUNT	bap
Feb 8	Abraham, s of Isaac & Mary DARBY	bur
Feb 10	Mary ASTON	bur
Feb 10	Mary GORTON	bur
Feb 17	Hatfield, d of John & Sarah FOLLOWS	bap

1788

Feb 17	Joseph, s of Joseph & Jane LAW	bap
Feb 24	James TALBOTT	bur
Feb 24	John, s of Benjamin & Elizabeth CLARK	bap
Feb 24	Kitty, d of William & Mary HUGHES	bap
Mar 9	Danl, s of John & Elizabeth GUTTRIDGE	bap
Mar 9	Elizabeth, d of Joseph & Mary WALTON	bap
Mar 10	Daniel, s of William & Sarah MOOR	bur
Mar 16	Hannah, d of James & Hannah HEELEY	bap
Mar 16	John, s of John & Mary ATTWOOD	bap
Mar 23	Hannah, d of William & Elizabeth BARNETT	bap
Mar 23	Mary, d of John & Hannah WHEAL	bap
Mar 23	Hannah, d of John & Hannah STAFFORD	bap
Mar 23	Thomas, s of John & Phebe GRAY	bap
Mar 23	John, s of William & Sarah GREENAWAY	bap
Mar 23	Nancy, d of Richard & Margaret REED	bap
Mar 23	Edward, s of John & Jemimah PRISSEN	bap
Mar 23	Joseph, s of Thomas & Elizabeth WHITEHOUSE	bap
Apr 2	Widow TIMMINS	bur
Apr 2	Aron SMITH	bur
Apr 4	Sarah, d of John & Hannah ROWLEY	bur
Apr 6	Isaac DUTTON	bur
Apr 6	Elizabeth, d of James & Martha GREEN	bap
Apr 6	William, s of William & Elizabeth JEWKS	bap
Apr 13	Timothy, s of Daniel & Betty SMITH, Born March 12th	bap
Apr 14	William, s of Thomas & Lydia TAYLOR, Born Feb 18th	bap
Apr 14	Phebe WARR	bur
Apr 14	Edward ALEXANDER	bur
Apr 16	Mary, wife of Joseph WHITEHOUSE	bur
Apr 20	James MILLS	bur
Apr 20	Mary, d of John & Hannah HODGSKINS	bap
Apr 25	Daniel, s of James & Eleanor MILLS	bur
Apr 25	Thomas WINNINGTON	bur
Apr 30	Barnabus, s of Joseph & Nancy CIVETER	bur
Apr 30	Sarah, d of Samuel & Sarah ROBERTS	bur
Apr 30	Joseph, s of Richard & Sarah INGRAM	bap
May 1	Samuel, s of William & Margaret SAUNDERS	bur
May 4	Samuel, s of Francis & Mary WHITEHOUSE	bur
May 4	Thomas, s of Joseph & Martha CADDRACK, Born Novr 11, 1787	bap
May 4	Amelia, d of Benjamin & Sarah HORTON	bap
May 4	James, s of Thomas & Elizabeth HORTON	bap
May 8	John NICHOLDS	bur
May 8	Ann CLIFT	bur
May 8	Isaac, s of Samuel & Elizabeth HICKMANS, Born Feb 26	bap
May 8	William, s of Joseph & Mary WILLEYS	bap
May 8	Thomas, s of John & Mary SMITH, Born April 3	bap
May 11	John DARBY	bur
May 11	Daniel, s of Daniel & Phebe MILLS	bap
May 11	Richard, s of George & Ann HOOLDRIDGE	bap
May 11	Joseph, s of Joseph & Ann LESTER	bap

1788

May 11	Mary, d of Joseph & Ann TURNER	bap
May 11	Phebe, d of Joseph & Mary GORTON	bap
May 12	William, s of Joseph & Lucy GEORGE	bap
May 15	William ROUND	bur
May 18	Lydia, d of James & Sarah RICHARDS	bap
May 20	Samuel JEVON	bur
May 20	Francis MILLS	bur
May 20	James, s of Thomas & Mary KENDRICK	bap
May 20	Catharine, d of Thomas & Sarah HILL	bap
May 25	Sarah, d of John & Mary SHARROTT	bur
May 25	Phebe, d of Thomas & Sarah MORRIS	bap
May 25	Titus, s of Richard & Elizabeth WAINWRIGHT	bap
May 25	William, s of William & Mary CLARK	bap
May 27	William WHEAL	bur
Jun 1	Thomas, s of Joseph & Sarah GRANGER	bur
Jun 4	William FOSTER	bur
Jun 4	William, s of Thomas & Sarah WHITEHOUSE	bap
Jun 4	Mariah, d of Isaac & Sarah GUTTRIDGE	bap
Jun 8	Mary, d of William & Margaret CUNLEY	bap
Jun 15	William, s of John & Jane GRIFFIS	bap
Jun 15	Hannah, d of William & Sarah TRUSTON	bap
Jun 17	Mary UNITE	bur
Jun 17	James, a bas begott Child of Mary UNITE	bap
Jun 17	Sarah, d of Richard & Sarah WHITEHOUSE	bap
Jun 22	Sarah, d of John & Charlotte WARD, Born June 20th	bap
Jul 1	Hannah PASKIN	bur
Jul 8	Nancy FISHER	bur
Jul 11	Hannah DARBY	bur
Jul 20	John, s of John & Sarah FISHER	bap
Jul 20	Jane, d of William & Mary FISHER	bap
Jul 20	Joseph, s of John & Sarah ROWLEY	bap
Jul 20	Sarah, wife of John WALTERHOUSE	bur
Jul 22	Ann SAUNDERS	bur
Jul 27	Thomas, s of George & Mary BRINLEY	bap
Jul 27	Hannah, wife of Edward WHITEHOUSE	bur
Jul 28	Mary, d of William & Hannah WHITEHOUSE	bap
Jul 31	Mary, wife of George BRINLEY	bur
Aug 3	William, s of Edward & Ann ROBERTS	bap
Aug 3	Ithiael, s of Ithiael & Mary SALLMON	bap
Aug 4	Thomas HODGYETTS	bur
Aug 10	Edward, s of Paul & Lydia GRIFFIS	bap
Aug 10	David, s of Abell & Martha HILL, Born July 2d, 1788	bap
Aug 10	Sarah, d of Edward & Elizabeth DUDLEY, Born March 21 1788	bap
Aug 10	Joseph, s of Thomas & Phebe BUNCE, Born July 3 1788	bap
Aug 10	Hannah PITEWAY	bur
Aug 17	William, s of William & Hannah FOSTER	bap
Aug 17	Hannah, d of James & Martha NOCK	bap
Aug 23	Joseph, s of John & Sophia LAW	bap
Aug 31	Samuel, s of William & Rebekah JEVON	bap

1788

Sep 7	Phebe, d of William & Rebekah ROUND	bap
Sep 7	John, s of David & Mary SMITH, Born June 1, 1788	bap
Sep 8	Ann ATTWOOD	bur
Sep 13	John ALEXANDER	bur
Sep 14	Richard EDWARDS	bur
Sep 16	Ann NICKOLDS	bur
Sep 16	Sarah ATTWOOD	bur
Sep 18	Mary CALLOWAY	bur
Sep 21	William, s of Thomas & Elizabeth MORRIS	bap
Sep 28	Edward, s of Richard & Sarah NIGHTINGALE, Born August 10th 1788	bap
Sep 28	Sarah, d of Thomas & Phebe NICKOLDS	bap
Oct 4	Eley, s of Benjamin & Sarah WHITEHOUSE, Born June 25, 1788	bap
Oct 4	Sarah, d of William & Mary GRATTON	bap
Oct 12	Daniel, s of Edward & Elizabeth MILLS	bap
Oct 12	William, s of Thomas & Elizabeth HUGHES	bap
Oct 12	Sarah, d of John & Rosannah RIDER	bap
Oct 12	Ann, d of Moses & Hannah TIMMINS	bap
Oct 16	Peter, s of Peter & Rachael ROWLEY	bap
Oct 16	Joseph PITEWAY	bur
Oct 26	Edward, s of Joseph & Rachael DUFFIELD, Born Feb 16 1788	bap
Oct 26	Samuel, s of Isaac & Sarah ASTON	bap
Oct 30	Job FISHER	bur
Nov 2	Elizabeth, d of Edward & Hannah MILLINGTON, Born July 11 1788	bap
Nov 2	Mary, d of William & Violette PARKES	bap
Nov 2	Daniel, s of Joseph & Sarah HILL	bap
Nov 2	Isaac, s of Thomas & Elizabeth HILL	bap
Nov 2	Samuel, s of Emanuel & Ann DARBY, Born January 28 1788	bap
Nov 2	Hannah, d of William & Ann SHELDON, Born Oct 14 1788	bap
Nov 2	Catharine, d of William & Martha INGRAM	bap
Nov 9	Daniel, s of Stephen & Mary HIPKISS, Born Sepr 21	bap
Nov 16	Sarah, d of Thomas & Hannah WHITEHOUSE	bap
Nov 16	Moses, s of Moses & Elizabeth HILL	bap
Nov 16	Mary, d of John & Phebe ASTON, Born Oct 28	bap
Nov 16	John, s of Daniel & Sarah NICKOLDS	bap
Nov 23	James FLETCHER	bur
Nov 23	Thomas, s of Thomas & Sarah SUTTON	bap
Nov 23	Margarett, d of Joseph & Elizabeth HODGSKINS	bap
Nov 23	Mary, d of Thomas & Mary WHEAL	bap
Nov 23	Daniel, s of Daniel & Nancy WHITEHOUSE	bap
Nov 23	Thomas, s of Thomas & Mary WILLIAMS	bap
Nov 23	Mary, d of Edward & Jane WITMORE	bap
Nov 23	Hannah, d of Michael & Elizabeth DUFFIELD	bap
Nov 23	John, s of John & Sarah WELLS, Born June 25th	bap
Nov 23	William, a bas begott Child of Mary WHITEHOUSE, Born Aug 17	bap
Nov 24	John, s of Samuel & Sarah BAYLEY, Born Aug 14	bap
Nov 24	Isaac, s of Thomas & Sarah TURNER, Born June 24 1785	bap

1788

Nov 24	Ellen, d of Thomas & Sarah TURNER, Born July 10th	bap
Nov 30	William ATTWOOD	bur
Nov 30	Sarah, d of Bayley & Sarah HILL	bap
Dec 7	James MILLARD	bur
Dec 7	John, s of John & Mary WOLLOWS	bap
Dec 14	William, s of Robert & Hannah SMITH	bap
Dec 14	Mary Ann, a bas begott Child of Ann BOWIN, Born Feb 1	bap
Dec 21	John NICKOLDS	bur
Dec 21	Andrew ROLINSON	bur
Dec 21	Mary WINNINGTON	bur
Dec 28	Hannah, d of John & Hannah ALEXANDER	bap
Dec 28	Stephen, s of Richard & Mary FISHER	bap
Dec 28	Samuel, s of Samuel & Phebe BECK	bap

1789

Jan 4	Martha, d of Joseph & Phebe CROFTS, Born Oct 30th 1788	bap
Jan 4	Elizabeth, d of Eutychus & Phebe FISHER	bap
Jan 5	William, s of Henry & Sarah KENDRICK, Born August 23 1788	bap
Jan 11	Edward, s of Gideon & Elizabeth GRISE	bap
Jan 11	Joice, d of Joseph & Sarah HORTON	bap
Jan 11	Joshua WHITEHOUSE	bur
Jan 18	Danl GRIFFIS	bur
Jan 18	Joseph HIPKISS	bur
Jan 18	Ellen, d of Luke & Nancy PHILIPS	bap
Jan 18	Joseph, s of Daniel & Sarah WARR	bap
Jan 25	Mary, wife of Philip RATHBONE	bur
Feb 1	John, s of William & Elizabeth INGLEY	bap
Feb 1	Anna, d of Joseph & Elizabeth BLAKESLEY	bap
Feb 8	Thomas, s of Joseph & Jane PERCALL	bap
Feb 8	Daniel, s of James & Eleanor MILLS	bap
Feb 8	Joseph, s of John & Sarah WHITEHOUSE	bap
Feb 8	James, s of William & Phebe ALLWRITT	bap
Feb 8	Eliz, d of Thomas & Mary SMITH	bap
Feb 13	Richard, s of Edward & Tamor WHITEHOUSE	bap
Feb 13	Daniel NICKOLDS	bur
Feb 13	Abraham TURNER	bur
Feb 16	Abraham, s of Abraham & Phebe WHITEHOUSE, born May 14 1788	bap
Feb 16	Hannah DARBY	bur
Feb 16	Joseph & Mary, bas begott Children of Hannah DARBY	bap
Feb 16	Edward, s of William & Eleanor GRIFFIS	bap
Feb 16	Dianna, d of Francis & Esther PAUMOR	bap
Feb 19	Amelia, d of Isaac & Hannah LAW, Born Novr 5 1785	bap
Feb 19	Edward DUDLEY	bur
Feb 19	Abraham, s of Robert & Phebe ONIONS	bap
Feb 22	Lett, d of Joseph & Nancy SOWER, Born November 15 1788	bap
Feb 23	Isaac, s of Isaac & Jane MILLS, Born No^v 5 1788	bap
Mar 1	Hannah DARBY	bur
Mar 1	Elizabeth TOMPSON	bur

Mar 1	Mary, d of William & Mary WRIGHT	bap
Mar 1	Sarah, d of Joseph & Ann CARTWRIGHT	bap
Mar 4	Samuel, s of Samuel & Phebe BECK	bur
Mar 4	Sarah, d of William & Sarah HEATH	bap
Mar 8	Sarah, d of Joseph & Sarah GRANGER	bap
Mar 8	Mary, d of John & Sarah HODGSKINS	bap
Mar 8	Jane WOODWARD	bur
Mar 8	Sarah RICHARDS	bur
Mar 12	Isaac GUTTRIDGE	bur
Mar 12	Sarah JONES	bur
Mar 12	John, s of Thomas & Sarah SMITH, Born Sep 11 1788	bap
Mar 13	Edward ASTON	bur
Mar 15	Thomas PARKES	bur
Mar 15	John, s of John & Ann MARTIN, born Feby 23	bap
Mar 15	William, s of John & Phebe HICKMANS	bap
Mar 18	Francis PAUMER	bur
Mar 20	Sarah GRISE	bur
Mar 22	Ann, d of Edward & Elizabeth FEREDAY	bap
Mar 22	William, s of William & Sarah WALKER	bap
Mar 22	Phebe, d of Benjamin & Ann MILLS	bap
Mar 22	Sarah, d of Peter & Mary MILLS	bap
Mar 22	Hannah, d of Thomas & Elizabeth DIXON	bap
Apr 1	Sarah MOOR	bur
Apr 1	Daniel, s of William & Sarah MOOR	bap
Apr 1	John, s of George & Elizabeth BALL	bap
Apr 1	Joseph & Mary, Twins of Samuel & Sarah FLETCHER	bap
Apr 12	William, s of William & Mary WHITEHOUSE	bap
Apr 12	Samuel, s of Joseph & Elizabeth MILLS	bap
Apr 12	John, s of John & Hannah WINNINGTON	bap
Apr 12	Phebe, d of Richard & Sarah BECK	bap
Apr 13	Mary, d of William & Hannah HOLYOAK, Born Dec 27, 1788	bap
Apr 19	Shusannah, d of William & Lydia EDWARDS	bap
Apr 19	James, s of Alexander & Mary MAC.MULLIN	bap
Apr 26	Samuel Midleton, s of John & Jane SPINK	bap
May 10	James, s of John & Martha PARTRIDGE	bap
May 10	Thomas, s of William & Elizabeth WHITEHOUSE	bap
May 10	Elizabeth, d of John & Lydia FURNEYFOOT	bap
May 10	Hannah, d of John & Sarah FISHER	bap
May 10	John, a bas begott Child of Mary PARTRIDGE	bap
May 12	Mary, d of Edward & Martha OWEN	bur
May 12	John, s of John & Hannah WHEAL	bap
May 12	Ann, d of James & Ann OWEN	bap
May 24	Mary, d of John & Elizabeth REED	bap
May 24	John, s of Daniel & Sarah NICKOLDS	bur

A Transcript of the Register of the Parish of Tipton Alias Tibbington
was Exhibited into the Deans Visitation held in the Court of Lichfield
being on May 30 1789

May 31	Jesse FISHER	bur
May 31	Robert HARPER	bur

1789

May 31	Elizabeth, d of Peter & Ann MILLS	bap
May 31	Mary, d of Abell & Ann WHITEHOUSE	bap
May 31	Ann, d of George & Lucy MARSHALL, Born Nov 12 1788	bap
May 31	Francis, s of Francis & Hannah WHITEHOUSE	bap
May 31	Richard, s of Joseph & Mary GORTON	bap
May 31	Hannah, d of Joseph & Elizabeth HORTON	bap
Jun 1	James, s of Benjamin & Sarah LAW, Born October 4 1787	bap
Jun 1	Sarah, d of Isaac & Mary DARBY, Born September 1 1787	bap
Jun 7	Maria, d of Joseph & Ann SIVATOR	bap
Jun 7	Ann, d of William & Phebe TURNER	bap
Jun 14	Samuel, s of Daniel & Hannah ROUND, Born March 30	bap
Jun 14	Edward, s of Edward & Mary DARBY, Born June 2	bap
Jun 14	Ruth, d of John & Elizabeth TURNER	bap
Jun 24	Elizabeth, d of Ann & William BLAKEMORE	bap
Jun 28	John, s of Samuel & Sarah ROBERTS	bap
Jun 28	Maria, d of Daniel & Sarah SHELDON	bap
Jul 5	James JONES	bur
Jul 5	Thomas, s of Samuel & Sarah NOCK, Born May 1, 1789	bap
Jul 5	Rosannah, d of David & Sarah JEVON	bap
Jul 12	William, s of Thomas & Sarah WAINWRIGHT	bap
Jul 12	Sarah, d of William & Nancy JOHNSON	bap
Jul 26	William, s of Joseph & Mary HODGYETTS, Born May 3^d	bap
Jul 26	William, s of Cornelias & Esther BAKER	bap
Jul 26	William, s of Thomas & Mary LITTLE	bap
Aug 5	Mary FISHER	bur
Aug 9	Daniel GORTON	bur
Aug 16	William, s of Edward & Mary STOCKWIN	bap
Aug 23	Thomas, s of Thomas & Catharine BAYLEYS, Born Aug 3, 1784	bap
Aug 23	Mary, d of Thomas & Catharine BAYLEYS, Born Jan 23, 1789	bap
Aug 23	Samuel, s of Samuel & Sarah WHITEHOUSE	bap
Aug 23	David, s of John & Sarah FISHER, Born April 12 1789	bap
Aug 23	Mary, d of John & Sarah FISHER, Born June 14 1785	bap
Aug 23	Thomasin, d of John & Sarah FISHER, Born Feb 8 1783	bap
Aug 23	William, s of Joseph & Mary HIPKISS, Born June 16 1789	bap
Aug 30	Joseph, s of John & Mary HARRISS, Born July 29	bap
Aug 30	Joseph, s of William & Ann WARD	bap
Aug 30	Thomas, s of Richard & Elizabeth EDWARDS	bap
Aug 30	Jeremiah, s of Enass & Hannah WHITEHOUSE	bap
Aug 30	Esther, d of Thomas & Sarah HILL	bap
Sep 6	John, s of Joseph & Ann SAUNDERS	bap
Sep 14	Hannah, a bas begott Child of Elizabeth BOTT, Born June 9	bap
Sep 14	Richard, s of Joseph & Mary GORTON	bur
Sep 17	William, s of Isaac & Martha TIMMINS	bap
Sep 17	Elizabeth, d of John & Sarah WAINWRIGHT	bap
Oct 4	William, s of Aron & Hannah SMITH	bap
Oct 4	Elizabeth, d of Joseph & Hannah ONIONS	bap
Oct 11	William, s of William & Elizabeth WORTON, Born April 19	bap
Oct 11	Ann, d of Samuel & Mary CLIFT, Born April 29	bap
Oct 11	Hannah EVINS	bur

1789

Oct 11	William, s of William & Sarah SINCOX	bap
Oct 15	Ann, d of Richard & Elizabeth EDWARDS	bur
Oct 18	William ATTWOOD	bur
Oct 18	Ann, d of Edward & Margaret FISHER	bap
Oct 18	Isaac, s of Joseph & Mary FISHER	bap
— Oct 25	Sarah, d of William & Phebe HODGSKINS	bap
Oct 25	Hannah, d of Richard & Hannah WHITEHOUSE	bap
Oct 25	John, s of John & Mary WHITEHOUSE	bap
Nov 8	Elizabeth, d of John & Ann SHELDON, Born July 11	bap
— Nov 11	Thomas PARREY	bur
Nov 11	John, s of Thomas & Elizabeth MILLARD, Born Sepr 15	bap
Nov 18	Eutychus FISHER	bur
Nov 29^{25}	Mary, d of Richard & Hannah EDWARDS	bap
Nov 29	Sarah, d of William & Mary LAW	bap
Nov 29	Edward, s of Joseph & Mary SMITH	bap
Nov 29	Benjamin, s of Benjamin & Sarah WHITEHOUSE	bap
Nov 29	Phebe, d of Richard & Elizabeth SAUNDERS	bap
— Dec 1	James FELLOWS	bur
Dec 6	Timothy SAUNDERS	bur
Dec 6	James, s of William & Mary WHITEHOUSE	bap
Dec 8	William HORTON	bur
Dec 13	Hannah, d of Jaby & Elizabeth FISHER	bap
Dec 13	Joseph, s of James & Hannah HEELEY	bap
Dec 20	Daniel, s of Daniel & Phebe WARR	bap
Dec 20	William, s of Joseph & Elizabeth FINNEY	bap
Dec 25	Joseph, s of Stephen & Mary FISHER	bap
Dec 28	Josiah, s of Joseph & Nancy FIELDHOUSE	bap

1790

Jan 3	Nathaniel, s of Nathaniel & Elizabeth HEELEY	bap
Jan 10	Nancy, d of Joseph & Susannah JONES	bap
Jan 10	Mary, d of Joseph & Hannah NICKOLDS	bap
Jan 10	Mary, d of Joseph & Jane CALLOWAY	bap
Jan 10	John ALEXANDER	bur
Jan 10	Joseph, s of Samuel & Mary WHITEHOUSE, Born Apl 5 1789	bap
Jan 10	Phebe, a bas begott Child of Sarah BURROWS	bap
Jan 10	Mary, a bas begott Child of Phebe BURROWS	bap
Jan 17	William, s of Joseph & Rachael DUFFIELD	bap
— Jan 17	Catharine, d of Richard & Sarah INGRAM	bap
Jan 31	Ann, d of Isaac & Hannah SMITH, Born May 21, 1789	bap
— Feb 7	John, s of William & Mary HUGHES	bap
Feb 9	Maria, d of Joseph & Eleanor FISHER, Born May 28	bap
Feb 9	Charlotte, d of Edward & Sarah SMITH, Born April 12th 1787	bap
— Feb 9	Sarah, wife of Joseph GRANGER	bur
Feb 11	Isaac FLETCHER	bur
— Feb 11	Elizabeth, d of Jonah & Ann PRICE	bap
Feb 21	Daniel, s of Samuel & Sarah SMITH	bap
Feb 21	Dorothy, d of Matthew & Ann HART	bap
Feb 21	Jane, d of John & Sarah HILL	bap

1790

Feb 21	Peter, s of Joseph & Sarah HILL, Born April 25 1783	bap
Feb 28	James, s of John & Mary ATTWOOD	bap
Feb 28	George, s of Richard & Betty SAUNDERS	bap
Feb 28	Sarah, s of Daniel & Phebe MILLS	bap
Feb 28	Mary FULLWOOD	bur
Feb 28	Sarah FOSTER	bur
Mar 14	Mary WHITEHOUSE	bur
Mar 14	Mary, d of Joseph & Elizabeth WHITEHOUSE	bap
Mar 14	Benjamin, s of Thomas & Phebe BUNCE, Born January 20	bap
Mar 14	William, s of Daniel & Ann TIMMINS	bap
Mar 14	Mary, d of Edward & Elizabeth WALL	bap
Mar 14	Joseph, s of James & Martha GREEN	bap
Mar 14	Nancy, d of Thomas & Mary SMITH	bap
Mar 14	Sarah, d of Samuel & Elizabeth MILLS	bap
Mar 21	Thomas, s of Joseph & Ann LESTER	bap
Mar 21	Whitehouse Henry, s of Emanuel & Nancy DARBY	bap.
Mar 25	Joseph, s of Joseph & Catharine DINESDALE	bap
Mar 25	Catharine, d of Edward & Mary ROBINSON	bap
Mar 30	John ELWELL	bur
Mar 30	Joseph CADRACK	bur
Mar 30	William WHITEHOUSE	bur
	[*At the start of the next page*: "Omitted being entered right"]	
Mar 23	Wm MILLS	bur
Mar 23	Amelia ARTIL	bur
Mar 23	William, s of Charles & Ann WEAVER, Born Novr 5, 1789	bap
Mar 23	James, s of John & Mary WITTALL	bap
Mar 24	John GRISE	bur
Mar 28	Charles, s of John & Catharine FISHER	bap
Apr 4	Thomas, s of David & Mary ROUND	bap
Apr 4	Saml, s of Joseph & Hannah SMITH	bap
Apr 4	Joseph, s of Elizabeth EDGE Bap^d a Bastard	bap
Apr 4	Francis, d of Samuel & Mary NOCK	bap
Apr 4	Hannah, d of James & Sarah RICHARDS	bap
Apr 4	Samuel ROUND	bur
Apr 4	Mary, d of John & Elizabeth ROUND	bap
Apr 8	Shusannah, wife of John HOLDEN	bur
Apr 8	Martha, d of John & Mary CASHMORE	bap
Apr 11	Hannah, d of William & Mary PERSHOUSE	bap
Apr 18	Abraham, a bas begot Child of Joice PICKIN	bap
Apr 18	Joseph, s of Richard & Sarah GRIFFIS, Born Dec 23 1789	bap
Apr 18	Sophia GRIFFIS	bur
Apr 22	Elizabeth FISHER	bur
Apr 22	Ambrose, s of John & Shusannah BLACKHAM	bap
Apr 28	Sarah PARKES	bur
May 2	Mary, d of Thomas & Sarah MORGAN	bap
May 2	James, s of Thomas & Maria WARTON	bur
May 2	Mary WHITEHOUSE	bur
May 2	James WHITEHOUSE	bur
May 6	Isaac, s of Isaac & Ann LAW	bap

May 6	John, s of Joseph & Mary WHITEHOUSE	bur
May 9	Mary, d of John & Susannah GREGORY	bap
May 11	William WAINWRIGHT	bur
May 11	George NICKLIN	bur
May 11	William, s of Daniel & Jane NICKLIN, Born Dec 11 1789	bap
May 11	Hannah, d of James & Elizabeth ROUND, Born Dec 22 1789	bap
May 12	Hannah, wife of Thomas WHITEHOUSE	bur
May 16	Ezekiel, s of Ezekiel & Elizabeth WALTERS	bap
May 18	James, s of John & Martha PARTRIDGE	bur
May 18	Hannah, d of John & Sarah FISHER	bur
May 23	Elizabeth, d of John & Sarah GIBBANS	bap
May 25	John WHESSON	bur
May 25	Mary, d of William & Sarah HOSBAND	bap
May 30	Samuel, s of Peter & Elizabeth SAUNDERS	bap
May 30	Benjamin, s of James & Elizabeth BENNETT	bap
Jun 7	Edward, s of William & Eleanor GRIFFIS	bur
Jun 7	Mary, d of Eutychus & Phebe FISHER	bap
Jun 28[sic]	Hannah, d of William & Mary FISHER	bap
Jun 12	John, s of Benjamin & Elizabeth GIBBANS	bap
Jun 25	Sarah FISHER	bur
Jul 4	William, s of David & Joice WALTERS	bur
Jul 4	William, s of David & Joice WALTERS	bap
Jul 4	Ann, d of James & Nancy CORNSFORTH	bap
Jul 4	Sarah, d of John & Hannah HOGSKINS	bap
Jul 8	Martha, d of William & Phebe HICKMANS	bap
Jul 8	Job, s of Joseph & Mary SMITH	bap
Jul 8	Hannah HICKMANS	bur
Jul 11	Nancy, d of William & Sarah ROUND	bur
Jul 11	Karl, d of John & Rosanna RIDER	bap
Jul 11	Benjamin, d of William & Sarah TURNER	bap
Jul 13	Jane, d of William & Mary TURNER	bap
Jul 13	Edward TIMMINS	bur
Jul 25	William, s of John & Elizabeth REED	bap
Jul 25	Alice DAVIS	bur
Jul 25	Joseph GRIFFIS	bur
Jul 28	Mary BECK	bur
Aug 1	Phebe, d of Benjamin & Sarah CRESSWELL	bap
Aug 4	Jeremiah WHITEHOUSE	bur
Aug 8	Hannah, d of William & Elizabeth HORTON, Born July 14	bap
Aug 8	Richard, a bas begot Child of Mary BOWIN	bap
Aug 29	Josiah, s of Thomas & Elizabeth MORRISS	bap
Aug 29	William, s of James & Martha NOCK	bap
Aug 29	Mary, d of John & Sarah ROWLEY	bap
Sep 12	Sarah ALLPORT	bur
Sep 12	Job, s of Job & Mary SMITH	bur
Sep 15	William HORTON	bur
Sep 19	Elizabeth GRIFFIS	bur
Sep 19	Mary, d of Abraham & Hannah FISHER	bap
Sep 19	Phebe, d of Abraham & Sarah WHITEHOUSE	bap

Sep 19	Elizabeth, d of John & Mary SHARROD	bap
Sep 19	Elizabeth, d of Jevin & Lucy OWEN	bap
Sep 21	Sarah, wife of John HODSKINS	bur
Sep 21	Sarah FISHER	bur
Sep 26	Sarah, d of Thomas & Elizabeth TILLEY, Born Aug 17 1790	bap
Sep 26	Phebe, d of Thomas & Elizabeth HUGHES, Born Aug 24 1790	bap
Oct 6	Joseph HOLLAND	bur
Oct 6	Phebe, d of Isaac & Hannah LAW	bap
Oct 10	William, s of Joseph & Rachel DUFFIELD	bur
Oct 10	Frances, d of David & Ann HIPKISS	bap
Oct 10	Hannah, d of John & Elizabeth GUTTRIDGE	bap
Oct 10	Stephen, s of Isaac & Sarah ASTON	bap
Oct 10	Joseph, s of Thomas & Lydia TAYLOR	bap
Oct 17	Elizabeth, d of William & Margaret CUNLEY, Born Oct 1, 1790	bap
Oct 18	Hannah, d of John & Rhody DOUTY	bap
Oct 18	Sarah, d of William & Phebe HODSKINS	bur
Oct 25	Elizabeth KIDSON	bur
Oct 25	Enock, s of John & Elizabeth PARTRIDGE	bur
Oct 25	Sarah, d of George & Lucy MARSHALL	bap
Oct 31	Sarah, d of Thomas & Elizabeth HORTON	bap
Nov 3	Ambrose, s of John & Susannah BLACKHAM	bur
Nov 3	Ann, d of James & Mary DARBY, Born Oct 16	bap
Nov 7	John, s of John & Elizabeth EDWARDS	bap
Nov 7	Jane, d of Joseph & Sarah HILL	bap
Nov 7	Hannah, d of Richard & Elizabeth WAINWRIGHT	bap
Nov 7	Mary, d of Benjamin & Nancy RUDGE	bap
Nov 14	Sarah, d of Joseph & Mary WORTON	bap
Nov 14	Ann, d of Thomas & Sarah SUTTON	bap
Nov 28	Rebekah COLE	bur
Nov 28	Ann, d of William & Mary LOW	bap
Nov 28	John, s of Robert & Hannah SMITH	bap
Nov 28	Hannah, d of Samuel & Sarah BAYLEYS	bap
Nov 28	Mary, d of Richard & Elizabeth EDWARDS	bap
Dec 2	John HICK	bur
Dec 5	Hannah MILLS	bur
Dec 7	Joseph, s of Samuel & Elizabeth HICKMANS, Born Oct 14	bap
Dec 7	Thomas PHILIPS	bur
Dec 7	Joseph, s of Michael & Sarah DUFFIELD	bur
Dec 12	Elizabeth, d of George & Elizabeth BALL	bap
Dec 15	Mary, d of John & Sarah ROWLEY	bur
Dec 15	John, s of Samuel & Sarah BAYLEYS	bur
Dec 19	Thomas, s of William & Hannah FOSTER, Born Oct 7, 1790	bap
Dec 25	James DREW	bur
Dec 25	Sarah, d of William & Elizabeth GEORGE	bap
Dec 26	Andrew, s of John & Lydia FURNEYFOOT	bap

Jan 2	Joseph, s of Joseph & Elizabeth HODSKINS	bap
Jan 2	Ann, d of Peter & Ann MILLS	bap

1791

Jan 5	Abraham, s of Abraham & Sarah TIMMINS	bap
Jan 5	Thomas WILLIAMS	bur
Jan 5	Mary DARBY	bur
Jan 16	Thomas, s of Thomas & Phebe NICKOLDS	bap
Jan 16	James, s of William & Mary WHITEHOUSE	bap
Jan 16	Rosannah, d of James & Eleanor MILLS	bap
Jan 19	Sarah DUDLEY	bur
Jan 19	Ann, d of James & Judith BAKER, Born Feb[y] 7, 1790	bap
Jan 23	Daniel, s of Joseph & Phebe CROFTS	bap
Jan 23	Mary, d of Edward & Elizabeth WHITEHOUSE	bap
Jan 25	Sarah MILLS	bur
Jan 25	Phebe, d of Richard & Elizabeth SAUNDERS	bur
Jan 25	Stephen, s of Edward & Elizabeth MILLS	bap
Jan 25	Simon, s of Isaac & Jane MILLS	bap
Jan 25	Maria, d of William & Eleanor GRIFFIS	bap
Jan 30	Ann, d of Joseph & Susanna DAVIS	bap
Feb 2	Samuel FISHER	bur
Feb 2	Nancy, d of Richard & Sarah WHITEHOUSE	bap
Feb 13	Thomas EDGE	bur
Feb 13	Thomas DREW	bur
Feb 13	William, s of Peter & Rachael ROWLEY	bap
Feb 17	Thomas GREYOR	bur
Feb 20	Hannah EVINS	bur
Feb 20	Samuel, s of John & Elizabeth BATE, Born Oct 1, 1790	bap
Feb 20	Phebe, d of Abraham & Elizabeth SHELDON	bap
Feb 22	Phebe SHARROTT	bur
Feb 22	Mary, d of William & Sarah WHITEHOUSE	bap
Feb 27	Hannah, d of Abell & Martha HILL, Born Feb[y] 1, 1791	bap
Mar 1	Mary, d of James & Ellzabeth ATTWOOD	bur
Mar 1	Nancy, d of Robert & Ann BETTY	bap
Mar 6	Hannah, d of James & Hannah FISHER, Born Feb 12 1791	bap
Mar 6	Mary, d of Benjamin & Sarah WESSON	bap
Mar 11	Richard TIMMINS	bur
Mar 13	Elizabeth, d of John & Mary HARRIS, Born Jan 27, 1791	bap
Mar 13	John, s of John & Ann SHELDON	bap
Feb 16[sic]	Isaac, s of William & Mary WRIGHT	bap
Mar 20	James Fletcher, s of Daniel & Phebe WARR	bap
Mar 20	William, s of William & Mary GRETTON, Born Feb[y] 17, 1791	bap
Mar 20	Hannah, d of Edward & Hannah MILLINGTON, Born Mar 1 1790	bap
Mar 27	Hannamariah, d of Benjamin & Hannah BAGLEY, Born Dec 21 1790	bap
Mar 27	Mary, d of William & Martha INGRAM	bap
Mar 27	Samuel, s of Peter & Elizabeth SANNDERS	bap
Mar 27	Maria, d of John & Hannah WHEAL	bap
Mar 27	Sarah, d of Jacob & Sarah MILLS, Born Feb[y] 24, 1790	bap
Mar 27	Sarah WHITEHOUSE	bur
Mar 27	Elizabeth BROOKS	bur
Mar 27	Joseph COLE	bur
Apr 3	Jeremiah, s of Isaac & Elizabeth WHITEHOUSE	bap

1791

Apr 3	Nancy, d of William & Phebe TURNER	bap
Apr 3	Hannah, d of Joseph & Mary GORTON	bap
Apr 3	Charlotte, d of Thomas & Sarah WHITEHOUSE	bap
Apr 3	Ann, d of Samuel & Phebe BECK	bap
Apr 13	Sarah, wife of John ONIONS	bur
Apr 13	Sarah, d of Henry & Sarah KENDRICK, Born Oct 13, 1790	bap
Apr 17	Zachariah, s of Moses & Elizabeth HILL	bap
Apr 17	William, s of William & Ann EDGE	bap
Apr 17	William, s of John & Phebe HICKMANS	bap
Apr 24	Joseph, s of Joseph & Sarah HORTON	bap
Apr 24	Paul, s of Paul & Lydia GRIFFIS	bap
Apr 24	Sophia, d of Gideon & Betty GRISE	bap
Apr 24	Mary, d of Richard & Margaret REED	bap
Apr 24	Stephen, s of Moses & Hannah TIMMINS	bap
Apr 24	Peter, s of Joseph & Phebe FLETCHER	bap
Apr 24	Stephen SMITH	bur
Apr 25	Widow BROAD	bur
May 1	John PARKES	bur
May 1	Mary FISHER	bur
May 1	Richard, s of John & Ann JUKES, Born Aug 1, 1789	bap
May 1	Jane, d of John & Ann JUKES	bap
May 1	Joseph, s of John & Ann LAW, Born Novr 15, 1790	bap
May 8	Elizabeth, wife of Joseph TURNER	bur
May 8	Elizabeth, d of Joseph & Elizabeth TURNER, Born Mar 20 1791	bap
May 8	Ann, d of Jeremiah & Mary WILLETTS, Born March 20 1791	bap
May 15	Sophia, d of Edward & Ann ROBERTS, Born March 11 1790	bap
May 15	William, s of John & Sophia LAW, Born Apr 1 [9?], 1790	bap
May 15	William SHELDON	bur
May 19	William, s of Joseph & Mary NICKLIN	bur
May 19	Thomas, s of Thomas & Sarah ELWELL, Born April 14, 1779	bap
May 29	Kitty, d of Thomas & Nancy FELLOWS	bap
Jun 12	Elizabeth, d of Thomas & Charlotte COTTOM	bap
Jun 12	Elizabeth, d of William & Phebe ALDRETT	bap
Jun 12	Mary, d of John & Ann MATTHEWS, Born Oct 23, 1790	bap
Jun 12	James, s of Thomas & Mary WHEAL	bap
Jun 12	Daniel, s of David & Ann WHITEHOUSE	bap
Jun 12	Ann NIGHTINGALE	bur
Jun 12	Joseph GREYER	bur
Jul 3	Job, s of Joseph & Mary SMITH	bap
Jul 5	William, s of Thomas & Mary WHEAL	bur
Jul 10	John WHITEHOUSE	bur
Jul 11	Hannah, d of Samuel & Mary WHITEHOUSE, Born Mar 15 1791	bap
Jul 11	Hannah, d of Thomas & Phebe WHITEHOUSE, Born Feby 2 1791	bap
Jul 11	Lydia, wife of Isaac WINNINGTON	bur
Jul 17	William, s of Alexander & Mary MACKMULLIN	bap
Jul 17	James, s of Samuel & Mary NOCK	bap
Jul 19	Joseph PASKIN	bur
Jul 21	Hannah MILLARD	bur

1791

Jul 21	David, s of Samuel & Sarah FLETCHER, Born Apl 26 1791	bap
Jul 27	Phebe WINNINGTON	bur
Jul 27	John ILLINGSLEY	bur
Jul 31	Timothy, s of Joseph & Rachael DUFFIELD, born July 13 1791	bap
Jul 31	Hannah WINNINGTON	bur
Jul 31	Richard NICKLIN	bur
Aug 5	Josiah, s of Joseph & Ann FIELDHOUSE	bur
Aug 5	Ann, d of James & Elizabeth ATTWOOD, Born Dec 25 1790	bap
Aug 7	Samuel, s of Samuel & Sarah SMITH, Born Apl 26 1791	bap
Aug 7	George, s of Daniel & Hannah ROUND, Born July 29 1791	bap
Aug 10	Sarah, d of Daniel & Elizabeth MILLS	bur
Aug 14	Hannah, d of Luke & Nancy PHILIPS	bap
Aug 24	Lucy, d of Thomas & Mary WHITEHOUSE	bur
Aug 24	William, a bas begott Child of Lettice SAULT	bap
Aug 24	Rosannah, d of William & Hannah HOLEYOAK	bap
Aug 28	Thomas GRIFFIS	bur
Aug 28	Thomas, s of Richard & Voialette PARKES	bap
Aug 28	Ambrose, s of William & Rebekah JEVON	bap
Aug 28	Ambrose, s of Richard & Sarah STANTON, Born July 31, 1791	bap
Sep 4	William, s of William & Phebe HODSKINS	bap
Sep 4	Joseph, s of William & Lydia EDWARDS	bap
Sep 4	Lydia, d of Joseph & Elizabeth SHELDON	bap
Sep 4	Ann, d of John & Charlotte WARD, Born May 22, 1791	bap
Sep 11	Maria, d of Benjamin & Sarah HORTON, Born Sep 3 1791	bap
Sep 11	Ellen Stevens WORSEY, d of Henry WORSEY & Mary STEPHENS	bap
Sep 18	Thomas, s of Thomas & Sarah MORGAN	bap
Sep 23	Lydia, d of Joseph & Elizabeth SHELDON	bur
Sep 25	Richard, s of Richard & Sarah INGRAM	bap
Sep 29	Thomas, s of Joseph & Sarah LESTER	bur
Oct 3	John, s of Francis & Hannah WHITEHOUSE	bap
Oct 3	Eeanor, d of Job & Mary WHITEHOUSE, Born Nov 26 1790	bap
Oct 3	Francis MILLS	bur
Oct 5	Samuel WHITEHOUSE	bur
Oct 5	Benjamin, s of Abraham & Phebe WHITEHOUSE, Born Oct 3 1790	bap
Oct 5	William, s of Richard & Hannah EDWARDS	bap
Oct 9	Joseph, s of Joseph & Ann CARTWRIGHT	bap
Oct 10	Sarah, d of Richard & Sarah WHITEHOUSE	bur
Oct 10	William, s of Cornelias & Esther BAKER	bur
Oct 10	Joseph, s of John & Sarah ROWLEY	bur
Oct 15	Mary, d of Joseph & Jane CALLOWAY	bur
Oct 18	Mary, d of James & Sarah WALL	bur
Oct 27	Daniel, s of Daniel & Sarah CALLOWAY	bur
Oct 30	Elizabeth, d of Thomas & Elizabeth HODSKINS	bur
Oct 30	William, s of Joseph & Mary HODGYETTS	bur
Oct 30	Sarah WHITEHOUSE	bur
Oct 30	William, s of William & Sarah JONES	bap
Oct 30	Mary, d of Benjamin & Ann MILLS, Born May 1 1791	bap

Oct 30	Pheby, d of William & Mary PERSHOUSE	bap
Nov 3	John SMITH	bur
Nov 3	John, a bas begott Child of Winneyfed WRIDER	bap
Nov 5	James, s of George & Ann BRINLEY	bap
Nov 5	Mary Ann, d of Benjamin & Hannah RICHARDS, Born Apl 3, 1791	bap
Nov 7	Mary, d of James & Sarah WALL	bur
Nov 7	John, s of Stephen & Mary HIPKISS	bur
Nov 20	Ann, d of William & Sarah SIMCOX	bap
Nov 20	Mary, d of John & Sarah HOTLEY	bap
Nov 23	Eleanor, d of Luke & Nancy PHILLIPS	bur
Nov 27	Joseph, s of Benjamin & Sarah MILLARD	bur
Nov 27	William, s of James & Nancy OWEN	bap
Nov 27	Hannah, d of Isaac & Mary DARBY	bap
Nov 27	Elizabeth, d of Michael & Elizabeth DUFFIELD	bap
Nov 27	Mary, d of James & Hannah HEELEY	bap
Nov 27	Sarah, d of Richard & Elizabeth SAUNDERS	bap
Dec 1	Sarah, d of William & Mary LAW	bur
Dec 1	John, s of William & Sarah GREENEWAY	bur
Dec 5	Sarah, d of William & Elizabeth WARTON	bur
Dec 5	Elizabeth, d of William & Elizabeth WARTON	bap
Dec 2[sic]	Mary WHITEHOUSE	bur
Dec 11	Sarah, d of Luke & Nancy PHILLIPS	bur
Dec 11	Sarah, d of Edward & Mary ROBERTS	bur
Dec 18	Benjamin MILLARD, Jun[r]	bur
Dec 18	Mary, d of Benjamin & Mary WHESSON	bur
Dec 22	William, s of Richard & Eleanor SHARROTT	bur
Dec 25	William, s of Cornelius & Esther BAKER	bap
~ Dec 25	Joseph, s of John & Sarah ROWLEY	bap
Dec 25	Mary, d of William & Hannah SHELDON	bap
Dec 25	Maria, d of Richard & Elizabeth TAYLOR	bap
Dec 25	Richard BECK	bur
Dec 25	Josiah, s of Enass & Hannah WHITEHOUSE	bur
Dec 25	Isiah, s of Enass & Hannah WHITEHOUSE	bap
Dec 25	Mary, d of David & Phebe SMITH, Born June 21 1787	bap
Dec 25	William, s of David & Phebe SMITH, Born Feb[y] 17 1789	bap
Dec 25	Hannah, d of David & Phebe SMITH, Born Oct 16 1791	bap

Jan 3	Joseph, s of Joseph & Rachael HIPKISS, Born Jan 11 1791	bap
Jan 5	Ann, d of James & Ann OWEN	bur
Jan 5	Elizabeth, d of Benjamin & Mary WHEAL, Born Apl 17, 1791	bap
Jan 8	Mary MATTHEWS	bur
Jan 11	Frances, d of David & Mary HIPKISS	bur
Jan 11	Mary, d of Sam[l] & Mary WHITEHOUSE	bur
Jan 15	Hannah, wife of Daniel ROUND	bur
Jan 15	Sarah, d of James & Rhody GUEST	bap
Jan 15	Joseph, s of Thomas & Sarah FISHER	bap
Jan 19	Mary, d of Joseph & Mary SMITH	bur

1792

Jan 22	Sarah FELLOWS	bur
Jan 22	Joseph, s of Edward & Tamor WHITEHOUSE	bur
Jan 25	John, s of Henry & Nancy TURNER	bap
Jan 25	Peter, s of Peter & Mary MILLS	bap
Jan 25	William ELWELL	bur
Jan 29	Mary, d of Thomas & Ann COTTRELL	bap
Jan 29	Elizabeth, d of Joseph & Ann LESTER	bap
Jan 29	Joseph, s of Thomas & Mary LITTLE	bap
Feb 3	George FOSTER	bur
Feb 3	William, s of Edward & Ann ROBERTS	bap
Feb 12	James, s of Thomas & Maria WORTON	bur
Feb 12	Ann, wife of Moses ROUND	bur
Feb 12	Sarah, d of John & Elizabeth SMITH, Born Oct 25, 1789	bap
Feb 12	John, s of John & Elizabeth SMITH, born Nov 15 1791	bap
Feb 16	Thomas, s of Thomas & Elizabeth WHITEHOUSE	bap
Feb 16	Jane, wife of Daniel PERSHOUSE	bur
Feb 19	Hannah, wife of Samuel MILLS	bur
Feb 19	William, s of Joshua & Hannah PARTRIDGE	bap
Feb 19	Mary, d of William & Ann WARD, Born Dec 10 1791	bap
Feb 26	Joseph, s of Joseph & Ann SIVITER	bap
Mar 4	Elizabeth, d of Joseph & Susannah JONES	bap
Mar 11	William, s of James & Nancy HORTON	bap
Mar 18	Philip, s of Samuel & Sarah ROBERTS	bap
Mar 18	Mary, d of Francis & Jane PIERCE	bap
Mar 18	John, s of John & Jane TAYLOR	bap
Mar 18	Sarah, d of Samuel & Elizabeth MILLS	bap
Mar 18	Elizabeth, d of John & Mary JONES	bap
Mar 18	Joseph, s of Joseph & Jane CALLOWAY	bap
Mar 25	Josiah, s of Samuel & Sarah NOCK	bap
Mar 27	Elizabeth, d of Richard & Sarah WHITEHOUSE	bur
Apr 1	Enock, s of Joseph & Sarah NOCK	bap
Apr 8	William, s of John & Mary ATTWOOD	bap
Apr 8	Edwd, s of Thomas & Elizabeth MORRISS	bap
Apr 8	Abel, s of Abraham & Ann GEORGE	bap
Apr 8	Abel, s of Abel & Sarah WHITEHOUSE	bap
Apr 8	Isaac, s of John & Mary WHITEHOUSE	bap
Apr 8	Elizabeth, d of Joseph & Elizabeth MILLS	bap
Apr 8	Phebe, d of James & Martha GREEN	bap
Apr 8	Mary, d of Joseph & Ann SAUNDERS	bap
Apr 8	Mary, d of John & Mary FIELDHOUSE	bap
Apr 8	Sarah, d of William & Ann WHITEHOUSE	bap
Apr 8	Sarah, d of Thomas & Mary ASPLEY	bap
Apr 8	Sarah, d of Richard & Mary HODGSKISS	bap
Apr 8	William, s of Daniel & Phebe MILLS	bap
Apr 11	William COOK	bur
Apr 11	Thomas, s of William & Hannah BROWN, Born Aug 12, 1784	bap
Apr 15	Elizabeth, d of Edward & Tamor WHITEHOUSE	bap
Apr 15	Moses WHITEHOUSE	bur
Apr 15	Frederick GUTTRIDGE	bur

1792

Apr 22	Sarah, d of Richard & Hannah WHITEHOUSE	bap
Apr 22	Samuel, s of Joseph & Ann FIELDHOUSE	bap
Apr 22	Sarah, d of Stephen & Mary FISHER	bap
Apr 24	Joseph WHEAL	bur
Apr 26	Elizabeth, d of Joseph & Elizabeth TURNER	bur
Apr 29	Enock, John & Phebe TURNER	bap
Apr 29	Moses, s of Samuel & Sarah SMITH	bap
Apr 29	Maria, d of Samuel & Elizabeth HILL	bap
Apr 29	Mary, d of John & Sarah WHITEHOUSE	bap
Apr 29	Elizabeth, d of James & Martha NOCK	bap
May 6	Mary, d of Thomas & Isabella BRADLEY, Born Mar 23	bap
May 13	Sarah, d of John & Mary CASHMORE	bap
May 13	Mary OWEN	bur
May 20	Jane, d of Edward & Jane WITTMORE	bap
May 20	Jane, d of Benjamin & Elizabeth GIBBONS	bap
May 27	Joseph, s of John & Nancy WHOLLEY, Born Sep 30 1791	bap
May 27	James, s of John & Lydia FURNEYFOOT, Born March 22 1792	bap
May 27	Zacharia, s of Benjamin & Mary ROUND	bap
May 27	Mary, a bas begott Child of Mary EDGE	bap
May 27	Mary Ann, d of Samuel & Ruth LESTER	bap
May 27	Thomas, s of Thomas & Lydia TAYLOR, Born Feby 22, 1792	bap
May 27	Shusannah, d of George & Mary GREYOR	bap
May 27	Daniel, s of Abraham & Sarah WHITEHOUSE, Born Dec 6 1791	bap
May 27	Nancy, d of John & Nancy WHOLLEY, Born Dec 7, 1789	bap
May 27	Edwd DARBY	bur
May 27	Mary, wife of Joseph WORTON	bur

A Transcript of the Register Book of the Parish of Tipton Alis Tibbington
was Exhibited into the Deans Visitation held in the Court of Lichfield
being on May the 30 1792

Jun 3	Hannah, d of John & Eleanor NICKOLDS	bap
Jun 3	Joseph, s of Joseph & Catharine MILLS	bap
Jun 3	Ann, d of Nathaniel & Elizabeth HEELEY, Born May 16	bap
Jun 10	Hattheld, d of John & Sarah FELLOWS	bur
Jun 10	Abraham, s of Ezekiel & Elizabeth WALTERS	bap
Jun 10	Jesse, s of Arther & Mary WHESSON	bap
Jun 10	Benjamin, s of John & Mary HORTON	bap
Jun 10	Ann, d of David & Mary ROUND	bap
Jun 10	Sarah, d of John & Hannah HODGSKINS	bap
Jun 10	Shusannah, d of William & Elizabeth BEDDOW	bap
Jun 13	George, s of John & Mary HARRISON	bur
Jun 13	Mary, d of John & Sarah WALTERHOUSE	bap
Jun 24	Hannah, d of Abraham & Hannah NICHOLDS	bap
Jun 24	Isaac, s of Isaac & Elizabeth FISHER	bur
Jun 26	Benjamin, s of Mary COLLINS	bur
Jun 26	Sarah FEREDAY, a bas begot Child of Ann BLACKHAM	bap
Jun 26	Ann, d of Richard & Elizabeth TAYLOR	bap
Jun 27	Ann, d of Abel & Mary ROUND	bur
Jun 27	Sarah, d of William & Sarah JONES	bap
Jul 15	Elisha, s of Richard & Sarah GRIFFIS	bap

1792

Jul 15	Thos, s of John & Mary WITTALL, Born Apl 26 1792	bap
Jul 15	Sarah, d of Joseph & Elizabeth HOLLAND	bap
Jul 22	John, s of Edward & Ann SMITH	bap
Jul 22	Thomas, s of Jonas & Ann PRICE	bap
Jul 22	John, s of John & Elizabeth REED	bap
Jul 22	Elizabeth, d of John & Mary WILLIAMS	bap
Jul 22	Sarah, d of William & Phebe HICKMANS	bap
Jul 22	Elizabeth, d of Joseph & Mary GORTON	bap
Jul 22	Mary, d of Thomas & Sarah SUTTON	bap
Jul 22	Mary, d of Joseph & Prudence HORTON	bap
Jul 24	Peter, s of Peter & Phebe FOX	bap
Jul 24	William, s of James & Lucy DARBY	bap
Jul 24	Elizabeth, d of Thomas & Sarah PARKES	bap
Jul 24	Hannah GUTTRIDGE	bur
Jul 31	John HICKMANS	bur
Jul 31	Nancy, d of George & Ann WHITEHOUSE	bap
Aug 5	James, s of Thomas & Phebe BUNCE	bap
Aug 12	John, s of John & Sarah GIBBONS	bap
Aug 12	Thomas, s of Thomas & Mary WILLOCK	bap
Aug 12	Hannah, d of James & Mary NOCK	bap
Aug 12	Hannah, d of Edward & Margarett FISHER	bap
Aug 13	Sarah STOKES	bur
Aug 18	Mary, d of John & Catharine INGRAM	bap
Aug 19	Joseph, s of Benjamin & Sarah CRESSWELL	bap
Aug 19	Thomas, s of Thomas & Elizabeth HUGHES	bap
Aug 26	John, s of Joseph & Lucy GEORGE	bap
Aug 26	William, s of Edward & Esther SMITH, Born Jan 31 1788	bap
Aug 26	Edward, s of Edward & Esther SMITH	bap
Aug 26	John, s of William & Sarah PARTRIDGE	bap
Aug 26	Edward, s of William & Eleanor JONES	bap
Aug 26	Mary, d of Isaac & Hannah SMITH, Born November 1790	bap
Aug 26	John, s of Isaac & Hannah SMITH	bap
Aug 26	Sarah DARBY	bur
Aug 26	Nancy, d of John & Mary WHOLLEY	bur
Sep 2	Samuel, s of Richard & Sarah BECK, Born July 20	bap
Sep 2	Isaac, s of Isaac & Elizabeth WHITEHOUSE	bap
Sep 2	David, s of Abraham & Elizabeth SHELDON	bap
Sep 2	Elizabeth, d of Joseph & Mary GORTON	bur
Sep 9	Phebe, d of John & Phebe ASTON	bap
Sep 16	Mary WHITEHOUSE	bur
Sep 16	Zachariah Parkes, s of Joseph & Mary SMITH	bap
Sep 19	Pamelia, d of Robert & Phebe ONIONS	bap
Sep 19	Thomas HOLLAND, s of Mary GRIFFIS, Wid:	bap
Sep 19	Mary GRICE	bur
Sep 19	Thomas, s of William & Eleanor BAKER	bap
Sep 19	Sarah, d of Joseph & Rachael HIPKISS	bap
Sep 19	Thomas, s of James & Hannah BAYLEYS	bap
Sep 23	Joseph, s of John & Mary HODGSKINS	bap
Sep 23	Benjamin, s of Benjamin & Ann RUDGE	bap

1792

Sep 30	William GRETON	bur
Sep 30	Mary TURNER	bur
Sep 30	Elizabeth SHELDON	bur
Oct 4	Phebe BATE	bur
Oct 4	Amelia, d of Thomas & Sarah TUDAR	bap
Oct 4	John, s of William & Eleanor GRIFFIS	bap
Oct 4	Sarah, d of William & Rebekah ROUND	bap
Oct 7	Samuel, s of Benjamin & Sarah WHITEHOUSE	bap
Oct 7	Phebe, d of David & Ann HIPKISS	bap
Oct 7	Sarah, d of Thomas & Eleanor LAW	bap
Oct 7	Phebe, wife of Dan' WHITEHOUSE	bur
Oct 7	Isaac, s of Joseph & Sarah FISHER	bur
Oct 9	Daniel, s of Joseph & Elizabeth SHELDON	bur
Oct 9	Thomas, s of George & Lucy MARSHALL	bap
Oct 14	Ralph, s of Samuel & Hannah SAXON	bap
Oct 21	Ann, d of John & Jane GRIFFIS	bap
Nov 3	Ann, d of Nathaniel & Elizabeth HEELEY	bur
Nov 3	Joseph, s of Isaac & Nancy LAW	bap
Nov 3	Joseph, s of William & Isabell GEORGE	bap
Nov 3	Sarah, d of Edward & Elizabeth WALL, Born July 20 1792	bap
Nov 3	Rosannah, d of Thomas & Elizabeth MILLARD	bap
Nov 3	Elizabeth, d of Isabell WHITEHOUSE	bap
Nov 13	Elizabeth, d of Joseph & Lucy GEORGE	bur
Nov 18	James, s of Joseph & Phebe CROFTS	bap
Nov 25	Joseph, s of Isaac & Mary BATE, Born Aug 25	bap
Nov 25	Thomas, s of Edward & Ann FEREDAY	bap
Nov 25	Abraham, s of James & Mary DARBY	bap
Dec 2	Daniel WHITEHOUSE	bur
Dec 8	John, s of Thomas & Isabell WESTWOOD	bur
Dec 16	George, s of George & Elizabeth BALL	bap
Dec 16	Isaac, s of Benjamin & Hannah MILLARD	bap
Dec 25	Thomas, s of William & Mary LAW	bap
Dec 25	John, s of Joseph & Elizabeth HODGSKINS	bap
Dec 25	William, s of Joseph & Elizabeth WHITEHOUSE	bap
Dec 25	Thomas, s of Thomas & Esther ALSOP	bap
Dec 25	Hannah, d of Joseph & Lettice LAW	bap
Dec 26	Benjamin NIGHTINGALE	bur
Dec 30	Joseph, s of John & Mary HODGSKINS	bur
Dec 30	John, s of Luke & Nancy PHILLIPS	bap
Dec 30	Ellnor, d of Joseph & Mary HOLLAND	bap
Dec 30	Joseph, s of John & Jane PARKES	bur

1793

Jan 6	John, s of John & Dorothy BADGER	bap
Jan 6	William, s of John & Sarah TIMMINS	bap
Jan 6	Abraham, s of Jesse & Mary WHITEHOUSE	bap
Jan 6	Joseph, s of John & Ann MARTIN	bap
Jan 6	William, s of John & Susannah GREGORY	bap
Jan 6	Abraham MILLS	bur

1793

Jan 6	Elizabeth, d of Joseph & Ann LESTER	bur
Jan 6	Joseph, s of William & Lydia EDWARDS	bur
Jan 13	Ann, d of William & Mary SHORTHOUSE	bap
Jan 13	Sarah MAULIN	bur
Jan 15	Henry, s of Samuel & Sarah NOCK	bur
Jan 15	Benjamin, s of Thomas & Jane PARKES	bur
Jan 15	Sarah, d of Jonas & Sarah PRICE	bur
Jan 27	Richard GRIFFIS	bur
Jan 27	John BANBURY	bur
Jan 27	Thomas, s of Joseph & Catharine COCKERIN	bap
Feb 10	Joseph, s of John & Ann MATTHEWS	bap
Feb 17	Nancy, d of Thomas & Elizabeth TILLEY	bap
Feb 17	Maria, d of Thomas & Sarah WHITEHOUSE	bap
Feb 17	Mary, d of George & Ann MARSHALL	bap
Feb 17	Mary, d of Edward & Sarah SHELDON	bur
Feb 19	Ann, wife of William EDGE	bur
Feb 19	Joseph, s of Moses & Hannah TIMMINS	bap
Feb 24	Ann, d of John & Elizabeth WINNINGTON	bur
Feb 26	Mary WHITEHOUSE	bur
Feb 27	Elizabeth NIGHTINGALE	bur
Mar 3	John DREW	bur
Mar 3	Daniel HARRISON	bur
Mar 3	Samuel, s of Richard & Mary BECK	bur
Mar 3	William & Mary, s & d of Elizabeth DREW	bap
Mar 3	William Horton, s of John & Mary HARRIS, Born Jan 13	bap
Mar 3	Sarah, d of James & Sarah RICHARDS	bap
Mar 3	Sarah, d of William & Hannah FOSTER	bap
Mar 3	Isaac, s of James & Rebekah WHITEHOUSE	bap
Mar 3	Mary, d of James & Sarah PERSHOUSE	bap
Mar 3	Thomas, s of Edward & Ann FEREDAY	bap
Mar 10	Daniel, s of Daniel & Sarah CALLOWAY	bap
Mar 10	William, s of Abraham & Hannah FISHER	bap
Mar 10	James, s of John & Mary WHITEHOUSE	bap
Mar 10	Nancy, d of James & Eleanor MILLS	bap
Mar 10	Ann, d of William & Elizabeth DARBY	bap
Mar 10	Moses, s of James & Elizabeth ROUND	bap
Mar 10	James, s of William & Sarah CONSTABLE	bap
Mar 10	Sarah, d of Joseph & Mary HOGYETTS, Born Mar 10 1792	bap
Mar 10	Isabell, wife of William SMITH	bur
Mar 17	William, s of William & Mary LORD, Born Feb 14, 93	bap
Mar 17	Elizabeth, d of Samuel & Elizabeth HICKMANS	bap
Mar 17	Isaac WHITEHOUSE	bur
Mar 17	James NOCK	bur
Mar 17	Mary, wife of Tho LITTLE	bur
Mar 22	William HODGYETTS	bur
Mar 24	Ann, d of Thomas & Elizabeth COLLINS	bap
Mar 24	John, s of Joseph & Jane WILKS	bap
Mar 24	Benjamin, s of Joseph & Rachael DUFFIELD	bap
Mar 24	Joseph, s of Joseph & Susannah DAVIES	bap

1793

Mar 24	Samuel, s of Samuel & Sarah BAYLEYS	bap
Mar 31	Sarah, d of John & Ann FOSTER	bap
Mar 31	Thomas, s of Robert & Hannah SMITH	bap
Mar 31	Richard, s of Thomas & Phebe WHITEHOUSE	bap
Mar 31	James, s of William & Mary WHITEHOUSE	bap
Mar 31	Shusannah, d of Thomas & Sarah LOWE	bap
Mar 31	Sarah, d of Thomas & Sarah MORGAN	bap
Mar 31	Maria, wife of Daniel & Ann TIMMINS	bur
Mar 31	Sarah, wife of Danl WARR	bur
Apr 7	Thomas EVINS	bur
Apr 7	Mary, wife of John WHITEHOUSE	bur
Apr 7	Thomas, s of James & Judith BAKER	bap
Apr 7	Ann, d of Isaac & Sarah ASTON	bap
Apr 9	Josiah, s of Samuel & Mary NOCK	bap
Apr 9	John, s of John & Ann LOWE	bap
Apr 9	Ann, d of Henry & Sarah KENDRICK	bap
Apr 9	John ROYLANDS	bur
Apr 9	John LOW	bur
Apr 10	John GREYOR	bur
Apr 10	Isaac, s of Richard & Elizabeth WAINWRIGHT	bap
Apr 10	Joseph, s of James & Sarah GUTTRIDGE	bap
Apr 14	John, s of Thomas & Charlotte COTTON	bap
May 5	Abraham, s of Peter & Ann HICKMANS	bap
May 19	Wid HICKMANS	bur
May 19	Rachael WARD	bur
May 19	Phebe, d of John & Mary CARTWRIGHT	bur
May 19	Mary, d of Joseph & Sarah FLETCHER	bap
May 19	Samuel, s of Benjamin & Sarah WHESSON	bap
May 19	Jane, d of Daniel & Jane NICKLIN	bap
May 20	William, s of John & Ann SHELDON	bap
May 20	Ann, d of Thomas & Sarah TURNER	bap
May 20	George, s of John & Mary FIELDHOUSE	bap
May 26	John, s of Aamass & Ann BUTLER	bap
May 30	Benjamin, s of John & Mary HORTON	bur
May 30	Pheby, d of William & Elizabeth TATE	bap
May 30	John, s of Sarah MILLINGTON	bap
Jun 2	Ruth, d of Thomas & Sarah KIRKOM	bap
Jun 5	Mary, wife of John HARRISS	bur
Jun 9	Thomas, s of Joseph & Mary WILLEY	bap
Jun 9	Mary, d of John & Sophia LAW	bap
Jun 9	William, s of John & Sophia LAW	bur
Jun 12	Edwd, s of Daniel & Sarah SHELDON	bur
Jun 16	Elizabeth, wife of Jabez FISHER	bur
Jun 16	Jeremiah WHITEHOUSE	bur
Jun 16	William, s of Peter & Ann MILLS	bap
Jun 21	Sarah, d of Thomas & Elizabeth HODGSKINS	bur
Jun 23	John, s of James & Hannah FISHER	bap
Jun 23	James, s of Joseph & Rebekah RHOADS	bap
Jun 25	Jane, d of Richard & Elizabeth SAUNDERS	bur

1793

Jun 28	Amelia, d of Daniel & Hannah ROUND	bur
Jul 1	Shusannah, wife of William JONES	bur
Jul 5	William SROPSHIRE	bur
Jul 5	Ann, d of Eliz: BOTT	bap
Jul 7	Edward, s of Daniel & Grace ROUND	bap
Jul 7	Rachael, d of Michael & Elizabeth DUFFIELD	bap
Jul 7	Mary, d of Moses & Elizabeth HILL	bap
Jul 14	William, s of William & Margarett COMLEY	bap
Jul 14	Benjamin, s of John & Sarah SAUNDERS	bap
Jul 21	Benjamin, s of William & Elizabeth HORTON, Born June 29	bap
Jul 21	Ann, d of Daniel & Mary ROUND	bap
Jul 24	Ann, wife of Charles LAW	bur
Jul 25	Samuel DARBY	bur
Aug 4	Joseph, s of William & Pheby BISSELL	bap
Aug 4	Mary, d of Thomas & Mary KENDRICK	bap
Aug 18	John, s of John & Shusannah Margarette WHITEHOUSE	bap
Aug 18	Thomas, s of Thomas & Mary SMITH, Born June 20	bap
Aug 18	Elizabeth, d of Joseph & Mary FISHER	bap
Aug 25	Ann, d of Samuel & Jane STOKES	bap
Aug 27	Edward, s of Daniel & Grace ROUND	bur
Aug 28	John BEAL	bur
Sep 8	Ann KIRK	bur
Sep 15	Sarah, d of Richard & Sarah WHITEHOUSE	bap
Sep 17	Mary FLETCHER	bur
Sep 22	Joseph, s of James & Hannah FISHER	bap
Sep 22	Sarah, d of Joseph & Jane LAW	bap
Sep 26	William Horton, s of John & Mary HARRISS	bur
Sep 29	Amelia, d of William & Mary FISHER	bap
Sep 29	Sarah, d of Richard & Sarah STANTON	bap
Sep 29	Maria, d of Thomas & Mary MILLINGTON	bap
Sep 29	William, s of William & Eleanor BAKER	bap
Oct 6	William, s of Peter & Mary MILLS	bap
Oct 6	Mary, d of Cornelias & Esther BAKER	bap
Oct 13	Thomas, s of George & Nancy BRINLEY	bap
Oct 13	Mary, d of Joshua & Hannah PARTRIDGE	bap
Oct 13	Elizabeth, d of Joseph & Ann CARTWRIGHT	bap
Oct 20	Edward GRIFFIS	bur
Oct 20	Pheby ROLINSON	bur
Oct 20	William, s of Edward & Ann ROBERTS	bap
Oct 20	Joseph, s of Edward & Martha HUMPHREYS	bap
Oct 20	Elizabeth, d of Edward & Elizabeth MILLS	bap
Oct 20	Sarah, d of William & Pheby HODGSKINS	bap
Oct 27	Thomas, s of John & Pheby MILLS	bap
Oct 27	William, s of Joseph & Mary MILLS	bap
Oct 27	Ann FISHER, d of Joseph & Dianna FISHER	bap
Nov 3	William, s of William & Lydia EDWARDS	bap
Nov 3	Richard, s of Richard & Hannah WHITEHOUSE	bap
Nov 3	Richard, s of Thomas & Pheby NICHOLDS	bap
Nov 10	Joseph MILLS	bur

<u>1793</u>

Nov 10	Mary, d of Peter & Rachel ROWLEY	bap
Nov 10	Mary, d of William & Ann PARKES	bap
Nov 24	Shusannah, d of Thomas & Elizabeth JONES	bap
Nov 24	George, s of Gidion & Elizabeth GRISE	bap
Nov 24	Sarah, d of John & Hannah HODGSKINS	bap
Nov 24	Sarah, d of Joseph & Nancy ASTON	bap
Nov 24	Susannah, d of Mary SHELDON	bap
Dec 1	Hannah, wife of Francis WHITEHOUSE	bur
Dec 1	Daniel WHEALE	bur
Dec 1	Maria WHEALE	bur
Dec 1	Daniel, s of John & Hannah WHEAL	bap
Dec 1	Joseph, s of Samuel & Lydia FREASON	bap
Dec 1	Elizabeth, d of Thomas & Elizabeth HILL	bap
Dec 1	Elizabeth, d of Joseph & Lucy SMITH	bap
Dec 1	Hannah, d of Francis & Hannah WHITEHOUSE	bap
Dec 8	Thomas, s of Thomas & Rachael HOUGHTON	bap
Dec 8	Elizabeth, d of Joseph & Sarah HORTON	bap
Dec 8	James, s of Daniel & Sarah WARR	bap
Dec 15	Nancy, d of Samuel & Sarah FLETCHER	bap
Dec 15	Ann, d of Thomas & Martha DANKS	bap
Dec 22	Jacob, s of Abraham & Sarah TIMMINS	bap
Dec 22	Gidion GRISE	bur
Dec 22	Richard, s of Thomas & Eleanor GRIFFIS	bur
Dec 25	Rebekah, d of Thomas & Lydia TAYLOR	bap
Dec 25	David, s of Eutychus & Pheby FISHER	bap
Dec 27	Ann HIPKISS	bur
Dec 29	Joseph, s of Francis & Jane PERCALL	bap
Dec 29	William, s of Daniel & Jane RHODEN	bap
Dec 30	Benjamin, s of William & Elizabeth HORTON	bur
Dec 30	Pheby PERSHOUSE	bur

<u>1794</u>

Jan 5	William, s of Thomas & Ann COTTRELL, Born Nov 3, 1793	bap
Jan 5	Joseph, s of Joseph & Mary SMITH	bap
Jan 8	Hannah TAYLOR	bur
Jan 8	Sarah SMTH	bur
Jan 8	Eleanor, d of Joseph & Eleanor FISHER	bap
Jan 12	Zachariah, s of Joseph & Catharine MILLS	bap
Jan 12	Sarah, d of James & Hannah HEELEY	bap
Jan 12	Elizabeth, d of Richard & Betty SAUNDERS	bap
Jan 19	Thomas PITCHFORK	bur
Jan 19	Ambrose, s of William & Sophia BATE	bap
Jan 19	Daniel, s of William & Sarah NIGHTINGALE	bap
Jan 19	Elizabeth, d of John & Mary HORTON	bap
Jan 19	Hannah, d of John & Sarah ONIONS	bap
Jan 28	Ann, wife of John NIMMS	bur
Feb 9	Mary, wife of Thomas WHEAL	bur
Feb 9	Aylce, wife of Thomas CARTWRIGHT	bur
Feb 9	William, s of William & Mary HUGHES	bap

1794

Feb 9	John, s of John & Sarah WHITEHOUSE	bap
Feb 9	Enock, s of Mary SHELDON	bap
Feb 9	Mary, d of William & Pheby ALLDRETT	bap
Feb 9	Hannah, d of Richard & Isabell TAYLER	bap
Feb 12	Mary, d of Thomas & Elizabeth HAUGHTON	bap
Feb 12	Elizabeth, wife of Thomas HAUGHTON	bur
Feb 16	William, s of David & Ann WHITEHOUSE	bap
Feb 23	Mary, wife of John STOKES	bur
— Feb 23	John, s of John & Mary WRIGHT	bap
— Feb 23	David, s of John & Pheby HICKMANS	bap
Feb 23	Ann, d of James & Pheby BATE	bap
Feb 23	Stephen, s of John & Rachael HIPKISS	bap
— Feb 23	Thomas, s of John & Mary BENNETT	bap
— Mar 2	John, s of Thomas & Elizabeth HUGHES	bap
Mar 2	Mary, d of William & Sarah EDGE	bap
Mar 2	Ann, d of John & Mary SMITH, Born Jany 2, 1792	bap
→ Mar 5	Ann, d of William & Sarah TURNER	bap
Mar 5	Hannah, wife of William BISSELL	bur
Mar 5	Mary WHITEHOUSE	bur
Mar 7	Sarah, d of William & Mary PERSHOUSE	bap
Mar 7	John, s of Thomas & Elizabeth MORRISS	bap
Mar 9	Benjamin, s of William & Sarah HORTON	bap
Mar 9	Sarah, d of William & Mary LAW	bap
Mar 16	Thomas, s of Edward & Mary LLOYD	bap
Mar 16	Elizabeth, d of Peter & Hannah BAKER	bap
Mar 16	Elizabeth, d of Thomas & Catharine HAMPTON	bap
— Mar 20	Pheby, d of Bayley & Sarah HILL	bap
Mar 23	Elizabeth, d of Joseph & Mary GORTON	bap
Mar 27	Pheby, wife of Joseph FLETCHER	bur
⌐ Mar 27	Prudence, d of Thomas & Sarah PARKES	bap
Mar 30	William, s of Edward & Elizabeth WHITEHOUSE	bap
▾ Mar 30	Edward, s of Joseph & Elizabeth SHARROTT	bap
Mar 30	Hannah, d of Benjamin & Ann MILLS	bap
Mar 30	David, s of Samuel & Sarah SMITH	bap
Apr 2	Sarah, d of John & Mary JONES	bap
Apr 7	Elizabeth, d of William & Margarett CUNLEY	bur
Apr 16	Thomas, s of Daniel & Pheby MILLS	bap
Apr 16	John, s of Richard & Elizabeth SAUNDERS	bap
Apr 16	Thomas, s of Thomas & Mary WHEEL	bap
Apr 16	Benjamin, s of Abraham & Elizabeth SHELDON	bap
Apr 16	Esther, d of Joseph & Hannah SMITH	bap
— Apr 16	Mary, d of Richard & Sarah INGRAM	bap
⌐ Apr 16	Hannah, d of Henry & Ann TURNER	bap
Apr 16	Sarah, d of William & Mary SHORTHOUSE	bap
⤙ Apr 27	Nancy, d of Samuel & Sarah NOCK	bap
Apr 27	Mary, wife of Arther WHESSON	bur
Apr 27	Mary Maria, d of Abraham & Nancy GEORGE	bap
Apr 27	Mary, wife of Joseph MILLS	bur
May 4	Thomas, s of John & Mary ATTWOOD	bap

1794

May 4	Elizabeth, d of George & Lucy MARSHALL	bap
May 5	Daniel, s of Samuel & Sarah ROBERTS	bap
May 5	Elizabeth, d of William & Mary TURNER	bap
May 5	Pheby, wife of Joseph STANLY	bur
May 9	Aylce, d of Thomas & Sarah PARKES	bap
May 11	Abel, s of James & Ann RICHARDS	bap
May 11	William, s of Thomas & Mary RICHARDS	bap
May 18	John, s of Joseph & Ann SIVITER, Born Apl 25	bap
May 18	William, s of Thomas & Catharine BAYLEYS, Born Apl 6	bap
Jun 1	Thomas, s of Joseph & Hannah BOTT	bap
Jun 1	Ann, d of Edward & Tamar WHITEHOUSE	bap
Jun 1	John, s of John & Sarah WHITEHOUSE	bap
Jun 1	James, s of John & Sarah FISHER	bap
Jun 1	Mary, d of Ithiel & Mary SALLMON	bap
Jun 5	Joseph SHELDON	bur
Jun 8	Edward, s of Edward & Mary DARBY	bap
Jun 8	Edward, s of Edward & Jane WITMORE	bap
Jun 8	Abraham, s of John & Mary WHITEHOUSE	bap
Jun 8	Hannah, d of James & Triphenia GUEST	bap
Jun 8	Mary, d of Thomas & Jane PARKES	bap
Jun 8	Nancy, d of John Pheby ASTON	bap
Jun 8	Sophia, d of Daniel & Jane NICKLIN	bap
Jun 13	Mary, d of Joseph & Mary WHITEHOUSE	bap
Jun 15	Mary, d of Edward & Hannah SMITH	bap
Jun 22	Joseph, s of William & Martha INGRAM	bap
Jun 22	John, s of John & Rachel COTTRELL	bap
Jun 29	Henry, s of Peter & Elizabeth SAUNDERS, Born April 24	bap
Jun 29	Thomas, s of William & Elizabeth BEDDOW	bap
Jul 6	Sarah, d of Abell & Martha HILL	bap
Jun 10	Elizabeth, wife of William WORSEY	bur
Jul 13	Benjamin, s of James & Ann HORTON	bap
Jul 20	Ann, d of John & Elizabeth SMITH	bap
Jul 20	Peter, s of Thomas & Hannah RUDGES	bap
Jul 20	Maria, d of George & Mary GREGORY	bap
Jul 20	Ann, d of Isaac & Martha TIMMINS	bap
Jul 20	Mary, d of John & Mary HODGSKINS	bap
Jul 24	Ann GREEN	bur
Jul 27	Benjamin WILLIAMS	bur
Jul 27	Hannah, d of James & Sarah FOSTER	bur
Jul 27	Timothy SMITH	bur
Jul 27	Sarah, d of Paul & Lydia GRIFFIS	bap
Jul 29	Mary BLOXWICH	bur
Aug 3	Thomas, s of William & Elizabeth ALLEN	bap
Aug 3	Henry, s of Joseph & Elizabeth HOLLAND	bap
Aug 3	Edward, s of John & Hannah HODGSKINS	bap
Aug 3	Andrew, s of John & Lydia FURNEYFOOT	bap
Aug 7	William MILLS	bur
Aug 7	Benjamin NOCK	bur
Aug 10	William, s of Joseph & Elizabeth WHITEHOUSE	bur

1794

Aug 10	Edward, s of Daniel & Mary FISHER	bap
Aug 17	Joseph, s of James & Sarah GUTTRIDGE	bur
Aug 17	John, s of Benjamin & Sarah CRESSALL	bap
Aug 17	Henry, s of John & Mary SAUNDERS	bap
Aug 24	William, s of John & Jane TAYLOR	bap
Aug 24	Mary, d of Frederick & Nancy MORRISS	bap
Aug 28	Mary, wife of Stephen HIPKISS	bur
Aug 28	Benjamin, s of John & Elenor NICHOLDS	bap
Aug 31	James, s of William & Ann WARD, Born Dec 31, 1793	bap
Aug 31	Phebe, d of Isaac & Elizabeth WHITEHOUSE, Born Dec 1, 1793	bap
Aug 31	William OSBOURN	bur
Sep 7	Edward, s of John & Elizabeth BROWN	bap
Sep 7	Maria, d of William & Esther TURNER	bap
Sep 14	Edward ROUND	bur
Sep 14	James, s of Luke & Mary PHILIPS	bap
Sep 21	Mary, d of Joshua & Jane WHITEHOUSE	bap
Sep 21	John SMALLMAN	bur
Sep 24	Samuel WHITEHOUSE	bur
Sep 28	John, s of John & Mary NOCK	bap
Sep 28	John, s of John & Mary NICKOLDS	bap
Sep 28	Martha, d of Thomas & Sarah SUTTON	bap
Oct 5	Nancy, d of John & Sarah ROWLEY	bap
Oct 5	Hannah, d of John & Mary HODGSKINS	bap
Oct 5	Hannah, d of Thomas & Eleanor WEBB	bap
Oct 12	Joseph, s of Jaby & Elizabeth FISHER	bur
Oct 12	Mary, d of Edward & Pheby WHITEHOUSE	bur
Oct 12	Mary DUNN	bur
Oct 12	Enass, s of Enass & Hannah WHITEHOUSE	bap
Oct 12	John, s of James & Martha NOCK	bap
Oct 12	Martha, d of James & Martha GREEN	bap
Oct 12	Hannah, d of Abraham & Sarah WHITEHOUSE	bap
Oct 19	Timothy KIDSON	bur
Oct 26	Elizabeth, d of Thomas & Elizabeth DANKS	bap
Oct 26	Edward FISHER	bur
Oct 30	George, s of Daniel & Hannah ROUND	bur
Oct 30	Sarah SHELDON	bur
Nov 2	Joseph, s of Stephen & Mary FISHER	bap
Nov 2	Mary, d of William & Eleanor BAKER	bap
Nov 2	Mary, d of Richard & Mary HODGSKISS	bap
Nov 9	Joseph, s of William & Ann WHITEHOUSE	bap
Nov 9	Mary, d of Joseph & Mary TURNER	bap
Nov 9	George, s of Joseph & Jane CALLOWAY	bap
Nov 20	Constant, d of John & Mary SHELDON	bap
Nov 20	Samuel, s of John & Catharine INGRAM	bap
Nov 20	Thomas RICHARDS	bur
Nov 20	Richard INGRAM, Jun[r]	bur
Nov 20	Joseph, s of Joseph & Sarah PENN	bap
Nov 23	Joseph, s of John & Elizabeth SAUNDERS	bap
Nov 23	Nancy, d of Daniel & Sarah MINCHER	bap

1794

Nov 27	Sarah DUDLEY	bur
Nov 27	John, s of Abraham & Sarah GEORGE	bur
Nov 30	Elizabeth, d of Joseph & Mary GORTON	bur
Nov 30	Nancy, d of William & Elizabeth HORTON	bap
Dec 2	Richard ALLIN	bur
Dec 7	Richard NICHOLIS	bur
Dec 7	Ann, wife of John JUKES	bur
Dec 16	Mary, d of Ithiael & Mary SALLMAN	bur
Dec 16	Ann BATE	bur
Dec 21	Joseph, s of Joseph & Rachael DUFFIELD, Born Decr 1	bap
Dec 25	Joseph SMITH	bur
Dec 25	Richard, s of John & Ann SHELDON	bap
Dec 25	Elizabeth, d of John & Ann SHELDON	bur
Dec 25	Jonas PRICE	bur
Dec 28	Lydia, d of Edward & Mary FISHER	bap
Dec 28	William, s of William & Phebe HICKMANS	bap
Dec 28	Thomas, s of Thomas & Elizabeth TILLEY	bap
Dec 28	Samuel, s of John & Mary FIELDHOUSE	bap
Dec 28	Zachariah, s of Joseph & Mary SMITH	bur
Dec 28	Elizabeth, d of Joseph & Lucy SMITH	bap

1795

Jan 4	Prudence PARKES	bur
Jan 4	John, s of Joseph & Nancy SIVITER	bur
Jan 4	Sarah LLOYD	bur
Jan 4	Sarah, d of John & Susannah BLACKHAM	bap
Jan 4	Sarah, wife of Daniel CALLOWAY	bur
Jan 11	Ann, d of Benjamin & Elizabeth GIBBONS	bap
Jan 11	Thomas BOLT	bur
Jan 13	Ann BRINLEY	bur
Jan 13	William, s of Abraham & Ann SHELDON	bur
Jan 25	Mary, d of James & Sarah GUTTRIDGE	bap
Jan 25	William NICKLIN	bur
Jan 25	Mary, d of Thomas & Jane PASKIN	bur
Jan 25	James, s of Joseph & Phebe GUTTRIDGE	bur
Feb 1	William, s of Daniel & Mary JEVON	bap
Feb 1	Elizabeth, d of Jonas & Ann PRICE	bap
Feb 2	Sarah GUTTRIDGE	bur
Feb 5	Abraham FISHER	bur
Feb 5	Hannah CALLOWAY	bur
Feb 5	Joseph, s of Robert & Ann BETTY	bap
Feb 8	Sarah CALLOWAY	bur
Feb 8	John, s of Edward & Elizabeth HARRIS	bap
Feb 15	Peter MILLS	bur
Feb 15	[Christian name erased] DARBY	bur
Feb 15	Hannah, d of James & Hannah HEELEY	bur
Feb 15	Edward, s of James & Ann FELLOWS	bap
Feb 15	Elizabeth, d of Samuel & Elizabeth HICKMANS	bap
Feb 19	Edward, s of Samuel & Mary NOCK, Born Dec 26 1792	bap

1795

Feb 19	John FISHER	bur
Feb 22	Sarah, d of William & Mary PERSHOUSE	bur
Feb 22	Nancy, d of John & Ann GREENEWAY, Born Jan 21[?]	bap
Feb 22	Sarah, d of George & Ann WHITEHOUSE	bap
Feb 25	Sarah WORTON	bur
Feb 25	William DREW	bur
Mar 1	Richard, s of John & Ann KENDALL	bap
Mar 1	Joseph, s of Samuel & Lydia FREASON	bur
Mar 5	Richard FOARD	bur
Mar 5	Hannah WHITEHOUSE	bur
Mar 5	Thomas, s of William & Hannah WHITEHOUSE	bap
Mar 5	Thomas, s of William & Elizabeth HOLLAND	bap
Mar 8	Joseph, s of John & Mary STOKES	bur
Mar 8	Jane, wife of Thomas PERRY	bur
Mar 8	Mary, d of William & Rebekah JEVON	bap
Mar 8	Samuel, s of Daniel & Grace ROUND, Born Nov 8, 1794	bap
Mar 8	John ASTON	bur
Mar 22	William HUGHES	bur
Mar 25	Joseph, s of Thomas & Isabella BRADNEY	bap
Mar 25	Abel, s of Joseph & Hannah GRISE	bap
Mar 25	Henry Whitehouse DARBY	bur
Mar 29	Hannah, d of Isaac & Mary DARBY	bur
Mar 29	Joshua, s of John & Sarah WESTWOOD	bap
Apr 5	Hannah, d of Joseph & Sarah HILL	bap
Apr 5	Thomas, s of Thomas & Phebe WHITEHOUSE, Born Jan 20/94	bap
Apr 5	Joseph, s of Benjamin & Nancy HILL, Born Jan 12, 94	bap
Apr 5	Mary, d of Thomas & Charlotte COTTOM	bap
Apr 5	Nancy, d of Richard & Mary JUKES	bap
Apr 5	Sarah, d of Edward & Margaret FISHER	bap
Apr 12	John WHITEHOUSE	bur
Apr 12	Ann JUKES	bur
Apr 12	Nancy Sitch, d of Edward & Lilia MILLINGTON	bap
Apr 12	Edward, s of Richard & Hannah WHITEHOUSE	bap
Apr 19	Edward, s of John & Elizabeth SHELDON	bap
Apr 19	Hannah, d of James & Sarah RICHARDS	bap
Apr 26	John, s of Thomas & Elizabeth SAMBRIDGE, Born Jan 29, 1792	bap
Apr 26	William, s of Thomas & Elizabeth SAMBRIDGE	bap
May 3	Sarah, d of Isaac & Sarah ASTON	bap
May 3	Sarah, d of John & Mary HORTON	bap
May 3	John, s of Robert & Phebe FULLWOOD	bap
May 6	William WHITEHOUSE	bur
May 6	Sarah SAUNDERS	bur
May 8	Ann ATTWOOD	bur
May 8	Mary, d of Samuel & Sarah ADCOCK	bur
May 10	William, s of Edward & Elizabeth WALL	bap
May 10	William, s of William & Elizabeth GEORGE	bap
May 10	Thomas, s of Thomas & Elizabeth MILLARD, Born Dec 4 1794	bap
May 14	Sarah OZBOURN	bur
May 14	Samuel, s of Thomas & Sarah TUDOR	bap

<u>1795</u>

May 14	Selvia, d of Samuel & Ann LEES	bap
May 16	Thomas BATE	bur
May 16	James ALLDIN	bur
May 24	Edward, s of Edward & Sarah JONES	bap
May 24	Zachariah Parkes, s of Joseph & Mary SMITH	bap
May 24	Sarah, d of William & Mary LOWE	bap
May 24	Nancy, d of William & Hannah MILLS	bap
May 24	Hannah, d of Peter & Ann MILLS	bap
May 24	Charles, s of Joseph & Susannah DAVIS	bap
May 31	Richard INGRAM	bur
Jun 7	John, s of Isaac & Ann LAW	bap
Jun 7	William DARBY	bur
Jun 8	Sarah INGRAM	bur
Jun 8	Moses, s of Moses & Hannah TIMMINS	bap
Jun 14	Martha, d of Thomas & Sarah NOONS	bap
Jun 21	Stephen, s of Abel & Hannah CADDICK	bap
Jun 21	Benjamin, s of John & Jane TINSLEY	bap
Jun 28	Thomas ELWELL	bur
Jun 28	Sarah TIMMINS	bur
Jun 28	Thomas, s of Joseph & Rachael HORTON	bap
Jun 28	Hannah, d of Joseph & Hannah SMITH, Born May 29	bap
Jun 30	William GRIFFIS	bur
Jun 30	George GORTON	Bur
Jul 2	Sarah, d of John & Mary HORTON	bur
	A Transcript of the Register Book of the Parish of Tipton alias Tibbington was Exhibited into the Deans Visitation held in the Court of Lichfield being on Monday July 20, 1795	
Jul 23	Joseph GUTTRIDGE	bur
Aug 3	Robert MARTIN married Elizabeth WILLSON by Banns	mar
Aug 4	Sarah FISHER	bur
Aug 9	Stephen, s of David & Mary HIPKISS	bur
Aug 9	Elizabeth, d of John & Ann MATTHEWS	bap
Aug 16	Sarah, d of John & Mary BISSELL	bap
Aug 16	David, s of Joseph & Phebe CROFTS	bap
Aug 16	William, s of James & Hannah FISHER	bap
Aug 23	Maria, d of Robert & Sarah BROWN	bap
Aug 23	Rachael, d of Joseph & Rachel HIPKISS	bap
Aug 23	Mary, d of Joseph & Mary HIPKISS	bap
Aug 23	Nancy Esther, d of John & Jane WOOD	bap
Aug 24	Elizabeth, d of Joseph & Mary PITCHFORK	bur
Aug 25	Thomas RAVENSCROFT	bur
Aug 28	Sarah, wife of Thomas LOWE	bur
Aug 30	Samuel, s of James & Mary COOKSEY, Born July 2	bap
Aug 30	Thomas, s of Joseph & Hannah BOTT	bap
Aug 30	Sophia, d of John & Sophia LAW, Born June 15	bap
Aug 30	Jane, d of Eutychus & Phebe FISHER, Born Aug 7th, 1795	bap
Sep 6	John WILKINSON	bur
Sep 13	Amelia, d of John & Sarah FISHER	bap
Sep 13	William, s of Charles & Sarah WOODCROFT	bap

1795

Sep 22	William SARGENT & Ann SPITTLE by Banns	mar
Sep 27	Joseph, s of Joseph & Lucy GEORGE	bap
Sep 27	Joseph, s of John & Mary HODGSKINS	bap
Sep 27	Elizabeth, d of Thomas & Sarah EVINS	bap
Oct 4	James JONES & Elizabeth BRINDLEY by Banns	mar
Oct 4	James, s of John & Sarah WHITEHOUSE	bap
Oct 4	Eleanor, d of William & Esther TURNER	bap
Oct 4	Rachael, d of James & Triephenia GUEST	bap
Oct 4	Sarah, d of Joseph & Elizabeth HODGSKINS	bap
Oct 11	Samuel, s of Richard & Sarah BECK	bap
Oct 18	John, s of William & Sarah EDGE	bap
Oct 18	Elizabeth, d of Joseph & Mary MILLS	bap
Oct 25	Maria, d of Benjamin & Sarah HORTON, Born Oct 19 1795	bap
Oct 25	Elizabeth, d of Joseph & Ann LESTER	bap
Nov 1	John TOY & Emma GUEST by Banns	mar
Nov 8	Matthew, s of Thomas & Catharine HAMPTON	bap
Nov 8	Richard, s of Joseph & Mary GORTON	bap
Nov 8	James, s of John & Ann WHEAL	bap
Nov 8	Ann, d of John & Elizabeth HORTON	bap
Nov 8	Charles, s of George & Ann MARSHALL	bap
Nov 8	Mary, d of James & Mary DARBY, Born Aug 30 1795	bap
Nov 8	Isabella, wife of William GEORGE	bur
Nov 8	Mary, wife of Thomas KENDRICK	bur
Nov 12	James ATTWOOD	bur
Nov 12	James, s of Robert & Hannah SMITH	bur
Nov 15	William GEORGE	bur
Nov 15	Samuel WILKS & Mary MASON by Banns	mar
Nov 15	Sarah, d of Thomas & Mary SMITH, Born Oct 19, 1795	bap
Nov 22	Sarah, d of George & Ann BRINLEY	bap
Nov 22	John SAUNDERS	bur
Nov 22	Elizabeth, d of Joseph & Lucy SMITH, Born Oct 27, 1795	bap
Nov 29	Francis WRIGHT & Margarette DIKE by Banns	mar
Nov 29	Timothy, s of Joseph & Lettice LOWE	bap
Nov 29	Joseph & Mary, twins of Thomas & Sarah WHITEHOUSE	bap
Nov 29	Joshua, s of John & Mary WHITEHOUSE	bap
Nov 29	Mary, d of Isaac & Mary BATE	bap
Nov 29	William, s of John & Phebe MILLS	bap
Nov 29	Abraham MILLS	bur
Dec 6	John, s of Benjamin & Sarah WHESSON	bap
Dec 13	Mary, d of Richard & Sarah STANTON	bap
Dec 13	Kezia, d of Joseph & Mary FISHER	bap
Dec 13	Joseph, s of Joseph & Elizabeth HORTON	bap
Dec 25	James, s of Thomas & Hannah KENNEDY	bap
Dec 25	Maria, d of Thomas & Nancy FELLOWS	bap
Dec 25	Amelia, d of John & Sarah TIMMINS	bap
Dec 25	Richard, s of Thomas & Sarah MORGAN	bap
Dec 25	Isaac, s of Richard & Violette PARKES	bap
Dec 25	John, s of Thomas & Elizabeth HILL	bap
Dec 25	Sarah, d of Thomas & Elizabeth TAYLOR	bap

Dec 25	Elizabeth, d of Eleanor CLEATON	bap
Dec 25	Hannah, d of Thomas & Esther ALSOP	bap
Dec 25	Joseph, s of Hannah ALSOP	bap
Dec 27	Daniel, s of Peter & Rachael ROWLEY	bap
Dec 27	John, s of William & Hannah FOSTER	bap
Dec 27	Sarah, d of Ithiel & Mary SALLMON	bap
Dec 27	Leah, d of William & Alice BUTTLER	bap

1796

Jan 3	Edward CHILDS & Alice ONIONS by Banns	mar
Jan 8	Thomas HICKMANS	bur
Jan 10	Isaac, s of Abel & Elizabeth FLETCHER	bap
Jan 10	George, s of George & Hannah WAIN	bap
Jan 10	Rosannah, d of James & Lettice RUBOOTOM	bap
Jan 10	Mary, d of Thomas & Sarah KIRKHAM	bap
Jan 10	Leah, d of Samuel & Sarah SMITH	bap
Jan 10	Elizabeth, d of Edward & Hannah SMITH, Born Nov 19 1795	bap
Jan 10	Elizabeth, d of Francis & Hannah ASTON	bap
Jan 10	Richard GORTON	bur
Jan 10	Nancy MINCHER	bur
Jan 14	Nancy WHESSON	bur
Jan 14	Ann, d of Joseph & Elizabeth PITT	bap
Jan 17	John WHESSON	bur
Jan 24	James, s of James & Sarah ASTON	bap
Jan 30	Elizabeth, d of Abraham & Elizabeth SHELDON	bap
Jan 30	Eleanor, d of Joseph & Sarah SHINGLETON	bap
Jan 30	William, s of Joseph & Sarah SHINGLETON, Bap at 2 years	bap
Jan 30	William PARKES	bur
Jan 30	Charles HICKMANS	bur
Feb 7	John NORRIS	bur
Feb 7	John, s of Joseph & Phebe BATE	bap
Feb 7	William, s of William & Phebe BISSELL	bap
Feb 7	Sarah, d of Joseph & Catharine COTTRELL	bap
Feb 7	Catharine, d of Cornelias & Esther BAKER	bap
Feb 7	Kitty, d of Joseph & Kitty MILLS, Born Jan 6	bap
Feb 12	Thomas HARRISON	bur
Feb 14	Ann, d of Joshua & Hannah PARTRIDGE	bap
Feb 16	Phebe WHESSON	bur
Feb 16	Isiah, s of William & Phebe ALLDRITT	bap
Feb 21	Hannah PITT	bur
Feb 21	Hannah WHITEHOUSE	bur
Feb 21	Thomas WHITEHOUSE	bur
Feb 21	Mary, wife of John HORTON	bur
Feb 21	Thomas, s of Emanuel & Ann DARBY, Born Jan 22 1792	bap
Feb 21	Hannah, d of Emanuel & Ann DARBY	bap
Feb 21	Edward, s of Joseph & Mary WOOD, Born Dec 20 1795	bap
Feb 21	Mary, d of William & Sarah WHITEHOUSE	bap
Feb 21	William, s of Thomas & Ann WOODALL, Born 1st	bap
Feb 21	Phebe, d of William & Mary SMITH, Born July 22, 95	bap

Feb 21	Shukey, d of John & Mary CASHMORE	bap
Feb 21	Nancy, d of William & Mary HUGHES	bap
Feb 24	Sarah, d of Jonah & Hannah CLARK, Born Jan 7, 1795	bap
Feb 28	Thomas ALLIN	bur
Mar 6	Thomas, s of Benjamin & Sarah DUNN, Born Dec 21, 1795	bap
Mar 6	Mary, d of John & Mary JONES	bap
Mar 6	Mary, d of Thomas & Elizabeth COLLINS	bap
Mar 6	Joseph, s of John & Susannah GREGORY, Born Apl 1, 1795	bap
Mar 6	Nancy, d of Thomas & Jane STILLARD	bap
Mar 6	John, s of William & Hannah SMITH, Born Apl 1 1793	bap
Mar 6	Mary LEAGG	bur
Mar 6	Ann WALTERHOUSE	bur
Mar 9	Samuel HICKMANS	bur
Mar 9	Isaac, s of Joseph & Ann ASTON, Born Feb 27, 1795	bap
Mar 9	Samuel, s of Benjamin & Joice FISHER	bap
Mar 20	Thomas, s of Thomas & Ann COTTRILL	bap
Mar 20	Elizabeth, d of John & Sarah BENNETT	bap
Mar 20	Phebe, d of Thomas & Phebe NICKOLDS	bap
Mar 27	Simeon, s of Daniel & Grace ROUND, Born Jan 13 1796	bap
Mar 27	Thomas, s of William & Mary SHORTHOUSE	bap
Mar 27	Sarah, d of Edward & Jane WITTMORE	bap
Mar 27	Elizabeth Whitehouse, d of Edward & Martha HUMPHREYS	bap
Mar 27	Elizabeth, d of Joseph & Elizabeth GRANGER	bap
Mar 27	Benjamin WOOLLEY & Ann EVINS by Banns	mar
Apr 3	Eleanor WILKINSON	bur
Apr 3	Barnet, s of Thomas & Rachael HOMER	bap
Apr 3	Phebe, d of William & Eleanor BAKER	bap
Apr 5	Jesse WORTON	bur
Apr 5	Benjamin, a bas begott Child of Isabell SMITH, Born Dec 19 1794	bap
Apr 5	Samuel, s of Thomas & Elizabeth MORRISS	bap
Apr 5	Elizabeth, d of Joseph & Marabele GUTTRIDGE	bap
Apr 11	Lydia EDWARDS	bur
Apr 17	Joseph HORTON	bur
Apr 17	Ann MILLS	bur
Apr 17	John, s of Joseph & Mary WARD	bap
Apr 21	Joshua WHITEHOUSE	bur
Apr 21	Phebe, d of Elizabeth WHITEHOUSE	bap
Apr 24	Samuel, s of John & Mary ATTWOOD	bap
Apr 24	Amelia, d of Richard & Elizabeth TAYLOR	bap
Apr 24	Daniel, s of Stephen & Phebe FOSTER	bap
Apr 29	Hannah NICKOLIS	bur
May 1	Sarah, d of Thomas & Elizabeth DANKS	bap
May 1	Eleanor, d of John & Rachael COTTRILL	bap
May 1	Maria TAYLOR	bur
May 5	William ROUND	bur
May 5	Ann PITCHFORK	bur
May 5	Nathaniel HEELEY	bur
May 5	Thomas, a bas begott Child of Elizabeth JUKES	bap

<u>1796</u>

May 5	Comfort, d of Joseph & Eleanor FISHER	bap
May 8	Sarah, d of Joseph & Mary GRIFFIS	bap
May 8	Sarah GRIFFIS	bur
May 8	Sarah, d of William & Sarah GREENEWAY	bap
May 8	John BAGNOLL & Phebe GRIFFIS by Banns	mar

[Note re the above entry, "John" is written in a darker ink over the word "Joseph"]

May 13	Joseph BOTT	bur
May 15	Thomas, s of Joseph & Ann CARTWRIGHT	bap
May 15	Joseph, s of William & Sarah TUCKLEY, Born Jan 11	bap
May 15	Daniel, s of Thomas & Elizabeth HUGHES	bap
May 15	Elizabeth, d of Thomas & Eleanor WEBB, Born July 28 1792	bap
Mar 15	William, s of John & Sarah MORRISS	bap
Mar 15	Benjamin, s of Daniel & Jane RHODEN	bap
May 15	Hannah, d of James & Martha GREEN	bap
Mar 15	Hannah, d of Francis & Jane PIERCE	bap
May 15	Thomas BUFF	bur
May 16	Henry, s of Joseph & Elizabeth HOLLAND	bap
May 19	Isaac FLETCHER	bur
May 19	Thomas SHARROTT	bur
May 19	Hannah RICHARDS	bur
May 22	Mary, d of John & Sarah EVINS	bur
May 22	Ann FULLWOOD	bur
May 29	John, s of John & Phebe MILLS	bap
May 29	Mary, d of Edward & Sarah WHITEHOUSE	bap
May 29	Mary Ann, d of Joseph & Ann FIELDHOUSE	bap
May 29	Benjamin, s of Simeon & Elizabeth FISHER	bap
May 29	Joseph SAUNDERS	bur
Jun 5	John, s of William & Elizabeth TATE, Born Apl 18 1795	bap
Jun 5	Sarah, d of John & Ann WILLDEY	bap
Jun 5	Joseph, s of Jeremiah & Mary WILLETTS	bap
Jun 9	Thomas MILLARD	bur
Jun 9	Hannah PINCHER	bur
Jun 10	Thomas DARBY	bur
Jun 12	John FOSTER	bur
Jun 12	Ann ROUND	bur
Jun 12	James, s of James & Rachael TATE, Born March 7	bap
Jun 12	Abraham, s of John & Sarah WHITEHOUSE	bap
Jun 13	William HICKMANS	bur
Jun 25	Phebe, d of John & Lydia FURNEYFOOT	bap
Jun 25	Thomas FULLWOOD	bur
Jun 25	Sarah WILLMORE	bur
Jun 28	John HALL	bur
Jun 30	Sarah TAYLOR	bur
Jun 30	Benjamin NICKOLDS	bur
Jul 3	Hannah CHARLOTON	bur
Jul 6	James KERRY	bur
Jul 6	Maria JAMES	bur
Jul 6	James, a bas begott Child of Sarah WEATLY	bap

1796

Jul 10	Mary WHITEHOUSE	bur
Jul 10	Thomas RHODEN	bur
Jul 17	Mary BROOKS	bur
Jul 17	Sarah SMITH	bur
Jun 17	Joseph PARKES	bur
Jul 17	Sarah LOWE	bur
Jul 17	John SHARROTT	bur
Jul 17	Elizabeth, d of Edward & Mary LLOID	bap
Jul 17	George, s of Thomas & Mary BATE	bap
Jul 20	Eve THOMAS	bur
Jul 20	William SAUNDERS	bur
Jul 24	Isiah, s of Isaac & Elizabeth WHITEHOUSE	bap
Jul 24	Joseph, s of John & Sarah MORFIELD	bap
Jul 24	James HEELEY	bur
Jul 24	Hannah JUKES	bur
Jul 28	Thomas WHITEHOUSE	bur
Jul 31	Lydia, d of John & Catharine INGRAM	bap
Jul 31	Joseph, s of Samuel & Jane STOKES	bap
Jul 31	Ann SMITH	bur
Aug 2	Catharine WINNINGTON	bur
Aug 4	Daniel MILLS	bur
Aug 10	Richard FULLWOOD	bur
Aug 10	Mary FISHER	bur
Aug 10	Joseph LAW	bur
Aug 14	Thomas BATE	bur
Aug 15	Thomas WILLIAMS & Hannah EDWARDS by Banns	mar
Aug 15	Charles HUMPHREYS	bur
Aug 21	Edward SLOIN & Ann MORRIS by Banns	mar
Aug 21	Mary, d of Peter & Ann MILLS	bap
Aug 27	John LAW	bur
Sep 4	William, s of John & Mary BARNES	bap
Sep 4	George, s of George & Ann GILL	bap
Sep 14	Ann, d of William & Sophia BATE	bap
Sep 14	Ankerwright FISHER	bur
Sep 18	Betty, d of Richard & Elizabeth SAUNDERS	bap
Sep 18	William, s of Ambrose & Hannah HUGHES	bap
Sep 18	Daniel, s of Benjamin & Sarah CRESSWELL	bap
Sep 25	Joseph, s of Edward & Jane JONES	bap
Oct 2	Sarah WHITEHOUSE	bur
Oct 2	Isaac, s of William & Sarah SMITH	bap
Oct 2	Nancy, d of William & Sarah RENOLDS	bap
Oct 2	Edward TIMMINS	bur
Oct 6	Eleanor MILLS	bur
Oct 9	James, s of James & Nancy HORTON	bap
Oct 9	John, s of Joseph & Rachael HIPKISS	bap
Oct 13	Joseph OWEN	bur
Oct 23	Isaac LAW	bur
Oct 23	William, s of Thomas & Hannah PORTER	bap
Oct 23	Maria, d of Stephen & Mary FISHER	bap

Oct 30	Henry, s of Edward & Elizabeth HARRISS	bap
Oct 30	Mary, d of Edward & Alice CHILDS	bap
Nov 1	Sarah MILLS	bur
Nov 1	George, s of George & Elizabeth BALL	bap
Nov 3	Elizabeth LESTER	bur
Nov 3	James, s of Robert & Mary EMERY	bap
Nov 9	William, s of John & Mary EVINS, Born May 16	bap
Nov 9	William GEORGE	bur
Nov 13	Thomas, s of John & Mary HODGSKINS	bap
Nov 13	John, s of Thomas & Catharine BAYLEYS	bap
Nov 20	Silvia, d of Joseph & Sophia BROOKS	bap
Nov 27	James, s of John & Eleanor NICKOLDS	bap
Nov 27	Maria HONE	bur
Dec 4	Mary WHITEHOUSE	bur
Dec 4	Mary, d of Thomas & Sarah BOTT	bap
Nov 4	William, s of David & Mary ROUND	bap
Dec 11	Mary HIPKISS	bur
Dec 11	Mary COTTOM	bur
Dec 14	John COTTOM	bur
Dec 14	Hannah, d of William & Sarah WILDAY	bap
Dec 14	John Millington, s of James & Phebe BATE	bap
Dec 18	John, s of George & Mary GREGORY	bap
Dec 18	Hannah, d of John & Ann PENN	bap
Dec 18	Richard FLETCHER	bur
Dec 18	Ann WHITEHOUSE	bur
Dec 18	Thomas TAYLOR	bur
Dec 18	Phebe BROOKHOUSE	bur
Dec 29	Sarah WHESSON	bur
Dec 29	Mary WHITEHOUSE	bur

Jan 1	John, s of Joseph & Mirandia STONE	bap
Jan 1	Phebe, d of Thomas & Esther TURNER	bap
Jan 1	Eleanor CLEATON	bur
Jan 4	Mary, d of John & Catharine [crossed out and "Ann" inserted above] SHELDON	bur
Jan 4	Hannah, d of Joseph & Hannah BOTT	bap
Jan 8	Sarah SMITH	bur
Jan 8	Ann, d of Thomas & Jane BOAD, Born May 20 1796	bap
Jan 12	John MILLS	bur
Jan 12	Mary, d of William & Hannah LAW	bur
Jan 15	Nancy HUGHES	bur
Jan 15	Thomas, s of Thomas & Eleanor WEBB, Born Jan 12	bap
Jan 22	Samuel, s of Abraham & Phebe WHITEHOUSE, Born Sep 4/96	bap
Jan 22	Joseph, s of Edward & Hannah SMITH, Born Dec 11 1796	bap
Jan 22	Richard, s of William & Sarah NIGHTINGALE	bap
Jan 22	Mary, d of Abraham & Lydia FISHER, Born Dec 25 1796	bap
Jan 26	Catharine, d of Cornelias & Esther BAKER	bur
Jan 26	Amilia, d of John & Sarah TIMMINS	bur

1797

Jan 26	Mary, d of Joseph & Rachael DUFFIELD	bap
Jan 26	Ann, d of John & Elizabeth SMITH	bap
Jan 26	Joseph, s of Joseph & Ann ASTON	bap
Jan 29	Rosannah, d of Benjamin & Mary HARTLAND	bap
Jan 29	Ann BOAD	bur
Feb 3	Rachael, d of James & Trinophenea GUEST	bur
Feb 5	Rachael, d of John & Elizabeth SAUNDERS	bap
Feb 5	Richard, s of William & Rebekah MORGAN	bap
Feb 9	Henry, s of Daniel & Mary WHITEHOUSE	bap
Feb 9	Sarah NOCK	bur
Feb 9	James SMITH	bur
Feb 12	John, s of John & Sarah FISHER	bap
Feb 15	Mary, d of Benjamin & Mary FEREDAY	bap
Feb 15	John, s of Edward & Elizabeth HARRISS	bur
Feb 19	James FISHER	bur
Feb 19	Abraham, s of Joseph & Mary JUKES	bap
Feb 19	Edward, s of John & Sarah HOMES	bap
Feb 19	Elizabeth, d of John & Sarah ROWLEY	bap
Feb 26	John FISHER	bur
Feb 26	John WARR	bur
Feb 26	John, s of John & Mary BISSELL	bap
Feb 28	Samuel WHITEHOUSE	bur
Mar 5	Richard, s of Richard & Sarah WHITEHOUSE	bur
Mar 5	Samuel, s of David & Ann HIPKISS	bap
Mar 8	Benjamin LITTLE	bur
Mar 8	Mary, d of James & Martha NOCK	bap
Mar 8	Shusannah, d of Thomas & Sarah PARKES	bap
Mar 13	Silvia, d of Peter & Elizabeth SAUNDERS, Born 26 Mar 96	bap
Mar 13	Joseph TURNER	bur
Mar 19	Joseph, s of James & Trioniphenia GUEST	bap
Mar 19	Ann, d of John & Mary FIELDHOUSE	bap
Mar 26	Amass, s of John & Mary WHITEHOUSE	bap
Mar 26	Thomas, s of Joseph & Elizabeth SHARRATT	bap
Apr 2	Samuel, s of George & Hannah CALLOWAY	bap
Apr 3	Stephen WHITEHOUSE	bur
Apr 7	John WHESSON	bur
Apr 7	Edward, s of Abraham & Nancy GEORGE, Born Nov[r] 13, 1796	bap
Apr 7	Joseph, s of David & Sarah MINCHER, Born Nov 16 1796	bap
Apr 9	John, s of Thomas & Elizabeth TILLEY	bap
Apr 13	Elizabeth GRICE	bur
Apr 13	Elizabeth, s of [crossed out], Ezekiel, s of Thomas & Sarah PARKES, Born Jan 8	bap
Apr 16	William, s of William & Mary PERSHOUSE, Born Feb 15	bap
Apr 16	James, s of James & Deborah NOCK, Born Feb[y] 22	bap
Apr 16	Amelia, d of Thomas & Mariah NORTON [WORTON?], Born March 10	bap
Apr 16	Richard, s of Richard & Mary FOSTER, Born Mar 8	bap
Apr 16	Mary, d of Joseph & Lettice LAW	bap
Apr 18	Margarett BRIANN	bur

Apr 18	William WHITEHOUSE	bur
Apr 18	Joseph, s of Joseph & Ann NOCK	bap
Apr 23	William, s of William & Sarah JOHNSON	bap
Apr 23	William, s of Benjamin & Sarah WHESSON	bap
Apr 28	John DUDLEY	bur
Apr 28	John, s of Thomas & Ann ALLEN	bap
Apr 28	John, s of Thomas & Sarah TUDOR	bap
May 7	John, s of Bayley HILL & Sarah his wife	bap
May 7	Isaac FLETCHER	bur
May 11	Phebe, d of James & Sarah GUTTRIDGE	bap
May 11	Daniel EVINS	bur
May 14	Ann, wife of William SMITH	bur
May 14	Mary Ann, d of William & Eleanor JONES	bap
May 14	Samuel, s of John & Jane TAYLOR	bap
May 14	Joseph, s of Joseph & Mary NIGHTINGALE, Born Dec 25 1794	bap
May 14	Mary Ann, d of Joseph & Mary NIGHTINGALE	bap
May 21	Samuel TAYLOR	bur
May 21	Richard, s of Richard & Mary FLETCHER	bap
May 25	Stephen, s of Joseph & Rachael HIPKISS	bur
May 28	William, s of Joseph & Lucy SMITH, Born May 2	bap
May 29	Stephen FISHER	bur
Jun 4	Mary, d of David & Ann WHITEHOUSE	bap
Jun 4	Esther, d of Eutychus & Phebe FISHER	bap
Jun 4	Elizabeth GRIFFIS	bur
Jun 5	James HORTON & Catharine JOHNSON by Banns	mar
Jun 5	Elizabeth, d of John & Mary SHELDON	bap
Jun 6	George CALLOWAY	bur
Jun 8	Mary KIDIAR	bur
Jun 11	Mary, d of Thomas & Phebe WHITEHOUSE, Born Apl 19	bap
Jun 11	George, s of William & Elizabeth TURNER, Born May 12	bap
Jun 18	Francis, s of William & Ann WARD, Born June 12	bap
Jun 19	Edward FEREDAY	bur
Jun 25	Uriah EDGE	bur
Jun 25	Thomas, a base begott Child of Hannah WHITEHOUSE	bap
Jun 25	Sarah, d of Thomas & Lydia TAYLOR	bap
Jun 28	Abraham EDWARDS	bur
Jul 2	Sarah SMITH	bur
Jul 9	Abraham NOCK	bur
Jul 9	Sarah, d of Joseph & Sarah HORTON	bap
Jul 16	Phebe, d of Daniel & Mary JEVON	bap
Jul 27	Thomas, s of Job & Sarah SHINGLETON	bap
Jul 27	Thomas, s of John & Ann ADAMS	bap
Jul 27	Richard, s of Thomas & Catharine ADAMSON	bap
Jul 27	Mary, d of William & Mary LOWE	bap
	[The next comment is entered at the top of the page:]	
	N.B. Tipton Church Consecrated August 10, 1797	
Jul 27	Simeon, s of Benjamin & Hannah RICHARDS	bap
Jul 27	Shusan, d of Thomas & Elizabeth WHITEHOUSE	bap
Jul 27	Nancy, d of John & Mary WRIGHT	bap

Jul 27	Sarah, d of John & Mary NOCK	bap
Jul 27	Elizabeth, d of William & Mary HOSBOURN	bap
Aug 6	Ephraim & Ann, s & d of Benjamin & Sarah SKIDMORE	bap
Aug 6	Thomas, s of Thomas & Sarah MASON	bap
Aug 6	John, s of William & Elizabeth GEORGE	bap
Aug 6	Rhody, d of Simeon & Ann BUTTLER	bap
Aug 6	Sarah, d of William & Mary MORRIS	bap
Aug 10	Tipton New Church Consecrated	
Aug 13	George, s of John & Mary LANKFORD	bap
Aug 20	William, s of Eader & Mary TIMMINS	bap
Aug 20	Sarah STATCHELL	bur
Aug 24	Thomas FISHER	bur
Aug 27	John STOKES	bur
Sep 10	Amelia, d of John & Elizabeth BARRETT	bap
Sep 10	Sarah, d of Edward & Jane WILLMORE	bap
Sep 10	Hannah, d of Abell & Sarah WHITEHOUSE	bap
Sep 10	Rosannah, d of Daniel & Jane NICKLIN	bap
Sep 10	John, s of John & Susannah GREGORY	bap
Sep 10	Josiah, s of Thomas & Mary HICKIN, Born Nov 12, 1796	bap
Sep 19	Hannah MILLARD	bur
Sep 19	John, a bas begott Child of Mary GEALEY	bap
Oct 1	Martha, d of Benjamin & Elizabeth TWIGG	bap
Oct 1	Elizabeth, d of Thomas & Eleanor LAW	bap
Oct 8	Mary, d of William & Ann WHITEHOUSE	bap
Oct 8	Mary, d of Edward & Margaritt FISHER	bap
Oct 15	William, s of Thomas & Mary WRIGHT	bap
Oct 15	Ann, d of Aamoss & Ann BUTTLER	bap
Oct 15	Phebe, d of Job & Mary WHITEHOUSE, Born Dec 25, 1795	bap
Oct 22	Edward, s of Edward & Elizabeth WHITEHOUSE	bap
Oct 22	Thomas, s of Thomas & Elizabeth DANKS	bap
Oct 29	Isaac, s of Isaac & Ann LAW	bap
Oct 29	John, s of John & Phebe MILLS	bap
Oct 29	Rosannah[?], d of Isaac & Martha TIMMINS	bap
Nov 5	Francis RALPH & Mary JACKSON by Banns	mar
Nov 5	Ann, d of John & Sarah WARR	bap
Nov 5	William, s of Samuel & Sarah FLETCHER	bap
Nov 5	Mary, d of William & Sarah JONES	bap
Nov 5	Abraham, s of Abraham & Elizabeth SHELDON	bap
Nov 5	John, s of Thomas & Mary BATE	bap
Nov 12	Sarah, d of Simeon & Elizabeth FISHER	bap
Nov 12	Martha, d of Sarah ALLEN	bap
Nov 12	Joseph, s of George & Ann WHITEHOUSE	bap
Nov 12	Phebe, d of James & Sarah RICHARDS	bap
Nov 12	Joseph, s of Joseph & Mary MILLS	bap
Nov 26	Samuel, s of John & Sarah MORRISS	bap
Dec 3	Joseph SMITH & Martha WHITEHOUSE by Banns	mar
Dec 3	Samuel LAW & Amelia JEVONS by Banns	mar
Dec 3	John, s of James & Hannah FISHER	bap
Dec 3	Mary, d of John & Mary BLACKHAM, Born Apl 28	bap

1797

Dec 10	Jane, d of George & Ann MARSHALL	bap
	[The next entry has been inserted]	
Dec 23	Thomas BODY & Ann ROUND by Banns	mar
Dec 25	Hannah PRICE	bur
Dec 25	John & Elizabeth, s & d of Thomas & Elizabeth WHITEHOUSE	bap
Dec 25	James, s of Joseph & Sarah HILL	bap
Dec 25	John, s of John & Sarah EVANS	bap
Dec 25	Michael, s of Richard & Mary HIPKISS, Born Sep 1 1792	bap
Dec 25	Esther SMITH	bur
Dec 30	Jane WHITEHOUSE	bur

1798

Jan 2	Joseph Moore, s of Jeremiah & Mary WILLETTS	bap
Jan 2	Silvia, d of John & Mary CASHMORE	bap
Jan 2	Thomas, s of John & Charlotte WARD	bap
Jan 2	Benjamin, s of John & Ann MATTHEWS	bap
Jan 2	Elizabeth, d of Benjamin & Sarah WHITEHOUSE	bap
Jan 2	John, s of Thomas & Charlotte COTTOM, Born Oct 10 1797	bap
Jan 2	John, s of William & Sarah WHITEHOUSE	bap
Jan 2	Mary, d of Richard & Mary WASSELL	bap
Jan 2	Elizabeth, d of Joseph & Catharine MILLS	bap
Jan 2	William *[crossed out and* "Benjamin" *inserted above]* MILLARD & Sarah PINFIELD by Banns	mar
Jan 18	Sarah, d of William & Mary NICKLIN *[entry inserted]*	bur
Jan 28	Richard MOORE & Francis BERRY by Banns	mar
Jan 19[sic]	Joseph SMITH *[entry inserted]*	bur
Jan 28[sic]	William John *[crossed out]*, s of John & Phebe HICKMANS	bap
Jan 21	Elizabeth, d of William & Sarah SMITH *[entry inserted]*	bur
Jan 28	Elizabeth, d of Abraham & Hannah BATE	bap
Jan 28	Mary, d of Thomas & Ann WOODALL	bap
Jan 31	William INGRAM	bur
Feb 4	John HORTON	bur
Feb 4	Joseph, s of Thomas & Jane STILLARD	bap
Feb 4	Mary, d of James & Hannah HEELEY	bap
Feb 4	Hannah, d of William & Mary SHORTHOUSE	bap
Feb 8	John GAILEY	bur
Feb 8	Thomas MILLS	bur
Feb 11	Isaac, s of Thomas & Sarah EVINS	bap
Feb 11	Isaac COTTRILL & Mary SMITH by Banns	mar
Feb 11	Sarah, d of William & Susannah SHORTHOUSE	bap
Feb 16	Phebe MILLS	bur
Feb 16	Nancey, d of William & Rebekah ROUND	bap
Feb 16	Phebe, d of Edward & Elizabeth MILLS	bap
Feb 16	Hannah, d of Isaac & Jane MILLS	bap
Feb 16	Phebe, d of Joseph & Prudence HORTON	bap
Feb 16	Joseph, s of William & Hannah MILLS	bap
Feb 16	Enock, s of Samuel & Elizabeth MILLS	bap
Feb 18	Elizabeth, d of George & Ann BRINLEY	bap
Feb 25	Elizabeth, d of William & Ann SARGENT	bap

1798

Feb 25	William, s of Richard & Sarah STANTON	bap
Feb 28	Ann, d of Thomas ALLIN	bur
Mar 1	Hannah BROWN	bur
Mar 1	Ann ROUND	bur
Mar 4	Phebe, d of Thomas & Hannah CANNADY	bap
Mar 4	Joseph, s of James & Rachael TATE	bap
Mar 4	Martha, d of Joseph & Elizabeth HODGYETTS	bap
Mar 4	William, s of William & Elizabeth BRETT	bap
Mar 5	Sarah HORTON	bur
Mar 5	William PARKES	bur
Mar 11	Elizabeth, d of John & Sarah GIBBINS	bap
Mar 11	John, s of William & Margarett CLIFFON	bap
Mar 11	William, s of Thomas & Elizabeth TAYLOR	bap
Mar 18	Sarah, d of Thomas & Elizabeth MORRISS	bap
Mat 18	William, s of George & Mary MARSHALL	bap
Mar 18	William, s of Joseph & Mary WOOD	bap
Mar 18	Moses, s of Moses & Sarah BUTTLER	bap
Mar 18	Mary, d of Joseph & Jane CALLOWAY, Bap Dec 14, 97	bap
Mar 18	Esther, d of George & Mary WEBSTER	bap
Mar 18	Mary, d of Robert & Hannah SMITH	bap
Mar 18	Mary, d of John & Ann LAW	bap
Mar 18	Rachael, d of William & Alice BUTTLER	bap
Mar 25	William, s of Joseph & Susannah DAVIS	bap
Mar 25	James, s of Peter & Mary ROUND	bap
Mar 25	Mary, d of William & Ellner BAKER	bap
Mar 25	William, s of Peter & Ann HICKMANS	bap
Apr 8	Edward, s of James & Mary DARBY	bap
Apr 8	Hannah, d of John & Sarah WALTERHOUSE	bap
Apr 8	Sarah, d of Joseph & Phebe CROFTS, Born July 1 1797	bap
Apr 8	John YORK & Jane TAYLOR by Banns	mar
Apr 8	Francis HOLDING & Ann FISHER by Banns	mar
Apr 8	William, s of Thomas & Sarah KIRKUM	bap
Apr 8	Ann Beck, d of William & Sarah WHITEHOUSE	bap
Apr 8	Rosannah, d of William & Sarah TUCKLEY, Born Mar 5	bap
Apr 8	Mary, d of James & Lettice RUBOTTOM	bap
Apr 10	Thomas COOK & Ann WHITEHOUSE by Banns	mar
Apr 15	Joseph, s of Joseph & Sarah BENNETT	bap
Apr 15	Henry WILLIAMS & Sarah COX by Banns	mar
Apr 19	Mary HORTON	bur
Apr 22	Rachael, d of Francis & Jane PIERCE	bap
Apr 22	Joseph, s of Joseph & Elizabeth SHELDON	bap
Apr 27 *[sic; entry squeezed in]* John BAILEY & Martha HORTON by Banns		mar
Apr 22	Sarah, d of Thomas & Jane KNOWLE	bap
Apr 22	Elizabeth, d of William & Elizabeth HORTON, Born Mar 26	bap
Apr 22	Jacob FORSTER & Sarah HOOLEY by Banns *[squeezed in]*	mar
Apr 27	Mary DARBY	bur
Apr 29	Thomas TILLEY	bur
Apr 29	Phebe, d of Abraham & Lydia FISHER	bap

1798

Apr 29	John FISHER & Lydia DARBY by Banns	mar
Apr 29	William GREEN & Sarah WINSER by Banns	mar
Apr 29	Abraham MILLS & Dinah BAKER by Banns	mar
May 1	James WHITEHOUSE & Mary HARPER by Banns	mar
May 6	Oliver PITT	bur
May 6	William KIRKIM	bur
May 6	Moses WALTON	bur
May 6	James, s of William & Phebe HODGSKINS	bap
May 6	John, s of Joshua & Hannah PARTRIDGE	bap
May 8	Hannah, d of Joseph & Hannah BOTT	bap
May 8	Ann, d of John & Sarah WHITEHOUSE	bap
May 8	John TILLEY	bur
May 11	Ann TUNKS	bur
May 17	Thomas WHITEHOUSE	bur
May 20	Catharine, d of John & Sarah WESTWOOD	bap
May 20	Nancy, d of John & Jane TAYLOR	bap
May 20	Thomas, s of Edward & Ann ROWLEY	bap
May 20	Lucy, d of William & Mary SMITH	bap
May 20	Nancy, d of William & Mary HUGHES	bap
May 20	William, s of Thomas & Elizabeth HUGHES	bap
May 23	Ann NICKLIN	bur
May 23	Joseph WHITEHOUSE	bur
May 27	Lydia, d of John & Mary BISSELL, Born Mar 3	bap
May 27	Edward, s of Joseph & Martha SMITH	bap
May 27	John WHITEHOUSE	bur
May 27	Sarah WHITEHOUSE	bur
May 27	John FISHER	bur
May 27	Edward, s of John & Sarah TIMMINS	bap
May 27	John, s of Isaac & Mary BATE	bap
May 27	Sarah, d of Samuel & Sarah THOMEY	bap
May 27	Hannah, d of Thomas & Phebe NICKOLIS	bap
Jun 1	Joseph ROUND	bur
Jun 3	Mary THOMAS	bur
Jun 10	Ann, d of William & Rebekah JEVON	bap
Jun 10	Joseph FISHER	bur
Jun 15	John, a bas begott Child of Mary PARKES	bap
Jun 17	John, s of John & Mary PENDENTON	bap
Jun 17	Thomas, s of Mary SHELDON	bap
Jun 17	John WHITEHOUSE	bur
Jun 21	Jacob OWEN & Mary UNDERHILL, by Lycence	mar
Jun 22	Thomas WEBB	bur
	[The handwriting changes at this point]	
Jun 22	Elisabeth WHITEHOUSE	bur
Jun 24	Richard SHEREWOOD & Ann TURNER by Banns *[squeezed in]*	mar
Jun 25[sic]	William HIPKISS	bur
Jun 24	Sara, d of Abraham & Phebe MILLS, Born June 9	bap
Jun 24	William, s of Daniel & Elisabeth ELWELL, Born Feb 13	bap
Jun 27	Rosanna, d of John & Elisabeth BROWN, Born Feb 3, 1797	bap
Jun 27	Joseph BAKER	bur

1798

Jun 27	Elisabeth ROWLEY	bur
Jun 27	Daniel PERSHOUSE	bur
Jun 27	Edward GREEN	bur

Here ends the Triennial Transcript from 1795 to 1798
[then the following note is crossed through:]
~~List of Marriages not registered from this time here,~~
~~them being Kept in a separate book used only for that purpose.~~

Jul 6	Mary DUFFIL	bur
Jul 6	James ROUND	bur
Jul 8	James, s of Joseph & Sarah PARTRIGE, Born June 14	bap
Jul 8	John, s of Charles & Elisabeth TITTLEY, Born June 27	bap
Jul 15	Maria, d of Joseph & Rachael HIPKISS, Born Jan 15	bap
Jul 15	Phebe, d of William & Ann PARKES, Born Apr 15	bap
Jul 15	Jane, d of John & Sara FISHER, Born June 7	bap
Jul 15	Thomas WORTON	bur
Jul 15	James PARTRIDGE	bur
Jul 22	Hannah, d of Joseph & Mary HODGATTS, Born May 14	bap
Jul 22	Elisabeth, d of Thomas & Ann COTTERELL, Born June 12	bap
Jul 22	John, s of Richard & Sellwynn NEWELL, Born July 14	bap
Jul 22	John, s of George & Mary WILKES, Born July 17	bap
Jul 22	Samuel MORRIS	bur
Jul 22	Joseph FULLWOOD	bur
Jul 22	David LAW	bur
Jul 23	Ann BATE	bur
Jul 29	Hannah WORTON	bur
Jul 29	Richard HADINSON	bur
Jul 29	Elizabeth, d of Benjamin & Joice FISHER	bap
Aug 1	Elisabeth WORTON	bur
Aug 3	Ann WARR	bur
Aug 5	John PARTRIDGE	bur
Aug 5	William DREW	bur
Aug 5	William, s of David & Sara JEVONS, Born July 8	bap
Aug 12	Joice, d of Peter & Ann MILLS, Born Aug 5	bap
Aug 12	James GUTTRIDGE	bur
Aug 19	John, s of William & Mary FISHER, Born July 18	bap
Aug 19	Edith, d of Edward & Hannah SMITH, Born July 19	bap
Aug 19	William, s of Samuel & Jane STOKES, Born Aug 7	bap
Aug 21	Joice PASKIN	bur
Aug 26	Ann SHELDON	bur
Aug 26	Hannah BOTT	bur
Aug 26	William, s of Thomas & Mary JERVIS, Born July 29	bap
Aug 26	Rosanna, d of Richard & Susanna DERBY, Born Aug 3	bap
Aug 26	Thomas, s of John & Mary OAKES, Born May 26	bap
Aug 26	William, s of William & Elisabeth TATE, Born July 25	bap
Aug 27	James, s of William & Hannah FORSTER, Born June 29	bap
Aug 27	Hannah FOSTER	bur
Sep 2	Edward CARTWRIGHT	bur
Sep 2	Simeon, s of Richard & Isabella TAYLOR	bap

Sep 9	George FREETH & Phebe DAVIES by Banns *[entry inserted]*	mar
Sep 9	Ann, d of George & Sara GILES	bap
Sep 11	Edward, s of John & Sara FERRIDAY, Born Dec 16, 1797	bap
Sep 11	William MILLS	bur
Sep 16	Sara GREENAWAY	bur
Sep 16	John, s of James & Ann HORTON, Born Sep 16	bap
Sep 16	Thomas BUNCH & Mary EDWARDS by Banns *[entry inserted]*	mar
Sep 23	Joseph, base S of Sara SHELDON, Born Sep 12	bap
Sep 23	Hannah, d of Thomas & Sara BOTT, Born Aug 30	bap
Sep 23	Hannah SHORTHOUSE	bur
Sep 23	James PERSHOUSE	bur
Sep 30	Edward JONES	bur
Sep 30	Edward PHILLIPS & Mary HORTHAN by Banns *[entry inserted]*	mar
Oct 7	William, s of Daniel & Mary WHITEHOUSE, Born Sep 15	bap
Oct 7	William, s of John & Elisabeth FISHER, Born Sep 30	bap
Oct 7	Enos, s of Enos & Hannah WHITEHOUSE, Born Mar 13	bap
Oct 7	Isaac, s of John & Sara ARNOLD	bap
Oct 7	Elisabeth WHITEHOUSE	bur
Oct 10	Lydia WHEATLEY	bur
Oct 10	James FORSTER	bur
Oct 16	Elisabeth ATTWOOD	bur
Oct 16	Thomas WHALE	bur
Oct 16	Daniel ROBERTS	bur
Oct 16	Sara, d of Peter & Elisabeth SAUNDERS, Born Oct 30 1797	bap
Oct 21	William, s of John & Mary HODGSKINS, Born Oct 2	bap
Oct 21	Esther, d of Richard & Martha HANCOX, Born May 19	bap
Oct 21	Honour, d of William & Amelia LOWE, Born Sep 30	bap
Oct 21	Daniel SHELDON & Rosannah WHITEHOUSE by Banns *[entry inserted]*	mar
Oct 23	John GAYLEY	bur
Oct 28	Joseph, s of William & Sara EDGE, Born Oct 15	bap
Nov 4	Joseph, s of William & Rachael NICKLIN, Born Sep 9	bap
Nov 4	William, s of William & Mary LAW, Born July 28	bap
Nov 4	Joseph, s of John & Ann SMITH, Born Feby 1	bap
Nov 4	Elisabeth, d of John & Mary BARNES, Born Feby 2	bap
Nov 4	John EDGE	bur
Nov 6	Thomas SHELDON	bur
Nov 7	Hannah WATERHOUSE	bur
Nov 11	Ann, d of James & Elizabeth DUFFIELD, Born Aug 6	bap
Nov 18	William, s of George & Hannah CALLAWAY, Born Nov 12	bap
Nov 18	Elisabeth, d of John & Catherine INGRAM, Born June 14, 1797	bap
Nov 18	Elisabeth, d of Joseph & Phebe STANTON, Born Nov 15	bap
Nov 18	Daniel, s of William & Rebecca STANTON, Born Oct 27	bap
Nov 18	Phebe, d of John & Mary WILLIAMS, Born Novr 2	bap
Nov 18	Charlotte WINNINGTON	bur
Nov 20	William MAWPAS	bur
Nov 25	Jinny PERRY	bur
Nov 25	James, s of Thomas & Hannah WOODALL, Born Nov 12	bap
Nov 25	Emanuel, s of John & Mary CHINTON, Born May 25	bap

1798

Nov 25	Sara, d of Richard & Elisabeth SAUNDERS, Born Oct 30	bap
Nov 25	Marianne, d of John & Ann WOOD, Born Aug 1	bap
Nov 25	Elizabeth, d of Joseph & Mary WARR, Born June 9	bap
Nov 25	John, s of Thomas & Jenny PERRY, Born Nov 18	bap
Nov 12[sic]	John SHORT & Rachel MALLORS, by Licence *[inserted]*	mar
Nov 29	Hannah FOSTER	bur
Dec 2	Ann BAKER	bur
Dec 2	William, s of Samuel & Ann SMITH, Born Nov[r] 13	bap
Dec 2	Samuel, s of Benjamin & Elisabeth BROWN, Born Mar 30	bap
Dec 2	James, s of James & Judith BAKER, Born Sep 9, 1797	bap
Dec 6	William FLETCHER	bur
Dec 6	Thomas WINNINGTON	bur
Dec 6	George ATTWOOD	bur
Dec 9	Benjamin, s of Benjamin & Ann MATTHEWS, Born Nov 14	bap
Dec 9	Hannah, d of James & Triaphenia GUEST, Born Nov 11	bap
Dec 9	John, s of Benjamin & Sara MILLARD, Born Nov[r] 4	bap
Dec 9	Eleanor, d of Edward & Alice CHILDES, Born July 30	bap
Dec 9	Isaac, s of Peter & Rachael ROWLEY, Born Dec[r] 4	bap
Dec 9	Sara, base Child of Mary NICKOLDS, Born Dec[r] 4	bap
Dec 16	Thomas, s of John & Mary PRICE, Born Dec[r] 10	bap
Dec 16	Thomas, s of Thomas & Mary PALMER, Born Nov 3	bap
Dec 16	John, s of Francis & Ann HORDERN	bap
Dec 16	Pheebe PERSHOUSE	bur
Dec 20	William, s of John & Mary FIELDHOUSE, Born Dec[r] 14	bap
Dec 20	Ann FIELDHOUSE	bur
Dec 23	Ann, d of Thomas & Ann BODY, Born Sep 30	bap
Dec 23	Joseph, s of Joseph & Hannah GRICE, Born Aug 5	bap
Dec 25	Robert SIMSON & Prudence HARRIS by Banns *[inserted]*	mar
Dec 26	Benjamin, s of Benjamin & Sara FERRIDAY, Born Mar 22	bap
Dec 26	Henry HAWKINS & Susannah CARTER by Banns *[inserted]*	mar
Dec 26	Joseph, s of James & Debora NOCK	bap
Dec 26	Aaron WHITEHOUSE	bur
Dec 26	Sara WOODALL	bur
Dec 30	Sara MILLS	bur
Dec 30	Elisabeth HODGSKINS	bur
Dec 30	William, s of Richard & Jane DAVIS, Born Nov[r] 19	bap
Dec 30	John, s of Peter & Mary MILLS, Born Nov[r] 27	bap
Dec 30	Elizabeth, d of Abraham & Mary BAKER, Born Dec 25	bap
Dec 30	Daniel, s of Samuel & Elizabeth COLLINS, Born Dec 5	bap

1799

Jan 4	Mary ASTLEY	bur
Jan 6	Mary BROWN	bur
Jan 6	John WHITEHOUSE	bur
Jan 6	John, s of Abiathar & Sara HANCOX, Born Oct 10, 1798	bap
Jan 6	Benjamin, s of Joseph & Ann FIELDHOUSE	bap
Jan 6	James, s of James & Sara CHARTER	bap
Jan 9	Joseph NICKLIN	bur
Jan 13	Susanna SMITH	bur

1799

⌐	Jan 13	Richard, s of Charles & Mary NEATH	bap
⌐	Jan 13	George, s of Samuel & Mary BAYLEY	bap
⌐	Jan 13	Thomas MASON & Margaret HARRISS by Banns *[inserted]*	mar
⌐	Jan 15	Thomas FORSTER	bur
	Jan 18	Phebe NICKLISS	bur
	Jan 20	Richard, s of John & Mary JONES, Born Oct 5 1798	bap
	Jan 20	Phoebe & Maria, twin d of Joseph & Ann CARTWRIGHT, Born Dec 30 1798	bap
	Jan 22	Samuel, s of Elisha & Priscilla WHITEHOUSE, Born Dec 7, 1798	bap
	Jan 22	Phoebe WHITEHOUSE	bur
	Jan 27	Hannah NICKLISS	bur
	Jan 27	Enock, s of Benjamin & Mary WATERS	bap
	Jan 27	Mary, d of Richard & Mary JUKES, Born Jan 5	bap
	Jan 27	Sara, d of James & Phœbe OSBOWIN	bap
	Feb 3	Ann, d of William & Phœbe BISSELL	bap
⌐	Feb 3	Francis WARD	bur
	Feb 3	Phœbe FERRIDAY	bur
	Feb 10	Mary GILES	bur
	Feb 10	John, s of Daniel & Rosanna SHELDON, Born Dec 11 1798	bap
⌐	Feb 10	Martha, d of Amos & Ann BUTLER, Born Jan 16	bap
	Feb 10	Richard HUBBARD & Mary ADAMS by Banns	mar
	Feb 10	Joseph, s of John & Ann DOUGHTY, Born Jan 14	bap
	Feb 10	Thomas, s of John & Ann SHELDON, Born Jany 2	bap
	Feb 10	Samuel, s of Samuel & Elisabeth SMITH, Born Nov 1, 1798	bap
	Feb 10	Catherine, d of George & Elisabeth BALL, Born Dec 15 1798	bap
	Feb 15	Maria HIPKISS	bur
⌐	Feb 17	John WRIGHT	bur
	Feb 17	William, s of John & Rachel COTTRELL, Born Jan 17	bap
	Feb 17	Isaiah, s of Joseph & Ann ASTON, Born July 4 1798	bap
	Feb 17	James FULLWOOD & Mary ROGERS by Banns *[inserted]*	mar
	Feb 20	Samuel CALLOWAY	bur
	Feb 24	Thomas SILK	bur
	Feb 24	Thomas, s of Joseph & Sara JOHNSON, Born Feb 2	bap
⌐	Feb 24	James, s of Thomas & Elizabeth HOLWEYHEAD, Born Feb 14	bap
	Mar 3	Joseph HORTON & Mary TURNBULL by Banns *[inserted]*	mar
	Mar 3	Samuel, s of Edward & Elisabeth WHITEHOUSE, Born Jan 31	bap
	Mar 3	John, s of William & Jane WHITEHOUSE, Born Jan 28	bap
	Mar 3	Ann, d of Joseph & Elisabeth SHERWOOD, Born Oct 18 1798	bap
	Mar 3	Nancy, d of Joseph & Elisabeth DUKES, Born Nov 18 1798	bap
	Mar 3	Stephen, s of John & Sara FISHER, Born Feb 9	bap
	Mar 3	Isaac, s of James & Mary WHITEHOUSE, Born Feb 13	bap
	Mar 3	Elisabeth, d of Richard & Sara SMITH, Born Oct 21, 1798	bap
	Mar 3	Hannah, base Child of Elisabeth WHITEHOUSE, Born Feb 14	bap
	Mar 3	Ann REYNOLDS	bur
	Mar 3	Isaac WHITEHOUSE	bur
	Mar 5	Mary CALLAWAY	bur
	Mar 8	Sara SKIDMORE	bur
	Mar 10	Joseph WINDSOR & Esther CADDICK by Banns *[inserted]*	mar
⌐	Mar 10	Joseph, s of Joseph & Mary WARD, Born Feb 18	bap

1799

Mar 10	William GUEST & Hannah EVANS by Banns *[inserted]*	mar
Mar 13	Sophia FISHER	bur
Mar 17	Rebecca, d of Thomas & Mary FELLOWS, Born Oct 2, 1798	bap
Mar 17	Mary, d of Thomas & Mary ATKISS, Born Jan 4	bap
Mar 17	Joseph, s of John & Eleanor NICHOLLS, Born Dec 1, 1798	bap
Mar 20	Richard WHITEHOUSE	bur
Mar 20	Joseph WHITEHOUSE	bur
Mar 22	Joseph TUCKLEY	bur
Mar 22	Harriet, d of Thomas & Eleanor WEBB, Born Mar 18	bap
Mar 24	John, s of Robert & Sara BOWYER, Born Mar 3	bap
Mar 24	Elisabeth, d of George & Mary GREGORY, Born Mar 1	bap
Mar 24	Samuel, s of James & Mary TILL, Born Jan 10	bap
Mar 24	Mary, d of Joseph & Rachael DUFFIELD, Born Mar 2	bap
Mar 24	Elisabeth, d of Thomas & Phebe PARKES, Born Jan 7	bap
Mar 24	Joseph, s of Joseph & Catherine COCKRAL	bap
Mar 24	Sara, d of Abel & Elisabeth FLETCHER, Born Dec 26 1798	bap
Mar 26	George CLIFFORD	bur
Mar 28	Rosanna TUCKLY	bur
Mar 31	Phœbe OSBORN	bur
Mar 31	Stephen FISHER	bur
Mar 31	Ann, d of William & Sara SMITH, Born Jan 27	bap
Mar 31	James ATTWOOD & Elizabeth BATE by Banns *[inserted]*	mar
Mar 31	John CROSS & Elizabeth SMITH by Banns *[inserted]*	mar
Apr 2	Benjamin HORTON	bur
Apr 7	Sophia, d of Thomas & Mary RICHARDS, Born Mar 21	bap
Apr 14	Susanna, d of Joseph & Sara TAILOR, Born Mar 20	bap
Apr 14	Maria, d of John & Sara GOULD	bap
Apr 14	Hannah GEALEY	bur
Apr 17	Margaret ELWELL	bur
Apr 30	Sara NICKLISS	bur
Apr 30	Ann FISHER	bur
Apr 30	Sara, d of John & Sophia LAW, Born April 4	bap
Apr 30	Zachariah, s of Joseph & Catherine MILLS, Born Apl 28	bap
May 5	Debora, df of Richard & Elisabeth ALLEN, Born Apl 14	bap
May 5	Maria, d of Thomas & Elisabeth TILLY, Born May 3	bap
May 5	Marianne, d of John & Mary DAINTY, Born Apl 11	bap
May 5	Mary, d of William & Sara ROUND, Born Feb 17	bap
May 10	Elisabeth SMITH	bur
May 12	Samuel FORSTER	bur
May 12	Thomas HODGSKINS	bur
May 12	John, s of Isaac & Margaret HADLEY, Born Apl 30	bap
May 12	Joseph, s of Joseph & Ann DUDLEY, Born May 4	bap
May 12	Benjamin, base Son of Phebe CALLOWAY, Born March 16	bap
May 12	Lucy, d of Richard & Ann BOOTH, Born March 27	bap
May 12	Thomas, s of William & Hannah HOPKINS, Born Apl 21	bap
May 13	John, s of Joseph & Elisabeth GALLOP, Born Apl 22	bap
May 13	John, s of Richard & Elisabeth TAILOR, Born Apl 25	bap
May 13	John PERRY	bur
May 13	Ann PARKES	bur

May 19	Phœbe DUFFIL		bur
May 19	Rowland, s of Robert & Mary MORRIS, Born Sep 24 1798		bap
May 19	John, s of William & Jane VIPOMD, Born Apl 1		bap
May 22	Joseph WHITEHOUSE		bur
May 26	Job SMITH		bur
May 26	Mary, d of Thomas & Lydia TAYLOR, Born May 4		bap
May 26	Sara, d of Benjamin & Ann SKIDMORE, Born May 12		bap
May 26	Sophia, d of Abraham & Ann GEORGE, Born April 21		bap
May 28	John FISHER		bur
Jun 2	John, s of John & Catherine LANGFORD, Born March 29		bap
Jun 2	Mary & Martha, twin d of Ithial & Mary SALMON, Born Dec 6 1798		bap
Jun 2	John, s of Richard & Elisabeth BOWEN, Born Jan 30		bap
Jun 2	Peter, s of Peter & Mary ROUND, Born May 9		bap
Jun 2	John, s of John & Sara MORRIS, Born March 20		bap
Jun 2	Mary, d of Charles & Hannah HILL, Born May 3		bap
Jun 2	Nancy, d of William & Sara WALKER, Born May 26		bap
Jun 9	Sara, d of William & Jane ALLENDER, Born Jan 29		bap
Jun 9	John COTTAM		bur
Jun 11	Mary GRIFFIS		bur
Jun 11	John LANGFORD		bur
Jun 13	James PANE & Betty PITT by Banns [inserted]		mar
Jun 13	Samuel HARGRIFF		bur
Jun 16	Phœbe MILLS		bur
Jun 16	Ann, d of Noah & Sara SMITH, Born April 28		bap
Jun 16	Mary, d of Daniel & Elisabeth SHELDON, Born June 2nd		bap
Jun 18	Sara GUTTRIDGE		bur
Jun 21	Thomas WHITEHOUSE		bur
Jun 23	Mariann, d of John & Mary BISSELL		bap
Jun 23	Henry Holland, s of Joseph & Hannah BOTT, Born Mar 31		bap
Jun 23	William, s of Thomas & Sara SMITH, Born Dec 10, 1783		bap
Jun 26	Edward ROUND		bur
Jun 26	Hannah HODGETTS		bur
Jun 30	Henry Holland BOTT		bur
Jun 30	Richard, s of Joseph & Mary GORTON		bap
Jun 30	Thomas, s of Thomas & Sara PARKES		bap
Jun 30	John, s of James & Hannah FISHER, Born June 8		bap
Jun 30	Ann, d of John & Sara BARNET		bap
Jul 1	Thomas SHELDON & Hannah BATE by Banns		mar
Jul 1	Mary, d of Thomas & Hannah SHELDON, Born Jan 21		bap
Jul 1	John PHILIPPS		bur
Jul 9	Nancy SMALLMAN		bur
Jul 14	John SILVESTER		bur
Jul 14	Jane, d of John & Jane DAWES, Born Feb 19		bap
Jul 14	Maria, d of Benjamin & Sara GRIFFITHS		bap
Jul 14	Michael, s of Thomas & Sara RAYBOULD, Born June 9		bap
Jul 16	Thomas PARRY & Sarah DARBY by Banns [inserted]		mar
Jul 21	Samuel, s of Benjamin & Elizabeth TWIGG, Born Mar 14		bap
Jul 21	James, s of Thomas & Mary BAGLEY, Born June 14		bap

1799

Jul 21	Ann, d of William & Sara REYNOLDS, Born May 28	bap
Jul 28	Mary, d of Simeon & Hannah BUTLER, Born June 20	bap
Jul 28	Ann, d of Simeon & Elisabeth FISHER, Born June 28	bap
Jul 28	Ann, d of Thomas & Ann THOMPSON, Born July 6	bap
Jul 28	Paul LANCASTER	bur
Jul 30	Elisabeth FORSTER	bur
Aug 4	Edward BOWKLEY & Mary COX by Banns *[inserted]*	mar
Aug 4	Mary, d of John & Ann ADAMS, Born July 22	bap
Aug 11	William SHORT	bur
Aug 18	George ALLINDER	bur
Aug 18	William MORRIS	bur
Aug 18	Stephen HIPKISS	bur
Aug 18	John, s of John & Ann THOMASON	bap
Aug 18	Richard, s of William & Sophia BATE, Born Feb 13	bap
Aug 21	Mary STOKES	bur
Aug 25	John, s of Henry & Esther WORTON, Born July 13	bap
Aug 25	Sara, d of Edward & Sara DUDLEY, Born June 27	bap
Aug 25	Thomas, s of William & Mary MORRIS, Born Aug 3	bap
Aug 25	Joseph DUFFEL & Mary WHITEHOUSE by Banns	mar
Aug 25	Timothy, s of John & Susanna GREGORY	bap
Aug 27	John FISHER	bur
Sep 1	Edward GRIFFIN & Mary WAKELAM by Banns *[inserted]*	mar
Sep 1	Joseph, s of John & Mary ROWLEY, Born Aug 25	bap
Sep 1	Elizabeth, d of Joseph & Sophia BROOKS, Born Aug 13	bap
Sep 8	Benjamin CARTWRIGHT	bur
Sep 8	Esther SMITH	bur
Sep 10	Thomas RICHARDS	bur
Sep 10	Sara, d of John & Mary WELCH, Born April 8	bap
Sep 15	George HOBSON & Mary GRATELY by Banns *[inserted]*	mar
Sep 15	John, s of George & Mary MARSHALL, Born July 14	bap
Sep 15	Jane, d of John & Sara ROWLEY, Born Sep 1	bap
Sep 15	Joseph, base child of Mary DUFFIL, Born Sep 1	bap
Sep 15	Sara, d of Joshua & Hannah PARTRIDGE, Born July 23	bap
Sep 22	Thomas, s of James & Sara BIRD, Born Aug 25	bap
Sep 22	Hannah, d of John & Mary LANGFORD, Born Feb 17	bap
Sep 22	Mary, d of William & Mary SHORTHOUSE, Born July 8	bap
Sep 22	Mary JEWKES	bur
Sep 22	Sara ASTON	bur
Sep 29	Hannah, d of Edward & Jane WHITMORE, Born Aug 25	bap
Sep 29	Martha, d of Daniel & Mary JAMES, Born Sep 4	bap
Sep 29	Ann, d of Robert & Ann GALLER, Born Sep 8	bap
Sep 29	John ALLEN & Susannah SMITH by Banns	mar
Oct 1	Ann ROBERTS	bur
Oct 6	John HEATH	bur
Oct 6	Sara, d of Thomas & Sara ELWELL, Born June 15	bap
Oct 6	Eliza, d of William & Mary OSBOND, Born Sep 11	bap
Oct 13	Edward, s of William & Mary SMITH, Born Sep 23	bap
Oct 13	Elisabeth, d of John & Eleanor DIXON, Born Aug 24	bap
Oct 17	John HODGSKINS	bur

1799

Oct 20	William, s of John & Sara WARR, Born July 15	bap
Oct 20	Benjamin, s of William & Sarah DANGERFIELD, Born Oct 12	bap
Oct 27	Lydia, d of Benjamin & Mary HARTLAND, Born Oct 2	bap
Oct 27	Elisabeth, d of William & Sara WHITEHOUSE, Born Sep 15	bap
Oct 27	Josiah, s of Joseph & Elizabeth TONKES, Born Aug 9	bap
Oct 27	Francis PIERCE	bur
Nov 3	Enoch MILLS	bur
Nov 3	Cornelius, s of Richard & Mary FORSTER, Born Nov 3/1798	bap
Nov 3	Samuel, s of Isaac & Jane MILLS, Born Sep 10	bap
Nov 3	Marianne, d of James & Ann PERRY, Born June 29	bap
Nov 4	William WALTERS	bur
Nov 5	Isaac BATE	bur
Nov 5	Elisabeth FISHER	bur
Nov 8	William FIELDHOUSE	bur
Nov 10	John LOWE	bur
Nov 10	John, s of Thomas & Elizabeth COLLINS, Born Oct 17	bap
Nov 10	John, s of John & Ann PEAT, Born Oct 5	bap
Nov 10	Joseph, s of Thomas & Ann WILLDAY, Born Oct 25	bap
Nov 24	Isaiah, s of Samuel & Mary MILLS, Born Nov 17	bap
Nov 24	Thomas, s of William & Elizabeth BRATT, Born Nov 19	bap
Nov 24	Jeremiah, s of Richard & Sara STANTON, Born Nov 17	bap
Nov 24	Abraham MALLEN	bur
Dec 1	Joseph STOKES & Phebe HURLEY by Banns *[inserted]*	mar
Dec 2	John SANDERS	bur
Dec 8	Samuel TIMMINS	bur
Dec 8	Thomas ROUND	bur
Dec 8	Joseph, s of Samuel & Sara FOREST, Born Aug 8	bap
Dec 8	Elisabeth Green, d of William & Mary MILLS, Born Nov 6	bap
Dec 8	William, s of Thomas & Elizabeth MORRIS, Born Nov 13	bap
Dec 8	Sara, d of Thomas & Ann MAWPAS, Born Novr 16	bap
Dec 11	Thomas Naylor FULLER & Marianne TRUEMAN, by Licence *[inserted]*	mar
Dec 22	Hannah, d of Thomas & Charlotte COTTOM, Born Oct 18	bap
Dec 22	Elisabeth, d of Samuel & Susanna FERRIDAY, Born Dec 16	bap
Dec 25	Edward, s of William & Phebe JONES, Born Sep 13	bap
Dec 25	Debora CORBETT	bur
Dec 27	Ann PASKIN	bur
Dec 27	John SMITH	bur
Dec 29	Ann WILLDAY	bur
Dec 29	Mary WHITEHOUSE	bur
Dec 29	Isaiah MILLS	bur
Dec 29	Aaron, s of Moses & Sara BUTLER, Born Novr 30	bap
Dec 29	Charlotte, d of Benjamin & Ann BLEWETT, Born Dec 11	bap
Dec 29	Rebecca, d of John & Elisabeth SAUNDERS	bap
Dec 29	George, base S of Elisabeth FIELD, Born Decr 11	bap
Dec 29	Sara, d of William & Sara NIGHTINGALE, Born Oct 7	bap
Dec 29	Joseph COTTON & Elizabeth HUMPHREYS by Banns *[inserted]*	mar
Dec 29	Aaron, s of John & Elizabeth SMITH, Born Oct 4	bap
Dec 29	Samuel, s of Samuel & Rebecca HIPKISS, Born Aug 20	bap

Jan 5	William WILLIAMS & Martha MOUNTFORD by Banns *[inserted]*	mar
Jan 5	Thomas, s of Edward & Margaret FISHER, born Dec 6, 1799	bap
Jan 5	Isaac, s of Joseph & Mary FISHER, Born Dec 15 1799	bap
Jan 5	Sara, d of David & Ann WHITEHOUSE, Born Oct 13, 1799	bap
Jan 5	Sara, d of John & Sara WHITEHOUSE, Born Dec 2, 1799	bap
Jan 5	Benjamin WHEAL & Mary NIGHTINGALE by Licence *[inserted]*	mar
Jan 5	Ann, d of Thomas & Sara COX, Born Dec 2, 1798	bap
Jan 5	Mary, d of William & Mary PERSHOUSE, Born Aug 11, 1799	bap
Jan 5	Thomas, s of Joseph & Sara SHINGLETON, Born Apl 16 1799	bap
Jan 12	Samuel, s of William & Elisabeth GEORGE, Born Novr 25 1799	bap
Jan 12	Isaac, s of John & Mary HODGSKINS, Born Dec 22 1799	bap
Jan 12	Ann, d of Thomas & Eleanor LAW, Born Novr 8, 1799	bap
Jan 19	Benjamin, s of Richard & Ann COOK, Born Dec 30 1799	bap
Jan 19	William, s of Joseph & Ann ASTON, Born Novr 28 1799	bap
Jan 26	Elisabeth, d of Pharaoh & Eleanor SMITH, Born Jan 8	bap
Jan 26	Mary, d of William & Hannah GUEST, Born Sep 9, 1799	bap
Jan 26	Mary, d of John & Elizabeth TURNER, Born Sep 19, 1799	bap
Jan 26	Eleanor, d of Thomas & Sara MORGAN, Born Dec 1, 1799	bap
Jan 26	Rosanna, d of William & Sara TUCKLEY, Born Jan 4	bap
Jan 26	Hannah, d of Richard & Silvia NEWIN, Born Dec 27, 1799	bap
Jan 26	John LORD	bur
Feb 2	Edward WHITEHOUSE	bur
Feb 2	Jenny CHATTERTON	bur
Feb 2	Elisabeth, d of William & ~~Mary~~ *[struck through]* Alice *[written above]* GAMMONS, Born Jan 22	bap
Feb 2	Phœbe, d of Thomas & Catherine WILLIS, Born Jan 19	bap
Feb 2	William, s of John & Mary WHITEHOUSE, Born Jan 15	bap
Feb 2	Sara, d of William & Eleanor JONES, Born Dec 29 1799	bap
Feb 4	Samuel SMITH	bur
Feb 4	William GRIFFIS	bur
Feb 7	William GIDDENS	bur
Feb 9	Hannah, d of Joseph & Sarah HORTON, Born Jan 7	bap
Feb 9	Joseph WHITEHOUSE	bur
Feb 11	Mary Nicklin HIPKISS	bur
Feb 16	Thomas TAYLOR	bur
Feb 16	Solomon WOODALL	bur
Feb 23	Jeremiah, s of Jeremiah & Mary WILLETS, Born Dec 25 1799	bap
Feb 23	Amos HODGSKINS & Frances SHELDON, by Banns *[inserted]*	mar
Feb 23	George, s of Joseph & Martha HURLEY, Born Jan 3	bap
Feb 23	Ann, d of John & Sarah FISHER, Born Jan 25	bap
Feb 23	James GUEST	bur
Feb 23	David LAW	bur
Feb 25	Phebe ROUND	bur
Feb 25	Thomas, s of Thomas & Sarah TUDOR, Born Apl 1, 1799	bap
Mar 2	Mary, d of Thomas & Elisabeth DANKES, Born Jan 4	bap
Mar 2	Thomas FERRIDAY	bur
Mar 2	Margaret NIGHTINGALE	bur
Mar 2	Hannah COLLINS	bur
Mar 6	Joseph WILLDAY	bur

1800

Mar 6	Abraham JUKES	bur
Mar 6	James SMITH	bur
Mar 9	David, s of David & Hannah HORTON, Born at Birmingham Oct 13 1799	bap
Mar 9	Charles, s of John & Sarah GIBBINS, Born Dec 12 1799	bap
Mar 12	Elizabeth GAMMONS	bur
Mar 19	Elizabeth ECCLES	bur
Mar 23	Mary, d of Richard & Amelia LAW, Born Jan 30	bap
Mar 23	Elizabeth, d of Edward & Sarah JONES, Born Jan 8	bap
Mar 23	Maryann, d of Joseph & Mary WARR, Born Mar 5	bap
Mar 23	Elizabeth, d of Samuel & Sarah THORNEY, Born Sep 10 1799	bap
Mar 23	Catharine, d of Edward & Mary HOLTON, Born Mar 2	bap
Mar 23	William, s of William & Sarah DUDLEY, Born Feb 9	bap
Mar 23	Mary WHESSON	bur
Mar 26	Thomas WHITEHOUSE	bur
Mar 30	Shusannah, d of William & Sarah HYDE, Born Mar 17	bap
Mar 30	James, s of Eutychus & Phœbe FISHER, Born Feb 28	bap
Mar 30	Sarah MILLS	bur
Apr 1	Thomas PORTER	bur
Apr 1	Samuel SATCHELL	bur
Apr 4	Phebe DUDLEY	bur
Apr 6	Edward, s of Jesse & Ann SIMMS, Born Feb 10	bap
Apr 6	Richard, s of Joseph & Lydia COWDRELL, Born March 16	bap
Apr 6	Elizabeth, d of William & Sarah ROBISON, Born Feb 11	bap
Apr 6	Elizabeth ROBISON	bur
Apr 6	Hannah HORTON	bur
Apr 6	Jeremiah PARKES	bur
Apr 13	Benjamin, s of William & Phoebe HODGSKINS, Born March 14	bap
Apr 13	Thomas, s of Thomas & Ann WOODALL, Born March 20	bap
Apr 13	Thomas, s of William & Hannah JEWKES, Born Novʳ 2 1799	bap
Apr 13	Mary SHELDON	bur
Apr 13	Joseph NICHOLLS	bur
Apr 20	William MORRIS	bur
Apr 20	John SMITH & Eleanor CHATTINGTON by Banns [inserted]	mar
Apr 20	Mary Ann, d of Charles & Hannah LEGER	bap
Apr 20	George, s of Richard & Mary JONES, Born Mar 20	bap
Apr 20	Mary, d of Benjamin & Elizabeth GIBBONS, Born Sep 29, 1799	bap
Apr 27	Phœbe, d of Abel & Hannah CADDICK, Born Mar 27	bap
Apr 27	Ann, d of Richard & Martha WASSALL, Born Apl 2	bap
Apr 27	William, s of Joseph & Mary SMITH, Born April 2	bap
Apr 27	Hannah, d of William & Esther TURNER, Born Mar 18	bap
Apr 27	John, s of Isaac & Ann LAW, Born Dec 26 1799	bap
Apr 27	Thomas MORRIS	bur
Apr 27	Joseph ASTON	bur
Apr 30	Abraham SHELDON	bur
May 4	Frances, d of Francis & Jane PIERCE, Born Apl 10	bap
May 4	Lydia, d of Daniel & Sarah MINCHER, Born Aug 26 1799	bap
May 8	William PARISH	bur
May 8	Edward NICKLIN	bur

1800

May 8	Hannah AUTHORN	bur
May 8	Thomas, s of Joseph & Elizabeth HODGSKINS, Born Apl 19	bap
May 11	Edward, s of Edward & Phebe WHITEHOUSE, Born Feb 20	bap
May 11	Elizabeth, d of John & Mary FURNEYFIELD, Born May 9	bap
May 11	Ann, d of Thomas & Hannah HICKMANS, Born Mar 4	bap
May 11	Phebe, d of Emanuel & Ann DERBY, Born Apl 13	bap
May 11	Sarah, d of Emanuel & Ann DERBY, Born Jan 22, 1798	bap
May 18	William GUTTRIDGE	bur
May 25	Thomas WHITEHOUSE	bur
May 25	William GUTTRIDGE, an infant	bur
Jun 1	Mary, d of Henry & Mary SMITH, Born May 31	bap
Jun 1	Robert LLOYD & Phebe ALLDRITT by Banns [inserted]	mar
Jun 1	Sarah, d of Benjamin & Nancy RUDGE, Born Apl 17	bap
Jun 1	Sarah, d of Joseph & Dina FISHER, Born Jan 14	bap
Jun 1	Eleanor, d of Thomas & Phebe NICKLISS, Born May 13	bap
Jun 1	Mary, d of William & Sarah ROBISON, Born May 5	bap
Jun 1	Sarah ROBISON	bur
Jun 1	Isaac FISHER	bur
Jun 2	James, s of Isaac & Elizabeth WHITEHOUSE, Born Mar 2	bap
Jun 2	Maryann, d of Isaac & Elizabeth WHITEHOUSE, Born March 29 1798	bap
Jun 4	James WHITEHOUSE & Ann WRIGHT by Licence [inserted]	mar
Jun 4	Thomas DERBY	bur
Jun 8	Catherine SMITH	bur
Jun 8	George FISHER	bur
Jun 8	Joseph, s of George & Mary WILKES, Born June 1	bap
Jun 8	Mary, d of Benjamin & Hannah RICHARDS, Born May 15	bap
Jun 13	Sarah BAYLEY	bur
Jun 13	George, s of Joseph & Hannah FEREDAY, Born Jan 10	bap
Jun 15	Thomas COX & Ann BEDWORTH by Banns [inserted]	mar
Jun 15	David FEREDAY	bur
Jun 15	Phebe TIMMINS	bur
Jun 15	James, s of James & Mary DARBY, Born Mar 27	bap
Jun 22	Hannah, d of Benjamin & Mary WALTERS, Born May 25	bap
Jun 22	Edward, s of Isaac & Martha TIMMINS, Born Mar 27	bap
Jun 22	Mary, d of John & Ann MATTHEWS, Born May 8	bap
Jun 22	Daniel, s of Abel & Sarah WHITEHOUSE, Born May 25	bap
Jun 22	Oliver PITT, an Infant	bur
Jun 22	Sarah REYNOLDS	bur
Jun 29	Joseph, s of Edward & Sarah GRIFFITHS, Born May 15	bap
Jul 6	Ann, d of Joseph & Mary DUFFIELD, Born May 23	bap
Jul 18	Joseph HODGSKINS	bur
Jul 18	Edward WHITEHOUSE	bur
Jul 20	Hannah, d of James & Sara RICHARDS, Born Jan 31	bap
Jul 20	Thomas, s of Joseph & Ann DUDLEY, Born July 11	bap
Jul 20	Edward FEREDAY & Isabel CHANNEY by Banns [inserted]	mar
Jul 20	Francis, s of John & Charlotte WARD, Born Mar 27	bap
Jul 20	Edward, s of Isaac & Mary BATE, Born June 20	bap
Jul 20	Richard, s of Edward & Alice GILES, Born July 2	bap

1800

Jul 20	Mary ALEXANDER	bur
Jul 22	Mary ROBISON	bur
Jul 25	James ONIONS	bur
Jul 27	Richard, s of William & Sarah WHITEHOUSE, Born Apl 9	bap
Jul 27	Richard, s of Richard & Maria DYSON, Born Apl 19	bap
Aug 3	Thomas, s of William & Sarah GUEST, Born July 3`	bap
Aug 3	Sarah, d of John & Sarah BENNET, Born July 8	bap
Aug 5	William ROBISON	bur
Aug 10	James FISHER	bur
Aug 10	Francis Inkinson, s of Benjamin & Eleanor BILL, Born June 12	bap
Aug 10	John, s of George & Catharine WILLETS, Born June 8	bap
Aug 10	Eleanor, d of John & Mary DUDLEY, Born July 26	bap
Aug 17	John, s of Peter & Ann MILLS, Born Aug 14	bap
Aug 17	Joseph, s of James & Mary WHITEHOUSE, Born July 23	bap
Aug 17	Thomas HARCOT & Mary FISHER by Banns [inserted]	mar
Aug 17	Eleanor DUDLEY	bur
Aug 24	William HILL & Hannah BISSELL by Banns [inserted]	mar
Aug 27	William REYNOLDS	bur
Aug 31	Thomas, s of Samuel & Jane SKELTON, Born Aug 8	bap
Aug 31	Joseph, s of John & Maria SHAW, Born Aug 9	bap
Aug 31	Elizabeth, d of Thomas & Sarah LOWNDES, Born June 20	bap
Aug 31	John, s of Amos & Frances HODGSKINS, Born May 18	bap
Sep 2	Nancy WORTON	bur
Sep 2	Sarah, d of Joseph & Prudence HORTON, Born May 17	bap
Sep 7	William, s of William & Sarah SMITH, Born June 28	bap
Sep 7	John, s of Samson & Catharine AUSTIN, Born Aug 23	bap
Sep 7	Samuel ADAMS & Sarah HARRISON by Banns [inserted]	mar
Sep 7	Daniel, s of James & Sarah GUTTRIDGE, Born July 22	bap
Sep 12	Jesse WHITEHOUSE	bur
Sep 17	John GIBBONS	bur
Sep 21	Abraham WHITEHOUSE & Phebe FOX by Banns [inserted]	mar
Sep 21	Thomas, s of Joseph & Sarah HUGHES, Born Apl 5	bap
Sep 21	William BATE & Molly BRADBURY by Banns [inserted]	mar
Sep 21	Pharoah, s of James & Mary STANSFIELD, Born Aug 7	bap
Sep 21	Sarah SMITH	bur
Sep 28	Enoch WHITEHOUSE	bur
Sep 28	Mary TIMMINS	bur
Sep 28	James, s of James & Martha GREEN, Born Sep 3	bap
Sep 28	Mary, d of Benjamin & Sarah WHITEHOUSE, Born Sep 5	bap
Oct 5	Ann, d of Edward & Hannah SMITH, Born Aug 3	bap
Oct 5	Thomas, s of Thomas & Phebe LEECH, Born Sep 7	bap
Oct 5	Nancy, d of John & True WHITEHOUSE, Born Sep 17	bap
Oct 5	Elizabeth, d of William & Mary MANNINGS, Born July 13	bap
Oct 5	Samuel, s of Samuel & Mary PASKIN, Born Sep 7	bap
Oct 5	Frances, d of Richard & Martha HANCOX, Born July 1	bap
Oct 12	Elizabeth, wife of Will[m] HORTON (Parish Clerk)	bur
Oct 12	Sarah, d of Peter & Mary MILLS, Born Sep 29	bap
Oct 16	Mary ROUND	bur
Oct 19	Thomas, s of Thomas & Mary JERVIS, Born Sep 27	bap

1800

Oct 19	Sarah, d of William & Ann BLANKLEY, Born Dec 6 17[??]	bap
Oct 19	Sarah, d of William & Sarah GREENAWAY, Born Oct 15	bap
Oct 20	Abraham MILLS	bur
Oct 20	Abraham, s of Abraham & Mary MILLS, Born May 22 1799	bap
Oct 20	Francis, s of Francis & Martha MILLS, Born Dec 18 1795	bap
Oct 26	Samuel ROUND	bur
Oct 26	Joseph GRIFFITHS	bur
Oct 26	Mary BATE	bur
Oct 26	Ann, d of Benjamin & Sarah FEREDAY, Born Mar 21	bap
Oct 29	Maria FLETCHER	bur
Oct 29	John PASKIN	bur
Nov 2	Anthony Lewis, s of Daniel & Jane NICKLIN, Born Mary 27	bap
Nov 2	Phebe, d of William & Rebecca JEVONS, Born Oct 14	bap
Nov 2	Joseph, s of Joseph & Sarah TAILOR, Born Oct 17	bap
Nov 2	Fanny, d of Thomas & Mary ATKISS, Born Oct 3	bap
Nov 2	John, s of William & Sarah EDGE, Born Oct 12	bap
Nov 2	Mary, d of Samuel & Sarah SOUTHALL, Born Sep 14	bap
Nov 5	Susannah WHITEHOUSE	bur
Nov 5	Jane ROWLEY	bur
Nov 9	George YORK & Sarah MILLS by Banns [inserted]	mar
Nov 11	Peter ROUND	bur
Nov 16	Luke BRIERLEY & Mary BLODWELL by Banns [inserted]	mar
Nov 16	Daniel, s of Daniel & Mary WHITEHOUSE, Born Oct 2	bap
Nov 16	Nancy, d of Thomas & Sarah WALKER, Born Aug 16	bap
Nov 16	Thomas SANDBIGE	bur
Nov 19	Leah, d of Amos & Ann BUTLER[?], Born Sep 18	bap
Nov 19	Mary, d of John & Mary EVANS, Born May 18	bap
Nov 19	John MILLS	bap

[lightly written at the top of the page:]

1857	1861
	59
	2

Nov 25	Joseph WHITEHOUSE	bur
Nov 30	John, s of Joseph & Martha ROTTON, Born Nov 1	bap
Nov 30	William BUNN	bur
Dec 7	Maria, d of William & Mary FISHER, Born Novʳ 7	bap
Dec 7	Joseph EDGE	bur
Dec 9	Ann GOODBY	bur
Dec 10	John CARTWRIGHT	bur
Dec 14	Samuel, a base Son of Elizabeth ALLEN, Born Dec 3	bap
Dec 16	James FRANCIS	bur
Dec 16	Abraham MILLS [entry inserted; date appears to have been altered from "14" to "16"]	bur
Dec 21	Daniel Collins, s of Abraham & Mary JEVONS, Born Nov 22	bap
Dec 21	Sarah, d of Abraham & Mary DANGERFIELD, Dec 2	bap
Dec 21	Edward BLOXWICH	bur
Dec 21	Mary GIBBONS	bur
Dec 21	Sarah HOSBOWIN	bur
Dec 25	Sarah, d of Joseph & Jane CALLOWAY, Born Nov 1	bap

1800

Dec 25	Isaac, s of John & Mary BISSELL, Born Dec 12	bap
Dec 25	Ann FEREDAY	bur
Dec 25	William SMITH	bur
Dec 28	William, s of Thos & Elizabeth HOLYHEAD, Born Dec 6	bap
Dec 28	Sarah, d of Richard & Rachel GOWER, Born Dec 16	bap
Dec 28	Ann ROBERTS	bur
Dec 28	Mary PRESTON	bur
Dec 28	Phebe DUDLEY	bur
Dec 28	Charles, s of James & Judith BAKER, Born May 20	bap
Dec 28	Ann, d of John & Mary WHITEHOUSE, Born Sep 27	bap
Dec 31	Eleanor NICKLISS	bur
Dec 31	Cornelius FELLOWS	bur
Dec 31	Sarah ARNOLD	bur
Dec 28[sic]	William CLARK & Elizabeth PRICHETT by Banns	mar

1801

Jan 1	Joseph SMITH & Susanna FISHER by Licence	mar
Jan 2	Ann EDGE	bur
Jan 4	Sarah, d of John & Sophia LAW	bap
Jan 4	Thomas HICKENBOTTOM	bur
Jan 4	William JONES	bur
Jan 4	Sarah HORTON	bur
Jan 4	Sarah TIMMINS	bur
Jan 4	Mary RICHARDS	bur
Jan 10	Thomas FEREDAY & Elizabeth NIGHTINGALE by Banns	mar
Jan 11	Stephen, s of Joseph & Elizabeth SHELDON, Born Nov 15 1800	bap
Jan 14	Thomas PARKES	bur
Jan 14	George FEREDAY	bur
Jan 14	Amelia BAILEY	bur
Jan 18	Samuel, s of Edward & Elizabeth MILLS	bap
Jan 18	Zachariah & Sarah, s & d of John & Phebe MILLS, Born Jan 16	bap
Jan 18	Isaac HODGSKINS	bur
Jan 18	Hannah SMITH	bur
Jan 18	Mary MILLS	bur
Jan 21	Eleanor FISHER	bap
Jan 21	Mary REWBERY	bur
Jan 25	Moses, s of Daniel & Elizabeth SHELDON, Born Jan 18	bap
Jan 25	Maria, d of Samuel & Hannah SHELDON, Born Jan 9	bap
Jan 25	Enoch & Noah, s of Joseph & Catharine MILLS, Born Jan 24	bap
Jan 25	John, s of Joseph & Elizabeth SHERWOOD, Born July 22 1782	bap
Jan 28	Daniel FISHER	bur
Jan 28	Rebecca NIGHTINGALE	bur
Jan 28	Benjamin LAW	bur
Jan 29	Martha FLETCHER	bur
Jan 29	James, s of Thomas & Elizabeth HUGHES, Born June 4 1800	bap
Feb 1	A Strange Man, much burnt at Mes^s PARKERS Furnace & brought to the Workhouse died Jan 27	bur
Feb 1	Edward MILLS	bur

Feb 1	Hannah KIMBERLEY	bur
Feb 1	Ann BUFF	bur
Feb 1	William, s of John & Elizabeth SHORT, Born June 6 1800	bap
Feb 1	Joseph, s of Hugh & Alice WELCH, Born Oct 15 1800	bap
Feb 3	Mary GRATTON	bur
Feb 8	Hannah Partridge RICHARDS	bur
Feb 8	Martha DARBY	bur
Feb 8	Maria, d of James & Nancy HORTON, Born Dec 28 1800	bap
Feb 10	Joseph LAW	bur
Feb 15	Jesse, s of Abraham & Lydia FISHER, Born Dec 31 1800	bap
Feb 15	Joseph GEORGE	bur
— Feb 15	Abraham TIMMINS	bur
Feb 18	John, s of Thomas & Catherine STORY, Born Mar 1 1799	bap
— Feb 18	Mary WRIGHT	bur
Feb 18	John SHELDON	bur
Feb 18	Noah MILLS	bur
Feb 20	Phebe DERBY	bur
⇀ Feb 22	Thomas, s of James & Deborah NOCK, Born Jan 19	bap
Feb 22	John, s of Cornelius & Esther BAKER, Born Jan 25	bap
Feb 22	Mary ALEXANDER	bur
Feb 22	William FISHER	bur
▬ Feb 22	James GREEN	bur
Feb 25	William SMITH	bur
Mar 1	John, s of John & Sarah HARTLEY, Born Feb 23	bap
Mar 1	Samuel, s of John & Jane TAILOR, Born Dec 17 1800	bap
Mar 1	Hannah, d of Thomas & Ann BODY, Born July 8 1800	bap
Mar 1	Sarah NICHOLAS	bur
Mar 1	Ann SMITH	bur
⤳ Mar 1	Joseph WEBB	bur
Mar 3	Jean TINSLEY	bur
Mar 8	Sarah, d of William & Elizabeth BRATT, Born Feb 15	bap
⤳ Mar 8	Joseph MOUNTFORD & Elizabeth BAYLEY by Banns	mar
⤳ Mar 12	George FOSTER	bur
Mar 12	John ASTON	bur
Mar 12	James SAMSON	bur
Mar 15	Eliza, d of Thomas & Ann CHAMBERS, Born Mar 2	bap
Mar 19	Joseph BARNETT	bur

	From 1798 ye Trienial Transcript Ends	
— Mar 26	Joseph SHELDON & Hannah HODGKINS by Licence	mar
Mar 29	Joseph DUFFILL	
Apr 1	Sara WHITEHOUSE	bur
Apr 1	William SMITH	bur
Apr 5	Joseph, s of Thomas & Ann COTTRELL, Born Mar 22	bap
Apr 5	John, s of John & Elizabeth SMITH, Born Decr 18, 1800	bap
Apr 5	Isaiah, s of Joseph & Ann SANDERS, Born Mar 3	bap
Apr 5	Edward, s of Samuel & Mary MILLS, Born Mar 20	bap
Apr 5	Samuel, s of William & Jane WHITEHOUSE, Born Mar 3	bap
Apr 5	Sarah RUBBOTTOM	bur

Apr 5	Sarah SANDERS	bur
Apr 5	Elizabeth MILLS	bur
Apr 5	Thomas WHALE	bur
Apr 5	Pharoah STANSFIELD	bur
Apr 5	Joshua WHITEHOUSE	bur
Apr 5	William SMITH	bur
Apr 8	Abraham BROWN	bur
Apr 8	Elizabeth BAILEY	bur

Exm^d May 21st J.F.

Apr 12	Edward, s of John & Phebe HICKMANS, Born Feb 19	bap
Apr 12	Ann, d of Peter & Ann HICKMANS, Born Feb 20	bap
Apr 12	Mary, d of Thomas & Jane STILLARD, Born Mar 11	bap
Apr 14	Elizabeth WARD	bur
Apr 14	Hopias MARTIN	bur
Apr 16	Mary SMITH	bur
Apr 19	Thomas, s of Robert & Phebe LLOYD, Born Sep 23 1800	bap
Apr 19	Elizabeth, d of Ithial & Mary SALMON, Born Apl 9	bap
Apr 19	Richard DANDLEY	bur
Apr 22	Elizabeth HODGSKINS	bur
Apr 22	Thomas LYON	bur
Apr 26	Hannah, d of Joseph & Hannah BOTT, Born Apl 1	bap
Apr 26	Letty, d of Joseph & Ann FIELDHOUSE, Born Apl 6	bap
Apr 26	John, s of Samuel & Maria WEST, Born Apl 7	bap
Apr 26	Peter ROUND	bur
Apr 26	William SHEREWOOD & Elizabeth WHITEHOUSE by Banns	mar
Apr 29	John SHORT	bur
Apr 30	Jeremiah LLOYD	bur
Apr 30	John PARTRIDGE	bur
May 3	Elizabeth, d of John & Sarah WESTWOOD, Born Apl 2	bap
May 3	Elizabeth, d of John & Mary FIELDHOUSE, Born Jan 14	bap
May 3	Thomas NOCK	bur
May 3	Elizabeth WORTON	bur
May 6	George BALL	bur
May 6	Rosannah, d of Thomas & Hannah KENNEDY, Born Nov 29 1800	bap
May 6	Mary, d of Joseph & Elizabeth GALLOP, Born Feb 25	bap
May 7	Margaret SALT	bur
May 8	Edward DUFFELL	bur
May 10	Maria, d of Joseph & Rachael HIPKINS, Born Aug 5 1800	bap
May 10	Sophia, d of Francis & Ann HOLDEN, Born Apl 17	bap
May 17	Joseph, s of James & Ann WHITEHOUSE, Born Apl 25	bap
May 19	Joseph DUDLEY	bur
May 19	Eleanor BAYLEY	bur
May 19	Thomas PARKES	bur
May 22	William INGRAM	bur
May 22	Hannah FREESON	bur
May 24	James DARBY	bur
May 24	Ann, d of Joseph & Martha SMITH, Born Apl 16	bap
May 26	Sarah GRIFFITHS	bur

1801

May 27	Hannah FISHER	bur
May 31	Samuel MARYGOLD & Mary ATKISS by Banns	mar
Jun 5	William HOLMES	bur
Jun 5	Mary SMITH	bur
Jun 7	Francis HORDEN	bur
Jun 11	Nancy WHITEHOUSE	bur
Jun 14	William WORTON & Sarah HAMER by Banns *[inserted]*	mar
Jun 14	Samuel s of George & Mary MARSHALL, Born June 9	bap
Jun 14	Isaac COURT & Charlotte HOWELL by Banns *[inserted]*	mar
Jun 16	Mary Ann, d of Thomas & Eleanor WEBB, Born May 27	bap
Jun 21	Mary, d of David & Hannah HORTON, Born at Birmingham May 6	bap
Jun 16[sic]	John GUTTRIDGE	bur
Jun 16	Ann WRIGHT	bur
Jun 21	James LATHAM & Maria MOUNTFORD by Banns *[inserted]*	mar
Jun 21	Thomas, s of Abraham & Mary BAKER, Born June 10	bap
Jun 21	Mary Rewberry, d of James & Phebe BATE, Born Jan 6	bap
Jun 28	Joseph HORTON	bur
Jun 30	Mary WHITEHOUSE	bur
Jul 3	Sarah GREENAWAY	bur
Jul 5	Mary, d of George & Ann BRINDLEY	bap
Jul 5	David, s of John & Ann SHELDON, Born July 3	bap
Jul 5	Samuel SHELDON	bur
Jul 8	Joseph MILLS	bur
Jul 8	Sarah PARKES	bur
Jul 12	Thomas, s of Thomas & Elizabeth EDWARDS, Born June 20	bap
Jul 12	John WILKINSON	bur
Jul 14	Mary COURTS	bur
Jul 19	Mary, d of James & Elizabeth ATTWOOD, Born Apl 30	bap
Jul 19	Susannah, d of William & Mary LOWE, Born June 22	bap
Jul 19	Samuel, s of Joseph & Marabell GUTTRIDGE, born Oct 26 1799	bap
Jul 19	Elizabeth, d of Charles & Hannah HILL, Born June 23	bap
Jul 19	Francis, s of William & Ann WARD, Born June 15	bap
Jul 19	Elizabeth WILKES	bur
Jul 21	Hannah BOTT	bur
Jul 26	Hannah, d of Daniel & Ann PRITCHETT, Born July 12	bap
Jul 26	Elizabeth Fletcher, d of John & Elizabeth SITCH, Born June 1	bap
Jul 28	Thomas HAWTHORN	bur
Aug 2	Edward EDWARDS & Mary TURNER by Banns *[inserted]*	mar
Aug 2	Thomas GRIFFITHS	bur
Aug 2	Lydia GRIFFITHS	bur
Aug 2	Samuel, s of James & Jane NOCK, Born June 19	bap
Aug 2	Mary, d of Abraham & Rosannah MILLS, Born July 20	bap
Aug 2	Joseph, s of Abraham & Mary NICHOLDS, Born July 14	bap
Aug 2	Lucy, d of Edward & Jane WHITMORE, Born July 20	bap
Aug 9	Sarah, d of Thomas & Mary BENNET	bap
Aug 9	William, s of John & Sophia LAW, Born June 2	bap
Aug 11	James COURTS	bur

1801

Aug 11	Mary BRINDLEY	bur
Aug 16	Thomas, s of Henry & Esther WORTON, Born July 13	bap
Aug 18	Joseph NOCK	bur
Aug 18	Jane BARNSLEY	bur
Aug 21	Phebe ROUND	bur
Aug 21	Hannah BOTT	bur
Aug 23	James DARBY	bur
Aug 23	Elizabeth BRUKES	bur
Aug 23	James, s of Philip & Ann WILLIAMS, Born Aug 1	bap
Aug 27	Hannah FOWNES	bur
Sep 3	John TINSLEY	bur
Sep 3	William CUNDLEY	bur
Sep 3	Betty TWIGG	bur
Sep 9	Daniel GUTTRIDGE	bur
Sep 13	Hannah, d of William & Sarah ROUND, Born July 1	bap
Sep 13	Rosannah, d of Thomas & Jane SMITH	bap
Sep 13	Elizabeth ONIONS	bur
Sep 14	Mary GALLOP	bur
Sep 20	William BAILEY & Mary JOHNSON by Banns *[inserted]*	mar
Sep 20	James BAGLEY	bur
Sep 25	Mary SALMON	bur
Sep 27	James, s of Richard & Betty ALLEN, Born Sep 6	bap
Sep 27	Elizabeth, d of Thomas & Ann DUDLEY, Born Sep 15	bap
Sep 27	George WHITEHOUSE	bur
Sep 27	Jonas ROUND	bur
Sep 28	Thomas PERRY	bur
Oct 1	James HUGHES	bur
Oct 4	Thomas, s of Henry & Sarah TAYLOR, Born July 31	bap
Oct 4	William, s of William & Mary MILLS, Born Aug 25	bap
Oct 4	John LAW	bur
Oct 11	Daniel WARR	bur
Oct 11	John, s of John & Ann PEAT, Born Sep 13	bap
Oct 13	Maria ROUND	bur
Oct 18	Sarah FEREDAY	bur
Oct 20	Zachariah MILLS	bur
Oct 23	Ann WHITEHOUSE	bur
Oct 25	Jane, d of Joseph & Dorothy HERVY	bap
Oct 26	John SHELDON	bur
Oct 26	Thomas, a base Son of Mary SHELDON	bap
Nov 1	Elizabeth, d of Richard & Mary HODGKISS, Born Sep 13	bap
Nov 1	William, s of Thos & Sarah BOTT, Born Sep 16	bap
Nov 4	Rachael GRIFFITHS	bur
Nov 8	Ann, d of John & Hannah CUMSTONE, Born June 8	bap
Nov 15	Hannah, d of Charles & Elizabeth HICKENBOTTOM	bap
Nov 15	Nancy, d of Joseph & Ruth WORTON, Born Oct 3	bap
Nov 17	Sarah WARR	bur
Nov 17	Mary ROUND	bur
Nov 22	Benjamin, s of Richard & Sylvia NEWEY, Born Oct 30	bap
Nov 22	John UNIT	bur

Nov 22	Edward BATE	bur
Nov 29	Elizabeth, d of Joseph & Mary WOOD	bap
Nov 29	Sarah, d of Job & Elizabeth BROOKES	bap
Dec 1	Hannah WHITEHOUSE	bur
Dec 2	James DARBY	bur
Dec 6	Elizabeth JORDEN	bur
Dec 20	Joseph, s of Peter & Ann MILLS, Born Dec[r] 11	bap
Dec 20	Elizabeth, d of William & Ann HUGHES, Born Nov 21	bap
Dec 20	Arabella, d of William & Phebe BISSELL, Born Dec 15	bap
Dec 20	Jane, d of Benj[n] & Mary HUGHES, Born Dec 23 1789	bap
Dec 20	Elizabeth, d of Thomas & Elizabeth BRATT, Born Nov 25	bap
Dec 20	Ann BLANKLEY	bur
Dec 25	Benjamin, s of Benj: & Ann BLEWIT, Born Sep 13	bap
Dec 25	John HORDEN	bur
Dec 27	Edward PRICE & Elizabeth BISSELL by Banns *[inserted]*	mar
Dec 27	Samuel STOKES & Jane MARSH by Banns *[inserted]*	mar

1802   1861
        58
         3

Jan 3	Lydia ASTON	bur
Jan 3	Harriot DAVIES	bur
Jan 10	Elizabeth, d of John & Mary BLACKHAM	bap
Jan 10	Joseph WHITEHOUSE	bur
Jan 12	Benjamin JORDEN	bur
Jan 12	Joseph SMITH	bur
Jan 17	William BLANKLEY	bur
Jan 17	Mary, d of Richard & Martha PERSALL	bap
Jan 18	Thomas BOTT	bur
Jan 19	Richard NICKLIN	bur
Jan 19	Jane SAINT	bur
Jan 24	William HODGSKISS & Dinah FISHER by Banns	mar
Jan 27	Eliza OSBORNE	bur
Feb 1	Joseph, s of Joseph & Mary HODGETTS	bap
Feb 1	Joseph HODGETTS	bur
Feb 2	Elizabeth, d of John & Sarah MORRIS	bap
Feb 2	Mary, d of William & Elizabeth TATE, born 14 Aug 1801	bap
Feb 2	John COTTRELL	bur
Feb 3	Elizabeth SHEREWOOD	bur
Feb 3	Elizabeth, d of Will[m] & Elizabeth SHAREWOOD, Born Jan 25	bap
Feb 7	Thomas, s of James & Sarah OSBORNE, Born Jan 31	bap
Feb 7	Edward SMITH	bur
Feb 7	William GLOVER	bur
Feb 7	William WILLINGTON	bur
Feb 7	Hannah LAW	bur
Feb 10	Rosanna RUBOTTOM	bur
Feb 14	Obadiah JOHNSON & Nancy DUDLEY by Banns	mar
Feb 16	Edward WALL	bur
Feb 21	Henry Nixon, s of Samuel & Sarah HODGKINS, Born 9th	bap

1802

Feb 21	Joseph, s of Daniel & Esther GRIFFITHS	bap
Feb 21	Mary, d of Thomas & Mary ELWELL, Born Jan 28	bap
Feb 21	Maryann, d of Jesse & Ann SIMS, Born Jan 9	bap
Feb 23	Phebe BAYLEYS	bur
Feb 28	James, s of John & Mary HINTON	bap
Feb 28	Richard, s of Robert & Ann CALLEAR	bap
Feb 28	Stephen, s of Samuel & Mary HICKMANS	bap
Feb 28	Mary, d of Joseph & Susannah TRANTER	bap
Feb 28	Maria, d of Joseph & Rachael DUFFEL	bap
Feb 28	Thomas WHITEHOUSE	bur
Mar 4	John DUFFEL	bur
Mar 7	John, s of Joseph & Hannah SHELDON, Born Feb 22	bap
Mar 7	Joseph, s of Robert & Mary GRANT, Born Oct 6 1801	bap
Mar 7	Hannah NEWEY	bur
Mar 14	William, s of John & Mary ROWLEY	bap
Mar 14	Martha, d of Abraham & Mary JEVON	bap
Mar 14	Hannah, d of John & Ann ADAMS	bap
Mar 14	Daniel SHELDON	bur
Mar 18	James NAILOR	bur
Mar 21	Richard, s of Richard & Mary JUKES	bap
Mar 28	Mary WHEAL	bur
Mar 28	David, s of Thomas & Elizabeth JONES	bap
Mar 28	William, s of William & Mary BUNCH	bap
Mar 28	Sarah, d of Elisha & Priscilla WHITEHOUSE	bap
Mar 28	Edward, s of Richard & Sarah MILLS	bap
Apr 2	James HERRING	bur
Apr 4	Joseph, s of Thomas & Susanna TAYLOR	bap
Apr 4	Elizabeth, d of James & Nancy NORTON	bap
Apr 4	Rachael, d of John & True WHITEHOUSE	bap
Apr 4	Phebe, d of Joseph & Hannah FEREDAY	bap
Apr 11	William CLEATON & Mary MILLS by Banns	mar
Apr 11	Sophia RICHARDS	bur
Apr 11	Rebecca WHITEHOUSE	bur
Apr 18	Edward DUDLEY & Elizabeth MEEK by Banns	mar
Apr 23	Sarah WEBB	bur
Apr 25	Zachariah WARD & Phebe COTTON by Banns	mar
Apr 25	William, s of William & Elizabeth BELCHER	bap
Apr 25	Sarah, d of William & Esther TURNER	bap
Apr 25	Sarah, d of John & Sarah ROWLEY	bap
Apr 25	Thomas, s of John & Maria SHAW	bap
Apr 25	William MILLS	bur
Apr 29	Elizabeth MARTIN	bur
May 2	Rachael, d of Henry & Violett HUGHES	bap
May 2	William & Sarah, s & d of William & Sarah WHITEHOUSE	bap
May 2	Elizabeth HARRIS	bur
May 2	Hannah COTTRELL	bur
May 2	Comfort FISHER	bur
May 5	Richard JONES	bur
May 7	Thomas BOWKLEY	bur

1802

	May 9	Sarah, d of Abraham & Sarah WHITEHOUSE	bap
	May 9	Mary, d of Joseph & Sophia BROOKS	bap
	May 12	Sophia LAW	bur
	May 12	Mary FISHER	bur
	May 16	Joseph, s of John & Mary JONES	bap
	May 16	David, s of William & Sarah DANGERFIELD	bap
	May 16	Sarah, d of John & Mary JEVONS	bap
	May 16	Ann, d of William & Sarah WORTON	bap
	May 23	Joseph CROMPTON	bur
~	May 23	Sarah BENNETT	bur
~	May 23	Obadiah HIGGINS & Elizabeth EDMONDS by Banns	mar
~	May 30	John, s of Daniel & Maria PARTRIDGE	bap
	May 30	Elizabeth, d of Edward & Elizabeth WHITEHOUSE	bap
~	Jun 1	Mary GUTTRIDGE	bur
~	Jun 6	Sarah, d of Amos & Ann BUTTLER	bap
	Jun 6	Thomas, s of Emanuel & Ann DERBY	bap
	Jun 6	Hannah, d of Joseph & Ann CARTWRIGHT	bap
	Jun 6	Thomas, s of Thomas & May WHITEHOUSE	bap
~	Jun 7	Joseph BIRCH & Sarah MASON by Banns	mar
~	Jun 7	James, s of William & Ann PERRY	bap
~	Jun 7	Harriot, d of Joshua & Hannah PARTRIDGE	bap
	Jun 7	Maryann, d of George & Mary GREGORY	bap
	Jun 7	John, s of William & Sarah GREENAWAY	bap
	Jun 13	John, s of Thomas & Ann WOODALL	bap
	Jun 14	Sarah FISHER	bur
	Jun 17	Hannah WHITEHOUSE	bur
	Jun 20	Sarah, d of Thomas & Mary LAPPAGE	bap
	Jun 20	Abraham, s of Abraham & Ann GEORGE	bap
	Apr 20	Thomas, s of Richard & Elizabeth SANDERS	bap
	Jun 20	Elizabeth, d of William & Elizabeth HORTON	bur
	Jun 20	John WILLINGTON & Mary PICKING by Banns	mar
	Jun 27	Elizabeth, d of Thomas & Sarah EVANS	bap
	Jun 27	Ann, d of Zachariah & Bettsy SHAW	bap
	Jun 27	Eleanor, d of William & Hannah HOLMES	bap
	Jun 27	George HURLEY	bur
	Jul 4	Joseph, s of William & Mary SHORTHOUSE	bap
	Jul 4	Thomas, s of Richard & Elizabeth WILSON	bap
	Jul 7	Ann REYNOLDS	bur
	Jan 9	Hannah BATE	bur
	Jul 14	William GREAER	bur
	Jul 14	Richard NICKLISS	bur
~	Jul 14	Zachariah, s of Richard & Mary FOSTER	bap
~	Jul 14	James, s of James & Ann PERRY	bap
	Jul 14	Mary, d of Isaac & Ann LAW	bap
~	Jul 18	John, s of John & Mary WRIGHT	bap
	Jul 18	Mary, d of Edward & Sarah TUCKLEY	bap
~	Jul 18	Richard BRADBURY & Hannah HALE by Banns	mar
	Jul 25	Nancy, d of Daniel & Sarah THOMPSON	bap
	Jul 25	Benjamin, s of Benjamin & Sarah BATE	bap

Jul 25	Ann SMITH	bur
Jul 25	Mary WHITEHOUSE	bur
Aug 1	Thomas LEEK & Ann BARRS by Banns	mar
Aug 1	Martha, d of Eutychus & Phebe FISHER	bap
Aug 1	Mary, d of Joseph & Elizabeth GALLOP	bap
Aug 1	Elizabeth EVANS	bur
Aug 1	Ann WHEAL	bur
Aug 8	Sarah, d of Charles & Nancy PARTRIDGE	bap
Aug 8	William EDWARDS	bur
Aug 10	Thomas WHITEHEAD	bur
Aug 15	Ann, d of Thomas & Elizabeth DANKS	bap
Aug 15	Mary, d of John & Ann COX	bap
Aug 19	Mary BROOKS	bur
Aug 19	Sophia FISHER, a base D^r of Sarah BENNETT	bap
Aug 22	Joseph, s of John & Elizabeth LIESTER	bap
Aug 22	Stephen, s of Joseph & Jane WHITEHOUSE	bap
Aug 22	William & Mary, s & d of Joseph & Mary WARD	bap
Aug 29	William OTTLEY	bur
Aug 29	Thomas SATCHELL	bur
Aug 29	William, s of William & Sarah ROBISON	bap
Aug 29	Henry, s of Henry & Mary WELCH	bap
Aug 29	William SHEREWOOD & Sarah DREW by Banns	mar
Sep 1	Mary NOCK	bur
Sep 5	William, s of Thomas & Elizabeth TILLEY	bap
Sep 5	Sophia, d of Thomas & Lydia TAYLOR	bap
Sep 7	Elizabeth ATTWOOD	bur
Sep 7	Joseph CHATER	bur
Sep 7	Sarah MILLS	bur
Sep 7	Edward, s of Benjamin & Sarah FEREDAY	bap
Sep 7	John, s of Daniel & Mary JEVON, Born June 22	bap
Sep 9	Benjamin HORTON	bur
Sep 9	Daniel, s of John & Mary DAINTY	bap
Sep 12	John DUFFELL	bur
Sep 12	Sarah LAW	bur
Sep 22	William EVANS	bur
Sep 26	Joseph, s of Joseph & Sarah BAGGETT	bap
Sep 27	Thomas GUTTRIDGE & Elizabeth BECK by Banns [inserted]	mar
Sep 28	John WARR	bur
Sep 28	John, s of John & Sarah WARR	bap
Sep 30	John LARNGLEAN	bur
Oct 3	Edward, s of James & Mary WHITEHOUSE, Born Sep 10	bap
Oct 3	Daniel MILLS	bur
Oct 10	Joseph BEADLEY & Elizabeth SALT by Banns [inserted]	mar
Oct 10	Elizabeth, d of George & Mary WILKES	bap
Oct 10	Daniel, s of Daniel & Elizabeth GORTON	bap
Oct 10	Daniel ETHERWAY & Elizabeth GUTTRIDGE by Banns [inserted]	mar
Oct 10	Mary WHITEHOUSE	bur
Oct 17	Ketura, d of William & Eleanor JONES	bap

<u>1802</u>

Oct 17	Benjamin, s of John & Elizabeth WHILE	bap
Oct 19	Mary ELWELL	bur
Oct 24	Mary, d of Jesse & Mary WHITEHOUSE	bap
Oct 24	Benjamin, s of Eder & Mary TIMMINS	bap
Oct 24	Sarah TIMMINS	bur
Oct 31	Thomas HAZLEHURST & Rosanna BOURNE by Banns [inserted]	mar
Oct 31	John Sych, s of George & Elizabeth DEELY	bap
Oct 31	Ruth, d of Thomas & Rebecca HARRIS	bap
Nov 7	Maria REWBRY	bur
Nov 7	John, a base son of Phebe WHITTALL	bap
Nov 7	Letitia, d of John & Lucretia KIRKAM	bap
Nov 7	Susannah, d of John & Elizabeth HORTON	bap
Nov 7	Phebe, d of Thomas & Sarah PARKES	bap
Nov 14	Martha, d of Benjamin & Mary WATERS	bap
Nov 14	Susanna, d of Thomas & Mary SHORTHOUSE	bap
Nov 15	William FISHER	bur
Nov 15	Elizabeth SHEREWOOD	bur
Nov 15	John, s of William & Mary LAW, Born Aug 22 1800	bap
Nov 21	Ketura JONES	bur
Nov 21	Amelia, d of Benjamin & Sarah COX	bap
Nov 28	Rachael, d of Edward & Isabel FEREDAY	bap
Nov 28	Isaac, s of Abel & Hannah CADDICK	bap
Nov 28	Hannah, d of Samuel & Mary PASKIN	bap
Nov 28	Mary, d of James & Sophia JONES	bap
Dec 1	Phebe ASTON	bur
Dec 1	William, s of William & Elizabeth HOLLAND	bap
Dec 5	Phebe, d of William & Sarah WALKER	bap
Dec 12	Hannah, d of James & Hannah FISHER	bap
Dec 12	Lydia, d of Samuel & Ann EDWARDS	bap
Dec 12	Sarah SMITH	bur
Dec 12	Richard BRIERLEY & Mary JENKS by Banns [inserted]	mar
Dec 19	Jacob, s of Isaac & Peggy HILL	bap
Dec 19	Ann, d of James & Ann WHITEHOUSE	bap
Dec 19	Mary & Sarah, twin d of Richard & Lucy DAVIES	bap
Dec 19	Henry REWBRY	bur
Dec 25	William MILLS & Penelope COPE by Banns [inserted]	mar
Dec 25	Job, s of Benjamin & Ann SKIDMORE	bap
Dec 25	Mary, d of Joseph & Elizabeth JUKES	bap
Dec 25	Mary, d of James & Hannah DOWNES	bap
Dec 25	Samuel, s of Samuel & Jane STOKES	bap
Dec 25	Jane, d of Samuel & Jane STOKES	bap
Dec 25	Sarah & Mary DAVIES	bur
Dec 25	Ann HART	bur
Dec 26	James, s of John & Sarah JONES	bap
Dec 26	Alexander, s of John & Jane SANKEY	bap
Dec 26	Mary, d of Joseph & Catharine COCKRAN	bap
Dec 26	Ann, d of Thomas & Sarah DANGERFIELD	bap
Dec 26	James, s of James & Elizabeth HOXLEY	bap

1802

Dec 26	Sarah, d of Richard & Sarah GRIFFITHS	bap
Dec 26	Maria, d of James & Sarah RICHARDS	bap
Dec 26	Eli, d of Joseph & Elizabeth WILLIAMS	bap
Dec 26	Sarah, d of John & Sarah BENNET	bap
Dec 28[sic]	Daniel WARR	bur
Dec 27	Edward WHITEHOUSE & Rebecca HOWES by Banns *[inserted]*	mar

[Very faint:]

1861	61
1802	1790
59	71

1803

Jan 2	Ann, d of Job & Mary SKIDMORE, baptis^d 23 years of age	bap
Jan 2	John DENIEL, from Cornwall	bur
Jan 9	Samuel ELWELL	bur
Jan 9	Charlotte HOLIHOCK	bur
Jan 9	William, s of Benjamin & Elisabeth SMITH	bap
Jan 16	Caroline, d of William & Mary OSBORN	bap
Jan 23	Thomas, s of George & Elizabeth BALL	bap
Jan 23	Thomas GARVIS	bur
Jan 23	Samuel WAGSTAFF & Rhoda SMITH by Licence	mar
Jan 26	Thomas BALL	bur
Jan 26	Jacob HILL	bur
Jan 26	Ann NIGHTINGALE	bur
Jan 30	Amos DARBY & Zeprah DARBY by Banns	mar
Jan 30	Mary, d of Thomas & Elizabeth EDWARDS	bap
Jan 30	Elizabeth, d of John & Charlotte WARD	bap
Jan 30	Maria, d of John & Elizabeth SMITH	bap
Jan 30	Martha, d of John & Hannah CUMSTONE	bap
Jan 30	Mary, d of Edward & Sarah COX	bap
Jan 30	Thomas NOCK	bur
Jan 30	Elizabeth GUTTRIDGE	bur
Feb 6	John, s of George & Mary ROBINSON	bap
Feb 6	William, s of William & Sarah TUCKLEY, Born Jan 11	bap
Feb 6	Sarah, d of Richard & Sarah SMITH	bap
Feb 6	John, s of Thomas & Phebe LEECH	bap
Feb 6	John, s of James & Sarah REWBRY, Born June 7 1802	bap
Feb 6	Joseph, s of James & Deborah NOCK, Born Jany 9	bap
Feb 6	Nancy, d of James & Sarah LUNN, Born Dec 26 1802	bap
Feb 6	Mary, d of John & Sarah REWBRY, Born May 26 1801	bap
Feb 6	John REWBRY Killed in the Coal Pitt	bur
Feb 6	John WRIGHT	bur
Feb 11	Samuel TURNER	bur
Feb 13	William Henry, s of William & Mary HORTON	bap
Feb 13	Elizabeth, d of William & Sarah EDGE, Born Dec 31 1802	bap
Feb 13	Richard, s of John & Elizabeth REED, Born Dec 15 1802	bap
Feb 13	James, s of Moses & Sarah BUTTLER, Born 6th	bap
Feb 13	Samuel, s of William & Elizabeth TURNER, Born Jan 15	bap
Feb 13	Benjamin LAW	bur

1803

Feb 13	James MILLARD	bur
Feb 18	Edward ROBERTS	bur
Feb 20	Maryann, d of James & Nancy HORTON	bap
Feb 27	Samuel HALL	bur
Feb 27	Maria, d of David & Hannah HORTON, Born at Birmingham Nov 30 1802	bap
Feb 27	John, s of Joseph & Sarah HORTON, Born Jan 7	bap
Feb 27	Samuel & Thomas, twin s of Samuel & Susanna FEREDAY	bap
Feb 27	Elizabeth, d of John & Mary SHELDON	bap
Feb 27	Nancy, d of John & Elizabeth STANTON	bap
Feb 27	Mary, d of Joseph & Phebe STANTON	bap
Feb 27	Phebe, d of John & Phebe MILLS	bap
Feb 27	Job CASHMORE & Sarah HEYNES by Banns	mar
Mar 1	Sarah SMITH	bur
Mar 3	William HEWITT	bur
Mar 3	Elizabeth, d of Charles & Susanna PERRY	bap
Mar 6	John TIMMINS & Mary ROBINSON by Banns	mar
Mar 6	Thomas, s of Thomas & Mary DOYNEY	bap
Mar 6	Mary, a base d of Martha LIESTER	bap
Mar 7	Michael LIESTER	bur
Mar 9	Elizabeth EVANS	bur
Mar 9	Hannah, d of Joseph & Catharine MILLS, Born Feb 6	bap
Mar 10	Sarah WHITEHOUSE	bur
Mar 13	John, a base son of Elizabeth ROBINSON	bap
Mar 13	Hannah, d of William & Elizabeth BRATT	bap
Mar 13	Hannah, d of George & Ann BRINDLEY	bap
Mar 13	William, s of William & Letitia SHELDON	bap
Mar 13	Mary, d of James & Margaret RAMSDEN	bap
Mar 13	Rachael, d of Thomas & Ann FEREDAY	bap
Mar 13	Martha EDGE	bur
Mar 13	Benjamin SMITH	bur
Mar 13	Ann CUMSTONE	bur
Mar 20	William BILLINGHAM & Mary PARTRIDGE by Banns	mar
Mar 20	Thomas, s of John & Susannah GREGORY, Born Jan 18	bap
Mar 20	John, s of James & Judith BAKER, Born Dec 25 1802	bap
Mar 20	John, s of William & Hannah HOGKISS, Born Feb 15	bap
Mar 20	Phebe, d of Thomas & Sarah GREEN, Born Jan 1	bap
Mar 20	Ann, d of James & Rebecca WHITEHOUSE	bap
Mar 20	Phebe, d of Isaac & Mary BATE, Born Novr 17 1802	bap
Mar 20	Joseph, s of John & Ann KING, Born Sep 2 1801	bap
Mar 20	David, s of Samuel & Elizabeth MILLS, Born Feb 1	bap
Mar 20	Jacob, s of Jacob & Phebe MILLS, Born Feb 4	bap
Mar 20	Maria, d of Richard & Martha WASSEL	bap
Mar 20	Sarah MILLS	bur
Mar 21	Thomas LION	bur
Mar 21	William, s of William & Mary LAW	bap
Mar 21	Edward, s of Peter & Mary MILLS	bap
Mar 22	Sarah WHITEHOUSE	bur
Mar 27	Julius GRAINGER & Sarah PRICE by Banns	mar

1803

Mar 27	Ann DREW	bur
Mar 27	Joseph WHITEHOUSE	bur
Mar 27	William, s of William & Mary MILLS, Born Jan 18	bap
Mar 27	Sarah, d of Thomas & Charlotte COTTON	bap
Mar 30	Edward MILLS	bur
Mar 30	Ann SMITH	bur
Mar 30	Thomas SHORT & Jane KINDON by Licence	mar
Mar 31	Daniel WHITEHOUSE & Lettice DARBY by Licence	mar
Apr 3	John WHITEHOUSE	bur
Apr 3	Sarah ROBERTS	bur
Apr 3	Mary, d of Thomas & Ann TOMASON	bap
Apr 3	James & Elizabeth, twins of James & Prissilla SHELDON, Born 2^d	bap
Apr 7	Mary HORDEN	bur
Apr 7	Elizabeth GRIFFITHS	bur
Apr 10	William, s of Edward & Margaret FISHER, Born Jan 3	bap
Apr 10	Samuel, s of William & Hannah WHILD, Born Mar 24	bap
Apr 10	Daniel, s of John & Sarah FISHER, Born Mar 11	bap
Apr 11	Jane LAW	bur
Apr 11	Mary OSBORN	bur
Apr 17	Mary, s base d of Ann EDWARDS	bap
Apr 17	Sarah, d of John & Mary TIMMINS, Born Mar 27	bap
Apr 17	Ann, d of Daniel & Sarah MINCHER, Born Mar 12	bap
Apr 24	George, s of William & Sarah SHEREWOOD, Born 1st	bap
Apr 24	John, s of Daniel & Mary WHITEHOUSE, Born 20th	bap
Apr 24	William LAVENDER & Ann HAMPTON by Banns	mar
May 1	Daniel, s of William & Jane WHITEHOUSE, Born Feb 26	bap
May 1	John, a base son of Hannah WHITEHOUSE	bap
May 1	David, s of James & Sarah GUTTRIDGE, Born Mar 8	bap
May 1	Sarah, d of Benjamin & Mary HARTLAND, Born Nov 17, 1802	bap
May 1	Ann, d of Joseph & Martha SMITH, Born Apl 15	bap
May 1	Amos, s of Amos & Francis HODGSKINS, Born Apl 18	bap
May 2	Benjamin LEMM & Mary WHITEHOUSE by Banns	mar
May 8	George, s of Thomas & Mary NASH, Born 1st	bap
May 8	Charlotte, d of John & Ann BARTLAM, Born Apl 2	bap
May 8	Edward, s of Edward & Sarah DUDLEY, Born Apl 17	bap
May 15	Thomas, s of John & Mary NOCK	bap
May 15	Mercy, d of James & Mary DOWERTY	bap
May 22	Lucy, d of Simeon & Hannah CORNFIELD	bap
May 22	Sarah, d of Joseph & Hannah BOTT, Born Apl 24	bap
May 22	Thomas PHILLIPS & Elizabeth FIELD by Banns	mar
May 22	John MARTIN & Mary FISHER by Banns	mar
May 29	Sarah, d of Thomas & Mary LUNN, Born 7th	bap
May 29	John, s of Daniel & Martha WHITEHOUSE, Born 5th	bap
May 29	Sarah, d of Daniel & Mary FISHER	bap
May 29	Ann, d of Hannah HOPKINS	bap
May 29	Elizabeth, d of Jeremiah & Isabella DAVIES, Born 2^d	bap
May 29	Job HICKMANS & Mary PENN by Banns	mar
May 29	George OSELAND & Ann COWDERELL by Banns	mar

May 29	John TIBBITTS & Hannah HUGHES by Banns	mar
Jun 5	Mary, d of Thomas & Mary JERVIS, Born May 13	bap
Jun 5	Phebe, d of Simeon & Elizabeth FISHER, Born May 16	bap
Jun 12	Thomas, s of Thomas & Elizabeth COLLINS, Born May 26	bap
Jun 12	John, s of Richard & Sarah REED, Born 2^d	bap
Jun 14	Ann DERBY	bur
Jun 19	Sarah, d of Richard & Amelia LAW, Born 5	bap
Jun 19	Benjamin DEVEY & Sarah DUDLEY by Banns	mar
Jun 26	Mary, d of Charles & Phillis LAW, Born Feb 13	bap
Jun 30	John DAVIES & Sarah EDWARDS by Licence	mar
Jul 3	Sarah, d of Joseph & Mary YATES, Born June 8	bap
Jul 3	Mary, d of Ambrose & Ruth TIMMINS, Born June 19	bap
Jul 6	Samuel BEARDS & Mary PYATT by Banns	mar
Jul 10	Mary, d of Joseph & Rebecca SMITH, Born Mar 16	bap
Jul 11	John GRANDFIELD & Elizabeth FORD by Banns	mar
Jul 17	Thomas, s of John & Jane TAYLOR, Born 7	bap
Jul 17	Nancy, d of Richard & Mary NICHOLLS, Born Jun 14	bap
Jul 17	Maryann, d of William & Rebecca DAVIES, Born Jan 17	bap
Jul 17	Edward, s of John & Lydia FERNYSILL, Born 15th	bap
Jul 19	William SHELDON	bur
Jul 24	Joseph MILLS & Sarah INGRAM by Banns	mar
Jul 24	Zacharias, d of Thomas & Sarah WALKER, Born 2^d	bap
Jul 24	Sarah, d of James & Jane NOCK, Born Apl 26	bap
Jul 24	John, s of William & Mary DUFFIELD	bap
Jul 24	Phebe, d of William & Rebecca ROUND, Born Apl 24	bap
Jul 24	Samuel, s of Joseph & Sarah JOHNSON	bap
Jul 24	John, s of John & Betty SHORT, Born June 22	bap
Jul 24	Ann, d of Joseph & Sophia BROOKS, Born 11th	bap
Jul 31	John, a base Son of Ann BOTT	bap
Jul 31	James, s of James & Sarah WHITE, Born 26th	bap
Aug 1	William WARD	bur
Aug 4	John SATCHELL	bur
Aug 4	William FISHER	bur
Aug 7	John, s of Job & Ann SMITH, Born July 18	bap
Aug 7	John DOVASON	bur
Aug 7	James WHITE	bur
Aug 7	Joseph, s of Joseph & Martha ROTTON, Born July 14	bap
Aug 7	Ann, d of John & Mary SKIDMORE	bap
Aug 14	John JOHNSON & Mary POWELL by Licence	mar
Aug 14	James HILL & Sarah BISSELL by Banns	mar
Aug 14	Daniel, s of Richard & Sylvia NEWAY, Born July 27	bap
Aug 14	Amelia, d of John & Ann MATTHEWS, Born July 9	bap
Aug 14	Hannah, d of William & Hannah WHITEHOUSE, Born Feb 7	bap
Aug 14	Edward, s of Edward & Mary WILLIAMS, Born May 9	bap
Aug 14	Thomas, s of Thomas & Eleanor WEBB, Born July 24	bap
Aug 14	Mary, d of Thomas & Phebe LLOYD, Born Sep[sic] 29	bap
Aug 14	Thomas, s of Willm & Hannah WHITEHOUSE, Born Jan 1801	bap
Aug 16	James BARNSLEY	bur
Aug 18	William SHELDON	bur

1803

Aug 18	Mary SMITH	bur
Aug 18	John, s of John & Catharine INGRAM, Born July 24 1799	bap
Aug 18	William, s of John & Catharine INGRAM, Born Jan 3 1802	bap
Aug 18	Abraham, s of John & Catharine INGRAM, Born June 29	bap
Aug 18	John, s of Phebe INGRAM, Born July 2	bap
Aug 21	Mary Ann, d of Abraham & Mary JEVONS, Born Aug 14	bap
Aug 21	James, s of William & Mary FISHER, Born July 31	bap
Aug 23	James HILL	bur
Aug 28	Martha, d of Charles & Elizabeth HICKABOTTOM, Born Apl 21	bap
Aug 28	William, S of Thomas & Jane STILLARD, Born 10th	bap
Aug 28	Rebecca, d of Henry & Violette HUGHES	bap
Aug 28	Maria, d of William & Sarah ROUND, born June 25th	bap
Aug 28	William WARD	bur
Sep 1	James OWEN	bur
Sep 1	Edward FIELD	bur
Sep 4	Elizabeth, d of John & Elizabeth WHITEHOUSE	bap
Sep 11	Samuel, s of Joseph & Sarah HICKABOTTOM, Born Aug 24	bap
Sep 11	Patiencegreen, d of Isaac & Elizabeth FISHER, Born May 13	bap
Sep 18	Obadiah, s of Robert & Mary MORRIS	bap
Sep 18	Jane, d of Edward & Sarah CRANAGE	bap
Sep 25	James HOLLIES & Elizabeth INGRAM by Banns	mar
Sep 23[sic]	Sarah WHITEHOUSE	bur
Sep 25	Sarah, d of Abraham & Mary BAKER, Born Sep 3	bap
Sep 28	Thomas HANDS & Ann SHELDON by Banns	mar
Sep 29	John SKELDING & Mary FISHER by Banns	mar
Oct 2	John OWEN & Lucy SMITH, by Licence	mar
Oct 2	James TURNBULL & Mary COTTON by Banns	mar
Oct 2	Samuel, s of Joseph & Hannah GRICE, Born Sep 13	bap
Oct 2	Elizabeth, d of George & Sarah BAYLEY, Born Aug 19	bap
Oct 2	James, s of James & Ann PLANT, Born Sep 16	bap
Oct 2	Maria, d of Thomas & Elizabeth HOLYHEAD, Born Sep 13	bap
Oct 9	Elizabeth, d of Joseph & Mary INGRAM, Born Sep 8	bap
Oct 9	Benjamin, s of Benjn & Elizabeth TWIGG, Born July 4	bap
Oct 9	Penelope ROUND	bur
Oct 16	Mary, d of Thomas & Sophia PARKES, Born Sep 23	bap
Oct 16	Peter, s of Thomas & Ann BODY, Born Mar 24	bap
Oct 16	John, s of Nathan & Mary HILL, Born Sep 29	bap
Oct 16	Sarah, d of Charles & Jane TITLEY, Born Oct 16 1802	bap
Oct 23	Hannah, d of Willm & Sarah WHITEHOUSE	bap
Oct 23	Henry, s of Henry & Esther NORTON, Born Oct 1	bap
Oct 20	Hannah NOCK	bur
Oct 30	William FORD & Elizabeth RUDGE by Banns	mar
Oct 30	David SANDERS & Sophia WHITEHOUSE by Banns	mar
Oct 30	Joseph, s of Joseph & Ruth WORTEN, Born Oct 27	bap
Oct 30	James, s of John & Ann ASTON, Born Aug 14	bap
Oct 30	Ann, d of Peter & Ann MILLS, Born Oct 24	bap
Oct 30	Mary Edwards, d of Richard & Joan DORRALL, Born Oct 13	bap
Oct 30	Sarah, d of Robert & Mary GRANT, Born Oct 1	bap
Oct 30	Sarah Mills, d of James & Mima WHITEHOUSE, Born Oct 2	bap

Nov 4	Joseph WORTEN	bur
Nov 6	Ann, d of Willm & Ann BISSELL, Born Oct 24	bap
Nov 6	Mary THOMAS	bur
Nov 6	John William, s of Phebe COLLINS, Born Oct 29	bap
Nov 13	Sarah, d of Richard & Sarah ASHTON, Born Oct 3	bap
Nov 13	Isaiah MORRIS	bur
— Nov 13	William, s of Amos & Ann BUTTLER, Born Oct 23	bap
Nov 13	Ann, d of Benjn & Barbara SIMCOX, Born Sep 4	bap
Nov 13	James, s of Willm & Nancy MILLARD	bap
↗ Nov 13	Samuel, s of Joseph & Mary HILL, Born Oct 25	bap
Nov 13	Mary, d of Thomas & Sarah TAYLOR, Born Oct 30	bap
Nov 18	Job WHITEHOUSE	bur
Nov 20	Thomas TAYLOR	bur
Nov 20	Mary STANTON	bur
Nov 20	Job, s of Job & Elizabeth BROOKS, Born Sep 1	bap
↜ Nov 20	Sarah, d of Richard & Elizabeth HOLYHEAD, Born Oct 30	bap
Nov 20	Sarah, d of Philip & Hannah EDWARDS, Born Oct 28	bap
Nov 27	John, s of James & Sarah OSBORN	bap
← Nov 27	John, s of Paul & Mary COX	bap
Nov 27	Martha, d of Samuel & Elizabeth COLLINS	bap
Nov 27	Jane, d of Edward & Susannah FRANCIS	bap
Nov 27	Joseph TAYLOR	bur
← Nov 27	Jenny EADES	bur
Nov 27	Mary WHITEHOUSE	bur
Dec 4	Mary, d of Daniel & Mary PRICHETT	bap
Dec 7	Thomas NICHOLLS	bur
Dec 8	Ann WHITEHOUSE	bur
Dec 8	Hannah BOTT	bur
Dec 11	William, s of Philip & Ann WILLIAMS, Born Nov 16	bap
Dec 11	Sarah, d of Edward & Rebecca WHITEHOUSE, Born Nov 23	bap
Dec 11	Thomas BODY	bur
Dec 11	Elizabeth BATE	bur
← Dec 11	George, s of John & Mary WRIGHT, Born Novr 20	bap
Dec 14	James FISHER	bur
Dec 18	Elizabeth PARRISH	bur
Dec 18	Sarah, d of Thomas & Elizabeth BRATT, Born Dec 14	bap
Dec 18	Phebe, d of Daniel & Elizabeth WHITEHOUSE, Born Dec 11	bap
Dec 18	Nancy, d of Edward & Sarah TUCKLEY, Born Novr 7	bap
Dec 25	Eleanor, d of John & Ann WILSON, Born June 23	bap
Dec 25	John, s of William & Ann ELWELL, Born Nov 22	bap
Dec 25	Joseph, s of Joseph & Mary WOOD, Born Oct 13	bap
Dec 25	Joseph, s of Abel & Sarah WHITEHOUSE, Born Nov 2	bap
Dec 25	Benjamin, a base Son of Ann STOKES	bap
Dec 25	John GREENAWAY	bur
↙ Dec 25	William INGRAM & Elizabeth ROBERTS by Banns	mar
Dec 25	Samuel STANTON & Mary DUFFIL by Banns	mar

1804

| Jan 1 | Joseph WHEALE & Sarah CORNFIELD by Banns | mar |

Jan 1	Joel DEELEY & Elizabeth FALKNER by Banns	mar
Jan 1	Elizabeth, d of Benjamin & Ann BLEWITT	bap
Jan 1	Richard, s of Richard & Mary HODGKISS	bap
Jan 1	Josiah, s of Joseph & Elizabeth WHITEHOUSE, Born Apr 14 1803	bap
Jan 1	James, s of Joseph & Sarah SHINGLETON	bap
Jan 1	David, s of Richard & Betty SANDERS, Born Dec 5 1803	bap
Jan 1	Joseph, s of John & Nancy HALL, Born Dec 20 1803	bap
Jan 2	John SIMKINS & Ann SMITH by Banns	mar
Jan 8	William SILVESTER & Mary SOUTHALL by Banns	mar
Jan 8	John HARTER & Elizabeth ALDRIDGE by Banns	mar
Jan 8	Joseph, s of Isaac & Sarah BENNETT, Born Jun 9 1803	bap
Jan 8	Mary, d of Thos & Ann HANDS, Born Dec 22 1803	bap
Jan 8	Joseph, s of John & Hannah TIBBETTS, Born Dec 18 1803	bap
Jan 8	Hannah, d of Thomas & Ann CHAMBERS	bap
Jan 8	Samuel, s of Thomas & Elizabeth FEREDAY, Born Dec 18 1803	bap
Jan 8	Elizabeth, d of Joseph & Mary DUFFIELD, Born Dec 17 1803	bap
Jan 11	Phebe FISHER	bur
Jan 15	Sarah, d of Samuel & Sarah INGRAM, Born 8th	bap
Jan 15	Susannah, d of Elijah & Ann WILCOX, Born Dec 27 1803	bap
Jan 15	Hannah, d of John & Mary HILTON, Born Dec 28 1803	bap
Jan 16	Edward, s of William & Mary PERSHOUSE	bap
Jan 17	Joseph MAWPER & Esther BUXTON by Banns	mar
Jan 20	Edwin Alexander, s of John & Sarah GWIMETT	bap
Jan 22	John, s of Joseph & Ann BUTTLER, born Nov 21 1803	bap
Jan 22	Lydia, d of John & Maria SHAW, born 16th	bap
Jan 22	Amelia, a base d of Sarah BENTON, born July 20 1803	bap
Jan 22	Maria, d of Thos & Sarah BOTT, Dec 21st born 1803	bap
Jan 22	Sarah, d of Edward & Mary FISHER, born Nov 13 1803	bap
Jan 22	Samuel, s of Samuel & Mary MILLS, born 11th	bap
Jan 22	Mary Ann, d of Thomas & Han^h KENEDAY, Born Nov 28 1803	bap
Jan 24	John BOTT	bur
Jan 24	John, s of John & Mary SHELDON, bapt ab^t 4 years old	bap
Jan 27	Joseph, s of Joseph & Hannah SHELDON	bap
Jan 29	Sarah, d of Thos & Mary TIMMINS	bap
Jan 29	Joseph, s of George & Hannah CALLOWAY, Born 18th	bap
Jan 29	Hannah, d of John & Mary JEVONS, Born Dec 22 1803	bap
Jan 29	John SANDERS & Maria TURNER by Banns	mar
Jan 29	Ann WHITEHOUSE	bur
Feb 1	Samuel MILLS	bur
Feb 5	Mary, d of Joseph & Sarah MILLS	bap
Feb 5	Mary, d of William & Mary WHITEHOUSE, Born Dec 26 1803	bap
Feb 5	Thomas WALTERS & Frances CRUMPT by Banns	mar
Feb 5	Lydia FISHER	bur
Feb 9	Nancy NICHOLLS	bur
Feb 10	Joseph SHELDON	bur
Feb 12	Phillis, d of Job & Sarah CASHMORE	bap
Feb 12	Joseph, s of Joseph & Ann DUDLEY	bap
Feb 12	Sarah, d of Joseph & Ann CADDICK	bap

<u>1804</u>

Feb 12	Daniel MILLS	bur
Feb 13	Sarah WHITEHEAD	bur
Feb 15	James WHITEHOUSE	bur
Feb 15	Dianna, d of Amos & Mary TRUEMAN	bap
Feb 15	Richard, s of John & Alse SHEREWOOD	bap
Feb 19	Ann, d of John & Mary GREATRER, Born Jan 27	bap
Feb 19	Peter FISHER	bur
Feb 20	Daniel HICKMANS	bur
Feb 20	Samuel, s of Joseph & Elizabeth SHEREWOOD	bap
Feb 21	Thomas SWIFT	bur
Feb 26	William, s of John & Hannah KING	bap
Feb 26	James, s of Thomas & Ann WOODALL	bap
Feb 26	Catharine, d of Thomas & Ann SHELDON	bap
Feb 26	Hannah HEYWOOD	bur
Feb 27	John FISHER & Elizabeth SHELDON by Banns	mar
Feb 28	William SWIFT	bur
Mar 4	Thomas ELWELL	bur
Mar 9	Sarah WHITEHOUSE	bur
Mar 9	Thomas, s of Robert & Susannah JONES	bap
Mar 11	Joseph, s of Joseph & Susannah TRANTER	bap
Mar 11	Ann, d of Thomas & Ann SHORT	bap
Mar 11	Mary, d of John & Elizabeth HORTON	bap
Mar 11	Sarah, d of Elijah & Prissilla WHITEHOUSE	bap
Mar 11	Mary, d of William & Elizabeth BELCHER	bap
Mar 12	Daniel GUTTRIDGE	bur
Mar 12	William INGRAM & Prissilla REED by Banns	mar
Mar 12	Abraham WHITEHOUSE	bur
Mar 22	Benjamin NICKLIN	bur
Mar 25	George, s of Robert & Ann CALLIER	bap
Mar 25	Hannah, d of Thomas & Hannah RABONE	bap
Mar 25	Mary, d of Thomas & Susannah PASKIN	bap
Mar 25	Abraham JUKES	bur
Mar 25	Thomas COX	bur

A Transcript of the Register of Tipton alias Tibbington was Exhibited into the Deans Visitation held in the Court of Lichfield being on June 27 1804

Mar 27	Joseph SHORTHOUSE	bur
Mar 27	John, s of John & Mary BLACKHAM	bap
Mar 27	Richard, s of Benjamin & Sarah FEREDAY	bap
Mar 29	John TURNER & Hannah BINKS by Banns	mar
Mar 29	Sarah, d of Samuel & Margaret BAYLEY	bap
Mar 29	John, s of John & Mary EVANS, Born Feb 26	bap
Apr 1	Sarah, d of James & Sarah CHATER	bap
Apr 1	Samuel, s of Daniel & Maria PARTRIDGE	bap
Apr 1	John, s of David & Sophia WHITEHOUSE	bap
Apr 1	Mary, d of John & Elizabeth PRESTON	bap
Apr 1	Sarah, d of George & Ann TURNER	bap
Apr 1	William, s of Thomas & Rosanna HAZLEDINE	bap
Apr 1	Phebe, d of Richard & Sarah GRIFFITHS	bap
Apr 1	Ambrose, s of Job & Mary WHITEHOUSE	bap

1804

Apr 1	Thomas, s of Thomas & Rachael RYLEY	bap
Apr 1	John, s of Edward & Ann HARRIS	bap
Apr 1	Elizabeth, d of Daniel & Rosanna SHELDON	bap
Apr 1	Thomas, s of Daniel & Rosanna SHELDON, About 2 years old	bap
Apr 1	William, s of Joseph & Joice TURNER, Born Mar 9	bap
Apr 1	Elizabeth, d of Joseph & Ann CARTWRIGHT, Born Jan 20	bap
Apr 2	Thomas SOUTHALL & Mary WHITTEN by Banns	mar
Apr 3	Joseph Taylor, s of Samuel & Sarah HODGKINS, Born Dec 16th 1803	bap
Apr 4	Mary WHITEHOUSE	bur
Apr 8	Hannah, d of John & Mary HORTON	bap
Apr 8	Daniel, s of Abraham & Susanna MILLS	bap
Apr 8	Susanna, d of Thomas & Susanna LEECH	bap
Apr 8	Rebecca COLE	bur
Apr 12	Joseph WRIGHT & Mary WHITEHOUSE by Licence	mar
Apr 12	Elizabeth INGRAM	bur
Apr 15	Samuel, s of Samuel & Mary HICKMAN	bap
Apr 15	Hannah, d of William & Mary SHELDON	bap
Apr 15	Joseph, s of William & Mary SHELDON	bap
Apr 15	James, s of Cornelius & Esther BAKER	bap
Apr 15	Mary, d of William & Catharine SMITH	bap
Apr 15	Elizabeth MILLS	bur
Apr 22	William, s of John & Mary JOHNSON, Born Feb 24	bap
Apr 22	Richard, s of Joseph & Elizabeth TONKS	bap
Apr 22	Eliza, d of William & Phebe BRAINE	bap
Apr 22	Mary, d of John & Cretia KIRKHAM	bap
Apr 22	John, s of Thomas & Elizabeth DANKS, Born Mar 29	bap
Apr 22	Nancy, d of Edward & Mary DANGERFIELD, Born Mar 24	bap
Apr 22	Joseph, s of Thomas & Mary BENNITT, Born Feb 24	bap
Apr 22	Joseph NOCK	bur
Apr 25	Elizabeth BANKING	bur
Apr 29	Richard PINNOCK & Rosanna BRITTIN	mar
Apr 29	William FIELD	bur
Apr 29	Joseph, s of George & Elizabeth DEELEY	bap
Apr 29	Martha, d of William & Mary LOWE	bap
Apr 29	William, s of George & Elizabeth BALL	bap
Apr 29	Jane, d of Jane PIERCE	bap
Apr 29	Joseph, s of Joshua & Hannah PARTRIDGE	bap
Apr 29	Thomas, s of John & Martha BUMFORD, Born Feb 17	bap
Apr 29	John Worton, s of Jos^h & Hannah ROUND, Born Mar 31	bap
May 1	Phebe WHITEHOUSE	bur
May 1	Daniel CALLOWAY	bur
May 1	Joseph, s of James & Sarah LUNN, Born Mar 18	bap
May 1	Richard Edward, s of Richard & Lucy DAVIES, Born Mar 25	bap
May 1	Mary, d of David & Mary SMITH, Born Feb 12 1803	bap
May 2	Ann BISSELL	bur
May 6	Edward, s of William & Sarah SHEREWOOD	bap
May 6	Maria, d of John & Sarah TIMMINS	bap
May 13	William, s of Henry & Ann JONES	bap

1804

May 13	Thomas, s of Richard & Ann COOK	bap
May 13	Mary, d of Richard & Elizabeth WILSON	bap
May 14	Thomas DAVIES	bur
May 14	William, s of Richard & Elizabeth BOWEN	bap
May 14	Mary, d of Samuel & Mary STANTON	bap
May 14	Mary STANTON	bur
May 17	Sarah FISHER	bur
May 20	Edward ROWLEY & Sarah BAKER by Banns	mar
May 20	George, s of George & Sarah COOPER	bap
May 20	James, s of James & Ann WORTON, Born May 2	bap
May 20	Susannah, d of James & Mary WHITEHOUSE, Born Apl 28	bap
May 20	Catharine, d of Isaac & Elizabeth WHITEHOUSE	bap
May 20	Abraham, s of Abraham & Sarah WHITEHOUSE	bap
May 20	Elizabeth, d of Isaac & Elizabeth WHITEHOUSE	bap
May 20	Mary, d of William & Sarah WORTON, Born Apl 18	bap
May 20	Thomas, s of Joseph & Jane WHITEHOUSE	bap
May 25	Richard BATE	bur
May 27	Benjamin, s of Benjamin & Ann MATHERS	bap
May 27	Ann, d of Benjamin & Ann MATHERS	bap
May 27	Hannah, d of Abraham & Elizabeth SHELDON)	bap
May 27	Sarah, d of Abraham & Elizabeth SHELDON) twines	bap
May 27	Francis, s of Joseph & Mary ADDENBROOKE	bap
May 28	Richard LAUD & Martha STEVENTON by Banns	mar
Apr 30	Samuel COLLINS	bur
May 30	Samuel BATE	bur
Mar 30	Sarah ROWLEY	bur
Jun 3	Edward, s of Thomas & Ann DUDLEY	bap
Jun 3	Benjamin, s of Thomas & Ellin LAW	bap
Jun 5	Robert PERSMORE	bur
Jun 6	Elizabeth, d of George & Mary MARSHALL, Born Jan 18	bap
Jun 10	John HALL	bur
Jun 10	Ann, d of Joseph & Phebe STANTON	bap
Jun 10	Maria, d of Thomas & Jane SMITH, Born Apl 2	bap
Jun 10	William, s of Eutychus & Phebe FISHER	bap
Jun 10	Ann, d of Thomas & Sarah KIRKHAM	bap
Jun 10	Elizabeth, d of Joseph & Jane CALLOWAY, Born May 21	bap
Jun 12	Edward WHITEHOUSE	bur
Jun 12	Philip MARTIN	bur
Jun 15	David DAVIES	bur
Jun 17	Phebe, d of William & Sarah WHITEHOUSE	bap
Jun 17	Thomas, s of John & Catharine LANKFORD	bap
Jun 17	Thomas, s of Benjamin & Ann BLUNT	bap
Jun 19	John GRIFFITHS	bur
Jun 24	John SHERWOOD & Sarah PERRY by Banns	mar
Jun 24	Rhoda, d of John & Sarah NEWEY	bap
Jun 24	Ann, d of Thomas & Lydia TAYLOR	bap
Jun 24	Amelia FISHER	bur
Jun 26	Mary DOUGHTY	bur
Jul 1	Daniel BATE & Sarah HADLEY by Banns	mar

1804

Jul 1	Nancy, d of Richard & Isbell TAYLOR	bap
Jul 1	Sarah, d of Joseph & Mary NIGHTINGALE, Born June 19	bap
Jul 1	Joseph MILLS	bur
Jul 4	Sarah NOCK	bur
Jul 5	James BURTON	bur
Jul 5	Charles LEAKIN	bur
Jul 6	Caleb WELCH	bur
Jul 8	Mary STANTON	bur
Jul 8	William, s of Samuel & Elizabeth WRIGHT	bap
Jul 8	Elizabeth, d of Richard & Rachael GOWER, Born June 9	bap
Jul 10	Richard BUNCH	bur
Jul 11	Andrew PARTRIDGE	bur
Jul 15	James, s of John & Nancy SPITTLE, Born Feb 8	bap
Jul 15	Sarah MILLER	bur
Jul 15	Carrolina OSBORNE	bur
Jul 19	William ALCOCK & Elizabeth EDWARDS by Licence	mar
Jul 24	Abraham, s of Isaac & Hannah DERBY	bap
Jul 22	Sarah, d of Benjamin & Sarah BATE	bap
Jul 22	Mary, d of Elias & Elizabeth AKER	bap
Jul 22	John, s of John & Mary ASTON	bap
Jul 22	Maria, d of John & Nancy SHENSTON	bap
Jul 22	John, s of Samuel & Jane STOKES	bap
Jul 24	Abraham, s of George & Mary FISHER	bap
Jul 24	John GWINNETT	bur
Jul 26	Joseph EVANS	bur
Jul 26	Frances, d of John & Sarah EVANS	bap
Jul 29	Phebe, d of John & Elizabeth LIESTER	bap
Jul 29	Elizabeth, d of William & Mary SHORTHOUSE	bap
Jul 30	Eli JEVON & Elizabeth ASTLEY by Banns	mar
Jul 30	Samuel LAWLEY & Susannah TAYLOR by Banns	mar
Jul 30	Joseph JONES & Mary KEMSTOR by Banns	mar
Aug 1	Charles Iliff AUSTIN	bur
Aug 1	Phebe LLOYD	bur
Aug 5	Elizabeth, d of John & Elizabeth SANDERS, Born Mar 30	bap
Aug 5	Henry, s of Edward & Sarah TAYLOR	bap
Aug 5	Rachael FEREDAY	bur
Aug 9	Thomas BATE	bur
Aug 10	John BOYLE	bur
Aug 10	Edwin STOCKWIN	bur
Aug 12	Thomas, s of Thomas & Ann PINCHER	bap
Aug 12	Thomas WOODERTS	bur
Aug 16	Rachel ROUND	bur
Aug 16	Joseph PEARSON	bur
Aug 17	John FISHER	bur
Aug 19	James, s of James & Ann WHITEHOUSE, Born July 21	bap
Aug 19	Joseph, s of Joseph & Elizabeth GALLOP, Born July 22	bap
Aug 19	Ann, a base d of Mary SHELDON	bap
Aug 19	James, s of John & Mary ROWLEY, Born July 23	bap
Aug 19	Samuel MORRIS	bur

<u>1804</u>

Aug 20	Benjamin ROUND	bur
Aug 20	Edward, s of Isaac & Jane MILLS	bap
Aug 21	Mariann EDWARDS	bur
Aug 22	Sarah HICKMANS	bur
Aug 23	Thomas WHITEHOUSE	bur
Aug 26	Stephen, s of John & Sarah JONES, Born 19th	bap
Sep 2	John POWELL & Hannah JOHNSON by Licence	mar
Sep 2	Sarah, d of Thomas & Mary ARCOT	bap
Sep 2	James, s of Edward & Sarah GRIFFITHS	bap
Sep 2	James, s of James & Elizabeth DUFFIELD	bap
Sep 2	Elizabeth, d of James & Sarah WHITE	bap
Sep 2	Phebe, d of Samuel & Mary PASKIN	bap
Sep 3	Moses COLLINS & Ann MASON by Banns	mar
Sep 6	James WHITEHOUSE	bur
Sep 9	Daniel, s of William & Sarah EDGE, Born July 26	bap
Sep 9	Sarah FELICITY, base d of Hannah FISHER	bap
Sep 9	Edward, s of John & Jane WILLIAMS, Born Aug 9	bap
Sep 9	Charlotte, d of William & Elizabeth FORD	bap
Sep 11	George SHELDON & Sarah BROOKS by Banns	mar
Sep 16	John, s of John & Mary SHELDON	bap
Sep 16	Maria, d of Richard & Elizabeth TURNER	bap
Sep 16	William, s of William & Elizabeth GRISNILL	bap
Sep 16	Joseph WILLIS	bur
Sep 17	Sarah ROWLEY	bur
Sep 23	George HOWELL & Sarah HICKMAN by Banns	mar
Sep 23	Lewis, s of Joseph & Elizabeth WILLIAMS	bap
Sep 25	William BLEWITT	bur
Sep 25	Mary HANDS	bur
Sep 30	Sarah & Elizabeth, twin d of Willm & Hannah WHITEHOUSE	bap
Sep 30	John Thomas, s of Thomas & Mary DANGERFIELD	bap
Sep 30	Mary, d of William & Mary MILLS, Born Sep 21	bap
Oct 3	Jenny ROBINSON	bur
Oct 7	David, s of Richard & Mary FOSTER	bap
Oct 7	Joseph, s of John & Sarah WHEALE	bap
Oct 7	Mary, d of Amos & Frances HODGSKINS, Born 5th	bap
Oct 14	Joseph, s of Richard & Mary JUKES	bap
Oct 15	William MINCHER & Prudence MARTIN by Banns	mar
Oct 21	John LAWRENCE & Ann WATTON by Banns	mar
Oct 21	William, s of Thomas & Ann TOMLINSON, Born 20th	bap
Oct 21	Phebe, d of Immanuel & Ann DERBY, Born Sep 30	bap
Oct 28	Pemiler, d of Joseph & Rachael DUFFIELD	bap
Oct 28	Hannah, d of Joseph & Elizabeth TILLEY	bap
Oct 28	Rosehannah, d of John & Mary JONES, Born Sep 27	bap
Oct 28	Mary MILLS	bur
Nov 1	Sarah CADDICK	bur
Nov 4	Hannah, d of Nathaniel & Susannah WEBB	bap
Nov 4	Mary, d of Sarah BARNS	bap
Nov 5	Thomas PRICE & Mary WEBB by Banns	mar
Nov 11	Elizabeth & Lucy, twin d of Joseph & Elizabeth CORBETT	bap

1804

Nov 11	Abraham, s of Benjamin & Rachel WHITEHOUSE, Born Oct 27	bap
Nov 13	Martin BRAWN & Sarah HICKABOTTOM by Banns	mar
Nov 18	John, s of Henry & Mary PITT, Born Oct 11	bap
Nov 18	Ann GREENAWAY	bur
Nov 21	Hannah BAKER	bur
Nov 25	Sarah, d of George & Sarah SHELDON	bap
Nov 25	John, s of Joseph & Elizabeth SHELDON	bap
Nov 29	Samuel NIGHTINGALE & Sarah WILLETTS by Banns	mar
Nov 29	Mary CADDICK	bur
Dec 2	Joseph HARTLAND & Elizabeth CAUSER by Banns	mar
Dec 2	Thomas BAKER	bur
Dec 2	Abraham FELLOWS	bur
Dec 6	Thomas WINN [entry inserted]	bur
Dec 9	David, s of Thomas & Ann FEREDAY	bap
Dec 16	Edward, s of Edward & Sarah COX, Born Nov 19	bap
Dec 16	Sarah, d of James & Mary ASTON, Born Nov 17	bap
Dec 18	John LEONARD & Sarah CADDICK, by Licence	mar
Dec 19	Thomas KENDRICK	bur
Dec 22	Henry HUDSON & Mary SMITH by Licence	mar
Dec 23	Samuel, s of John & Elizabeth FISHER, Born 15th	bap
Dec 23	Henry, s of Jesse & Mary WHITEHOUSE, Born 9th	bap
Dec 23	Clarissa, d of James & Phebe BATE	bap
Dec 23	Samuel, s of James & Deborah NOCK, Born Nov 4	bap
Dec 25	Abraham, s of Benjamin & Mary WALTERS, Born Nov 24	bap
Dec 25	Samuel, s of John & Elizabeth SMITH, Born Nov 27	bap
Dec 25	Elizabeth, d of William & Elizabeth DERBY	bap
Dec 30	Joseph LUNN	bur

[Note in a different hand:] The Marr Reg commenced in 1754 ends with entry dated 18 Dec 1804

1805

Jan 6	Richard JONES & Ann COPE by Banns	bap
Jan 6	Richard, s of William & Prissilla INGRAM	bap
Jan 6	Hannah, d of Samuel & Maria SIMCOX	bap
Jan 6	Thomas, s of James & Nancy HORTON, Born Dec 1 1804	bap
Jan 6	John OSBORNE	bur
Jan 9	William HARRISON	bur
Jan 13	Richard GWINNETT	bur
Jan 13	Elizabeth, d of William & Elizabeth BRATT, Born 4th	bap
Jan 13	Joseph, s of Richard & Sarah REED, Born Dec 7, 1804	bap
Jan 15	Thomas HODGKINS	bur
Jan 17	Mary OWEN	bur
Jan 20	Benjamin, s of John & Sarah BENNITT	bap
Jan 20	Mary, d of William & Letice SHELDON	bap
Jan 21	Thomas POOL & Jane GILLAM by Banns	mar
Jan 22	John PERRY	bur
Jan 27	Sarah, d of Joseph & Ann SMITH	bap
Jan 27	Benjamin, s of Edar & Mary TIMMINS	bap
Jan 27	Charles, s of Joseph & Ann SMITH	bap

1805

Jan 27	John, s of William & Phebe HODGKINS, Born Dec 26 1804	bap
Jan 27	John, s of James & Sophia JONES	bap
Jan 27	Sarah, d of Thomas & Susannah TAYLOR	bap
Feb 3	Thomas, s of John & Maria SANDERS	bap
Feb 3	Mary, d of Daniel & Mary WHITEHOUSE, Born Jan 24	bap
Feb 3	James, s of John & Nancy DOUGHTY	bap
Feb 3	Sarah, d of Thomas & Betty EDWARDS	bap
Feb 3	Sarah, d of James & Hannah FISHER	bap
Feb 3	Isaac, s of Isaac & Sarah BENNETT, Born Dec 18 1804	bap
Feb 3	Ann, d of John & Ann ADAMS	bap
Feb 3	Thomas, s of Charles & Susannah PERRY	bap
Feb 3	Phebe, d of Thomas & Elizabeth TILLEY	bap
Feb 3	Betty, d of Richard & Mary NICHOLDS	bap
Feb 3	Nancy, d of Samuel & Mary TAYLOR	bap
Feb 3	Sarah, d of William & Hannah WILDE	bap
Feb 3	George FISHER	bur
Feb 5	John REYNOLDS	bur
Feb 6	Nancy, d of Edward & Elizabeth FEREDAY	bap
Feb 6	Hannah WHITEHOUSE	bur
Feb 6	Ambrose, s of John & Mary BLACKHAM, Born Jan 16	bap
Feb 6	Ann, d of William & Mary LAW, Born July 1804	bap
Feb 7	Mary COCKRAN	bur
Feb 10	Mary Ann, d of John & Hannah POWELL	bap
Feb 12	John COLLINS	bur
Feb 17	Joseph, s of Joseph & Sarah HUGHES	bap
Feb 17	David, s of Peter & Ann HICKMAN	bap
Feb 17	Daniel, s of Daniel & Martha WHITEHOUSE, Born Jan 3	bap
Feb 17	Nancy, d of John & Hannah TIBBITTS, Born Jan 19	bap
Feb 17	Sarah, d of Isaac & Ann SMITH, Born June 4 1804	bap
Feb 17	Edward GOODMAN	bur
Feb 17	Ann PASKIN	bur
Feb 17	Ann OWEN	bur
Feb 17	John SHELDON	bur
Feb 17	Clarissa BATE	bur
Feb 19	Samuel BLASE	bur
Feb 24	Rebecca, d of Thomas & Rebecca HARRIS	bap
Feb 24	Sarah, d of John & Hannah POTTS	bap
Feb 24	Susannah, d of Thomas & Sarah EVANS	bap
Feb 24	John, s of John & Maria PLANT	bap
Feb 24	Martha, d of Nicklis & Sarah WOOD, Born Jan 29	bap
Feb 26	Thomas HAND	bur
Mar 3	Edward, s of Samuel & Susannah FEREDAY	bap
Mar 3	Henry, s of Thomas & Sarah PARKES	bap
Mar 3	Mary BAGLEY	bur
Mar 6	Abraham INGRAM	bur
Mar 6	William, s of Joseph & Catharine MILLS, Born Feb 5	bap
Mar 10	Esther, d of Charles & Elizabeth HICKABOTTOM	bap
Mar 10	Martha WHITEHOUSE	bur
Mar 10	Joseph COTTRILL	bur

1805

Mar 10	Sarah, d of Isaac & Ann LAW	bap
Mar 17	Mary Maria, d of Thomas & Sarah ADAMS	bap
Mar 17	Amelia, d of Thomas & Lydia TAYLOR	bap
Mar 17	William, s of John & Charlotte WARD, Born Feb 14	bap
Mar 17	William, s of James & Martha BARTLAM	bap
Mar 17	Hannah, d of Richard & Mary HODGSKISS	bap
Mar 17	Phebe, d of Edward & Phebe WHITEHOUSE	bap
Mar 19	Phebe WHITEHOUSE	bur
Mar 19	Nancy, d of Joseph & Mary GRIFFITHS, Born Apl 13, 1804	bap
Mar 24	Maria, d of James & Rebecca WHITEHOUSE	bap
Mar 24	Esther, d of Joseph & Martha SMITH	bap
Mar 24	Edward, s of Samuel & Sarah THORNEYCROFT, Born Nov 19 1803	bap
Mar 24	George, s of Daniel & Elizabeth GORTON	bap
Mar 24	William, s of John & Maria SHAW	bap
Mar 24	Thomas, s of Jeremiah & Isabella DAVIS	bap
Mar 24	Richard, s of William & Sarah HARTILL	bap
Mar 24	William, s of Daniel & Esther GRIFFITHS	bap
Mar 24	Hannah, d of Thomas & Sarah BILL	bap
Mar 24	Joseph TATE	bur
Mar 25	John ELWELL	bur
Mar 29	John BATE & Mary DARBY by Banns	mar
Mar 29	Henry HAZLEHURST	bur
Mar 31	James, s of Francis & Sarah PICKARD	bap
Mar 31	Samuel, s of James & Sarah BAYLEY	bap
Mar 31	William WOOD	bur
Mar 31	William BLASÉ	bur
Mar 31	Enoch, s of Benjamin & Hannah PARTRIDGE	bap
Mar 31	Benjamin, s of William & Phebe BISSELL	bap
Mar 31	Henry, s of Thomas & Mary MARSH	bap
Apr 2	Elizabeth CALLOP	bur
Apr 3	John WILLIAMS	bur
Apr 7	Catharine WHITEHOUSE	bur
Apr 7	Samuel SMITH	bur
Apr 7	Hannah, d of John & Phebe MILLS, Born Feb 27	bap
Apr 10	Joseph WHEAL	bur
Apr 11	Ann SHELDON	bur
Apr 14	Samuel, s of Samuel & Ann EDWARDS	bap
Apr 14	Sarah, d of William & Sarah TUCKLEY, Born Mar 22	bap
Apr 14	Elizabeth, a base d of Sarah SKELETON, 4 years old	bap
Apr 14	Mary Ann, d of John & Phebe COTTRILL	bap
Apr 14	Hannah, d of Thomas & Sarah BLASE, Born Mar 31	bap
Apr 14	Abraham, s of Hedar & Mary TIMMINS	bap
Apr 14	Samuel, s of Samuel & Elizabeth GROVES, Born Mar 28	bap
Apr 14	Elizabeth, d of Joseph & Elizabeth JEWKES	bap
Apr 14	Ann, d of Thomas & Mary PAINE, Born Mar 14	bap
Apr 14	Phebe, d of Edward & Margarett FISHER, Born Feb 4	bap
Apr 15	Samuel BATE & Nancy ALLEN by Banns	mar
Apr 18	Abraham PARKES	bur

1805

Apr 21	Ann, d of Abraham & Ann BATE	bap
Apr 21	Harriott, d of John & True WHITEHOUSE	bap
Apr 21	Cathrine SHELDON	bur
Apr 24	John FEREDAY	bur
Apr 24	Sarah FEREDAY, baptized about 28 years old	bur
Apr 27	Ellis OWEN & Jane FISHER by Banns	mar
Apr 28	Isaac, s of Isaac & Mary BATE	bap
Apr 28	William, s of Joseph & Sarah HICKABOTTOM	bap
Apr 28	Esther, d of Daniel & Jane RHODEN	bap
Apr 28	Edward, s of Joseph & Rebecca SMITH	bap
Apr 28	Rebecca, d of Abraham & Mary JEVON, Born Mar 31	bap
Apr 28	Ann WHITEHOUSE	bur
Apr 28	Mary SMITH *[Entry squeezed in]*	bur
Apr 30	Joseph STEVENSON & Rose BURTON by Licence	mar
Apr 30	Hannah WHEAL	bur
➤ Apr 30	Timothy, s of Edward & Lucy TURNER	bap
⇗ May 1	Mary HICKMANS	bur
May 3	John FIELDHOUSE	bur
May 5	James, s of Daniel & Sarah THOMPSON	bap
May 5	Joice, d of John & Elizabeth WILLIAMS	bap
May 5	James, s of Joseph & Rachael HIPKINS, Born May 29 1804	bap
➤ May 5	Elizabeth, d of Thomas & Hannah RAYBONE	bap
May 5	Sarah, d of Thomas & Phebe WHITEHOUSE,	bap
➤ May 5	Thomas, s of James & Habijul PRICE	bap
May 5	Phebe, d of Joseph & Rachel HIPKINS, Born July 26 1802	bap
May 5	Isaac LAW	bur
May 5	Sarah SHELDON	bur
May 6	John PARKES & Sarah POWESS by Banns	mar
May 9	Joseph, s of John & Elizabeth SKIDMORE, Born Aug 11 1803	bap
May 12	Hannah, d of Edward & Lettice WHITEHOUSE	bap
➤ May 12	Mary, d of William & Elizabeth TURNER	bap
May 12	Elizabeth, d of Abraham & Ann LAW	bap
➤ May 12	Hannah, d of Thomas & Sarah GREEN	bap
May 12	William CLEATON	bur
➤ May 12	James GUTTRIDGE	bur
May 12	Maria FEREDAY	bur
➤ May 12	William, s of John & Sarah ROWLEY	bap
May 12	Sarah, d of John & Hannah ASTON	bap
May 12	Esther, d of William & Jane WHITEHOUSE	bap
May 12	John, s of Joseph & Sarah SHINGLETON	bap
➤ May 12	Homer, d of William & Prudence MINCHER	bap
➤ May 12	Thomas, s of Paul & Mary COX	bap
May 12	Mary Ann, d of William & Mary WILLIAMS	bap
➤ May 12	Sarah, d of Nathan & Mary HILL	bap
May 12	Mary CARTWRIGHT	bur
May 14	Jane MOESLEY	bur
May 16	Joseph WHITEHOUSE	bur
May 16	James BAKER	bur
May 19	Thomas, s of John & Mary BISSELL, Born Feb 25 1802	bap

1805

May 19	Isaac, s of John & Mary BISSELL, Born Mar 11 1803	bap
May 19	Susanna, d of John & Mary BISSELL, Born Nov 9 1804	bap
May 19	Sarah CUTTLER	bur
May 19	Sarah JONES	bur
May 20	William EYARE & Frances ROUND by Banns	mar
May 20	William ASTON & Fanny HICKIN by Banns	mar
May 21	Elizabeth EVANS	bur
May 22	Sarah SHELDON	bur
May 23	Ann Maria HALL	bur
May 24	William JONES	bur
May 26	Laban, s of Henry & Violette HUGHES	bap
May 26	Abraham, s of Abraham & Maria PARKES	bap
May 26	Sarah, d of James & Susanna DALE	bap
May 26	Elizabeth, d of Edward & Sarah DUDLEY, Born Feb 21	bap
May 26	Edward WHITEHOUSE	bap
May 27	William WILLINGTON	bur
May 29	Sarah ASTON	bur
Jun 2	John, s of Joseph & Mary SMITH, Born Apl 26	bap
Jun 2	Daniel, s of Daniel & Lettice WHITEHOUSE	bap
Jun 2	George, s of Thomas & Lettice THORNECROFT, Born Oct 9 1803	bap
Jun 2	Joseph, s of Ambrose & Ruth TIMMINS, Born May 13	bap
Jun 2	Aaron, s of Moses & Sarah BUTTLER	bap
Jun 2	John, s of James & Sarah HANCOCKS, Born May 11	bap
Jun 2	Phebe, d of John & Ann LAW	bap
Jun 2	William, s of Benjamin & Ann MATTHEWS, Born May 17	bap
Jun 2	William, s of Thomas & Lettice THORNECROFT, Born Mar 13	bap
Jun 3	James SHINGLETON	bur
Jun 4	Thomas HILL & Hannah LEISTER	mar
Jun 4	Phebe WHITEHOUSE	bur
Jun 6	John DREW	bur
Jun 12	Mary CORNFIELD	bur
Jun 12	Nancy JEWKES	bur
Jun 13	Phebe LAW	bur
Jun 16	Sarah, d of Richard & Selvy NEWEY	bap
Jun 16	John, s of John & Hannah CUMSTONE	bap
Jun 16	John, s of James & Rosanna WALLIS	bap
Jun 17	John LATHAM & Catharine FISHER by Banns	mar
Jun 17	John WETHAM & Sarah TURNER by Banns	mar
Jun 17	William DUFFIELD & Betsy PARKES by Banns	mar
Jun 18	Sarah WHITEHOUSE	bur
Jun 21	John THOMAS & Prudence NIGHTINGALE by Banns	mar
Jun 21	Nancy GRIFFITHS	bur
Jun 22	Joseph TEATOM	bur
Jun 23	Mary, d of Samuel & Jane HARTSORN, Born May 1	bap
Jun 23	Rosehannah, d of James & Lucy DERBY	bap
Jun 23	Ann, d of David & Mary PHILLIPS	bap
Jun 23	Mary PRESTON	bur
Jun 24	Ambrose BLACKHAM	bur

Jun 25	Sarah INGRAM		bur
Jun 26	Edward MILLS		bur
Jun 29	Elizabeth NICKLIN		bur
Jun 30	Naomia, s[sic] of Abr^ham & Nancy GEORGE		bap
Jun 30	Joseph, s of Benjamin & Sarah COX		bap
Jun 30	Leah, d of Daniel & Sarah MINCHER		bap
Jun 30	Charlotte, d of William & Maria DANKS		bap
Jun 30	Thomas ALLENDER		bur
Jun 30	Samuel ROBERTS		bur
Jul 4	George ROBERTS		bur
Jul 7	Isaac, s of William & Elizabeth STANTON, Born June 12		bap
Jun 7	Samuel WHITEHOUSE		bur
Jul 12	Joseph GRIFFITHS		bur
Jul 14	Joseph, s of Joseph & Eleanor WEBB, Born Jun 21		bap
Jul 14	Ann, d of Abel & Hannah CADDICK		bap
Jul 14	Thomas, s of Samuel & Margarett BAYLEY		bap
Jul 14	Elizabeth, d of William & Phebe MORRIS, Born May 9		bap
Jul 14	Mary Ann, d of William & Rebecca ROUND, Born Mar 22		bap
Jul 14	Isaiah ALDWRIGHT		bur
Jul 15	Charles RICHARDSON & Mary HORTON by Banns		mar
Jul 21	Phebe, d of Peter & Mary MILLS, Born 8th		bap
Jul 21	William, s of William & Dinah HODGSKISS		bap
Jul 21	James, s of Thomas & Elizabeth HUGHES, Born Apl 15		bap
Jul 21	Elizabeth, d of John & Ann NEWTON		bap
Jul 21	Amelia, d of Henry & Mary NOCK, Born 14th		bap
Jul 21	Isaac WINNINGTON		bur
Jul 28	Richard HARPER & Ann PORTER by Banns		mar
Jul 28	Mary, d of John & Sarah FISHER		bap
Jul 28	William, s of Thomas & Mary LAPPAGE		bap
Jul 28	James, s of Thomas & Hannah HEELEY		bap
Jul 28	Sarah, d of Richard & Joan DORRALL		bap
Jul 28	David, s of William & Sarah WALKER		bap
Jul 29	Joseph CLEMSON & Ann BAKER by Banns		mar
Jul 30	Samuel FEREDAY		bur
Aug 2	John LINFORD		bur
Aug 2	John FISHER		bur
Aug 4	Elijah HUNT & Ann DUDLEY by Banns		mar
Aug 4	Richard, s of Richard & Hannah Baker BIRD		bap
Aug 4	Maria, d of Joseph & Elizabeth HODGKINS		bap
Aug 4	Ann, d of James & Prissilla SHELDON		bap
Aug 4	Muschamp, s of David & Mary JEVON		bap
Aug 4	Ann, d of Richard & Mary PASKIN		bap
Aug 4	Mary, d of James & Sarah HOSBORN		bap
Aug 5	Hannah BLAZE		bur
Aug 6	Thomas FEREDAY		bur
Aug 9	Thomas WHITEHOUSE		bur
Aug 9	John HODGSKINS		bur
Aug 11	Joseph WHITEHOUSE & Nancy LAW by Banns		mar
Aug 11	William, s of John & Sarah SHEREWOOD, Born June 24		bap

1805

Aug 11	John, s of Joseph & Jane WHITEHOUSE	bap
Aug 11	Rachael, d of Edward & Phebe WHITEHOUSE	bap
Aug 11	Henry, s of Joseph & Mary ADDENBROOKE	bap
Aug 12	Sarah BOTT	bur
Aug 13	Samuel FEREDAY	bur
Aug 14	Sarah PERKES	bur
Aug 14	Ann, d of James & Elizabeth HOLLIES	bap
Aug 14	Maria, d of Richard & Amelia FISHER	bap
Aug 14	Sarah, d of Samuel & Sarah PERKES	bap
Aug 16	Elizabeth WALL	bur
— Aug 16	John HODGKINS	bur
Aug 16	William BALL	bur
Aug 18	Richard, s of James & Catharine WORTON, about 19 years near old	bap
Aug 18	Martha, d of David & Hannah GRICE	bap
Aug 18	Rosehannah, d of David & Hannah GRICE	bap
Aug 18	Catharine, d of John & Sushannah WILKES	bap
Aug 23	James FISHER	bur
— Aug 25	Sarah, d of James & Ann PERRY	bap
Aug 25	Ann PASKIN	bur
— Aug 25	George, s of Richard & Ann GARBITT	bap
Aug 25	Thomas, s of Thomas & Hannah JAMES	bap
Aug 25	Thomas, s of Samson & Catharine AUSTIN, Born July 27	bap
— Aug 25	Elizabeth, d of Thomas & Hannah GREEN	bap
Aug 25	Eliza, d of James & Christiana AUSTIN, Born July 22	bap
— Aug 25	Elizabeth, d of Isaac & Elizabeth HICKMANS, Born Dec 3 1804	bap
Aug 28	John FIELDHOUSE	bur
Aug 28	David SHELDON	bur
Aug 28	William SATCHELL	bur
Sep 1	Richard FISHER & Sarah HARRISON by Banns	mar
— Sep 1	James, s of John & Mary MOORE	bap
Sep 1	Job, s of Joseph & Susannah DAVIES	bap
Sep 1	Joseph, s of Joseph & Hannah WHITEHOUSE	bap
Sep 1	David FEREDAY	bur
Sep 2	Amelia FISHER, d of Sarah BENTON	bap
— Sep 8	Joseph PAINE & Eleanor POTTER by Banns	mar
Sep 8	Samuel, s of Thomas & Elizabeth WHITEHOUSE	bap
Sep 8	Elizabeth, d of Joseph & Ann SMITH	bap
Sep 9	Joseph CANDLING & Ann SMITH by Banns	mar
Sep 9	Esther, d of John & Garroway BLACKHAM, Born Feby 19 1796	bap
Sep 15	Mary Ann, d of Thomas & Elizabeth STEPHENSON	bap
Sep 15	James, s of Joseph & Ann CADDICK	bap
— Sep 15	Mary Ann, d of James & Jane NOCK, Born July 14	bap
Sep 15	James, s of Joseph & Sarah BAGGOTT	bap
Sep 16	George BETREDGE & Ann ADAMS by Banns	mar
— Sep 18	Elizabeth PERRY	bur
Sep 19	Stephen JONES	bur
Sep 22	Mary, d of Thomas & Mary TILTINGTON	bap
Sep 22	Mary, d of Ellis & Jane OWEN	bap

1805

Sep 22	John, s of James & Ann AMOSS	bap
Sep 22	Ann, d of Thomas & Ann COTTRILL	bap
Sep 23	John REA & Sarah HORTON by Banns	mar
Sep 23	John GRICE & Ann Emma MULLEY by Banns	mar
Sep 24	John ELWELL	bur
Sep 29	Benjamin, s of Joseph & Catharine COCKRAM	bap
Sep 29	John, s of John & Elizabeth SANDERS	bap
Sep 29	Edward, s of William & Maria FISHER	bap
Sep/29	Hannah, d of James & Jane ATTWOOD	bap
Sep 29	Rebecca, d of Joseph & Eleanor PEARSON	bap
Sep 29	Phebe, d of John & Mary BATE	bap
Sep 29	Ann, d of John & Elizabeth PRESTON	bap
Oct 2	Thomas STEPHENS	bur
Oct 3	Rebecca, d of James & Rebecca COLEMAN, Born May 21, 1798	bap
Oct 5	Catharine JINKS	bur
Oct 6	Thomas, a base S of Prissilla RIDDING, abt 7 yrs old	bap
Oct 6	Martha SHORT	bur
Oct 6	Jane SMITH	bur
Oct 6	Mary, d of Joseph & Hannah BOTT, Born Sep 25	bap
Oct 6	Charles, s of Benjamin & Elizabeth MORRIS	bap
Oct 6	Rachael, d of William & Sarah ROUND	bap
Oct 9	Thomas SHELDON	bur
Oct 10	Elizabeth WHITE	bur
Oct 12	Elizabeth SHELDON	bur
Oct 13	John, s of William & Ann MILLARD	bap
Oct 13	Jane, d of Richard & Sarah PARTRIDGE	bap
Oct 13	Mary, d of Joseph & Elizabeth HAMPTON	bap
Oct 13	Sarah, d of George & Sarah BAYLEY	bap
Oct 13	John, s of George & Nancy BRINDLEY	bap
Oct 13	Elizabeth SHORTHOUSE	bur
Oct 14	Elizabeth, d of Samuel & Mary CLIFT, Born Dec 1 1783	bap
Oct 17	William ROUND	bur
Oct 20	Phebe, d of James & Hannah DOWNS, Born July 26	bap
Oct 20	Henry, s of Henry & Sarah WILLIAMS	bap
Oct 20	Mary, d of John & Catharina LATHAM	bap
Oct 20	Mary, d of Edward & Sarah GLAZE	bap
Oct 20	Sarah, d of John & Susannah PASKIN, Born May 9	bap
Oct 20	George, s of George & Mary GREGORY, Born Sep 5	bap
Oct 20	Phebe MILLS	bur
Oct 22	Henry TAYLOR	bur
Oct 27	Thomas DAVIES	bur
Oct 27	Joseph HUGHES	bur
Oct 27	Sarah, d of Joseph & Susannah WISE	bap
Oct 27	Joseph, s of Joseph & Ruth WORTON	bap
Oct 28	George HUNSTONE	bur
Oct 29	Ann HOLLIES	bur
Nov 3	Eleanor, d of Richard & Ann JONES, Born Oct 7	bap
Nov 3	Betsy, d of Richard & Elizabeth BOWEN	bap

Nov 3	Edward, s of William & Maria JASPER, Born May 13	bap
Nov 3	Hannah, d of Thomas & Elizabeth HOLLIHEAD	bap
Nov 3	Sarah, d of Joseph & Sophia BROOKES	bap
Nov 3	James, s of James & Sarah LUNN	bap
Nov 3	Walter HODGKINS	bur
Nov 3	Phebe SMITH	bur
Nov 4	Joshua HOYLE & Hannah HORTON by Banns	mar
Nov 4	Richard WARD & Hannah BUTTLER by Banns	mar
Nov 6	William THOMPSON	bur
Nov 10	Thomas WESTWOOD & Sarah FIELD by Banns	mar
Nov 10	Thomas, s of John & Mary GRIFFITHS	bap
Nov 10	Thomas, s of Thomas & Mary HANDS	bap
Nov 10	John BUTTLER	bur
Nov 13	Mary MORRIS	bur
Nov 15	Thomas MILLS	bur
Nov 17	Isaac ASTON & Bessy BYRCH by Licence	mar
Nov 17	Richard MILLINGTON & Jane BARNETT by Banns	mar
Nov 17	Joseph, s of Joseph & Joice TURNER, Born Oct 28	bap
Nov 17	Sarah, d of Thomas & Carey HOPKINS	bap
Nov 17	Mary GORTON	bur
Nov 18	John EVANS & Sarah SHELDON by Banns	mar
Nov 24	Joice FISHER	bur
Nov 24	John, s of John & Cretia KIRKHAM	bap
Nov 24	Sarah, d of Richard & Sarah MILLS	bap
Nov 24	Ruth, d of Abraham & Sarah WHITEHOUSE	bap
Nov 24	Sarah, base d of Mary EDWARDS	bap
Nov 25	Richard NEWTON & Sophia SUMMERFIELD by Banns	mar
Nov 28	John SMITH	bur
Dec 1	Elizabeth, d of Thomas & Mary POWELL	bap
Dec 1	Isaac, s of Joseph & Sarah FISHER	bap
Dec 3	Samuel ROSE	bur
Dec 4	William DERBY	bur
Dec 5	Edward, s of Edward & Rebecca WHITEHOUSE	bap
Dec 5	Mary Ann, d of John & Ann HICKINBOTTOM	bap
Dec 8	Martha, d of John & Jane SANKEY	bap
Dec 8	David Wilday, s of William & Mary HORTON	bap
Dec 8	Benjamin, s of Richard & Amelia LAW	bap
Dec 8	Samuel, s of William & Sarah BACHE	bap
Dec 8	Elisha, s of Elisha & Prissilla WHITEHOUSE	bap
Dec 8	Phebe TATE	bur
Dec 8	John LLOYD	bur
Dec 15	Henry, s of Jesse & Ann SIMS, Born July 21	bap
Dec 15	Phebe, d of Job & Ann SMITH	bap
Dec 15	Mary, d of Thomas & Hannah KENDRICK	bap
Dec 15	Sarah GUTTRIDGE	bur
Dec 15	Hannah LAW	bur
Dec 17	Joseph LIESTER	bur
Dec 17	Mary LATHAM	bur
Dec 22	Richard INGRAM & Halse HENLEY by Banns	mar

Dec 22   William, s of John & Dorothy WEBB   bap
Dec 22   Moses, s of Thomas & Sarah TUADAL   bap
Dec 22   Mary, d of Joseph & Mary WOOD   bap
Dec 24   John EVANS & Ann CARTWRIGHT by Banns   mar
Dec 25   Samuel BAILEY   bur
Dec 25   John, s of John & Ann GRICE   bap
Dec 25   Jerusha, s of Simeon & Hannah CORNFIELD   bap
Dec 25   Sarah, d of Richard & Pemilar GRIFFITHS   bap
Dec 25   Daniel, s of John & Sarah WATERHOUSE, Born Sep 18, 1784 bap
Dec 29   William COTTRILL   bur
Dec 29   Ann LAWRENCE   bur
Dec 29   Lucy WHITMORE   bur
Dec 29   Joseph, s of Samuel & Rebecca HIPKISS   bap
Dec 29   Mary, d of Richard & Elizabeth FIELD   bap
Dec 31   Isaac LAW   bur

Jan 2   Sarah GRIFFITHS   bur
Jan 2   Elizabeth LAW   bur
Jan 3   John BAKER & Maria BLODWELL by Banns   mar
Jan 5   Hannah, base d of Ann BOTT   bap
Jan 5   John, s of John & Jane WILLIAMS, Born at Oldbury   bap
Jan 5   Edward FEREDAY   bur
Jan 5   John SMITH   bur
Jan 12   James, s of William & Hannah RYLEY   bap
Jan 12   Thedoni, d of Aaron & Hannah STEPHENS   bap
Jan 12   Ann WHITEHOUSE   bur
Jan 12   Harriott WHITEHOUSE   bur
Jan 15   Richard INGRAM   bur
Jan 15   John, s of Joseph & Sarah MILLS   bap
Jan 19   John, s of Francis & Sarah SMITH   bap
Jan 19   William, s of William & Ann ALLEN   bap
Jan 19   James, s of Francis & Sarah SMITH   bap
Jan 19   Susannah, d of Joseph & Susannah TRANTER   bap
Jan 19   Obedience, d of Samuel & Mary ROSE   bap
Jan 19   William SULTCH   bur
Jan 19   Thomas STILLARD   bur
Jan 19   Mary FIELD   bur
Jan 19   William, s of John & Rhoda SMITH, Born Dec 1 1805   bap
Jan 19   Richard, s of Thomas & Sarah WILLIAMS   bap
Jan 26   William Horton, s of Joshua & Hannah HOYLE   bap
Jan 26   David, s of Richard & Martha WASSALL   bap
Jan 26   Phebe, d of Edward & Elizabeth WHITEHOUSE   bap
Jan 26   James, s of Thomas & Elizabeth COLLINS   bap
Jan 26   James, s of James & Susannah HARTLAND   bap
Jan 26   Harriott, d of Richard & Elizabeth LANKFORD, ab^t 15 yrs old   bap
Jan 30   John REED   bur
Jan 30   Lucy WOODALL   bur
Jan 30   Rebecca HUGHES   bur

1806

Feb 2	Mary, d of John & Elizabeth FISHER, Born Jan 29	bap
Feb 2	Mary, d of Richard & Mary STANTON	bap
Feb 2	Zachariah, s of Joseph & Sarah WARD	bap
Feb 2	Isaac, s of William & Elizabeth FORD	bap
Feb 7	Joseph FULWOOD	bur
Feb 9	Thomas HADLENTON & Elizabeth HORTHON by Banns	mar
Feb 9	Edward, s of Joseph & Mary MALE	bap
Feb 9	Rachael ROUND	bur
Feb 10	Charles MILLYARD & Mary STEPHENSON by Banns	mar
Feb 10	Thomas EADES & Sarah PEARSON by Banns	mar
Feb 10	Phebe JEVON	bap
Feb 14	Phebe Caddick, d of William & Phebe BRAINE	bap
Feb 16	Elizabeth, d of Thomas & Sarah BOTT	bap
Feb 16	Sarah, d of Thomas & Hannah WOODHALL	bap
Feb 16	John, s of John & Mary HILL	bap
Feb 16	Mary Ann, d of Abraham & Mary BAKER	bap
Feb 16	Maria FISHER	bur
Feb 17	Abel GROVSNOR & Martha STOKES by Banns	mar
Feb 18	Hannah SHELDON	bur
Feb 19	Mary CLARE	bur
Feb 20	Ann, d of Isaac & Bessey ASTON, Born Jan 23	bap
Feb 23	Mary Ann, d of Joseph & Mary PASKIN	bap
Feb 23	Elizabeth, base d of Charlotte STOKES	bap
Feb 23	Thomas, s of Thomas & Sarah SKIDMORE	bap
Feb 23	Sarah, d of Daniel & Rose SHELDON	bap
Feb 23	Margaret SANDERS	bur
Feb 23	Samuel SANDERS	bur
Feb 26	Jane Taylor, d of Samuel & Sarah HODGKINS, Born Nov 8 1805	bap
Feb 28	William MAIPAS	bur
Mar 2	Thomas, s of Thomas & Sophia PARKES	bap
Mar 2	Maria, d of Richard & Rachael GOWER	bap
Mar 2	Rhoda, d of Richard & Betty SANDERS	bap
Mar 2	Hannah, d of John & Mary ROWLEY	bap
Mar 4	Enoch PARTRIDGE	bur
Mar 5	Henry HOLIOKE	bur
Mar 9	Benjamin GREEN & Mary SMITH by Banns	mar
Mar 9	Hannah Maria, d of John & Mary JOHNSON	bap
Mar 9	Josiah TONKS	bur
Mar 16	John WHITEHOUSE & Elizabeth WHITEHOUSE by Banns	mar
Mar 16	William EBB & Susannah MARSON	mar
Mar 16	Samuel, s of John & Mary SHEERWOOD, nine years old [crossed out]	bap
Mar 16	Thomas, s of John & Mary SHEERWOOD, nine years old	bap
Mar 16	Richard, s of John & Mary SHEERWOOD, three years old	bap
Mar 16	Mary, d of John & Mary SHEERWOOD, six years old	bap
Mar 16	John, s of William & Sarah SHEERWOOD	bap
Mar 16	John, s of Joseph & Sarah COX, Born Feby 3	bap
Mar 16	Edward, s of Joseph & Ann WHITEHOUSE, Born Dec 31, 1805	bap

<u>1806</u>

Mar 16	James, s of John & Mary SKIDMORE	bap
Mar 16	Job, base s of Susannah SKIDMORE	bap
Mar 16	Elijath TWIGG	bur
Mar 20	Thomas WHEALE	bur
Mar 23	Isaac, s of Isaac & Elizabeth WHITEHOUSE, Born Feb 15	bap
Mar 23	Mary MILLS	bur
Mar 23	James ATTWOOD	bur
Mar 30	Hannah, d of Charles & Philliss LAW	bap
Mar 30	Elizabeth, d of Samuel & Elizabeth GOLD, 2 yrs & 10 mths old	bap
Mar 30	Ann, d of Samuel & Elizabeth GOLD	bap
Mar 30	Nancy, d of John & Elizabeth SMITH	bap
Mar 30	Mary, d of Joseph & Ann CANDLING	bap
Mar 30	Hannah, d of John & Alse SHEARWOOD	bap
Mar 30	Thomas COOPER	bur
Mar 30	Mary KIRKHAM	bur
Mar 31	Mary, d of Joseph & Susanna SMITH, of Coesly	bap
Apr 5	Henry HARRISON	bur
Apr 6	Mary, d of Joseph & Jane WHITEHOUSE	bap
Apr 6	William, s of John & Mary SMITH, Born Decr 14 1803	bap
Apr 6	Sarah, d of William & Ann ELWELL	bap
Apr 6	Isaac, s of John & Ann NEWTON	bap
Apr 6	John, s of Samuel & Sarah THORNEYCROFT, Born Feb 9	bap
Apr 6	Henry, s of Eutychus & Phebe FISHER	bap
Apr 6	John, s of John & Kitty LANKFORD	bap
Apr 6	Rachael, d of James & Mary WHITEHOUSE	bap
Apr 6	Elizabeth, d of John & Elizabeth THOMAS	bap
Apr 6	Ann, d of Benjamin & Mary WHEALE	bap
Apr 10	Joseph SHELDON	bur
Apr 10	Edward, s of Joshua & Hannah PARTRIDGE	bap
Apr 13	Ann, d of Daniel & Mary PRITCHARD	bap
Apr 13	Thomas, s of John & Eleanor ROBERTS	bap
Apr 14	William PARTRIDGE	bur
Apr 18	Sarah MILLS	bur
Apr 18	Thomas LION	bur
Apr 20	Mary, d of Samuel & Mary HICKMANS	bap
Apr 20	Ann Maria, d of John & Sarah NEWAY	bap
Apr 20	Mary, d of William & Prissilla INGRAM	bap
Apr 20	William, s of George & Ann TURNER	bap
Apr 20	William, s of Joseph & Martha ROUGHTON	bap
Apr 20	Edward, s of Joseph & Ann HARTWELL	bap
Apr 20	William, s of William & Sarah WHITEHOUSE, Born Mar 24[?]	bap
Apr 27	Sarah, d of Philip & Ann WILLIAMS	bap
Apr 27	Samuel, s of Samuel & Mary MILLS	bap
Apr 27	Edward WHITEHOUSE	bur
Apr 27	Ann PUGH	bur
May 4	Henry, s of David & Hannah HORTON, Born Birmingham Mar 3	bap
May 4	Sarah, d of John & Elizabeth HORTON, Born Mar 31 1805	bap
May 4	Maria, d of Job & Elizabeth BROOKS	bap
May 4	Mary, base d of Mary NOCK	bap

1806

May 4	Sarah, d of Edward & Sarah TUCKLEY, Born Mar 27	bap
May 4	William FLETCHER	bur
May 4	Samuel MILLS	bur
May 11	John, s of William & Sarah PHAYSEY	bap
May 11	Rachael, d of Thomas & Mary BRETTELL	bap
May 11	Mary Ann, d of Abiather & Sarah HANCOX	bap
May 11	Richard OWEN	bur
May 13	William ASTLEY & Elizabeth ROBINSON by Banns	mar
May 13	William COOKSEY	bur
May 25	Joseph, s of John & Nancy SHENTON, Born Apl 22	bap
May 25	Hannah & Martha, twin d of Cornelius & Esther BAKER	bap
May 25	Edward, s of John & Ann HUMPHRIES	bap
May 25	Ann, d of Thomas & Ann FEREDAY	bap
May 25	Maria, d of William & Elizabeth GRINSILL	bap
May 25	Joseph, s of John & Sarah ROGERS	bap
May 25	Mary Ann, d of James & Deborah NOCK	bap
May 25	Mary Ann, d of Thomas & Sarah WESTWOOD	bap
May 25	William, s of Abraham & Elizabeth SHELDON	bap
May 25	Joseph, s of Benjamin & Mary HARTLAND, Born Mar 9	bap
May 26	John BRION & Mary HOLLAND by Banns	mar
May 26	William, s of Joseph & Hannah SMITH, Born Jan 5	bap
May 26	Hannah, d of Joseph & Mary SMITH	bap
May 28	William ROBERTS & Elizabeth LAWLEY by Banns	mar
May 28	Ann WHITEHOUSE	bur
Jun 1	Richard, s of Edward & Sarah GRIFFITHS	bap
Jun 1	Richard LANKFORD	bap
Jun 3	Grace NICKLIN	bur
Jun 5	Richard GWINNETT, was Drowned	bur
Jun 8	Ann, d of John & Mary BELCHER	bap
Jun 8	Isaac, s of Isaac & Elizabeth FISHER	bap
Jun 8	Benjamin, s of William & Mary SKELDON	bap
Jun 8	Mary, d of Joseph & Hannah ROUND	bap
Jun 8	Leah, d of Thomas & Mary HARCOTT	bap
Jun 9	Edward PETERS & Phebe TROWMAN by Banns	mar
Jun 15	Mary LAW	bur
Jun 15	Ann, d of John & Ann LAW, Born May 29	bap
Jun 15	Sarah, d of Henry & Esther WARTON, Born May 29	bap
Jun 15	Edward, base Son of Phebe COLLINS, Born Feb 2	bap
Jun 15	Maria, d of Thomas & Sarah WALKER, Born May 17	bap
Jun 19	John FISHER	bur
Jun 19	Joseph, s of Joseph & Sarah RUBERY, Born Nov 8 1804	bap
Jun 22	William PERSHOUSE (Overseer of Poor)	bur
Jun 22	James, s of James & Ann WHITEHOUSE, Born May 24	bap
Jun 22	Mary, d of John & Mary EVANS	bap
Jun 22	William, s of William & Sarah BERBRIDGE, Born Nov 16 1803	bap
Jun 22	Nancy, base d of Mary DARBY	bap
Jun 24	Joseph YATES	bur
Jun 24	John BRINDLEY	bur
Jun 24	Elizabeth WHESSON	bur

Jun 29	Sarah TIMMINS	bur
Jun 29	Ann, d of Thomas & Lydia MANSLEY	bap
Jun 29	William & Margarett, twin s & d of Thomas & Martha DANKS	bap
Jun 29	William Henry, s of Joseph & Sarah HORTON, Born May 26	bap
Jun 29	Edward, s of William & Phebe HODGKINS	bap
Jun 30	William ROGERS & Elizabeth DAVIES by Banns	mar
Jul 2	Richard GRIFFITHS	bur
Jul 6	Sarah LEWIS	bur
Jul 6	Henry, s of Joseph & Phebe STANTON, Born 3^d	bap
Jul 6	Elizabeth, d of Edward & Elizabeth MARTIN	bap
Jul 6	Joseph, s of Joseph & Nancy DUDLEY, Born June 3	bap
Jul 8	Benjamin, s of W^m & Mary UNDERHILL, Born Mar 12 1800	bap
Jul 8	Esther, d of W^m & Mary UNDERHILL, Born Mar 17 1797	bap
Jul 8	Fanny, d of W^m & Mary UNDERHILL, Born Dec 8 1795	bap
Jul 8	Phebe, d of W^m & Mary UNDERHILL, Born Sep 26 1794	bap
Jul 8	James Evan, s of W^m & Mary UNDERHILL, Born Mar 21 1793	bap
Jul 8	Thomas, s of W^m & Mary UNDERHILL, Born Mar 19 1791	bap
Jul 8	Elizabeth, d of W^m & Mary UNDERHILL, Born Apl 9 1788	bap
Jul 8	William, s of W^m & Mary UNDERHILL, Born Nov 23 1783	bap
Jul 8	Lucy, d of W^m & Mary UNDERHILL, Born Jun 30 1775	bap
Jul 9	Moses WHITEHOUSE	bap
Jul 13	Joseph, s of Edward & Mary FISHER	bap
Jul 13	Sarah, d of Edward & Ann HARRIS	bap
Jul 13	Sarah, d of Benjamin & Sarah FEREDAY, Born Decr 8, 1805	bap
Jul 13	Susannah, base child of Sarah RUBERY, 2 years old	bap
Jul 13	Sarah, d of John & Hannah FURNIFILL, Born June 24	bap
Jul 20	Christopher, s of Thomas & Ann CHAMBERS	bap
Jul 20	Mary, d of Samuel & Mary NOCK	bap
Jul 20	Hannah, d of Thomas & Sarah EADES	bap
Jul 20	Benjamin, s of William & Mary LAW, Born Nov 11 1805	bap
Jul 21	Joseph SHELDON & Sarah LIESTER by Banns	mar
Jul 27	Richard, s of Samuel & Hannah HALL	bap
Jul 27	Thomas, s of Thomas & Mary BENNITT	bap
Jul 27	Alley, d of Joseph & Ann CARTWRIGHT	bap
Jul 28	William CORBITT & Lucy CARTWRIGHT by Banns	mar
Jul 28	David GUTTRIDGE & Mary JACKSON by Banns	mar
Aug 1	Mary PARTRIDGE	bur
Aug 3	Daniel, s of John & Sarah JONES, Born July 12	bap
Aug 3	Lucy, d of John & Ann MATTHEWS, Born July 15	bap
Aug 3	Ann SHELDON	bur
Aug 10	Francis, s of Richard & Elizabeth WHITEHOUSE	bap
Aug 10	Mary Ann, d of Henry & Elizabeth HOLLAND	bap
Aug 10	William, s of Joseph & Hannah DUDLEY	bap
Aug 15	Robert LLOYD	bur
Aug 15	John PHILLIPS, base son of Phebe CALLOWAY	bap
Aug 16	John ALEXANDER	bur
Aug 17	Joseph, s of Joseph & Mary YATES	bap
Aug 17	Thomas, s of Thomas & Elizabeth BRATT	bap
Aug 17	Maria, d of John & Eleanor WHITEHOUSE	bap

Aug 17	Eliza, d of William & Sarah WHITEHOUSE	bap
Aug 19	Noah BATE	bur
Aug 24	Edward, s of John & Margarett HATTON	bap
Aug 31	Sarah, d of James & Ann SATCHELL	bap
Aug 31	Mary, d of Richard & Sarah STEVENTON	bap
Aug 31	James, s of Thomas & Sarah EVANS	bap
Aug 31	Mary Ann, d of George & Hannah CALLOWAY, Born 15th	bap
Aug 31	Phebe, d of John & Maria PLANT	bap
Sep 2	Joseph FEREDAY	bur
Sep 7	Benjamin BROOKS & Susanna COX by Banns	mar
Sep 7	Sarah, d of Samuel & Mary BAGLEY	bap
Sep 7	John DARBY	bur
Sep 7	Jane, d of Thomas & Elizabeth DANKS, Born Aug 11	bap
Sep 14	Maria, d of Peter & Ann MILLS, Born 13th	bap
Sep 14	John, s of James & Elizabeth GOUGH	bap
Sep 14	Mary Ann, d of William & Elizabeth ROBERTS	bap
Sep 14	Frances, d of John & Susannah GREGORY, Born Apl 23	bap
Sep 14	Charles CLEAMENS	bur
Sep 17	Benjamin GRIFFITHS	bur
Sep 21	Samuel, s of Nathan & Mary HILL	bap
Sep 21	Mary Ann, d of John & Mary WRIGHT	bap
Sep 21	Mary, d of William & Sarah HICKMANS	bap
Sep 24	Thomas KNOWLES & Sarah TURNER by Banns	mar
Sep 28	Joseph SMITH & Rosanna SANSOME by Banns	mar
Sep 28	Joseph, s of John & Mary SHELDON	bap
Sep 28	Mary, d of George & Mary FISHER	bap
Sep 28	Ann, d of Thomas & Ann ANGSLEY, Born Sep 6	bap
Sep 28	Issabella, d of Charles & Elizabeth HICKABOTTOM	bap
Sep 30	Anthony HIDE	bur
Oct 5	Sarah, d of John & Sarah REUBERY, 14 years old	bap
Oct 5	Absalom, s of Thomas & Mary ARCHE	bap
Oct 5	William, s of William & Mary CLARKSON	bap
Oct 5	Eleanor, d of John & Eleanor ROBERTS	bap
Oct 5	Thomas JONES	bur
Oct 12	Phebe, d of Joseph & Hannah GRICE	bap
Oct 14	William LAW	bur
Oct 16	Emmanuel MATHIAS	bur
Oct 19	Dinah, base d of Sarah CLARKE	bap
Oct 19	Mary Ann, d of Mark & Sarah CARTWRIGHT	bap
Oct 19	William, s of William & Ann ONIONS	bap
Oct 20	Job JONES & Mary JONES by Banns	mar
Oct 26	Daniel, s of William & Rebecca ROUND	bap
Oct 26	Sarah, d of Joseph & Sarah HUGHES	bap
Oct 26	Ruth, d of Richard & Jane LANGDON	bap
Oct 27	Samuel HADLEY & Nancy JOHNSON by Banns	mar
Nov 2	Hannah, d of James & Sarah HANCOCK	bap
Nov 2	Richard, s of William & Elizabeth WALTERS	bap
Nov 2	David, s of Edward & Phebe WHITEHOUSE	bap
Nov 2	Hannah Naylor, d of William & Hannah GUEST, Born Sep 26	bap

Nov 2	Mary Ann, d of John & Ann STANLEY		bap
Nov 2	John, s of Thomas & Sarah ROWLEY		bap
Nov 2	Sarrah, d of John & Margaret HEELEY		bap
Nov 6	Mary DUDLEY		bur
Nov 9	Richard HUNT & Phillis TROWMAN by Banns		mar
Nov 9	James, s of John & Sarah TIMMINS		bap
Nov 9	Nancy, d of John & Mary JEVON		bap
Nov 14	Elizabeth SHARRATT		bur
Nov 16	Elizabeth, d of John & Patience WARD		bap
Nov 16	Edward, s of Charles & Elizabeth HOXLEY		bap
Nov 16	Hannah, d of James & Sophia JONES		bap
Nov 17	William CHATTIN & Phebe SMITH by Banns		mar
Nov 17	Mary TIMMINS		bur
Nov 23	Edward, s of Robert & Mary DAVIES		bap
Nov 23	Benjamin, s of William & Margarett WILLIAMS		bap
Nov 23	Hannah, d of Joseph & Ann HOLLOWAY		bap
Nov 23	Betsey, d of James & Nancy PLANT		bap
Nov 24	James HADLEY & Sarah FISHER by Banns		mar
Nov 26	Ann TIBBITTS		bur
Nov 27	Job SMITH		bur
Nov 30	Joseph WARR		bur
Nov 30	Anthony, s of William & Lydia LOWE, Born Nov 6		bap
Nov 30	Mary Ann, d of John & Mary HILTON, Born Nov 7		bap
Nov 30	Joseph, s of Joseph & Elizabeth TONKS, Born Oct 9		bap
Nov 30	Thomas, s of John & Catharine LATHAM		bap
Nov 30	Thomas, s of Richard & Sarah REED, Born Novr 4		bap
Nov 30	John, s of John & Nancy DOUGHTY		bap
Nov 30	Mary, d of Richard & Sarah GRIFFITHS, Born May 21		bap
Dec 6	Hannah WHITEHEAD		bur
Dec 6	Edward Ebenezer FISHER		bur
Dec 9	William PRICE		bur
Dec 14	Eliza, d of John & Hannah POWELL		bap
Dec 14	Bridget DARBY		bur
Dec 14	Joseph WARTON		bur
Dec 14	Richard MORRIS		bur
Dec 14	Anthony LOWE		bur
Dec 14	Samuel, s of James & Sarah CHATER		bap
Dec 14	James, s of James & Hannah FISHER		bap
Dec 14	Mary, d of Benjamin & Ann BLEWITT		bap
Dec 14	Sarah, d of Abraham & Maria PARKES		bap
Dec 14	Richard, s of John & Hannah ASTON		bap
Dec 14	Elizabeth, d of Thomas & Hannah GREEN		bap
Dec 17	Stephen MILLS		bur
Dec 21	Joseph WARD & Ann WALDRON by Banns		mar
Dec 21	William, s of John & Hannah TIBBITTS, Born Nov 12		bap
Dec 21	Hannah, d of Samuel & Mary INGRAM, Born Dec 9		bap
Dec 21	Elizabeth, d of John & Patience WILLIAMS		bap
Dec 21	Samuel, s of William & Ann WHITEHOUSE		bap
Dec 21	Robert MOORE		bur

<u>1806</u>

Dec 22	William MORRIS & Mary ROUND by Banns	mar
Dec 25	John YORK	bur
Dec 25	Mary, d of Benjamin & Ann BLEWITT	bap
Dec 25	William, s of Thomas & Martha LEE	bap
Dec 25	Sarah, d of George & Hannah PADDOCK	bap
Dec 25	Thomas, s of William & Hannah WHILE	bap
Dec 25	Phebe, d of John & Hannah WHITEHOUSE	bap
Dec 28	Nancy, d of William & Mary MILLS	bap
Dec 28	Nancy, d of Benjamin & Catharine PLANT	bap
Dec 28	Benjamin, s of John & Maria SHAW	bap
Dec 28	Frances, d of Abiather & Sarah HANCOX	bap
Dec 29	John WHITEHOUSE & Phebe WHITEHOUSE by Banns	mar
Dec 29	John GUTTRIDGE & Maria LAW by Banns	mar
Dec 30	William SMITH	bur
Dec 31	John BANNISTER & Hannah ASTON by Banns	mar
Dec 31	John HINTON & Ann NEWBY by Banns	mar
Dec 31	James EVANS	

[Written very faintly:]

1828

<u>1807</u>

21

<u>1807</u>

Jan 4	Joseph, s of William & Sarah LEWIS, Born Nov 1, 1806	bap
Jan 4	Hannah, base d of Maria DEALEA	bap
Jan 4	John, s of John & Sarah WHEALE	bap
Jan 4	William, s of William & Nancy DEALEA, Born June 23 1804	bap
Jan 4	Ann BELCHER	bur
Jan 4	James WILLIS	bur
Jan 5	Francis LEWIS & Martha EVANS by Banns	mar
Jan 5	Sarah HUGHES	bur
Jan 6	Ann FEREDAY	bur
Jan 11	Martha BATE	bur
Jan 11	William, s of Richard & Hannah WARD	bap
Jan 11	Thomas, s of George & Sarah MARSH	bap
Jan 12	Thomas CLARKE & Hannah INGRAM by Banns	mar
Jan 12	Mary WHITEHOUSE	bur
Jan 13	Eli OSBORNE	bur
Jan 13	Hannah WHITEHOUSE	bur
Jan 13	Mary BLASE	bur
Jan 14	John BOYLE	bur
Jan 18	Mary, d of James & Ann WARTON	bap
Jan 18	Martha, d of Edward & Elizabeth REED	bap
Jan 18	Charlotte Sarah, d of William & Hannah LAWRENCE	bap
Jan 19	Thomas PERRY & Elizabeth MORTON by Banns	mar
Jan 19	Martin PITT & Eleanor HARTSHORN by Banns	mar
Jan 19	George WITHERS	bur
Jan 19	Mary LEA	bur
Jan 25	William GIDDINS & Ann PARKES by Banns	mar

Jan 25	Gideon, s of Robert & Mary GRANT	bap
Jan 25	Billa, d of Samuel & Jane STOKES, Born Feb 26 1806	bap
Jan 25	Joseph, s of George & Sarah SHELDON	bap
Jan 25	Susannah, d of John & Mary BLACKHAM, Born June 24 1806	bap
Jan 25	Joseph, s of John & True WHITEHOUSE	bap
Jan 25	Sarah, d of John & Ann WILSON, Born July 13, 1805	bap
Jan 25	Isaac LAW	bur
Jan 25	Dorothy CHAMBERS	bur
Jan 26	Charles BROOKE & Jane CRUMPTON by Banns	mar
Jan 27	Richard MORLEY & Mary DAVIS by Banns	mar
Jan 28	Samuel FISHER, s of Sarah BENTON by Ab^m FISHER	bap
Jan 28	Thomas EVANS	bur
Jan 28	Richard GRIFFITHS	bur
Jan 28	John GRIFFITHS	bur
Jan 28	John SIMMONS	bur
Feb 1	Sarah, d of Henry & Sarah TAYLOR	bap
Feb 1	Noah, s of William & Elizabeth BRATT	bap
Feb 1	Thomas, s of Thomas & Elizabeth FEREDAY	bap
Feb 1	Mary, d of Abraham & Hannah LAW	bap
Feb 1	Mary Ann, d of John & Elizabeth LIESTER	bap
Feb 1	John, s of John & Clare STANLEY	bap
Feb 2	David LLOYD & Shusannah HARTWELL by Banns	mar
Feb 4	Pharoah BAKER	bur
Feb 4	Mary ROBERTS	bur
Feb 4	Mary HODGKINS	bur
Feb 8	Phebe JOHNSON	bur
Feb 8	Harriott, d of Samuel & Ann GUEST	bap
Feb 8	James, s of William & Elizabeth STEVENTON	bap
Feb 8	Mary, d of Joseph & Elizabeth TILLEY	bap
Feb 10	George PITT & Ann LLOYD by Banns	mar
Feb 15	James, s of James & Ann SATCHELL	bap
Feb 15	Charles, s of John & Phebe COTTRILL	bap
Feb 15	Joshua, s of Joseph & Jane CALLOWAY	bap
Feb 15	Nancy, d of Thomas & Mary MORRIS, Born Dec 8, 1806	bap
Feb 15	Maria, d of George & Sarah JONES, Born Feby 9	bap
Feb 15	Josiah, s of William & Phebe MORRIS, Born Feb 9	bap
Feb 15	Mary Ann, d of John & Maria SANDERS	bap
Feb 15	John, s of William & Ann GUEST, Born Dec 13 1806	bap
Feb 17	William GARRAT & Phebe HAWTHORN by Banns	mar
Feb 19	Leah MINCHER	bur
Feb 22	Phebe, d of Peter & Mary BANKS	bap
Feb 22	Ann MORRIS	bur
Feb 22	Eliza, d of John & Phebe MILLS, Born Jan 24	bap
Feb 22	Joseph, s of Edward & Phebe WHITEHOUSE	bap
Feb 24	John LAW	bur
Feb 25	Maria, d of John & Sarah GWINNETT, Born Aug 11, 1806	bap
Feb 25	Hannah WHITEHOUSE	bur
Feb 27	John ROUND	bur
Mar 1	Amos JONES & Mary WILLIAMS by Banns	mar

Mar 1	Edward MARTIN	bur
Mar 1	Thomas, s of Daniel & Martha WHITEHOUSE	bap
Mar 4	Benjamin SIMMONS	bur
Mar 8	William, s of William & Ann BISSELL	bap
Mar 8	Rose, d of Edward & Sarah DUDLEY	bap
Mar 8	Hannah, d of Thomas & Lydia TAYLOR	bap
Mar 8	Hannah, d of Joseph & Ann FOSTER	bap
Mar 8	Elizabeth, d of Joseph & Mary MILLARD, Born Feb 20 1803	bap
Mar 8	Elizabeth, d of John & Elizabeth TURNER	bap
Mar 8	William Henry, s of William & Sarah ROUND	bap
Mar 8	Martha, d of John & Mary HORTON	bap
Mar 8	Reuben, s of James & Sarah OSBORNE	bap
Mar 8	David, s of James & Nancy HORTON	bap
Mar 8	Phebe, d of Thomas & Phebe WHITEHOUSE	bap
Mar 8	Mary, d of William & Ann WHITEHOUSE	bap
Mar 8	Elizabeth, d of Thomas & Hannah JAMES	bap
Mar 8	Daniel, s of Abraham & Mary JEVON, Born Feb 13	bap
Mar 8	Benjamin HUSEY	bur
Mar 8	John BUNCH	bur
Mar 9	Benjamin EVANS & Sarah FISHER by Banns	mar
Mar 11	Mary SHORTHOUSE	bur
Mar 12	Shusannah TURNER	bur
Mar 12	Jane TAYLOR	bur
Mar 14	Esther, d of William & Hannah WHITEHOUSE, Born Feb 15	bap
Mar 15	Martha BAKER	bur
Mar 19	John PERSHOUSE, base s of Mary GAILY, Born Novr 27, 1806	bap
Mar 22	Richard, s of Richard & Selvia NEWELL, Born Feb 24	bap
Mar 22	John, s of Thomas & Mary PENN	bap
Mar 22	Timothy, base s of Mary WESTWOOD	bap
Mar 22	Mary, d of John & Elizabeth JESSON	bap
Mar 22	John COOKE	bur
Mar 22	Sarah EDGE	bur
Mar 23	Sarah SMITH	bur

Exhibited into the Court of Litchfield June 19, 1807

Mar 24	James ASTON & Ann BAKER by Banns	mar
Mar 27	William CONSTABLE & Elizabeth JONES by Banns	mar
Mar 27	Richard WHITEHOUSE & Sarah BULLOWS by Banns	mar
Mar 27	Mary, d of William & Susanna HOLLIES	bap
Mar 27	Edward, s of Edward & Sarah ROWLEY	bap
Mar 29	Ann, d of John & Jane WILLIAMS, Born Feb 27	bap
Mar 29	Edward, s of Edward & Elizabeth FEREDAY	bap
Mar 29	Joseph, s of Richard & Mary FOSTER	bap
Mar 29	Mary, d of Jeremiah & Isabella DAVIS	bap
Mar 29	Isaac, s of William & Ann THOMAS	bap
Mar 29	Elizabeth, d of John & Mary EVANS	bap
Mar 29	Ann Maria, d of Samuel & Ann EDWARDS	bap
Mar 29	Ann, d of George & Alice CRUMP	bap
Mar 29	Robert, s of Thomas & Ann FERN	bap

1807

Mar 29	Ann, d of Elijah & Ann WILCOX, Born 13th	bap
Mar 29	Hannah, base d of Sarah WHITEHOUSE	bap
Apr 1	Benjamin LAW	bur
Apr 1	Ann PRICE	bur
Apr 2	Elizabeth PASKIN	bur

[The edge of this page is frayed and some of the dates obliterated]

	Ann, d of John & Sarah BENNITT	bap
	Barbara, d of Joshua & Hannah HOYLE	bap
	James, s of Thomas & Mary LAPPAGE, Born Apl 1	bap
Apr 10	William BLACKHAM	bur
Apr 11	James BAKER & Hannah GRICE by Banns	mar
Apr 12	John DERBY & Sarah WHITEHOUSE by Banns	mar
Apr 12	Henry, s of Henry & Violette HUGHES	bap
Apr 12	Isaac GUTTRIDGE	bur
Apr 12	Hannah LAW	bur
Apr 12	William, s of William & Mary MANNING	bap
Apr 12	John, s of William & Mary MANNING	bap
Apr 12	Elijah, s of Thomas & Susanna TAYLOR	bap
Apr 12	Mary, d of James & Martha BARTLAM	bap
Apr 12	Roseanna, d of Thomas & Ann THOMMINSON	bap
Apr 12	Harriott, d of George & Sarah COOPER	bap
Apr 12	Mary PERSHOUSE	bur
Apr 13	Sarah, d of Joseph & Hannah SHELDON	bap
Apr 14	Henry HAZLEHURST	bur
Apr 16	John OWEN	bur
Apr 16	Susanna FEREDAY	bur
Apr 19	Phebe BRAINE	bur
Apr 19	Benjamin & Ann, twin s & d of John & Ann SKIDMORE	bap
Apr 19	Abraham, s of John & Mary TIMMINS	bap
Apr 19	Mary Ann, d of John & Ann CLARKE	bap
Apr 19	Mary WHITEHOUSE	bur
Apr 19	Mary Ann ROUND	bur
Apr 19	Thomas ROLLASON	bur
Apr 19	Sarah, d of George & Elizabeth BALL	bap
Apr 19	Elizabeth, d of John & Elizabeth HORTON	bap
Apr 19	Ann, d of Thomas & Ann MAWPAS	bap
Apr 19	Mary Ann, d of Thomas & Mary NASH	bap
Apr 19	Sarah Ann, d of William & Sarah DANGERFIELD	bap
Apr 23	John WHITEHOUSE	bur
Apr 24	Edwd Fisher SMITH	bur
Apr 26	Mary Ann, d of David & Francis HIPKINS	bap
Apr 26	Sarah, d of Joseph & Martha SMITH	bap
Apr 26	John, s of Robert & Mary GELEA	bap
Apr 26	Mary Ann, d of Henry & Mary NOCK	bap
Apr 26	Daniel, s of John & Hannah COMPSTONE	bap
Apr 26	Sarah, d of Joseph & Jane WHITEHOUSE	bap
Apr 29	James WHITEHOUSE	bur
Apr 30	Eliza WHITEHOUSE	bur
May 3	Sarah, d of William & Elizabeth BELCHER, Born Apl 10	bap

1807

	May 3	Lydia, d of Thomas & Eleanor LAW, Born Mar 16	bap
	May 3	Joseph, s of Joseph & Mary WARR, Born Apl 5	bap
	May 5	John WARR	bur
	May 5	Isabel, d of Sarah WARR (a base child)	bap
	May 5	Elizabeth, d of John & Mary BATE, Born Mar 29	bap
	May 7	Mary WHITEHOUSE	bur
	May 10	Betsey BOWEN	bur
	Mazy 12	Mary WHITMORE	bur
	May 13	John SHELDON	bur
	May 14	David WHITEHOUSE	bur
	May 15	Daniel COMPSTONE	bur
	May 17	Elizabeth, d of Edward & Ann CLARKE	bap
	May 17	Sarah, d of Benjamin & Rachel WHITEHOUSE	bap
~	May 17	John, s of John & Hannah POTT	bap
~	May 17	William, s of William & Prudence MINCHER	bap
	May 17	Benjamin, s of Daniel & Mary WHITEHOUSE, Born May 13	bap
	May 17	Solomon, s of Edward & Elizabeth STANHOPE, Born Apl 8	bap
	May 17	Ann, d of Daniel & Letty WHITEHOUSE	bap
	May 17	George ALLENDER	bur
	May 17	Abraham WHITEHOUSE	bur
	May 18	Richard MILICHIP & Prudence SMITH by Banns	mar
~	May 24	Philip, s of Daniel & Maria PARTRIDGE	bap
~	May 24	Henry, s of Amos & Frances HODGSKINS	bap
	May 24	Sabrain, d of Thos & Ann WHITEHOUSE	bap
	May 24	Sarah RUEBOTTOM	bur
	May 24	Hannah GRIFFITHS	bur
	May 25	Edward GEARY & Sarah SOCKET by Banns	mar
~	May 26	Mary INGRAM	bur
	May 26	Mary GRIFFITHS	bur
~	May 26	Alice GUTTRIDGE	bur
	May 26	Edward WHITEHOUSE	bur
	May 31	Daniel, s of Daniel & Mary WARR	bap
	May 31	Joseph, s of John & Maria TAYLOR	bap
	May 31	Mary, d of Richard & Elizabeth TAYLOR	bap
	May 31	Abraham PASKIN	bur
~	Jun 2	Abraham PARKES	bur
	Jun 7	Ann SKIDMORE	bur
	Jun 7	Elizabeth, d of Richard & Mary JUKES	bap
	Jun 7	Ruth, d of Richard & Eleanor WHITEHOUSE	bap
	Jun 7	Maryann, d of Thomas & Sarah EVANS	bap
	Jun 7	Thomas, s of Joseph & Elizabeth SHEREWOOD	bap
~	Jun 7	Joseph PARKES	bur
~	Jun 9	William HUGHES & Ann LLOYD by Banns	mar
	Jun 9	Edward PETERS & Isabell FISHER by Banns	mar
	Jun 10	Thomas WHITEHOUSE	bur
	Jun 12	Ann WELCH	bur
~	Jun 14	James, s of Thomas & Eleanor WEBB	bap
	Jun 14	Sarah, d of Richard & Sarah MILLS, Born Apl 10	bap
	Jun 14	John, s of Job & Sarah CASHMORE	bap

1807

Jun 14	Maria, d of Thomas & Jane STILLARD, Born May 25	bap
Jun 14	Sophia, d of Richard & Ann JONES	bap
Jun 14	John, s of John & Mary JONES, Born May 1	bap
Jun 14	Sarah LOWE	bur
Jun 19	John, s of Thomas & Mercy POWELL, Born May 26	bap
Jun 21	Phebe, d of Daniel & Esther GRIFFITHS	bap
Jun 21	William, s of William & Jane WHITEHOUSE	bap
Jun 21	Thomas, s of James & Sarah RHUBERY, Born 9th	bap
Jun 21	Sarah, d of Peter & Margarett TAYLOR	bap
Jun 21	John, s of John & Deborah GREGORY	bap
Jun 21	Elizabeth, d of Joseph & Mary PASKIN	bap
Jun 25	Elizabeth SHELDON	bur
Jun 28	Samuel Smith, s of Benjamin & Sarah LOWE, Born Oct 1806	bap
Jun 28	Sarah, d of John & Catharine JINKS, Born 8th	bap
Jun 28	Henry, s of Richard & Sophia PRICE	bap
Jun 29	Richard STOCKTON & Ann YORK by Banns	mar
Jul 2	Joseph ASTON	bur
Jul 2	Joseph, s of James & Mary STANTON, Born June 7	bap
Jul 2	Abraham HIPKISS	bur
Jul 5	Mary Ann, d of William & Maria DANKS	bap
Jul 5	Mary PASKIN	bur
Jul 5	Hannah HARPER	bur
Jul 5	William, s of John & Elizabeth HYDE	bap
Jul 5	William, s of Charles & Shusannah PERRY	bap
Jul 5	Thomas, s of Joseph & Hannah WALTERS	bap
Jul 6	Robert JOHNSON & Mary JEWIS by Banns	mar
Jul 10	Paul EVANS & Ann GRIFFITHS by Banns	mar
Jul 12	Abraham HARTLAND & Elizabeth HAYES by Banns	mar
Jul 12	Thomas, s of Samuel & Mary TAYLOR	bap
Jul 12	George HEYWARD	bur
Jul 12	Lette RUEBOTTOM	bur
Jul 16	Elizabeth FISHER	bur
Jul 18	William HYDE	bur
Jul 19	John CARTWRIGHT & Ann BROWN by Banns	mar
Jul 19	Isaac, s of Isaac & Hannah DARBY	bap
Jul 19	Ann, d of Thomas & Sarah LONES	bap
Jul 19	George, s of George & Elizabeth HAYNES	bap
Jul 20	George WEAVER & Mary JONES by Banns	mar
Jul 22	Ann HARDEN	bur
Jul 22	Roseanna DARBY	bur
Jul 26	William GARNER & Elizabeth LANE by Banns	mar
Jul 26	Elizabeth, d of Thomas & Rebecca HARRIS	bap
Jul 26	Henry, s of William & Sarah WALKER	bap
Jul 26	John, s of Job & Hannah SMITH	bap
Jul 26	Elizabeth, d of Joseph & Ann SMITH	bap
Jul 26	Mary, d of Edward & Letticia WHITEHOUSE	bap
Jul 27	Ann WHITEHOUSE	bur
Jul 27	John HALL	bur
Jul 28	Jane HARTSHORNE	bur

1807

Aug 2	John, s of Edward & Mary ALEXANDER, Born May 30 1804	bap
Aug 2	Edward, s of Edward & Mary ALEXANDER, Born June 21 1805	bap
Aug 2	Francis, s of Edward & Mary ALEXANDER, Born Apl 21 1807	bap
Aug 2	William, s of Joseph & Rebecca SMITH, Born July 8	bap
Aug 2	Joseph, s of John & Ann HARRIS	bap
Aug 2	Mary, d of Thomas & Elizabeth TILLEY, Born July 10	bap
Aug 4	John HODGKINS & Mary PERSHOUSE by Licence	mar
Aug 6	Mary Ann, d of James & Mary ASTON, Born July 13	bap
Aug 9	Sarah, d of William & Sarah SHEREWOOD	bap
Aug 9	William, s of Richard & Ann PEASE, Born July 17	bap
Aug 9	Thomas SMITH	bur
Aug 9	Joseph TURNER	bur
Aug 9	Sarah GREENAWAY	bur
Aug 11	Francis CONNOP & Elizabeth PANE by Banns	mar
Aug 11	John BADGER & Hannah BUTLER by Banns	mar
Aug 13	Thomas, s of Isaac & Betsey ASTON, Born July 19	bap
Aug 16	David, s of David & Hannah WASSELL, Born July 20	bap
Aug 16	Nancy, d of George & Ann BRINDLEY	bap
Aug 16	William, s of William & Rebecca ROUND, Born June 20	bap
Aug 23	Rachael, d of James & Sarah RICHARDS	bap
Aug 23	Scisily, d of Edwᵈ & Mary TIMMIN	bap
Aug 24	Thomas LEACH & Maria WARTON by Banns	mar
Aug 24	Joseph MASON & Hannah HENLEY by Banns	mar
Aug 25	Elisha JACKSON & Rachael BIRD by Licence	mar
Aug 30	Samuel CADDICK & Roseannah TRANTER by Banns	mar
Aug 30	Nancy, d of Joseph & Susannah TRANTER	bap
Aug 30	Benjamin, s of Benjamin & Mary WALTERS	bap
Sep 2	Mary WHITEHOUSE	bur
Sep 2	Benjamin WHEALE	bur
Sep 6	Joseph, s of Daniel & Elizabeth GORTON	bap
Sep 6	Elizabeth, d of Edward & Mary DANGERFIELD	bap
Sep 6	Maria, d of Robert & Sarah FULWOOD	bap
Sep 6	Jane, d of Richard & Mary HODGKISS	bap
Sep 6	Joseph, s of James & Elizabeth FISHER	bap
Sep 6	John, s of Benjamin & Rachael WHEALE	bap
Sep 10	John GREGORY	bur
Sep 11	Reuben OSBORNE	bur
Sep 13	James, s of William & Rebecca DAVIES	bap
Sep 13	Henry Nock, s of Samuel & Maria SIMCOX	bap
Sep 13	Mary Ann, d of Thomas & Mary PUGH	bap
Sep 13	John, s of Joseph & Sarah HICKABOTTOM	bap
Sep 13	Susannah, d of George & Mary PERRY	bap
Sep 20	Sarah, d of Daniel & Sarah MINCHER	bap
Sep 20	Mary, d of John & Sarah BEDWORTH	bap
Sep 20	Mary, d of Paul & Mary COX	bap
Sep 20	Richard, s of John & Ann ADAMS	bap
Sep 20	John, s of John & Catharine STANTON, Born Sep 13	bap
Sep 20	Thomas PERRY	bur
Sep 27	Elizabeth, d of William & Elizabeth CONSTABLE, Born 24ᵗʰ	bap

~ Sep 27	Mary, d of Daniel & Susannah WEBB	bap
Sep 27	Thomas, s of Thomas & Hannah RABONE	bap
Sep 27	Sarah, d of Joseph & Sarah BAGGIT	bap
Sep 27	Maria & Richard, Twin s & d of Richard & Isabella TAYLOR	bap
Sep 27	Samuel BAGNALL	bur
Sep 29	Hannah SMITH	bur
Sep 30	Ruth WHITEHOUSE	bur
Oct 4	William, s of William & Ann MILLARD	bap
Oct 4	William, s of David & Margarett MORRISS	bap
Oct 4	Joseph, s of Samuel & Elizabeth GROVES	bap
~ Oct 4	Eliza, d of John & Elizabeth WHILE	bap
Oct 4	Samuel, s of William & Sarah LAW, about 17 years old	bap
Oct 11	Mary, d of Samuel & Rebecca HIPKISS	bap
Oct 11	Kitty, d of Richard & Ann WARTON	bap
Oct 11	Abraham DARBY	bur
~ Oct 12	William PARKES & Nancy HODGETS by Banns	mar
Oct 18	Thomas TURTON & Ann GREENWOOD by Banns	mar
Oct 18	John, s of John & Mary GRIFFITHS	bap
Oct 18	James, s of Stephen & Sarah FISHER	bap
Oct 18	Sarah, d of Samuel & Ann DUDLEY	bap
Oct 18	Maria, d of Samuel & Ann DUDLEY	bap
Oct 18	Heman, s of Richard & Jone DORRELL	bap
Oct 18	Sarah, d of William & Sarah BLACKHAM	bap
Oct 18	William, base s of Mary JEVON	bap
~ Oct 18	Sarah, d of Michael & Elizabeth PRICE	bap
~ Oct 25	Maria, d of John & Eleanor SIMMETER	bap
Oct 25	Thomas, s of Zachariah & Roseanna STEVENSON	bap
Oct 25	John, s of George & Ann BAXTER	bap
Oct 25	Thomas, s of Jeremiah & Hannah FIRKIN	bap
Oct 25	William DARBY	bur
~ Nov 1	John, s of Joseph & Ann WARD, Born Oct 13	bap
Nov 1	David, s of David & Ann FEREDAY	bap
Nov 1	James, base s of Sarah BLUNT	bap
Nov 1	Ann, d of Richard & Elizabeth LANKFORD, 9 yrs & 11 months old	bap
Nov 1	Richard, s of John & Kitty LANKFORD	bap
Nov 5	Peggy WHITEHOUSE	bur
Nov 6	Emma & William, twin d & s of William & Margaret FOSBROOK	bap
Nov 6	Margaret FOSBROOK	bur
Nov 8	James, s of James & Sarah SHINGLETON, Born Oct 16	bap
Nov 8	Sarah, d of Richard & Elizabeth LANKFORD, ab^t 21 years old	bap
Nov 8	John, s of Joseph & Jane WHITEHOUSE	bap
Nov 8	Elizabeth, d of James & Sarah AMOSS	bap
~ Nov 8	Edward, s of William & Elizabeth TURNER	bap
~ Nov 8	Thomas, s of Thomas & Sarah EADES	bap
Nov 8	Joseph, s of Daniel & Elizabeth WHITEHOUSE, Born 1st	bap
Nov 8	John, s of John & Elizabeth ROUND	bap
Nov 10	John HOBSON & Martha WHITEHOUSE by Banns	mar
Nov 10	William JOINER & Mary WHITEHOUSE by Banns	mar

Nov 11	William NICHOLAS	bur
Nov 12	Ambrose TIMMINS	bur
Nov 15	Joseph, s of William & Prissilla INGRAM	bap
Nov 15	Mary, d of George & Nancy YORK	bap
Nov 15	Sarah, d of John & Cretia KIRKHAM	bap
Nov 15	George Miner, s of Benjamin & Ann MATHERS	bap
Nov 22	Mark, s of Thomas & Ann FEREDAY	bap
Nov 22	John, s of John & Susanna PASKIN, Born July 11	bap
Nov 22	Mary, d of Richard & Mary NICHOLLS	bap
Nov 23	Samuel HORTON & Nancy RUDGE by Banns	mar
Nov 23	John DAVIS & Mary RUDGE by Banns	mar
Nov 23	Edward FEREDAY	bur
Nov 25	Daniel WHITEHOUSE	bur
Nov 28	William FOSBROOK	bur
Dec 1	John SMITH & Phebe HARGROVE by Banns	mar
Dec 3	Thomas CLARKE	bur
Dec 6	Abraham TIMMINS	bur
Dec 7	Isaac BAKER	bur
Dec 8	Thomas MAYBUREY & Maria HUGHES by Banns	mar
Dec 10	Thomas GRATTON	bur
Dec 13	Joseph GIBBINS & Elizabeth HOLLEHEAD by Banns	mar
Dec 13	Joseph SMITH & Mary MUMFORD by Banns	mar
Dec 13	Sarah, d of Samuel & Elizabeth GOULD	bap
Dec 13	Edward HARTSHORN	bur
Dec 13	Ann, d of William & Elizabeth FORD	bap
Dec 20	George BUSBAY & Elizabeth GREEN by Banns	mar
Dec 20	Charles, s of Richard & Lucy DAVIS, Born June 25	bap
Dec 20	William, s of James & Sarah LUNN, Born Nov 30	bap
Dec 20	Elizabeth, d of Joseph & Joice TURNER, Born Nov 28	bap
Dec 20	Daniel, s of Daniel & Mary JEAVONS, Born Nov 18	bap
Dec 20	James JONES	bur
Dec 25	James, s of Joseph & Elizabeth WALTON, Born Nov 15	bap
Dec 25	Thomas, s of William & Rosefiana WRIGHT, Born Oct 17	bap
Dec 25	Joseph, s of John & Elizabeth SHORT	bap
Dec 25	John, s of Edward & Ann BENNITT, Born Oct 2	bap
Dec 27	Moses CHATTIN & Elizabeth GREEN by Banns	mar
Dec 27	Caleb, s of Samson & Catharine AUSTIN, Born Oct 21	bap
Dec 27	James, s of James & Mary JEWKES, Born Nov 9	bap
Dec 27	Israel, s of Joseph & Elizabeth WILLIAMS	bap
Dec 27	William, s of Abraham & Ann GEORGE	bap
Dec 27	Ann, d of Richard & Mary STANTON	bap
Dec 27	Thomas, s of Thomas & Roseanna HAZELHURST	bap
Dec 27	Delila, d of Simeon & Hannah CORNFIELD	bap
Dec 27	Hannah, d of Joseph & Elizabeth JEWKES	bap
Dec 27	Francis MILLS	bur
Dec 27	John WALKER	bur
Dec 27	Phebe HAYWOOD	bur
Dec 28	Samuel LAW & Mary SKIDMORE by Banns	mar
Dec 30	Henry GUEST	bur

Dec 31	William NORTON	bur
Dec 31	James PRICE	bur

1808

Jan 3	John TRUEMAN & Sarah PERRY by Banns	mar
Jan 3	Richard, s of John & Hannah WHEALE	bap
Jan 3	Benjamin, s of Francis & Elizabeth CONNOP	bap
Jan 3	Mary MILLS	bur
Jan 3	Ann MINCHER	bur
Jan 3	Hannah WHEALE	bur
Jan 7	Richard NIGHTINGALE	bur
Jan 7	Benjamin WILLIS	bur
Jan 10	Isabell WARR	bur
Jan 10	Benjamin Sitch, s of George & Elizabeth DEELEY, Born Dec 12 1807	bap
Jan 10	Maria, d of Joseph & Sophia BROOKES, Born Dec 12 1807	bap
Jan 17	Sarah, d of Francis & Esther NICKLISS	bap
Jan 17	Daniel, s of William & Sophia EVANS, Born Dec 19 1807	bap
Jan 17	Elizabeth, d of Edward & Mary HOLT	bap
Jan 17	Ann LAW	bur
Jan 17	Thomas, s of Richard & Elizabeth BOWEN	bap
Jan 17	George, s of Edward & Phebe SMITH, Born Nov 18, 1807	bap
Jan 17	James, s of Thomas & Mary FITHON, Born Nov 2 1807	bap
Jan 17	Sarah, d of Joseph & Hannah WHITEHOUSE	bap
Jan 20	George ROBINSON	bur
Jan 24	Robert GROOM & Mary BRANT by Banns	mar
Jan 24	Benjamin, s of Samuel & Mary BOTT, Born 5th	bap
Jan 24	Samuel, s of Abel & Hannah CADDICK	bap
Jan 24	Joseph, s of Henry & Sarah WILLIAMS	bap
Jan 24	Mary, d of Robert & Hannah EDMUNDS	bap
Jan 24	Hannah, d of Joseph & Hannah BOTT, Born Dec 24 1807	bap
Jan 29	James HIPKISS & Jane HACKET by Banns	mar
Jan 27[sic]	Mary Ann KITSON	bur
Jan 31	Benjamin MILLS & Phebe ASSON by Banns	bap
Jan 31	Samuel BETTS & Mary LOWE by Banns	bap
Jan 31	William, s of William & Mary COOK	bap
Jan 31	Ann Maria, d of Samuel & Mary ROSE	bap
Jan 31	Isaac, s of Richard & Hannah Baker BIRD	bap
Jan 31	Joseph, base s of Sarah WORTON	bap
Jan 31	John, s of Joseph & Mary WOOD	bap
Jan 31	Hannah, d of John & Elizabeth FISHER	bap
Jan 31	Sarah, d of Thomas & Mary MORRIS, Born Dec 19 1807	bap
Feb 3	Job DAVIS	bur
Feb 7	William, s of William & Lydia LOWE, Born Jan 9	bap
Feb 7	William, s of Edward & Mary HILL	bap
Feb 7	Mary Ann, d of John & Sarah SHEREWOOD, Born Jan 16	bap
Feb 7	Elizabeth, d of John & Hannah COOPER	bap
Feb 7	Joannah, d of Benjamin & Elizabeth TWIGG	bap
Feb 9	Thomas MOORE	bur

1808

Feb 14	Benjamin, s of James & Lettice TURNER	bap
Feb 14	Mary Ann Whitehouse, d of Thomas & Ann KENT	bap
Feb 14	Elizabeth, d of John & Ann WILSON, Born Jan 15	bap
Feb 14	John, s of John & Mary WHITEHOUSE, about 20 years old	bap
Feb 15	Jonas WARR & Jane GRIFFITHS by Banns	mar
Feb 17	William ROUND	bur
Feb 19	Thomas WEBB	bur
Feb 21	Edward, s of James & Ann WHITEHOUSE	bap
Feb 21	James Lawley, s of William & Sarah PHASELY	bap
Feb 21	James, s of Joseph & Mary HILL, Born Jan 17	bap
Feb 21	Hannah, d of Joseph & Mary SMITH	bap
Feb 21	Mary, d of Thomas & Lydia MANSLEY	bap
Feb 21	Job, s of Isaac & Ann SMITH	bap
Feb 21	Ann, d of Samuel & Elizabeth COLLINS	bap
Feb 21	Thomas, s of John & Mary MOORE	bap
Feb 21	Mary, d of Thomas & Sarah JEWKS	bap
Feb 22	Thomas HUGHES & Elizabeth BILLINSLEY by Banns	mar
Feb 22	Charles BEARDS & Elizabeth REEVES by Banns	mar
Feb 28	Levi, s of Thomas & Dianna ROBINSON, Born 6th	bap
Feb 28	Hannah, d of Isaac & Elizabeth WHITEHOUSE, Born Jan 30	bap
Feb 28	Sarah, d of James & Abigal PRICE	bap
Feb 28	William, s of William & Mary HOSBORNE	bap
Feb 28	Maria TAYLOR	bur
Feb 28	Sarah PARTRIDGE	bur
Mar 3	Sarah BLACKHAM	bur
Mar 6	Lettice, d of Edward & Elizabeth LAW	bap
Mar 6	Joseph, s of William & Elizabeth HANCOX	bap
Mar 8	Peter MILLS & Elizabeth EDWARDS by Banns	bap
Mar 13	Sarah GRIFFITHS	bur
Mar 13	James, s of Abraham & Roseanna MILLS	bap
Mar 13	Mary Ann, d of John & Catharine JACKSON	bap
Mar 13	Hannah, d of Abraham & Mary JEVON, Born Feb 8	bap
Mar 13	Phebe, d of John & Hannah BUNCH	bap
Mar 13	Margaret, d of Edward & Margaret FISHER, Born Dec 20 1807	bap
Mar 13	Betsey, d of Thomas & Elizabeth HOLLIHEAD	bap
Mar 13	Mary Ann, d of John & Hannah TIBBITS	bap
Mar 13	William, d of Paul & Ann EVANS, Born Jan 16	bap
Mar 13	Roseanna, d of Joseph & Sarah MILLS, Born Jan 12	bap
Mar 13	Eliza, d of Joseph & Mary GRIFFITHS, Born Dec 5 1807	bap
Mar 13	Abraham, s of James & Shusanna HARTLAND, Born Jan 13	bap
Mar 13	John PHILLIPPS	bur
Mar 15	William GRIFFITHS	bur
Mar 18	George, s of William & Phebe BRAIN, Born April 1807	bap
Mar 20	Hannah, d of Joseph & Ann CADDICK	bap
Mar 20	William, s of James & Mary WHITEHOUSE	bap
Mar 25	Phebe GWINNETT	bur
Mar 27	Thomas FLAVEL & Ann FELLOWS by Banns	mar
Mar 27	Aaron TIMMINS & Mary STEVENS by Banns	mar
Mar 27	John, s of Joseph & Hannah GREENAWAY	bap

1808

Mar 27	Elizabeth, d of Thomas & Rachael HANCOX, Born Feb 3	bap
Mar 27	Isaiah, s of Roger & Phebe BROACHER, Born 18th	bap
Mar 27	Mary Ann, d of Thomas & Sarah TUDER	bap
Mar 27	Frederick, s of John & Sarah MORRIS	bap
Mar 27	Ann, d of Joseph & Sarah MILLS	bap
Mar 27	John, s of John & Ann DREW, Born Oct 27, 1807	bap
Mar 27	John WARTON	bur
Mar 27	William SMITH	bur
Mar 27	Eleanor WHITEHOUSE	bur
Mar 28	William GRIFFITHS & Mary MILLS by Banns	mar
Mar 28	Thomas HADNEY & Fanney STONE by Banns	mar
Mar 31	Sarah GRIFFITHS	bur
Apr 3	John CARTWRIGHT & Hannah MILLS by Banns	mar
Apr 3	Elizabeth, d of John & Ailse SHEREWOOD, Born Mar 17	bap
Apr 3	William WHITEHOUSE	bur
Apr 5	William MORRIS	bur
Apr 10	Edward DAVIS & Mary TURNER by Banns	mar
Apr 10	Daniel, s of Joseph & Mary WARD	bap
Apr 10	Elizabeth, d of Richard & Amelia LAW	bap
Apr 10	Ann, d of Richard & Elizabeth FIELD, Born Mar 6	bap
Apr 10	Mary, d of James & Roseanna WILLIES	bap
Apr 10	Francis, s of John & Mary ROBINSON	bap
Apr 10	Sarah, d of Richard & Ann THOMPSON	bap
Apr 17	John, s of John & Maria SHAW, born Mar 16	bap
Apr 17	Thomas, s of Thomas & Elizabeth HARRISON, 2 years old	bap
Apr 17	Rebecca & Isaac, twin d & s of Thomas & Sarah BOTT	bap
Apr 17	Sophia, d of Robert & Mary GRANT	bap
Apr 17	Nancy, d of John & Ann WOODBURN	bap
Apr 17	William, s of Joseph & Mary FLEET	bap
Apr 17	David, s of Job & Elizabeth BROOKS	bap
Apr 17	Jesse, d of David & Mary JEVONS	bap
Apr 17	Elizabeth, d of James & Debora NOCK	bap
Apr 17	Mary, d of John & Elizabeth HIDE	bap
Apr 17	Ann, d of John & Mary GREEN	bap
Apr 17	Ann, d of Joseph & Catharine COCKRAN	bap
Apr 17	John WILLINGTON	bur
Apr 18	William RHODES & Elizabeth MARTIN by Banns	mar
Apr 18	Sophia DARBY	bur
Apr 19	William FOSTER & Jane BIDEL by Banns	mar
Apr 19	Daniel HICKMANS	bur
Apr 24	Ann, d of John & Hannah CUMPSTON	bap
Apr 24	William, s of Thomas & Mary ARCUT	bap
Apr 24	John, s of John & Sarah JONES	bap
Apr 24	Thomas, s of Joseph & Sarah PERRINS	bap
Apr 27	Sophia GRANT	bur
May 1	Josiah, s of Joseph & Sarah HUGHES	bap
May 2	John BATTY & Phebe HARRISS by Banns	mar
May 2	Thomas WHITEHOUSE	bur
May 3	Joseph CHAMBERS & Hannah STOKES by Banns	mar

1808

May 4	William, s of John & Mary SIMSON	bap
May 4	Daniel, s of Daniel & Phebe WHITEHOUSE, aged 27 years	bap
May 4	John, s of Daniel & Peggy WHITEHOUSE, aged near 12 years	bap
May 5	Joseph, s of William & Sarah TUCKLEY, Born Nov 9 1807	bap
May 5	Sarah FELLOWS	bur
May 8	Judith, d of George & Mary FISHER	bap
May 15	Hannah, d of Elisha & Prissilla WHITEHOUSE	bap
May 15	Prissilla, d of John & Ann EVANS	bap
May 15	Sarah, d of Ambrose & Ruth TIMMINS	bap
May 17	Joseph MORRIS	bur
May 17	John TAYLOR	bur
May 22	Maria MORRIS	bur
May 22	Ann, d of Daniel & Lucy WORLEY	bap
May 22	Nathaniel, s of John & Margarett HEELY	bap
May 27	Samuel BATE	bur
May 29	Harriot, d of William & Mary DUFFIELD	bap
May 29	Elizabeth, d of Benjamin & Sarah FEREDAY	bap
May 29	Phebe, d of Edward & Phebe WHITEHOUSE	bap
May 29	Mary, d of James & Nancy PLANT	bap
May 29	Ann, d of Charles & Elizabeth HICKABOTTOM	bap
May 29	John, s of Edward & Prissilla SMITH	bap
May 29	Francis, d of Edward & Prissilla SMITH, aged 5 years	bap
May 30	Nathaniel ARCH & Sarah WARD by Banns	mar
May 31	Shusanna EDGE	bur
Jun 5	Thomas, s of Edward & Elizabeth PETERS	bap
Jun 5	Maria, d of George & Sarah BUFF, Born Apl 30	bap
Jun 5	Samuel, s of William & Sarah WHITEHOUSE	bap
Jun 5	Ann, base d of Ann JEWKS	bap
Jun 5	John, s of Edward & Elizabeth STANHOPE, Born May 12	bap
Jun 5	Elizabeth, d of Joseph & Sarah FISHER	bap
Jun 5	Ann, base d of Elizabeth GEORGE	bap
Jun 5	John, s of John & Prudence THOMAS	bap
Jun 5	Mary, d of Joseph & Mary MILLS	bap
Jun 5	Thomas, s of Nathan & Mary HILL	bap
Jun 5	John, s of John & Eleanor ROBERTS	bap
Jun 5	William, s of William & Ann COOPER	bap
Jun 5	Nicholis, s of Nicholis & Sarah WOOD	bap
Jun 5	Levi, s of Benjamin & Sarah COX	bap
Jun 5	Ruth, d of William & Elizabeth DARBY	bap
Jun 5	John, s of Richard & Nancy GARBIT	bap
Jun 5	Elizabeth, d of Joseph & Rhoda ASTON	bap
Jun 5	Samuel, s of John & Lucy GARDENER	bap
Jun 5	Joseph, s of Joseph & Elizabeth Ann BANNER	bap
Jun 6	William UNIT & Mary FELLOWS by Banns	mar
Jun 6	Edward FINCH	bur
Jun 7	Nancy MILLS	bur
Jun 9	John LAW	bur
Jun 12	Mary & Hannah, twin d of Henry & Hannah JONES	bap
Jun 12	Mary, d of Edward & Mary FISHER	bap

1808

Jun 12	John, s of John & Ann SPITTLE, Born Nov 11 1807	bap
Jun 12	Thomas, s of John & Rhoda SMITH, Born May 22	bap
Jun 12	Charles, s of Charles & Phillis LAW	bap
Jun 12	Ann, d of James & Elizabeth HICKMANS	bap
Jun 12	Edward, s of Joseph & Ann WHITEHOUSE, Born Mar 6	bap
Jun 12	Samuel, s of Josiah & Hannah GRINSILL	bap
Jun 12	Jane, d of James & Jane NOCK, Born March 25	bap
Jun 12	Ann COLEY	bur
Jun 14	Abraham FISHER & Sarah BENTON by Banns	mar
Jun 19	Jane, d of William & Sarah HARTELL, Born June 20 1806	bap
Jun 19	Phebe, d of James & Hannah DOWNS, Born Feb 16	bap
Jun 19	William, s of William & Sarah HARTELL, Born Jan 6	bap
Jun 19	Elizabeth, d of Thomas & Elizabeth BILL	bap
Jun 19	William, s of Aaron & Mary TIMMINS	bap
Jun 19	Richard, s of Richard & Mary BRITTLE	bap
Jun 20	Lucy, d of Joseph & Elizabeth MOSS, Born Apl 13, 1806	bap
Jun 20	Thomas Powell, s of Joseph & Elizabeth MOSS	bap
Jun 23	Joseph PRESTON	bur
Jun 26	George, s of James & Mary SCHOLEFIELD	bap
Jun 26	John, s of John & Lucy DARBY	bap
Jun 26	Henry, s of Philip & Ann WILLIAMS	bap
Jun 26	William, s of Samuel & Mary HARPER	bap
Jun 26	Mary Ann, d of John & Mary GRIFFITHS	bap
Jun 26	Sarah, d of Joseph & Sophia HOLT, Born 16th	bap
Jun 26	Margaret, d of Samuel & Mary ROBERTS	bap
Jun 26	James, s of Joseph & Mary FISHER	bap
Jun 26	Ann, d of William & Ann ELWELL	bap
Jul 3	Thomas ASTON & Sarah FRANKS by Banns	mar
Jul 3	William, s of Samuel & Sarah FEREDAY	bap
Jul 3	Mary, d of Benjamin & Mary HARTLAND	bap
Jul 3	Joseph, s of William & Ann ALLIN	bap
Jul 3	Mary, d of David & Hannah GRICE	bap
Jul 4	William FIRKIN	bur
Jul 10	John Phillips, s of William & Sarah JEWKS	bap
Jul 10	Mary, d of John & Ann KING	bap
Jul 10	Edward, s of Joseph & Rachael DUFFIELD, Born May 4	bap
Jul 13	Mary BODY	bur
Jul 17	George COTTERILL & Elizabeth PITT by Banns	mar
Jul 17	Julia, d of Joseph & Sarah WHEALE	bap
Jul 17	Elizabeth, d of James & Ann PERRY	bap
Jul 17	Ann, d of James & Ann SATCHELL	bap
Jul 18	William GRIFFITHS & Shusanna SKIDMORE by Banns	mar
Jul 19	John HICKMANS & Elizabeth MULLINER by Banns	mar
Jul 24	Joseph STOKES & Mary GRIGG by Banns	mar
Jul 24	Sarah, d of William & Sarah HILL	bap
Jul 24	Thomas, s of James & Sarah ROBINSON	bap
Jul 24	William, s of John & Martha BUMFORD	bap
Jul 24	Sarah Taylor, d of Samuel & Sarah HODGKINS, Born Ap 23	bap
Jul 24	Sophia, d of John & Eleanor WHITEHOUSE	bap

Jul 24	John, s of Benjamin & Ann BLEWITT, Born 8th	bap
Jul 25	John TURNER & Dinah PAGE by Banns	mar
Jul 25	Joseph JEVONS & Mary JAMES by Banns	mar
Jul 25	George HASLEHURST & Elizabeth BEDFORD by Banns	mar
Jul 26	Paul ELWELL & Elizabeth EDWARDS by Banns	mar
Jul 27	Abraham TIMMINS	bur
Jul 28	William LEES	bur
Jul 31	John BINTT & Mary WOODHALL by Banns	mar
Jul 31	Richard HADLINGTON & Mary GRIFFIN by Banns	mar
Jul 31	Thomas, s of William & Mary SKELDING	bap
Jul 31	Constant, d of Daniel & Roseanna SHELDON	bap
Jul 31	Mary, d of Benjamin & Sarah GRIFFITHS	bap
Jul 31	Martha, d of Richard & Elizabeth OWEN	bap
Jul 31	Ann, d of Joseph & Ann CARTWRIGHT	bap
Jul 31	Mary, d of Joseph & Ann SMITH	bap
Aug 1	Richard PAGE	bur
Aug 2	Thomas DUFFIN & Eleanor CASHMORE by Banns	mar
Aug 2	Sarah CALLEY	bur
Aug 4	John TAYLOR	bur
Aug 6	John EDWARDS & Ann WILLIAMS by Licence	mar
Aug 7	Martha, d of Samuel & Shusanna MAYBUREY	mar
Aug 9	Julia WHEALE	bur
Aug 11	James MORRIS	bur
Aug 14	Maria, d of Jesse & Mary WHITEHOUSE	bap
Aug 14	Nancy, d of Abraham & Elizabeth SHELDON	bap
Aug 14	Sarah, d of Charles & Hannah JONES	bap
Aug 14	George, s of Thomas & Sarah GREEN	bap
Aug 15	John PUGH & Sarah HILL by Banns	mar
Aug 18	Elizabeth EDWARDS	bur
Aug 21	Charles, s of Joseph & Ann VERNON	bap
Aug 21	Arter, s of Arter & Frances WHESSON	bap
Aug 21	James, s of Thomas & Maria BAGNALL, Born July 23	bap
Aug 21	Harriott, d of John & Mary SHELDON	bap
Aug 21	Eleanor, d of John & Patience WARD	bap
Aug 21	Nancy, d of Thomas & Sarah BUTLER	bap
Aug 21	Elizabeth, d of Joseph & Sarah WARD	bap
Aug 22	Orolando POWELL	bur
Aug 25	Daniel ROUND	bur
Aug 27	Job DAVIS & Hannah DICKENS by Banns	mar
Aug 28	John, s of Thomas & Elizabeth HARRISON	bap
Aug 28	James, s of James & Sarah COOKSEY	bap
Aug 28	Rebecca, d of William & Hannah WHITEHOUSE	bap
Aug 28	Philliss, d of Richard & Philliss WHITEHOUSE	bap
Aug 28	Samuel, base s of Ann GREEN	bap
Aug 28	Roseanna, d of James & Sarah OSBORNE	bap
Aug 28	Sarah WHITEHOUSE	bur
Aug 29	Joseph MILLINGTON & Martha BAGLEY by Banns	mar
Sep 4	Thomas BARRAT & Roseanna WILLIAMS by Banns	mar
Sep 4	John, s of Benjamin & Hannah PARTRIDGE	bap

~	Sep 4	Nancy, d of Thomas & Cara HOPKINS	bap
	Sep 4	Mary, d of William & Elizabeth RICHARDS	bap
	Sep 4	Daniel, s of Thomas & Elizabeth COLLINS	bap
	Sep 4	Thomas, s of Richard & Jane LANGDON	bap
	Sep 4	John, s of William & Elizabeth ROBERTS	bap
	Sep 4	William OSBORNE	bur
	Sep 5	Joseph WHITEHOUSE & Hannah JAMES by Banns	mar
	Sep 9	Comfort SKIDMORE	bur
—	Sep 11	Sarah HALL	bur
	Sep 11	William, s of Richard & Sarah ROW, Born Aug 4	bap
	Sep 11	Elizabeth, d of John & Mary HARRIS	bap
	Sep 11	Ann, d of Thomas & Sarah BILL	bap
~	Sep 11	Maria, d of Joseph & Marrable GUTTRIDGE, Born Feb 1	bap
	Sep 12	William MORGAN & Elizabeth HARPER by Banns	mar
	Sep 13	Samuel Whittfield DANKS & Hannah SMITH, by Licence	mar
	Sep 16	Isaac MILLS & Ann WHITEHOUSE by Banns	mar
	Sep 16	Mary Ann BAKER	bur
	Sep 18	Elizabeth, d of Joseph & Nancy HOLLOWAY	bap
	Sep 18	Mary, d of Josiah & Mary FISHER	bap
	Sep 18	Eliza, d of Richard & Mary PASKIN	bap
	Sep 18	James, s of Henry & Esther WARTON, Born Aug 25	bap
	Sep 19	Joseph HEELEY & Hannah MILLINGTON by Banns	mar
—	Sep 19	John BODEN & Ann RODEN by Banns	mar
~	Sep 19	Joseph SHAW & Ann DOWLEY by Banns	mar
	Sep 20	Sarah BROOKS	bur
	Sep 25	Solomon WHIELD & Elizabeth HOLDEN by Banns	mar
	Sep 25	Thomas, s of Abraham & Ann BATE	bap
	Sep 25	Sarah, d of William & Sophia BATE	bap
—	Sep 25	Edward, s of Benjamin & Sarah LOWE	bap
	Sep 25	Joseph, s of Job & Elizabeth SHELDON, Born Aug 27	bap
	Sep 25	John, s of James & Mary STANTON	bap
	Sep 25	William BISSELL	bur
	Sep 25	Ann ASTON	bur
	Sep 25	Mary WHITEHOUSE	bur
	Sep 28	Maria BROOKS	bur
~	Oct 2	Joseph, s of Isaac & Sarah TIMMINS, Born Sep 20	bap
~	Oct 2	Thomas, s of John & Sarah WHEALE, Born Sep 23	bap
	Oct 2	Joseph, s of Joseph & Hannah ROUND, Born Sep 8	bap
~	Oct 3	Thomas SMITH & Mary TURNER by Banns	mar
	Oct 4	Honor TUDOR	bur
	Oct 9	Mary Ann, d of Benjamin & Hannah BLUNT	bap
	Oct 9	William, s of John & Hannah CARTWRIGHT	bap
~	Oct 9	Maria, d of Joseph & Susanna WISE	bap
	Oct 9	William, s of Thomas & Eleanor DUFFIN	bap
~	Oct 9	Abraham, s of Isaac & Isabella TIMMINS	bap
~	Oct 9	John, s of John & Prissilla SOUTHALL	bap
	Oct 9	Sarah HARRIS	bur
	Oct 10	William GARNER & Elizabeth ROGERS by Banns	mar
~	Oct 10	Tobias MITCHELL & Eleanor ROGERS by Banns	mar

Date	Name	Type
Oct 11	Catharine WORTON	bur
Oct 12	Joseph ROBINSON	bur
Oct 16	William, s of John & Elizabeth SMITH	bap
Oct 16	Hannah, base d of Mary NOCK	bap
Oct 16	John, s of James & Prissilla SHELDON	bap
Oct 16	Isaiah, s of Moses & Mary ROUND	bap
Oct 23	William MILLS & Elizabeth SPITTLE by Banns	mar
Oct 23	Eliza, d of Joshua & Hannah PARTRIDGE	bap
Oct 23	Richard, s of Thomas & Maria SMITH	bap
Oct 23	Joseph, s of John & Sarah HART	bap
Oct 23	Frances, d of Thomas & Sarah PERRINS	bur
Oct 23	Ailce CARTWRIGHT	bur
Oct 24	John HARRISON & Rebecca CHARTER by Banns	mar
Oct 27	Joseph ASTON & Hannah CADDICK by Licence	mar
Oct 28	Mary WILLIAMS	bur
Oct 30	Joseph, s of Edward & Mary WHITEHOUSE	bap
Oct 30	Joseph, s of Joseph & Elizabeth BRADLEY, ab^t 6 yrs old	bap
Oct 30	Nancy, d of Noah & Sarah TIMMINS	bap
Oct 30	Eliza, d of James & Sophia JONES	bap
Oct 30	Elizabeth, d of John & Deborah GREGORY	bap
Oct 30	Jane, d of Edward & Sarah TOOKLEY	bap
Oct 30	Elizabeth, d of James & Elizabeth WALTERS	bap
Oct 30	Roseanna, d of Joseph & Ann DUDLEY	bap
Oct 30	Sarah, d of Thomas & Nancy DUDLEY	bap
Oct 30	William GRIFFITHS	bur
Oct 31	Richard OWEN	bur
Nov 6	Ann, d of William & Martha ELLET, Born May 24	bap
Nov 6	Harriott, d of Thomas & Hannah MATHEWS	bap
Nov 6	John, s of Thomas & Hannah MATHEWS	bap
Nov 6	Mary, d of Abraham & Maria PARKES	bap
Nov 6	Adam, s of George & Mary GREGORY	bap
Nov 6	Jesse, d of Robert & Susanna JONES	bap
Nov 6	William Partridge, s of Thomas & Martha LEES	bap
Nov 7	Mary Ann, d of Francis & Mary TWIST	bap
Nov 7	Tobias MITCHELL	bur
Nov 8	Elizabeth JONES	bur
Nov 13	Samuel, s of Richard & Selvia NEWELL	bap
Nov 13	John, s of John & Hannah LAW	bap
Nov 13	Mary Ann, d of Nathaniel & Sarah ARCH	bap
Nov 13	Mary, d of Thomas & Sarah ROSE	bap
Nov 13	Thomas, s of Thomas & Mary ELWELL	bap
Nov 13	John, s of Abel & Eleanor EGGINTON	bap
Nov 13	Mary, d of Richard & Pemila GRIFFITHS	bap
Nov 13	Mary GRIFFITHS	bur
Nov 16	Sarah ELWELL	bur

[The next entry, made at the bottom of the page, is crossed through:]

	~~William TURNER & Amelia WHITEHOUSE~~	~~mar~~
Nov 20	Ann, d of Thomas & Ann WOODHALL	bap
Nov 22	William TURNER & Amelia WHITEHOUSE by Banns	bap

Nov 22	Sarah HEELEY	bur
Nov 27	Josiah OAKLEY & Phebe WHITEHOUSE by Banns	mar
Nov 27	Mary Ann, d of Thomas & Rachel RYLEY	bap
Nov 27	Eliza, d of John & Elizabeth JONES	bap
Nov 27	Ann, d of John & Mary BLACKHAM	bap
Nov 27	John Horton, s of Joshua & Hannah HOYLE	bap
Nov 27	Richard, d of John & Mary EVANS, Born July 20	bap
Nov 27	Jemmima, d of John & Ann CLERK	bap
Nov 27	Ann, d of William & Rose Sophia Ann WRIGHT	bap
Nov 28	Sarah JONES	bur
Dec 4	Joseph ADLINGTON & Mary HOBSON by Banns	mar
Dec 4	Edward, s of Thomas & Margarett COOPER	bap
Dec 4	Catharine, d of Edward Elizabeth MARTIN	bap
Dec 4	Joseph, s of Joseph & Nancy WHITEHOUSE	bap
Dec 4	William, s of John & Rachel GILES	bap
Dec 4	Maria, d of William & Ann PHIPPS	bap
Dec 4	Phebe, d of William & Margaret WILLIAMS	bap
Dec 4	John, s of John & Mary JEVONS	bap
Dec 4	Samuel, s of Edward & Sarah DUDLEY	bap
Dec 5	John PRICE & Mary SHELDON by Banns	mar
Dec 8	Eliza, d of Edward & Sarah ASTON, Born Nov 11	bap
Dec 11	Samuel SUTTON & Sarah WARD by Banns	mar
Dec 11	John, s of Thomas & Hannah CLERK	bap
Dec 11	Ann GEORGE	bur
Dec 11	Francis KEMP	bur
Dec 11	Harriott, d of John & Mary BATE, Born Nov 27	bap
Dec 12	Joseph CLEWLEY & Ann HICHENNER by Banns	mar
Dec 14	Samuel NEWELL	bur
Dec 15	Harriott PLATT	bur
Dec 18	Thomas, s of Joseph & Phebe STANTON	bap
Dec 18	Mary Ann, d of Joseph & Mary PASKIN	bap
Dec 18	Samuel, s of Samuel & Ann MORRIS	bap
Dec 18	Ann KEMP	bur
Dec 18	Mary TROWMAN	bur
Dec 18	John BLACKHAM	bur
Dec 24	Eleanor LAW	bur
Dec 25	Richard RUSTON & Ann TAYLOR by Banns	mar
Dec 25	Isaiah, s of Joseph & Henrietta PARKES	bap
Dec 25	Thomas, s of Joseph & Martha MILLINGTON	bap
Dec 25	William, s of William & Betsey DUFFIELD	bap
Dec 25	Richard, s of Richard & Sarah GRIFFITHS	bap
Dec 25	Edward, s of Richard & Sarah NIGHTINGALE	bap
Dec 25	Lydia, d of David & Francis HIPKINS, Born 16	bap
Dec 25	William, s of John & Prudence THOMAS	bap
Dec 25	Mary, d of Abraham & Mary BAKER	bap
Dec 25	James, s of John & Phebe MILLS	bap
Dec 25	Joseph, s of Thomas & Ann COTTERILL	bap
Dec 25	James, s of Thomas & Elizabeth COX	bap
Dec 25	Mary Ann, d of Thomas & Sarah WALKER	bap

<u>1808</u>

Dec 26	William RYLEY & Sarah JOHNSON by Banns	mar
Dec 26	Daniel FLETCHER & Francis TURNER by Banns	mar
Dec 27	Ralph BROWN & Elizabeth ARCH by Banns	mar
Dec 27	James MORRIS	bur
Dec 31	Charles WHITEHEAD	bur

Here ends this Register

1809

Jan 1	Maria, d of William & Elizabeth BRATT	bap
Jan 1	William, s of James & Ann WALTON	bap
Jan 1	Eliza, d of Samuel & Mary INGRAM	bap
Jan 8	Joseph, s of Thomas & Elizabeth DANKS	bap
Jan 8	Benjamin, s of John & Sarah BUTTLER	bap
Jan 8	Francis, s of Joseph & Elizabeth WHITEHOUSE	bap
Jan 8	John, s of William & Hannah HOLLAND	bap
Jan 9	Thomas LEADBETTER & Ann MEER, by Banns	mar
Jan 11	Francis SHELDON	bur
Jan 11	Ann, d of Thomas & Hannah CLARK	bap
Jan 12	Samuel WHITEHOUSE	bur
Jan 15	Hannah, d of William & Ann HIPKINS	bap
Jan 15	Thomas, s of John & Patience WILLIAMS	bap
Jan 15	David, s of Edward & Sarah GOODYER	bap
Jan 15	Elizabeth, d of John & Maria PLANT	bap
Jan 15	Sarah, d of Samuel & Maria SIMCOX	bap
Jan 15	Abraham, s of Richard & Mary FOSTER	bap
Jan 15	Edward GRIFFITHS	bur
Jan 18	Isaac FLETCHER	bur
Jan 22	John OCROFT & Elizabeth RALLEY, by Banns	mar
Jan 23	Thomas WEBSTER & Mary TONKS, by Banns	mar
Jan 24	True WHITEHOUSE	bur
Jan 29	William SMITH & Ann OSBORNE, by Banns	mar
Jan 29	Sarah, d of Samuel & Mary HARRISON	bap
Jan 29	John, s of Samuel & Ann DUDLEY, Born 6th	bap
Jan 29	Elizabeth, d of William & Mary DOWNING	bap
Jan 29	Sarah, d of William & Sarah BLACKHAM	bap
Jan 29	Elizabeth, d of Thomas & Eleanor GRIFFITHS	bap
Jan 29	Sarah, d of Elijah & Ann WILCOX, Born 13	bap
Jan 29	James, s of Thomas & Elizabeth FEREDAY, Born 5th	bap
Feb 5	John, s of Thomas & Mary BENNITT	bap
Feb 5	Thomas, s of Thomas & Sarah ROWLEY	bap
Feb 5	Solomon PARKES	bur
Feb 5	Isaac BOTT	bur
Feb 5	William WHITEHOUSE	bur
Feb 6	Charles HILL & Phebe INGRAM, by Banns	mar
Feb 12	Samuel, s of Griffin & Mary MITCHELL	bap
Feb 12	Elizabeth, d of Richard & Elizabeth JACKSON	bap
Feb 12	Clementina, d of John & Elizabeth BEDDOE	bap
Feb 12	Sarah, d of William & Elizabeth WALTERS	bap
Feb 12	John, s of James & Hannah GRIFFITHS	bap
Feb 12	Julia, d of Thomas & Hannah RABONE	bap
Feb 13	Thomas STEPHENSON & Jane GREEN, by Banns	mar
Feb 14	Thomas JEWKES	bur
Feb 16	Ann MILLS	bur
Feb 17	Edward GUEST	bur

	Feb 19	Sarah, d of Richard & Sarah STEVENTON	bap
	Feb 19	Joseph, s of Thomas & Sarah EADES	bap
	Feb 19	John, s of John & Elizabeth PRESTON	bap
	Feb 19	Abraham, s of Daniel & Mary WHITEHOUSE, Born 16th	bap
	Feb 19	Prudence, d of Joshua & Phebe FLETCHER	bap
	Feb 19	Jane, d of John & Clare STANLEY	bap
	Feb 19	Isaiah JEWKES	bur
	Feb 20	Thomas BAYNES & Phebe EARP by Banns	mar
	Feb 24	Eliza FIELD	bur
	Feb 26	Anchor, d of James & Elizabeth FISHER	bap
	Feb 26	Elizabeth, d of Thomas & Hannah MOTTRAM	bap
	Feb 26	Mary Ann, d of John & Sarah BAGNALL	bap
	Feb 26	John, s of Henry & Sarah LEWIS	bap
	Feb 26	John, s of Thomas & Mary NASH	bap
	Feb 26	John, s of John & Sarah DOWLEY	bap
	Feb 26	William, s of Thomas & Emey JONES, Born 22nd	bap
	Feb 27	Morris HARRISON	bur
	Feb 28	Edward WHITEHOUSE	bur
	Feb 28	Thomas Smith, s of Thomas & Sarah BELL, Born Sep 4 1807	bap
	Feb 28	Charles, s of Joseph & Hannah JONES, Born May 14 1808	bap
	Feb 28	Mary HIPKISS	bur
	Mar 2	Hannah, d of Thomas & Mercy POWELL	bap
	Mar 5	Joseph DAINTY & Elizabeth STEVENS by Banns	mar
	Mar 5	George BODEN & Mary HODGETTS by Banns	mar
	Mar 5	Thomas, s of John & Susanna GREGORY, Born Mar 23 1808	bap
	Mar 5	Elizabeth, d of Richard & Sarah REED	bap
	Mar 5	Mary, d of Edward & Elizabeth REED	bap
	Mar 5	Ann, d of Stephen & Maria CRESSWELL, Born Feb 24	bap
	Mar 5	Samuel, s of Samuel & Mary TONKS	bap
	Mar 5	Diana KIMBERLEY	bur
	Mar 6	Mary OSBORNE	bur
	Mar 7	Maria WHITEHOUSE	bur
	Mar 8	Charles PRICE	bur
	Mar 9	Mary FISHER	bur
	Mar 12	Benjamin, s of Daniel & Sarah TOMSON	bap
	Mar 12	Sarah, d of Edward & Mary BROWN	bap
	Mar 12	Richard, s of Benjamin & Sarah DUNN	bap
	Mar 12	Maria, d of Thomas & Mary STINSON	bap
	Mar 12	Ann, d of Ralph & Ann KELSON	bap
	Mar 12	Elizabeth, d of Daniel & Martha WHITEHOUSE	bap
	Mar 12	Joseph, s of Edward & Ann CLARK	bap
	Mar 12	Abraham, s of Isaac & Mary BATE	bap
	Mar 12	Lucy MATTHEWS	bur
	Mar 12	Jane, base d of Hannah FISHER	bap
	Mar 13	George DEAKIN	bur
	Mar 14	Harriott, d of John & Hannah POWELL	bap
	Mar 15	Benjamin NICKLIN	bur
	Mar 19	Esther, d of Abiathar & Sarah HANCOX	bap
	Mar 19	Robert, s of John & Sarah BENNITT	bap

1809

Mar 19	Margarett, d of David & Peggy MORRIS	bap
Mar 19	Mary, d of William & Esther FOSBROOK	bap
Mar 19	James, s of James & Hannah DALE	bap
Mar 19	Henry, s of George & Elizabeth BALL	bap
Mar 19	James, s of William & Susannah GRIFFITHS, Born 5th	bap
Mar 19	Mary Ann, d of James & Hannah BARKEBY[?]	bap
Mar 19	Thomas, s of William & Elizabeth ROGERS, Born Feb 19	bap
Mar 20	Elizabeth CONSTABLE	bur
Mar 23	Sarah STEVENTON	bur
Mar 23	Margarett MORRIS	bur
— Mar 26	Solomon, s of Thomas & Sophia PARKES	bap
Mar 26	George SCHOLEFIELD	bur
Mar 26	Harriott WHITEHOUSE	bur
Mar 27	Thomas BALL & Rebecca NEWTON by Banns	mar
Mar 30	Abraham WHITEHOUSE	bur
Apr 2	James PERRY & Elizabeth HARRISON by Banns	mar
— Apr 2	Sarah, d of Richard & Martha WASSELL	bap
— Apr 2	John, s of David & Hannah WASSELL	bap
— Apr 2	Esther, d of Thomas & Elizabeth HOLIHEAD	bap
Apr 2	William, s of Joseph & Jane WHITEHOUSE	bap
Apr 2	Charlotte, d of Joseph & Ann HARTWELL	bap
Apr 2	John, s of John & Elizabeth LESTER	bap
— Apr 2	Samuel, s of Amos & Francis HODGSKINS	bap
Apr 2	Elizabeth, d of John & Margery HATTON	bap
Apr 2	Isaiah, s of William & Elizabeth BELCHER, Born Mar 19	bap
Apr 2	Thomas, s of James & Sarah CHATER	bap
Apr 2	Samuel, s of Samuel & Elizabeth COLLINS	bap
Apr 2	Joseph, s of Obadiah & Nancy JOHNSON	bap
Apr 2	Daniel ROUND	bur
Apr 3	Thomas SMITH & Mary BARNS by Banns	mar
— Apr 3	Thomas KENDALL & Susannah WESTWOOD, by Banns	mar
— Apr 3	Richard PARTRIDGE & Ann LOWE by Banns	mar
Apr 4	Sarah FALKNALL	bur
Apr 9	Phebe, d of Thomas & Hannah TILLEY, Born Novr 10 1808	bap
✓ Apr 9	Mary Ann, d of Benjamin & Sarah PRICE, Born Dec 22 1808	bap
— Apr 9	Nancy, d of William & Prissilla INGRAM	bap
— Apr 9	Rebella, d of John & Sarah TIMMINS	bap
Apr 9	Sarah, d of John & Mary HIGGINS	bap
Apr 9	Daniel WILLIAMS	bur
— Apr 10	John FELLOWS & Sarah LAW by Banns	mar
Apr 13	Mary WHITEHOUSE	bur
Apr 16	Richard ELLIS & Aylce DAINTY by Banns	mar
Apr 16	William, s of Thomas & Susannah TAYLOR	bap
Apr 16	Edward, s of Thomas & Mary PUGH, Born Mar 23	bap
— Apr 16	Samuel TIMMINS	bur
Apr 16	Joseph TAYLOR	bur
Apr 18	George EVANS	bur
Apr 20	James BOTT & Mary WATERHOUSE, by Banns	mar
Apr 20	Helen, d of Joseph & Hannah ASTON	bap

1809

Apr 23	Rebecca, d of Samuel & Mary MILLS	bap
Apr 23	Julia, d of Thomas & Jane NOCK	bap
Apr 23	Richard, s of William & Elizabeth STANTON, Born Mar 30	bap
Apr 23	Phebe, d of James & Hannah FISHER, Born 3^d	bap
Apr 23	Elizabeth, d of William & Sarah SHEREWOOD	bap
Apr 23	Tabiatha, d of Uriah & Jane PLATT	bap
Apr 23	William, s of Isaac & Sarah WILKINSON	bap
Apr 24	Edward WHITEHOUSE & Jane GREEN by Banns	mar
Apr 26	Joseph INGRAM	bur
Apr 30	Ann, d of David & Sarah CALLOWAY	bap
Apr 30	Elizabeth, d of George & Sarah JONES	bap
Apr 30	Samuel, base s of Ann WHITEHOUSE	bap
Apr 30	Edward, s of James & Jane HARRISON	bap
Apr 30	William ADAMS	bur
Apr 30	Mary FEREDAY	bur
May 1	Thomas HICKMANS	bur
May 5	Benoni FISHER & Martha WILLETS by Licence	mar
May 7	Elizabeth, d of William & Maria HICKABOTTOM	bap
May 7	John, s of William & Prudence MINCHER	bap
May 7	Elizabeth, d of Gideon & Mary WHITEHOUSE	bap
May 7	Mary, d of Thomas & Sarah EVANS	bap
May 7	Elizabeth BALL	bur
May 8	Hannah Maria HODGKINS	bur
May 8	Amelia WALTON	bur
May 9	Edward WHITEHOUSE	bur
May 11	Thomas BATE	bur
May 12	John CRESWELL	bur
May 14	Mary BRAIN	bur
May 14	Mary, d of Thomas & Sarah POOL	bap
May 14	Thomas, s of Thomas & Mary LAPPAGE	bap
May 14	Mary & Ann, twin d's of John & Ann ROUPER, Born 7th	bap
May 14	Henry GROUTAGE	bur
May 14	Elizabeth EVANS	bur
May 21	Thomas PASKIN & Ann ASTON, by Banns	mar
May 21	Mary Ann, d of John & Mary SMITH	bap
May 21	William, s of William & Rebecca DAVIS	bap
May 21	Ann, base d of Mary SKIDMORE	bap
May 21	Thomas, s of Thomas & Ann CHAMBERS	bap
May 21	Thomas, s of Thomas & Hannah KENNEDY	bap
May 21	Mary, d of Joseph & Elizabeth TONKS	bap
May 21	James Hinds, s of James & Mary PASSFIELD	bap
May 22	Thomas DAVIS & Sarah DANKS by Banns	mar
May 23	William HATTON & Rebecca ADAMS by License	mar
May 23	Joseph GORTON	bur
May 23	Jane MERCY	bur
May 27	Daniel, s of Jonas & Jane WARR	bap
May 27	James, s of Thomas & Phebe WHITEHOUSE	bap
May 27	Ann, d of Richard & Ann JONES	bap
May 27	Joseph & Mary, twin s & d of Thomas & Mary WHITEHOUSE	bap

<u>1809</u>

May 27	Elizabeth GREGORY	bur
Jun 1	John KING	bur
Jun 4	William, s of James & Sarah WHITAKER, Born Decr 17, 1807	bap
Jun 4	Mary Ann, d of John & Ann HARRIS	bap
Jun 5	Thomas KENDRICK	bur
Jun 11	Edward, s of Thomas & Eleanor WEBB, Born May 20	bap
Jun 11	Ann, d of John & Eleanor MAURICE	bap
Jun 11	William, s of Edward & Phebe WHITEHOUSE	bap
Jun 11	John, s of George & Phebe BANISTON	bap
Jun 11	Daniel, s of George & Sarah SHELDON	bap
Jun 13	Thomas CLARKE & Maria JUKES by Banns	mar
Jun 14	Sarah NIGHTINGALE	bur
Jun 16	Samuel TURNER	bur
Jun 16	Mary LOWE	bur
Jun 18	Thomas POOL & Maria FRANKS by Banns	mar
Jun 18	Joseph NEEDAM & Sarah TAYLOR by Banns	mar
Jun 18	Hannah, d of Benjamin & Sarah MILLARD	bap
Jun 18	Stephen, s of William & Jane WHITEHOUSE, Born May 15	bap
Jun 18	Mary, d of Edward & Sarah ROWLEY	bap
Jun 18	Ann, d of John & Mary JOHNSON, Born April 6	bap
Jun 18	John, s of John & Mary HILTON, Born May 20	bap
Jun 18	Thomas STREET	bur
Jun 18	Maria SMITH	bur
Jun 21	Rhoda DOUGHTY	bur
Jun 23	Nancy PARKES	bur
Jun 25	Richard, s of John & Mary INGRAM	bap
Jun 25	Catharine, d of Thomas & Elizabeth BRATT	bap
Jun 25	Thomas, s of Thomas & Rebecca BALL	bap
Jun 25	William, s of John & Ann ASTON	bap
Jun 25	Thomas, s of John & Nancy DOUGHTY	bap
Jun 25	Ann EDWARDS	bur
Jun 27	Hannah NICKLIN	bur
Jul 2	Sarah, d of George & Sarah GILES	bap
Jul 2	Elizabeth, d of Richard & Ann HILL	bap
Jul 2	David, s of John & Mary HORTON	bap
Jul 2	Mary, d of William & Elizabeth CONSTABLE	bap
Jul 2	Mary MILLS	bur
Jul 4	James HORTON, 6 years Sexton of this Parish	bur
Jul 7	Scottsenea, d of Thomas & Jane SHORT	bap
Jul 7	Martha, d of Thomas & Jane SHORT	bap
Jul 9	Julia, d of Joseph & Sarah HORTON, Born June 7	bap
Jul 9	Mary Ann, d of John & Prudence JEVONS, Born June 17	bap
Jul 9	Hannah, d of John & Maria LANDER	bap
Jul 9	Roseanna OSBORNE	bur
Jul 10	John WHITE & Sarah WOOLEY by Banns	mar
Jul 10	Edward RAY & Mary LOUCH by Banns	mar
Jul 11	Thomas JONES & Hephzibah HORTON by Licence	mar
Jul 12	Joseph FLETCHER	bur
Jul 15	Clara MILLINGTON	bur

	Jul 16	Benjamin, s of Benjamin & Ann HOLLOWAY	bap
	Jul 16	Mary Ann, d of Daniel & Hannah TIMMINS	bap
	Jul 17	Joanna TWIGG	bur
	Jul 18	James INGRAM	bur
	Jul 18	Phebe FISHER	bur
	Jul 19	Prissilla GUTTRIDGE	bur
	Jul 19	Hannah WHITEHOUSE	bur
	Jul 23	Robert MORRIS & Nancy WARD by Banns	mar
	Jul 23	Sarah, d of Thomas & Mary ARCH, Born June 14	bap
	Jul 23	Jane & Maria, twin d of Edward & Mary DANGERFIELD	bap
	Jul 23	Rachael, d of George & Hannah CALLOWAY, Born April 15	bap
	Jul 23	John, s of James & Elizabeth WILLIAMS, Born Decr 25 1808	bap
	Jul 23	Esther, d of Benjamin & Sarah BATE, Born March 1	bap
	Jul 23	Mary, d of Francis & Ann SKELDING, Born Novr 12, 1808	bap
	Jul 23	Elizabeth, d of Thomas & Lettice SIMES, Born June 21	bap
	Jul 26	Mary DARBY	bur
	Jul 26	George DUDLEY	bur
	Jul 27	John SMITH & Mary ROUND by Banns	mar
	Jul 27	Elizabeth GUTTRIDGE	bur
	Jul 30	Ambrose, s of Solomon & Hannah TIMMINS	bap
	Jul 30	Isaiah, s of Michael & Phebe LAUGHTON	bap
	Jul 30	Thomas, s of Thomas & Sarah WHITEHOUSE, Born Feby 22, 1803	bap
	Jul 30	Joseph, s of Thomas & Sarah WHITEHOUSE, Born Feby 22, 1807[?]	bap
	Jul 30	Sarah TIMMINS	bur
	Aug 4	David MILLS	bur
	Aug 4	Phebe, d of Joseph & Mary GRIFFITHS, Born April 25	bap
	Aug 6	Daniel HUNT & Martha DUDLEY by Banns	mar
	Aug 6	Richard, s of Richard & Sarah MILLS	bap
	Aug 6	Sarah, d of Job & Hannah SMITH	bap
	Aug 6	Thomas, s of Isaac & Jane Ann TURNER	bap
	Aug 6	Jane, d of Richard & Sarah POWELL	bap
	Aug 6	James, s of James & Sarah HANCOX	bap
	Aug 13	Joseph MARTIN	bur
	Aug 13	Sophy, d of Joseph & Martha SMITH	bap
	Aug 13	Job, s of George & Ann CADDICK	bap
	Aug 13	Caroline Clara, d of James & Nancy HORTON	bap
	Aug 13	Harriott, d of Thomas & Ann WHITEHOUSE	bap
	Aug 15	John PARKES & Betty HADLEY, by Banns	mar
	Aug 17	Charles FISHER & Mary GRIFFITHS by Banns	mar
	Aug 20	John PASMOR & Elizabeth SWADLE by Banns	bap
	Aug 20	Isaac, s of Abraham & Aylce WATERHOUSE	bap
	Aug 27	James, s of James & Mary CADDICK	bap
	Aug 27	Hannah, d of John & Mary BARNETT	bap
	Aug 27	Nancy, d of John & Mary WRIGHT	bap
	Aug 27	Sarah, d of Charles & Mary ASH	bap
	Aug 27	Martha, d of Daniel & Ann DUDLEY	bap
	Aug 27	Job CADDICK	bur

Aug 27	Thomas SHINGLETON	bur
Sep 3	Richard HICKMAN & Elizabeth KEELING, by Banns	mar
Sep 3	Jane, d of William & Ann MILLARD	bap
Sep 3	Thomas, s of Francis & Ann CHAMBERS	bap
Sep 3	Mary Ann, d of Charles & Susanna PERRY	bap
Sep 3	John, s of Edward & Isabell PETERS	bap
Sep 3	Samuel, s of Samuel & Sarah THORNEYCROFT, Born June 10	bap
Sep 4	Ann MATTHEWS	bur
Sep 10	Benjamin, s of William & Sarah ROUND	bap
Sep 10	Enoch, s of James & Ann SAMBROOK	bap
Sep 12	Samuel MASON & Ann SLATER, by Banns	mar
Sep 12	Griffin MITCHEL	bur
Sep 14	Ann BATE	bur
Sep 17	Martha, d of Daniel & Maria PARTRIDGE	bap
Sep 17	William, s of Edward & Charlotte JAY	bap
Sep 17	Edwards, s of Edward & Charlotte JAY	bap
Sep 17	Joseph, s of Joseph & Ruth WORTON	bap
Sep 17	Rachael, d of William & Ann DUNN	bap
Sep 20	John TAYLOR	bur
Sep 24	James REDGEWAY & Martha BUTTLER by Banns	mar
Sep 24	John, s of John & Elizabeth SANDERS	bap
Sep 24	Moses, s of Joseph & Sarah BAGGOTT	bap
Sep 24	Henry, s of William & Naomi HIGGS	bap
Sep 24	Ann, d of William & Maria WHITEHOUSE	bap
Sep 24	Thomas, s of Richard & Sophia PRICE	bap
Sep 27	Julia NOCKE	bur
Oct 1	William SMITH & Ann GWINNETT by Licence	mar
Oct 1	Thomas WARD & Mary DICKENSON by Banns	bap
Oct 1	Thomas DAVIS & Hannah FISHER by Banns	mar
Oct 1	Samuel BAGNALL	bur
Oct 1	Benjamin, s of Thomas & Elizabeth STEVENSON	bap
Oct 1	Roseanna, d of Francis & Sarah GRIFFITHS	bap
Oct 1	Jacob, s of Isaac & Hannah DARBY	bap
Oct 1	Elizabeth, d of John & Ann TAYLOR	bap
Oct 8	Dinah, d of Henry & Violette HUGHES	bap
Oct 8	Mary, d of Daniel & Lettice WHITEHOUSE	bap
Oct 8	Elizabeth ROBERTS	bur
Oct 11	Daniel DANGERFIELD & Elizabeth BURN by Banns	mar
Oct 15	Joseph, s of Benjamin & Rachael WHITEHOUSE, Born Sep^t 27	bap
Oct 15	Eliza, d of William & Sarah PHASEY	bap
Oct 15	William, s of John & Ann SMITH	bap
Oct 16	William SHEREWOOD & Roseanna MILLS by Banns	mar
Oct 16	William PIERSELL & Eleanor COX by Banns	mar
Oct 17	James HOSBORN	bur
Oct 18	William KEY & Elizabeth PALMER by Banns	mar
Oct 19	Sarah WHITE	bur
Oct 22	John ADCOCK & Ann BROWN by Banns	mar
Oct 22	Benjamin, s of Joseph & Susanna TRANTER	bap
Oct 22	Henry, s of Joseph & Hannah BOTT, Born Sep 23	bap

Oct 22	Joseph, s of Joseph & Elizabeth SHEREWOOD	bap
Oct 22	Elizabeth, d of Abraham & Hannah LAW	bap
Oct 22	Mary Ann, d of Joseph & Elizabeth WALTON	bap
Oct 23	William GUEST & Hannah DIGORY by Banns	mar
Oct 25	Thomas BRETTEL	bur
Oct 28	Richard BAGNALL	bur
Oct 29	Leticia, d of John & Cretia KIRKHAM Born the 1st	bap
Oct 29	Ann, d of Joshua & Sarah HACKETT	bap
Oct 29	Mary, d of Joseph & Ann HILL	bap
Oct 29	Sarah WALTERS	bur
Oct 30	Benjamin ROCK & Ann HADLEY by Banns	mar
Oct 30	John WESTWOOD & Esther OAKLEY by Banns	mar
Oct 31	David ROUND	bur
Nov 5	Joseph, s of Joseph & Joice TURNER	bap
Nov 5	Abraham, s of Abraham & Sarah WHITEHOUSE	bap
Nov 5	Henry, s of William & Maria JASPER	bap
Nov 5	Sophia, d of Robert & Mary GRANT	bap
Nov 5	William, s of Samuel & Mary JENKIN	bap
Nov 5	Mary Ann, d of James & Sarah LUNN	bap
Nov 5	Edward GRIFFITHS	bur
Nov 5	Thomas CHAMBERS	bur
Nov 8	Sophia LAW	bur
Nov 12	Mary, d of William & Sarah TIMMING	bap
Nov 12	Jane, d of John & Susanna PASKIN, Born Aug 15	bap
Nov 12	John, s of Richard & Ann RUSTON	bap
Nov 13	Joseph LAW & Hannah BARNETT by Banns	,ar
Nov 14	Ann BOTT	bur
Nov 14	Phebe, d of George & Mary FISHER	bap
Nov 15	Thomas TUDER	bur
Nov 19	William HARPER & Hannah WOODHALL by Banns	mar
Nov 19	Thomas WILKINSON & Hannah CARTWRIGHT by Banns	mar
Nov 19	Phebe, d of Richard & Mary JEWKES, Born Oct 28	bap
Nov 19	Joseph, s of Daniel & Elizabeth ELWELL, Born Sep 27	bap
Nov 19	David, s of John & Mary WHITEHOUSE, 18 years old	bap
Nov 21	William ROUND	bur
Nov 23	William HYDE	bur
Nov 23	Henry, s of Joseph & Kitty MILLS, Born Feby 23, 1807	bap
Nov 23	Moses, s of Joseph & Kitty MILLS, Born Oct 7	bap
Nov 24	Sarah BUNN	bur
Nov 26	James, s of Thomas & Sarah JEWKES	bap
Nov 26	Mary, d of Nicholis & Sarah WOOD	bap
Nov 26	Job, s of Paul & Mary COX	bap
Nov 26	Abraham BAKER	bur
Dec 3	Sarah, d of Charles & Mary FISHER	bap
Dec 7	Emma, d of James & Mary ASTON	bap
Dec 7	John CHAMBERS	bur
Dec 7	Sarah WILLIS	bur
Dec 10	William THOMPSON & Elizabeth MEACHEL by Banns	mar
Dec 10	Joseph PIGGOT & Sarah HILL by Banns	mar

1809

Dec 10	Isaac, s of Samuel & Mary BOTT	bap
Dec 10	Jonothan, s of Joseph & Mary PRICE	bap
Dec 13	John TIMMINS	bur
Dec 17	John SHENTON & Hannah HARTILL by Banns	mar
Dec 20	Anchor FISHER	bur
Dec 20	John LAW	bur
Dec 22	Martha WHEALE	bur
Dec 24	Maria, d of James & Evies WOODWARD	bap
Dec 24	Cornelias Granger, s of Thomas & Phebe WESTWOOD	bap
Dec 24	Edward, s of Abraham & Sarah WHITEHOUSE	bap
Dec 24	John, s of Abraham & Sarah FISHER	bap
Dec 24	Jacob, s of Abraham & Sarah FISHER	bap
Dec 24	Mary Ann, d of Joseph & Ann SANDERS, Born Novr 25	bap
Dec 24	Ann, d of James & Martha BARTLAM	bap
Dec 24	James, s of John & Maria SHAW	bap
Dec 24	Mary Ann, d of Henry & Sarah HARRISS	bap
Dec 24	Samuel MILLS	bur
Dec 25	John, s of John & Nancy SHENTON, Born Sep 16	bap
Dec 25	Edward, s of Samuel & Rebecca HIPKISS	bap
Dec 25	Mary, d of Samuel & Mary TAYLOR	bap
Dec 25	Joseph, s of Francis & Elizabeth CONNOP	bap
Dec 25	Nancy, d of Joseph & Sarah MILLS	bap
Dec 25	Joseph, s of Thomas & Elizabeth TILLEY	bap
Dec 25	John, s of John & Sarah BEDDOE	bap
Dec 25	George, s of George & Elizabeth DEELEY	bap
Dec 31	Richard, s of Daniel & Elizabeth GORTON	bap
Dec 31	James, s of Richard & Elizabeth WHITEHOUSE	bap
Dec 31	Mary, d of Samuel & Sarah FEREDAY	bap

1810

Jan 1	John HODSON & Elizabeth VINSIM by Banns	mar
Jan 1	An, d of John & Hannah HODGSKISS	bap
Jan 1	Joseph, s of James & Sarah PERSHOUSE, Born April 16, 1805	bap
Jan 2	Elizabeth TIMMINS	bur
Jan 4	Phebe SMITH	bur
Jan 7	Ann, d of Thomas & Mary SHELDON	bap
Jan 7	James, s of Joseph & Ann FEREDAY, Born Oct 6	bap
Jan 7	Eliza, d of Joseph & Ann SMITH	bap
Jan 7	Mary, d of Robert & Ann MORRISS	bap
Jan 7	Ann, d of Thomas & Mary JONES	bap
Jan 7	John Edwards, s of Richard & Jane DORRELL	bap
Jan 7	John SHEREWOOD	bur
Jan 7	Elizabeth JONES	bur
Jan 10	George DEELEY	bur
Jan 13	James (a stranger) a Boy who was drowned in the Canal	bur
Jan 14	Henry, s of James & Deborah NOCK	bap
Jan 14	Thomas, s of Thomas & Ann KENT	bap
Jan 14	Henry, s of John & Hannah BUNCH	bap
Jan 14	Thomas, s of Benjamin & Elizabeth YATES	bap

<u>1810</u>

Jan 14	Joseph TILLEY	bur
Jan 14	Adam TAYLOR	bur
Jan 14	Sarah DANKS	bur
Jan 16	Thomas TINSLEY	bur
Jan 16	John MORRIS	bur
Jan 16	Elizabeth ASTON	bur
Jan 21	James, s of Joseph & Hannah ASHFORTH	bap
Jan 21	John HODGSKINS	bur
Jan 21	John, s of George & Nancy BRINDLEY, Born 16th	bap
Jan 21	Isaac, base s of Elizabeth LAW	bap
Jan 21	Sarah FISHER	bur
Jan 21	Elizabeth FLETCHER	bur
Jan 22	John WHITEHOUSE & Sarah SIMKIN by Banns	mar
Jan 23	John MARTIN & Ann PRICE, by Banns	mar
Jan 24	Elizabeth MILLS	bur
Jan 24	Miram TAYLOR	bur
Jan 28	William, s of John & Elizabeth HORTON, Born Dec 11 1809	bap
Jan 28	Mary, d of James & Mary WHITEHOUSE	bap
Jan 28	Elizabeth, d of John & Mary GUTTRIDGE	bap
Jan 28	Lettice, d of John & Ann EVANS	bap
Jan 28	Ann Maria TAYLOR	bur
Jan 30	Samuel BATE	bur
Feb 1	Nancy TAYLOR	bur
Feb 4	Richard, s of Michael & Elizabeth SANDERS	bap
Feb 4	James, s of Joseph & Elizabeth NOCK	bap
Feb 9	Margaret LEECH	bur
Feb 11	Jesse, s of Jesse & Mary WHITEHOUSE	bap
Feb 11	Thomas, s of William & Phebe EDWARDS	bap
Feb 11	William, s of William & Elizabeth TURNER	bap
Feb 11	Celina, d of Simon & Elizabeth BLEWITT	bap
Feb 11	Samuel MITCHELL	bur
Feb 12	Samuel THROPP & Catharine EVANS By Banns	mar
Feb 12	Robert SMITH & Catharine HACKWOOD by Banns	mar
Feb 13	Phebe WHITEHOUSE	bur
Feb 13	Ann CARTWRIGHT	bur
Feb 14	David CALLOWAY	bur
Feb 14	John HUMPHREY	bur
Feb 16	Mary WHITEHOUSE	bur
Feb 18	Mary Ann, d of Simeon & Mary WILKES	bap
Feb 18	William, s of James & Sarah OSBORNE	bap
Feb 18	Sarah, d of William & Hannah TAYLOR	bap
Feb 18	Abraham WHITEHOUSE	bur
Feb 19	Benjamin WARRINGTON & Sarah WOOD by Banns	mar
Feb 22	William JONES	bur
Feb 25	Mary Ann, d of James & Elizabeth HAWLEY	bap
Feb 25	Sarah, d of William & Mary DOWNING	bap
Feb 25	Sarah, d of Thomas & Jane STILLARD	bap
Feb 25	Fanny, d of John & Catharine JENKS	bap
Feb 25	John, s of Joseph & Mary SMITH	bap

<u>1810</u>

Feb 25	Richard, s of Richard & Sarah STEVENTON	bap
Feb 25	Mary Ann, d of James & Mary STANTON	bap
Feb 25	Thomas, s of Richard & Ann JUKES	bap
— Feb 25	Elizabeth, d of William & Elizabeth MOORE	bap
Feb 25	William, s of William & Hannah WHITEHOUSE	bap
— Feb 26	William HALL & Jane JACKSON by Banns	mar
Mar 4	William, s of Job & Sarah CASHMORE	bap
Mar 4	Leah, d of John & Sarah NICKLIN	bap
Mar 4	William, s of William & Sushannah HOLLINGS	bap
Mar 4	Edward, s of Edward & Hannah YORK	bap
Mar 4	Sarah, d of Samuel & Mary LAW	bap
Mar 4	Sarah, d of Joseph & Hannah GREENAWAY	bap
Mar 4	Elizabeth, d of Joseph & Rebecca SMITH, Born Jan 4	bap
Mar 4	Sarah, d of James & Mary SCHOLEFIELD	bap
⌐ Mar 4	John PARKES	bur
Mar 4	Elizabeth FEREDAY	bur
Mar 5	Henry RYLEY & Elizabeth ACKERS by Banns	mar
Mar 6	Charles HICKABOTTOM [entry squeezed in]	bur
⚥ Mar 8	Ann BUTLER	bur
Mar 11	Ambrose, s of Samuel & Mary Ann STOCKWIN	bap
◄ Mar 11	Thomas, s of John & Hannah POTTS	bap
Mar 11	John, s of William & Sarah JEWKES, Born Feby 10	bap
Mar 11	Elizabeth, d of William & Maria DANKS	bap
— Mar 11	Henry, s of Samuel & Patience NOCK, Born Decr 23, 1809	bap
Mar 11	Thomas, s of Thomas & Ann FEREDAY	bap
— Mar 11	Mary, d of Joseph & Ann WARD	bap
Mar 11	Phebe, d of James & Mary JEWKS	bap
Mar 12	John CADDICK & Mary CADDICK by Licence	mar
Mar 13	Mary WOODMAN	bur
— Mar 15	Nancy INGRAM	bur
Mar 16	Edward FISHER	bur
Mar 18	Thomas, s of William & Rebecca HATTON	bap
Mar 18	John, s of John & Charlotte DAVIS	bap
Mar 18	Hannah, d of James & Ann SATCHELL	bap
Mar 18	Mary, d of William & Ann ALLEN	bap
Mar 18	Daniel, s of Joseph & Hannah WALTERS	bap
Mar 18	Mary, d of John & Ann WALL	bap
Mar 18	Joseph, s of Joseph & Sarah HICKABOTTOM	bap
Mar 18	Sarah, d of William & Sarah HAND	bap
Mar 21	Samuel MORRIS	bur
Mar 22	Edward DAVIES & Elizabeth NICKLIN by Licence	mar
Mar 22	Hannah BOTT	bur
➤ Mar 25	Charles, s of Nathaniel & Sarah LEADBETTER	bap
Mar 25	William, s of Edward & Ann HARRIS	bap
Mar 25	Martha, d of Charles & Ann WARWICK	bap
Mar 25	Samuel, s of Thomas & Ann SHRED	bap
Mar 25	Martha, d of John & Hannah TIBBITS	bap
Mar 25	Catharine, d of Samson & Catharine AUSTIN, Born Jan 4	bap

Mar 25	John, s of Thomas & Mary Ann HEATHCOCK,	
	Born Oct 30 1809	bap
Mar 25	Isaac TIMMINS	bur
Mar 25	Cecila TIMMINS	bur
Mar 25	Sarah WHITEHOUSE	bur
Mar 25	Rebecca WHITEHOUSE	bur

A Transcript of the Register Book of Tipton alias Tibbington was
Exhibited into the Deans Visitation held in the Court of Lichfield being on
Friday the 8th day of June 1810

Mar 27	Martha REED	bur
Mar 29	Joseph HART	bur
Apr 1	Thomas PHILLIPS & Elizabeth BAGGOT by Banns	mar
Apr 1	Charles HAWKINS	bur
Apr 1	Elizabeth, d of John & Nancy BALL	bap
Apr 1	Mary, d of John & Mary TAYLOR, Born Jan 24	bap
Apr 1	Edward, s of Joseph & Mary WRIGHT	bap
Apr 1	William, s of Francis & Esther NICHOLLS	bap
Apr 1	Phebe, d of Joseph & Mary PASKIN	bap
Apr 1	Abraham, s of William & Hannah JEWKES	bap
Apr 1	William, s of William & Ann SOUTHALL	bap
Apr 1	Benjamin, s of Isaac & Ann SMITH	bap
Apr 1	Samuel, s of John & Mary JONES, Born March 3	bap
Apr 1	Daniel, s of Thomas & Sarah CORFIELD	bap
Apr 1	Joseph, s of Joseph & Elizabeth TILLEY, Born Jany 27 1809	bap
Apr 1	Naney, d of Joseph & Mary LEE	bap
Apr 1	Joseph DAVIS	bur
Apr 3	James TANGE & Sarah SMITH by Banns	mar
Apr 3	William JONES & Catharine REEVES by Banns	mar
Apr 3	Henry BOTT [entry inserted]	bur
Apr 4	William DARBY	bur
Apr 8	Henry FELLOWS & Margarett TAYLOR by Banns	mar
Apr 8	Elizabeth, d of James & Hannah DOWNS, born Feb 10	bap
Apr 8	Hannah, d of Benjamin & Mary WALTERS, Born Mar 8	bap
Apr 8	Elizabeth, d of Abraham & Elizabeth SHEARWOOD	bap
Apr 8	Tabiatha, s of Cornelias & Esther BAKER, Born Mar 8	bap
Apr 10	Isaiah TIMMINS	bur
Apr 11	Benjamin WHITEHOUSE	bur
Apr 11	Simon HARCOT	bur
Apr 11	Elizabeth BOTT	bur
Apr 13	Nancy BRINDLEY	bur
Apr 15	John GREENAWAY	bur
Apr 16	Catharine COCKRAN	bur
Apr 22	Edward ANDERSON & Ann OAKLEY by Banns	mar
Apr 22	Abraham SAYES & Sarah BURTON by Banns	mar
Apr 22	Rebecca, d of Thomas & Mary HOLYHEAD	bap
Apr 22	Thomas, s of John & Hannah GOODHALL	bap
Apr 22	Ann, d of Daniel & Jane RHODEN	bap
Apr 22	Charlotte, d of John & Hannah GOODHALL	bap
Apr 22	Nancy, d of Daniel & Sarah WHITEHOUSE	bap

1810

Apr 22	William, s of Joseph & Sarah FISHER	bap
Apr 22	Mary, d of Daniel & Sarah WATERHOUSE	bap
— Apr 22	Michael, s of Richard & Mary HODSGKISS	bap
Apr 22	John, s of William & Jemmima ROWETT	bap
Apr 22	Henry, s of James & Maria FISHER	bap
Apr 22	Maryann, d of William & Sarah WHITEHOUSE	bap
Apr 22	James Cook, s of Thomas & Esther JONES	bap
Apr 22	Mary LANGFORD	bur
Apr 22	Benjamin BOTT	bur
Apr 22	William HOYLE	bur
Apr 23	George HOMER & Ann HOLT by Banns	mar
Apr 24	Michael HAMLINTON	bur
Apr 24	Thomas BRATT	bur
Apr 25	Esther BOWEN	bur
Apr 27	Clement DAVIS	bur
Apr 29	William, s of William & Ann PADMORE	bap
Apr 29	Maryann, d of William & Elizabeth HANCOX	bap
— Apr 29	Isaiah, d of Thomas & Hannah EADES	bap
Apr 29	Sarah, d of William & Henrietta EDGE	bap
Apr 29	James COOKSEY	bur
May 2	Henry BALL	bur
May 4	Mary BAKER	bur
May 6	Sarah, d of John & Ann ADAMS	bap
— May 6	Thomas, s of Richard & Margarett GREEN	bap
May 6	Eliza, d of Joseph & Sarah SHINGLETON	bap
May 6	Thomas, s of William & Sophia EVANS	bap
May 6	Isaac, s of Joseph & Rachael DUFFIELD	bap
May 6	Richard BATE	bur
May 6	Josiah FISHER	bur
May 6	Maria TITTERTON	bur
May 6	Samuel FISHER	bur
May 8	Mary MORRIS	bur
May 9	Mary NORTON	bur
— May 13	Mary HODGKINS	bur
May 13	Benjamin, s of John & Sarah JONES	bur
May 13	Nancy, s of Edward & Mary FISHER	bap
May 13	Sarah, d of Robert & Catharine SMITH	bap
⁓ May 14	Thomas IRONS & Elizabeth LOWE, by Banns	mar
May 15	Thomas NORTON	bur
May 18	James MORRIS	bur
May 18	Roseanna WHITEHOUSE	bur
May 18	Harriott SHELDON	bur
— May 20	John, s of Joseph & Marrable GUTTRIDGE	bap
May 20	Elizabeth, d of David & Susannah LLOYD	bap
May 22	Maryann PASKIN	bur
May 23	Lucilla SMITH	bur
— May 24	John HODGKINS	bur
May 25	Susannah, d of Thomas & Sarah BELL, Born Jan 25	bap
May 25	William HAMMERSLEY	bur

1810

May 27	William STOCKWIN & Phebe COOPER by Banns	mar
May 27	William BATE	bur
May 27	Thomas BLAZE	bur
May 27	William WHITAKER	bur
May 27	John FISHER	bur
May 27	William DUFFIELD	bur
May 27	Francis CUMSTONE	bur
May 29	Joseph FLETCHER	bur
May 29	William KEY	bur
May 29	Sarah FISHER	bur
May 30	Ann CUMSTONE	bur
Jun 1	Thomas BAGNALL	bur
Jun 3	James MILLS & Sarah GRIFFITHS by Banns	mar
Jun 3	Agnes, son(sic) of Robert & Mary CALLER	bap
Jun 3	David, s of David & Margarett MORRIS	bap
Jun 3	Simeon, s of Benjamin & Ann BISSELL	bap
Jun 3	Joseph & Nancy, twin s & d of Joseph & Nancy HOLLOWAY	bap
Jun 3	Mary, d of John & Lucy GARDNER	bap
Jun 3	Elizabeth, d of John & Elizabeth DAVIS	bap
Jun 3	Daniel, s of Daniel & Sarah MINCHER, Born Dec 1 1809	bap
Jun 3	Joseph, s of Joseph & Mary CLUET, Born March 4	bap
Jun 4	Thomas PINSON	bur
Jun 5	William ELLMES	bur
Jun 6	Zachariah WARD	bur
Jun 9	Charles VERNUM	bur
Jun 10	John, s of John & Elizabeth FISHER	bap
Jun 10	Harriott, d of John & Mary SMITH	bap
Jun 10	William, s of William & Elizabeth BATE	bap
Jun 10	John, s of Edward & Elizabeth ROBINSON	bap
Jun 10	Richard, s of John & Mary GRIFFITHS	bap
Jun 10	Phebe, d of John & Hannah COOPER	bap
Jun 10	Susanna, d of Richard & Ann GARBIT	bap
Jun 10	Ann Lester, d of Henry & Sarah LEWIS	bap
Jun 10	Charles, s of Thomas & Elizabeth HARRISON	bap
Jun 10	Thomas, s of Samuel & Elizabeth GROVES	bap
Jun 10	Mary, d of William & Mary MANNING	bap
Jun 10	Maria, d of Thomas & Ann MAUPASS	bap
Jun 10	Roseanna, d of Thomas & Sarah MORRALL	bap
Jun 10	Thomas, s of James & Elizabeth WALTERS	bap
Jun 11	Abraham WHITEHOUSE & Charlotte RUSSELL by Banns	mar
Jun 11	James BAGNALL & Sarah JAME, by Banns	mar
Jun 11	James DAVIS & Mary DUDLEY by Banns	mar
Jun 13	Harriot BATE	bur
Jun 13	John WALLEY	bur
Jun 11	John PRESSON	bur
Jun 17	James, s of Thomas & Lydia TAYLOR	bap
Jun 17	Sarah, d of Joseph & Nancy DUDLEY	bap
Jun 18	Phebe FISHER	bur
Jun 19	Samuel HODGKINS	bur

1810

Jun 20	Susanna GOODWIN	bur
Jun 24	David DICKEN & Mary WHEALE by Banns	mar
Jun 24	Richard, s of Richard & Mary STANTON	bap
Jun 24	Mary, d of William & Elizabeth FORD	bap
Jun 24	Mary, d of John & Margery HATTON	bap
Jun 24	Sarah BROOKS	bur
Jun 24	Sarah LAW	bur
Jun 24	David HORTON	bur
Jun 25	Thomas TAYLOR & Elizabeth STONE by Banns	mar
Jun 27	William STANFIELD	bur
Jun 27	Sarah BLACKHAM	bur
Jun 27	Sarah FEREDAY	bur
Jul 1	John Frederick ROUVIER	bur
Jul 1	Thomas SHORT	bur
Jul 1	Abatha, s of Thomas & Rachel HANCOX	bap
Jul 1	William, s of John & Esther DARBY	bap
Jul 2	Elizabeth CLARK	bur
Jul 3	Thomas TAYLOR & Sarah GRIFFITHS by Banns	mar
Jul 6	Michael DUFFIELD	bur
Jul 6	Ann MORRIS	bur
Jul 6	Joseph WHITEHOUSE	bur
Jul 8	Isaac, s of William & Sarah HICKMANS, Born Mar 10, 1808	bap
Jul 8	John, s of John & Margarett HEELEY	bap
Jul 8	George, s of Thomas & Dianna ROBINSON	bap
Jul 8	Roseanna, d of John & Sarah WHITEHOUSE	bap
Jul 8	Henry James, s of Henry & Mary NOCK	bap
Jul 8	Hannah, d of John & Margarett HEELEY	bap
Jul 8	John, s of Daniel & Mary WARR	bap
Jul 11	John GRIFFITHS	bur
Jul 13	John MINCHER	bur
Jul 15	Sarah, d of James & Mary FULLWOOD, Born April 25, 1809	bap
Jul 15	Richard, s of John & Sarah GWINNETT, Born March 31, 1809	bap
Jul 15	Joseph, s of William & Elizabeth STEPHENSON	bap
Jul 15	Henry, s of Thomas & Mary PUGH	bap
Jul 15	Lydia, d of Paul & Ann EVANS	bap
Jul 15	John, s of James & Sarah ROBERTS	bap
Jul 16	John GREEN & Lydia HARPER by Banns	mar
Jul 16	Thomas PAINTER & Mary PEMBERTON by Banns	mar
Jul 17	Mary BYRCH	bur
Jul 17	Thomas, s of Thomas & Sarah ROSE	bap
Jul 20	James WHITAKER	bur
Jul 20	Ann THOMAS	bur
Jul 22	Maryann, d of William & Jane RYLEY	bap
Jul 22	John, s of William & Mary STRETTON	bap
Jul 22	Joseph & Sarah, twin s & d of Thomas & Susanna STEVENS	bap
Jul 22	Eliza, d of William & Sebrea CADDICK	bap
Jul 22	Florentine, d of Thomas & Ann LEADBETTER	bap
Jul 22	Mary, d of Daniel & Roseanna SHELDON	bap
Jul 22	Elizabeth, d of John & Ann CADDICK	bap

<u>1810</u>

Jul 22	Sarah, d of William & Ann COOPER	bap
Jul 22	William PARTRIDGE	bur
Jul 23	John TITLEY	bur
Jul 23	Mary WARD	bur
Jul 24	Richard LAW	bur
Jul 24	Hannah MILLARD	bur
Jul 25	Elizabeth JONES	bur
Jul 26	Samuel DUDLEY	bur
Jul 26	Isaac GUTTRIDGE	bur
Jul 28	John WHITEHOUSE	bur
Jul 28	Sarah WHITEHOUSE	bur
Jul 29	Joseph, s of Joseph & Mary HILL	bap
Jul 29	Thomas, s of John & Ann SIMCOX	bap
Jul 29	George, s of Thomas & Hannah DAVIS	bap
Jul 29	Sarah NIBB	bur
Jul 29	Joseph WHITEHOUSE	bur
Aug 1	John ROBERTS	bur
Aug 2	Nathaniel Thomas DAVIS & Hannah MORRIS by Licence	mar
Aug 3	Jacob FISHER	bur
Aug 3	David WHITEHOUSE	bur
Aug 5	Eliza, d of Philip & Mary PARTRIDGE	bap
Aug 5	Joseph, s of John & Catharine STANTON	bap
Aug 5	Hannah, d of Isaac & Isabella TIMMINS	bap
Aug 5	Ann, d of James & Prisilla SHELDON	bap
Aug 5	Samuel, s of John & Patience WARD	bap
Aug 5	William, s of Elisha & Prisilla WHITEHOUSE	bap
Aug 5	Thomas, s of Daniel & Mary WHITEHOUSE	bap
Aug 5	William, s of Henry & Sarah WILLIAMS	bap
Aug 5	Margarett FISHER	bur
Aug 5	Lydia WHITEHOUSE	bur
Aug 9	Edward WEBB	bur
Aug 11	Thomas HIPPING	bur
Aug 12	Ann, d of Lawrence & Ann HARTSHORN	bap
Aug 12	Mary, d of Edward & Prisilla SMITH	bap
Aug 12	John, s of George & Nancy YORK	bap
Aug 12	William, s of Henry & Esther WARTON	bap
Aug 12	Thomas WHITAKER	bur
Aug 16	John WHEALE	bur
Aug 19	Hannah WHITEHEAD	bur
Aug 19	Ann, d of Henry & Letticia WILLIAMS	bap
Aug 19	Mary Ann, d of Joseph & Jane WHITEHOUSE	bap
Aug 19	John, s of Thomas & Roseanna SHEREWOOD	bap
Aug 19	Moses, s of Joseph & Hannah GRICE	bap
Aug 19	Cornelius, s of John & Ann GRANGER	bap
Aug 21	Samuel FISHER	bur
Aug 21	John FISHER	bur
Aug 22	Catharine INGRAM	bur
Aug 22	Martha, d of John & Mary INGRAM	bap
Aug 22	William TURNER	bur

1810

Aug 23	Francis WHITEHOUSE	bur
Aug 23	Ann HARTSHORN	bur
Aug 24	Emma PHILLIPS	bur
Aug 25	John DOUGHTY	bur
Aug 26	William, s of William & Cara HOPKINS	bap
Aug 26	Ann, d of John & Elizabeth HYDE	bap
Aug 26	Henry, s of Benjamin & Sarah PIERCE	bap
Aug 26	Mary, d of Richard & Hannah WARD	bap
Aug 26	Halley, d of Joseph & Ann CARTWRIGHT	bap
Aug 26	Hannah, d of John & Eleanor ROBERTS	bap
Aug 26	Isaac Hill, s of James & Sarah COOKSEY	bap
Aug 26	Phebe, d of James & Rebecca WHITEHOUSE	bap
Aug 26	William FEREDAY	bur
Aug 26	Phebe FISHER	bur
Aug 26	Mary WHITEHOUSE	bur
Aug 26	Susanna LAWRANCE	bur
Aug 26	Sarah PRICE	bur
Aug 28	Hannah HIPKINS	bur
Aug 29	Henry HODGKINS	bur
Aug 29	Maryann JONES	bur
Aug 30	John, s of Jacob & Margaret OWEN, being ab^t 27 years of age	bap
Aug 30	Ann, d of James & Sarah EVANS, being about 41 years of age	bap
Aug 30	Phebe, d of James & Sarah EVANS, being about 40 years of age	bap
Aug 31	Hannah JUKES	bur
Sep 2	Harriott, d of Thomas & Roseanna HAZELHURST	bap
Sep 2	John, s of Joseph & Hannah LAW	bap
Sep 2	Charles, s of Charles & Elizabeth HICKABOTTOM	bap
Sep 2	Prudence FLETCHER	bur
Sep 2	Phebe WHITEHOUSE	bur
Sep 2	Mary SHEARWOOD	bur
Sep 2	Ambrose BLACKHAM	bur
Sep 3	Evan EVANS & Casiah JONES by Banns	mar
Sep 4	Esther SHELDON	bur
Sep 4	Joseph WILLIS	bur
Sep 5	James DALE	bur
Sep 7	Phebe NICKLIN	bur
Sep 7	Maryann PIERCE	bur
Sep 9	James BRADSHAW & Rebecca ROUPER by Banns	mar
Sep 9	Julia, d of Thomas & Jane NOCK	bap
Sep 9	Henry, s of James & Jane NOCK, Born Aug 17	bap
Sep 9	Phebe, d of Edward & Phebe WHITEHOUSE	bap
Sep 9	Rebella, d of Edward & Mary WHITEHOUSE	bap
Sep 9	Sarah, d of Job & Ann CADDICK	bap
Sep 9	Noah FLETCHER	bur
Sep 9	Amelia HALL	bur
Sep 10	David ROUND & Ann NIGHTINGALE by Banns	mar
Sep 12	James FEREDAY	bur
Sep 13	Ann GRANGER	bur

1810

Sep 14	Ann HYDE bur	
Sep 14	Job BROCKHOUSE	bur
Sep 16	Thomas, s of Job & Jane PEARCE	bap
Sep 16	Elizabeth, d of Thomas & Maria SMITH	bap
Sep 16	John, s of John & Mary JONES	bap
Sep 16	Joseph, s of Isaac & Sarah TIMMINS	bap
Sep 16	Maria, d of John & Mary WHITEHOUSE	bap
Sep 16	Elizabeth, d of George & Ann LOWE	bap
Sep 16	Thomas, s of Samuel & Sarah EVANS	bap
Sep 16	Mary BARNWELL	bur
Sep 19	Roseanna MILLS	bur
Sep 23	John BIRD & Hannah EDWARDS by Banns	mar
Sep 23	Roseanna, d of Joseph & Sarah MILLS	bap
Sep 23	Charles, s of Joseph & Ann CARTWRIGHT	bap
Sep 23	John, s of John & Sarah SMITH	bap
Sep 23	Tabiatha PLATT	bur
Sep 25	Jesse FOLEY & Mary Cythea HOPKINS by Banns	mar
Sep 27	John GRIFFITHS	bur
Sep 28	Isaiah WHITEHOUSE	bur
Sep 30	Phebe, d of Job & Elizabeth SHELDON	bap
Sep 30	William, s of William & Elizabeth WALTERS	bap
Sep 30	Zachariah, s of William & Sarah GRIFFITHS	bap
Sep 30	Ann, d of Joseph & Jane SANDERS	bap
Sep 30	Margarett, d of William & Esther FOSBROOK	bap
Oct 1	Francis WHITEHOUSE	bur
Oct 2	Benjamin WHITEHOUSE	bur
Oct 4	Edward SMITH	bur
Oct 6	Edward FISHER (14 years Church Warden)	bur
Oct 7	Lydia FISHER	bur
Oct 7	William, s of William & Elizabeth ROGERS	bap
Oct 7	Maryann, d of John & Mary JEVON	bap
Oct 7	Edward, s of Edward & Ann WHITEHOUSE	bap
Oct 7	Richard, s of Richard & Elizabeth FIELD	bap
Oct 7	Elizabeth, d of John & Phebe MILLS	bap
Oct 7	William, s of Thomas & Maryann HEATHCOCK	bap
Oct 7	Ann, d of Edward & Elizabeth ROBERTS	bap
Oct 7	Roseanna, d of Joshua & Ann TOLLEY	bap
Oct 7	Thomas MIDDLETON	bur
Oct 7	Mary ANDREWS	bur
Oct 14	William HOWELL & Elizabeth LAWLEY by Banns	mar
Oct 14	Samuel ASTON	bur
Oct 14	Elizabeth, d of John & Ann JONES	bap
Oct 14	John, s of William & Hannah HARRINGTON	bap
Oct 14	Thomas, s of Simeon & Hannah CORNFIELD	bap
Oct 14	John DAWLEY	bur
Oct 14	Jon MARTIN	bur
Oct 15	William THOMAS & Ann HUGHES by Banns	mar
Oct 15	Rachael GRIFFITHS	bur
Oct 16	Isaac Hill COOKSEY	bur

1810

Oct 16	Mary Ann TIBBETS	bur
Oct 19	Charlotte GUEST	bur
Oct 21	Ann, d of Samuel & Charlotte CUTLER	bap
Oct 21	Lydia, d of Samuel & Hannah DANGERFIELD	bap
Oct 21	Ann, d of James & Roseanna WOLLEY	bap
Oct 21	Prudence, d of Abel & Hannah CADDICK	bap
Oct 21	Sarah, d of James & Martha DELEHAY	bap
Oct 21	John, s of William & Sarah SHEARWOOD	bap
Oct 21	Edward, s of Thomas & Ann ADAMS	bap
Oct 21	John GUTTRIDGE	bur
Oct 21	William CHATTIN	bur
Oct 21	Hannah HEELEY	bur
Oct 23	Stephen HIPKINS & Nancy BAKER by License	mar
Oct 24	Daniel EVANS	bur
Oct 24	Mary HANCOX	bur
Oct 28	Lot ROBINSON & Rhoda DARBY by Banns	mar
Oct 28	Ann, d of Samuel & Ann DUDLEY	bap
Oct 28	William, s of Daniel & Esther GRIFFITHS	bap
Oct 28	Thomas, s of James & Sarah STEPHENTON	bap
Oct 28	Evan EVANS	bur
Oct 28	Elizabeth HARPER	bur
Oct 28	William ROBERTS	bur
Oct 29	Charles DOUGHTY & Elizabeth FELLOWS by Banns	mar
Oct 30	Thomas WHITEHOUSE	bur
Nov 4	Thomas BUTLER & Hannah GRIGG by Banns	mar
Nov 4	William FAWKES & Maria WILLIAMS by Banns	mar
Nov 4	Thomas PINSON & Sarah COX by Banns	mar
Nov 4	Elizabeth, d of Thomas & Sarah ROWLEY	bap
Nov 4	Richard, s of Isaac & Mary HENSHALL	bap
Nov 4	Mary, d of Richard & Elizabeth OWEN	bap
Nov 4	Nancy, d of Richard & Amelia LAW	bap
Nov 4	Edward, s of Joseph & Mary GRIFFITHS	bap
Nov 4	John, s of Thomas & Elizabeth LISMORE	bap
Nov 4	John, s of John & Mary WHITEHOUSE	bap
Nov 4	Edward, s of Samuel & Sarah LEECH	bap
Nov 4	Jane, d of Abraham & Hannah BATE	bap
Nov 4	Hannah, d of Thomas & Mary GREEN	bap
Nov 5	James HUTTON & Lucy CLIFT by Banms	mar
Nov 6	Ann HOWELLS	bur
Nov 7	John PUGH	bur
Nov 9	Jemmima CLARK	bur
Nov 11	Thomas ROSS	bur
Nov 11	Jeremiah, s of John & Sarah HANBURY	bap
Nov 11	Sarah TIMMINS	bur
Nov 13	Thomas FAIRFIELD	bur
Nov 15	Nancy WHITEHOUSE	bur
Nov 18	John HONES & Susanna INGRAM by Banns	mar
Nov 18	Hannah, d of William & Ann ELWELL	bap
Nov 18	James OSBORNE	bur

<u>1810</u>

Nov 18	Levi ROBINSON	bur
Nov 18	William, s of John & Mary ROBINSON	bap
Nov 18	John, s of Richard & Jane LANGDON	bap
Nov 18	William, s of William & Susanna GRIFFITHS	bap
Nov 18	Selenia, d of Joseph & Mary LAMBETH	bap
Nov 18	Mary Ann, d of Joseph & Sophia BROOKS	bap
Nov 19	George HOLDEN & Mary STANDLEY by Banns	mar
Nov 20	Joseph TIMMINS	bur
Nov 25	William TURNER	bur
Nov 25	Elizabeth GUTTRIDGE	bur
Nov 25	Samuel, s of Samuel & Maria SIMCOX	bap
Nov 25	James, s of John & Elizabeth SMITH	bap
Nov 25	John, s of Thomas & Mary TOOKEY	bap
Nov 25	Samuel, s of William & Rebecca ROUND, Born Sep 6, 1809	bap
Nov 25	Mary Ann, d of Thomas & Rose BARRAT, Born July 13, 1809	bap
Nov 26	Mary GRATTON	bur
Dec 2	Esther MARTIN	bur
Dec 2	John, s of Thomas & Eleanor DUFFIELD	bap
Dec 2	Joseph, s of John & Sarah SHEW	bap
Dec 2	Sarah, d of William & Mary REECE	bap
Dec 2	Charlotte, d of Joseph & Mary DEBBS	bap
Dec 2	Richard BAYLEY	bur
Dec 2	William SMITH	bur
Dec 2	Samuel WARR	bur
Dec 2	Sarah BATE	bur
Dec 3	Samuel HALE & Nancy HORTON by Banns	mar
Dec 5	Elizabeth SHARP	bur
Dec 5	Esther, d of Thomas & Elizabeth SHARP	bap
Dec 6	Selina, d of Edward & Sarah ASTON, Born Nov 7	bap
Dec 6	Phillip PARTRIDGE	bur
Dec 9	John HOLMES	bur
Dec 9	William MILLS	bur
Dec 9	Thomas, s of John & Mary SHELDON	bap
Dec 9	Joseph, s of Thomas & Elizabeth FEREDAY, Born Nov 17	bap
Dec 9	Benjamin, s of John & Rhoda SMITH, Born Nov 17	bap
Dec 9	Martha, d of Joseph & Elizabeth TURNER	bap
Dec 10	Thomas VAUGHAN & Elizabeth EVANS by Banns	mar
Dec 11	Hannah INGRAM	bur
Dec 12	Elizabeth GUTTRIDGE	bur
Dec 13	Joseph WHITEHOUSE	bur
Dec 14	Ann JONES	bur
Dec 16	William, s of Samuel & Ann MORRIS	bap
Dec 16	Maria, d of Thomas & Sarah TAYLOR	bap
Dec 16	Joseph, s of Joseph & Lucy ROBINSON	bap
Dec 16	Jesse, s of David & Frances HIPKINS	bap
Dec 16	Jane, d of Thomas & Hannah MOTTRAM	bap
Dec 17	Abraham ELWELL & Martha COX by Banns	mar
Dec 23	Elizabeth, d of James & Sarah RUBERY	bap
Dec 23	James, s of James & Elizabeth FISHER	bap

1810

Dec 23	Elizabeth, d of James & Mary BOTT	bap
Dec 23	William, s of Daniel & Mary BARNETT	bap
Dec 23	Richard, s of William & Julia WILLIAMS	bap
Dec 23	Joseph, s of Edward & Elizabeth LAW	bap
Dec 23	Ann, d of Daniel & Hannah TIMMINS	bap
Dec 23	Rebecca, d of Richard & Mary NICKLISS	bap
Dec 23	Isaiah, s of Thomas & Nancy TIMMINS	bap
Dec 24	Edward DAVIS & Susanna CARTWRIGHT by Banns	mar
Dec 25	John WARD & Hannah WHITEHOUSE by Banns	mar
Dec 25	Benjamin CASTRAY & Sarah ROUND by Banns	mar
Dec 25	Ambrose STANTON & Ann PRICE by Banns	mar
Dec 25	Henry, s of William & Mary HARRIS	bap
Dec 25	Sarah, d of Thomas & Mary WILLIAMS	bap
Dec 25	James, s of Joseph & Mary FISHER	bap
Dec 25	Richard, s of Benjamin & Elizabeth NICKLIN, Born Oct 18	bap
Dec 25	William, s of James & Abigal PRICE, Born March 15	bap
Dec 26	William GUTTRIDGE	bur
Dec 27	John GREENAWAY & Elizabeth GEORGE by Banns	mar
Dec 28	Fanny WATERFIELD	bur
Dec 30	Lucy, d of Joseph & Elizabeth WILLIAMS, Born Sep 2, 1809	bap
Dec 30	Samuel, s of James & Elizabeth GOUGH, Born Sep 2	bap
Dec 30	Sarah EDWARDS	bur

1811

Jan 1	James HICKMANS	bur
Jan 6	Martha INGRAM	bur
Jan 6	Casiah, d of John & Mary BLACKHAM	bap
Jan 6	Maria, d of Samuel & Sarah SUTTON	bap
Jan 9	Benjamin SMITH	bur
Jan 10	William, s of Thomas & Mercy POWELL	bap
Jan 10	Lucy ALEXANDER	bur
Jan 13	Elizabeth HODGKINS	bur
Jan 13	William, s of William & Prissilla INGRAM	bap
Jan 13	William, s of William & Elizabeth ROBERTS	bap
Jan 13	Thomas, s of Joseph & Mary WOOD	bap
Jan 13	John, s of Michael & Phebe LAWTON	bap
Jan 13	Maria, d of John & Mary CADDICK	bap
Jan 13	David DRYDEN	bur
Jan 13	John LEWIS	bur
Jan 13	Nancy HOLLOWAY	bur
Jan 15	Ann WHITEHOUSE	bur
Jan 15	George JONES	bur
Jan 15	William TAYLOR	bur
Jan 20	Sarah DUDLEY	bur
Jan 20	James, s of Isaac & Mary PRICE, Born Dec[r] 27, 1808	bap
Jan 20	Rebecca, d of Isaac & Mary PRICE, Born Dec 24, 1810	bap
Jan 20	Mary, d of William & Ann WHITEHOUSE	bap
Jan 20	William, s of James & Sussana HARTLAND	bap
Jan 27	Mary Ann, d of Joseph & Ann CADDICK	bap

<u>1811</u>

Jan 27	John, s of William & Margarett WILLIAMS	bap
Jan 27	Martha, d of Joseph & Mary FISHER	bap
Jan 27	Nancy, d of Daniel & Martha WHITEHOUSE	bap
Jan 27	Maria, d of Samuel & Sarah TILSLEY	bap
Jan 27	Eliza, d of Thomas & Rachel RYLEY	bap
Jan 28	Thomas RUSTON & Hannah BOUGH by Banns	mar
Jan 30	Mary, d of John & Hannah WILLIAMS	bap
Jan 30	William ELWELL	bur
Feb 3	Hannah GORTON	bur
Feb 3	Ann HODGKISS	bur
Feb 3	George Edwin, s of George & Elizabeth DEELEY	bap
Feb 4	William ALLEN & Catharine BANBURY by Banns	mar
Feb 6	Richard WILLIAMS	bur
Feb 7	John SMITH	bur
Feb 10	Ann, d of John & Hannah THORNEYCROFT	bap
Feb 10	Stephen, s of Thomas & Hannah RABONE	bap
Feb 10	Sarah, d of William & Ann MILLARD	bap
Feb 10	Mary, d of Ralph & Ann KELSELL	bap
Feb 11	Robert OWEN & Mary ELWELL by Banns	mar
Feb 11	Thomas ELLIS & Rebecca PAINTER by Banns	mar
Feb 12	Thomas HARRIS & Hannah BROFON by Banns	mar
Feb 17	Mary, d of Thomas & Sarah BOTT	bap
Feb 17	Elisha, d of Benjamin & Sarah MILLARD	bap
Feb 17	Eleanor, d of Thomas & Elizabeth LAW	bap
Feb 17	Maria, d of Edward & Sarah TOOKLEY	bap
Feb 24	Thomas DAVIS & Elizabeth DANKS by Licence	mar
Feb 24	George, s of Nathaniel & Susanna WEBB	bap
Feb 24	Moses, s of Abraham & Elizabeth SHELDON	bap
Feb 24	Mary, d of Abraham & Elizabeth SHELDON, abt 10 yrs old	bap
Feb 24	Charles, s of Samuel & Ann GUEST	bap
Feb 24	John, s of John & Ann EVANS	bap
Feb 24	Martha, d of John & Ann WILSON	bap
Feb 24	Joseph, s of Stephen & Maria CRESWELL	bap
Feb 24	Abraham TIMMINS	bur
Feb 24	David JONES	bur
Feb 24	Mary FISHER	bur
Feb 27	Joseph SHEREWOOD	bur
Mar 3	Mary, d of Benjamin & Sarah WARRINGTON	bap
Mar 3	Samuel, s of William & Phebe MILLS	bap
Mar 3	Benjamin, s of William & Margaret IKIN	bap
Mar 3	Ann, d of William & Mary TIMMINS	bap
Mar 3	Henry, s of Robert & Susanna JONES, Born Nov 27 1810	bap
Mar 3	William, s of Thomas & Eleanor PARTON	bap
Mar 3	Maryann, d of William & Sarah TIBBITS	bap
Mar 4	Evan DAVIS & Elizabeth HADLEY by Banns	mar
Mar 5	William BELCHER	bur
Mar 6	Hannah ELWELL	bur
Mar 6	William WHESSON	bur
Mar 10	Edward, s of Thomas & Hannah TILLEY, Born Nov 4 1810	bap

Mar 10	Richard, s of David & Hannah WASSELL	bap
Mar 10	Richard, s of John & Ann THOMPSON, Born Dec 16 1810	bap
Mar 10	John, s of Thomas & Sarah NICHOLLS	bap
Mar 10	Ann, d of James & Catharine MERREY	bap
Mar 10	Hannah, d of Thomas & Sarah NICHOLLS	bap
Mar 10	Maria, d of Thomas & Sarah BUTLER	bap
Mar 10	Thomas, s of Ralph & Elizabeth BROWN	bap
Mar 10	William, s of William & Sarah KING	bap
Mar 10	Susanna, d of Thomas & Margarett COOPER	bap
Mar 10	Sarah, d of Francis & Ann CHAMBERS	bap
Mar 11	Thomas HUBBARD & Elizabeth HAMLET, by Banns	mar
Mar 13	Catharine MARTIN	bur
Mar 13	Sophia SMITH	bur
Mar 13	Sarah CARTWRIGHT	bur
Mar 15	Mary WILLIAMS	bur
Mar 17	Phebe, d of Thomas & Mary HARCOTT	bap
Mar 17	Sarah, d of Solomon & Hannah TIMMINS	bap
Mar 17	Jemmima, d of Joshua & Hannah PARTRIDGE	bap
Mar 17	Gideon, s of Gideon & Mary WHITEHOUSE	bap
Mar 17	Edward, s of Edward & Isabello PETERS	bap
Mar 17	William, s of Thomas & Sarah JEWKES	bap
Mar 17	John, s of Richard & Esther ASHTON, Born Jany 30 1810	bap
Mar 17	Thomas, s of Thomas & Sarah LONES, Born Dec 16 1810	bap
Mar 17	Thomas, s of Thomas & Hannah MATHERS [a faint "w" appears to have been written over the "RS"]	bap
Mar 17	Daniel, s of Joseph & Elizabeth SHELDON	bap
Mar 17	Mary HITCHEN	bur
Mar 17	Edward BROWN	bur
Mar 24	Thomas PIERCE	bur
Mar 24	James, s of Martin & Sarah BROWN	bap
Mar 24	John, s of Henry & Sarah HARRISS	bap
Mar 24	Harriott, d of Richard & Mary PASKIN	bap
Mar 24	Joseph, s of Abraham & Maria PARKES	bap
Mar 24	Joseph, s of William & Mary EADES	bap
Mar 24	Elizabeth, d of Daniel & Rachel FISHER	bap
Mar 24	Mary, d of Thomas & Mary ELWELL	bap
Mar 24	William, s of George & Ann CADDICK	bap
Mar 24	Richard, s of Richard & Penila GRIFFITHS	bap
Mar 24	Joseph, s of John & Lydia WHITEHOUSE	bap
Mar 24	Josiah James, s of Thomas & Ann WHITEHOUSE	bap
Mar 25	Thomas DARBY & Sarah HOBSON by Banns	mar
Mar 25	Samuel OAKLEY & Mary ADLINGTON by Banns	mar
Mar 29	Sarah NIGHTINGALE	bur
Mar 31	Eliza, d of John & Prudence JEVONS	bap
Mar 31	Sarah Gill, d of Thomas & Elizabeth COX	bap
Mar 31	Joseph, s of Silas & Hannah STONES	bap
Apr 3	John MACCLANE & Barbara SHEDDEN by LIcence	mar
Apr 3	Mary BLACKHAM	bur
Apr 4	Isaac, s of Joseph & Hannah ASTON, Born Mar 6	bap

Apr 5	Elizabeth FISHER	bur
Apr 7	Thomas, s of Thomas & Ann DANGERFIELD	bap
Apr 7	Frances, d of John & Maria GOULD	bap
Apr 7	William, s of Richard & Sarah REED	bap
Apr 7	William, s of Daniel & Lucy WORLEY	bap
Apr 7	Sarah, d of Joseph & Ann SMITH	bap
Apr 7	Sarah, d of Benjamin & Hannah BLUNT	bap
Apr 7	James DAVIS	bur
Apr 7	Phebe PASKIN	bur
Apr 7	Harriott PASKIN	bur
Apr 10	Joseph MORRIS	bur
Apr 14	William HUGHES	bur
Apr 14	Mary, d of William & Lucy BAGNALL	bap
Apr 14	Joseph, s of Joseph & Elizabeth WALTON	bap
Apr 14	John, s of William & Mary NIGHTINGALE	bap
Apr 14	Joseph & Mary, twin s & d of Thomas & Elizabeth BILL	bap
Apr 14	Sarah, d of John & Maria SANDERS	bap
Apr 14	Edward, s of Eutychus & Phebe FISHER	bap
Apr 14	Francis, s of Francis & Hannah BEDDOE	bap
Apr 14	Jane, d of George & Mary NICKOLAS	bap
Apr 14	Maryann, d of Samuel & Mary LAW	bap
Apr 14	Ann SANDERS	bur
Apr 17	John WESTWOOD & Maria JEFFRIES by Banns	mar
Apr 17	Mary ELWELL	bur
Apr 17	Catharine WINNINGTON	bur
Apr 21	John DUTTON & Elizabeth RADNELL by Banns	mar
Apr 21	James ALEXANDER	bur
Apr 21	Sarah, d of Richard & Sarah NIGHTINGALE	bap
Apr 21	Thomas, s of Joseph & Ann WHITEHOUSE	bap
Apr 23	Isaiah, s of Joseph & Hannah ROUND	bap
Apr 24	Thomas LAPPAGE	bur
Apr 28	James STEACEY & Sarah WHITEHOUSE by Banns	mar
Apr 28	Daniel SMITH, a base s of Amelia MEREDITH, Born Feb 21 1802	bap
Apr 28	John, s of Nathaniel & Sarah ARCH	bap
Apr 28	Fanney, d of William & Prudence MINCHER	bap
Apr 28	Roseanna MILLS	bur
Apr 28	Thomas EDWARDS	bur
May 1	James WILKINSON	bur
May 1	William WHITEHOUSE	bur
May 5	William, s of Jonas & Jane WARR	bap
May 5	Sarah, d of James & Nancy WARTON	bap
May 5	Maria, d of Samuel & Maria INGRAM	bap
May 5	Elizabeth, d of Thomas & Eleanor JONES	bap
May 5	Edward, s of William & Elizabeth BELCHER	bap
May 5	Ann CADDICK	bur
May 7	Mary MILLS	bur
May 7	William CADDICK	bur
May 8	Thomas YATES	bur

1811

May 9	James FEREDAY	bur
May 12	John, s of John & Harriott PIERCE, Born Decr 25 1810	bap
May 12	Uriah, s of Uriah & Jane PLATT	bap
May 12	Henry, s of William & Hannah HOLLAND	bao
May 12	Thomas, s of John & Hannah POWELL	bap
May 12	Phebe, d of James & Ann PERRY	bap
May 12	Job, s of Richard & Mary FOSTER	bap
May 12	Josiah, s of Samuel & Mary TONKS	bap
May 12	Samuel, s of Joseph & Elizabeth TONKS	bap
May 12	Abel Armstrong, s of Abel & Eleanor EGGINTON	bap
May 12	Elizabeth, d of James & Ann WILKINSON	bap
May 12	Michael, s of Thomas & Mary LEISTER	bap
May 19	Joseph Horton, s of Joshua & Hannah HOYLE	bap
May 19	Elizabeth, d of James & Ann SATCHELL	bap
May 19	Peter, s of Peter & Ann HICKMANS	bap
May 19	Abraham, s of John & Mary BATE	bap
May 21	John ELWELL & Ann WILLETTS by Licence	mar
May 22	Jane, d of William & Maria MORRISS	bap
May 23	John LAW	bur
May 26	Thomas HOPKINS	bur
May 26	Lydia EVANS	bur
May 26	Richard, s of Thomas & Elizabeth TILLEY	bap
May 26	Sarah, d of William & Ann PHIPPS	bap
May 26	Maryann, d of James & Elizabeth HICKMANS	bap
May 26	Mary, d of Thomas & Nancy DAVIS	bap
May 26	Nancy, d of Thomas & Eleanor WEBB	bap
May 31	Richard BAYLIS	bur
Jun 2	Edward WARR & Harriott EASTTON by Banns	mar
Jun 2	John, s of Joseph & Hannah BOTT	bap
Jun 2	Thomas, s of Benjamin & Elizabeth BENNITT	bap
Jun 2	Benjamin, a base son of Elizabeth FULLWOOD	bap
Jun 2	James, s of John & Eleanor MORRIS	bap
Jun 2	Elizabeth, d of Thomas & Ann WHITEHOUSE	bap
Jun 2	Moses, d of William & Elizabeth BRATT	bap
Jun 2	Joseph, s of John & Elizabeth PRESTON	bap
Jun 2	John, s of Joseph & Ann VERNON[?]	bap
Jun 2	John, s of John & Margarett COTTON	bap
Jun 2	Mary, d of Richard & Ann HILL	bap
Jun 2	Mary, d of John & Rebecca MILLWARD	bap
Jun 2	Mary Ann LAW	bur
Jun 3	Joseph SMITH & Ann PARSONS by Banns	mar
Jun 3	John, s of Joseph & Phebe CROFTS, Born Aug 29 1808	bap
Jun 3	Robert, s of William & Sarah WILLIAMS	bap
Jun 3	Joseph, s of William & Hannah ROUND	bap
Jun 3	Joseph, s of Joseph & Phebe CROFTS	bap
Jun 4	Ann DREW	bur
Jun 9	William, s of William & Mary PATE	bap
Jun 9	Elizabeth, d of Randle & Catharine CLARK	bap
Jun 9	Joseph SHEREWOOD	bur

Jun 10	Benjamin HORTON	bur
Jun 12	Elizabeth DUDLEY	bur
Jun 12	Esther RICHARDS	bur
Jun 12	George WHITEHOUSE	bur
Jun 16	Martha, d of James & Hannah FISHER	bap
Jun 16	William, s of John & Sarah DIGGERY	bap
Jun 16	Mary, d of James & Mary PASSFIELD	bap
Jun 16	Elizabeth, d of Thomas & Catharine WAKEFIELD	bap
Jun 19	Mary SMITH	bur
Jun 23	Joseph, s of George & Jane MORRIS	bap
Jun 23	Richard, s of George & Sarah JONES	bap
Jun 25	Hannah WILDAY	bur
Jun 26	John DUFFIN	bur
Jan 26	Esther WHITEHOUSE	bur
Jun 28	Betsey WILDAY	bur
Jun 28	Benjamin DUDLEY	bur
Jun 30	Eliza, d of Jonah & Ann DAVIS	bap
Jun 30	Eliza, d of Joseph & Elizabeth JEWKES	bap
Jun 30	Hannah Mills, d of Daniel & Elizabeth GORTON	bap
Jun 30	Sarah, d of Joshua & Ann NORTON	bap
Jun 30	Daniel, s of John & Siganda DAVIS	bap
Jun 30	Ann, d of John & Sarah PUGH	bap
Jun 30	Ann, d of Abraham & Ann GEORGE	bap
Jul 1	Thomas HARDY	bur
Jul 1	Mary BAGNALL	bur
Jul 4	Joseph HOLLOWAY	bur
Jul 7	Henry CHALLENDER & Mary WOODWARD by Banns	mar
Jul 7	Elizabeth, d of James & Ann WHITEHOUSE	bap
Jul 7	Thomas, s of Edward & Mary CARTWRIGHT	bap
Jul 7	John, s of Thomas & Hannah PACKETT	bap
Jul 7	Thomas, s of Thomas & Martha LEE	bap
Jul 7	Thomas, s of Charles & Mary ROGERS	bap
Jul 14	Elizabeth, d of John & Maria GUTTERIDGE	bap
Jul 14	James, s of John & Sarah BENNETT	bap
Jul 16	James LINES & Rebecca SANDERS by Banns	mar
Jul 16	Hannah SMITH	bur
Jul 17	Elizabeth ASTON	bur
Jul 18	Mary RYLEY	bur
Jul 18	John WHEALE	bur
Jul 19	Elizabeth WHITEHOUSE	bur
Jul 21	William, s of James & Sarah DUNN	bap
Jul 21	John, a base son of Hannah NIGHTINGALE	bap
Jul 21	Thomas, s of John & Martha CLULO, Born May 20 1809	bap
Jul 21	Ann, d of Joseph & Hannah WHITEHOUSE	bap
Jul 21	Joseph, s of William & Sarah HARTILL	bap
Jul 21	Francis, s of Francis & Ann SKELDIN	bap
Jul 22	George INCHER & Sarah SMITH by Banns	mar
Jul 22	John HOOD & Sarah INGRAM	mar
Jul 25	William SMITH	bur

Jul 28	Sarah, d of Thomas & Mary HEMMINGS	bap
Jul 28	Hannah, d of John & Hannah COMPSTON	bap
Jul 28	Charlotte, Benjamin & Susanna BROOKS	bap
Jul 28	Sarah, d of Richard & Eleanor WHITEHOUSE	bap
Jul 29	Abraham DUFFIELD	bur
Jul 29	William TIMMINS	bur
Jul 30	James GILBERT & Hannah NICKLIN by Licence	mar
Jul 31	Sarah BLACKHAM	bur
Aug 1	Phebe CARTWRIGHT	bur
Aug 1	William WARTON	bur
Aug 4	Sebrah, d of Edward & Mary MOODY	bap
Aug 4	William EDWARDS	bur
Aug 5	Jane ROUND	bur
Aug 7	Thomas WALTERS	bur
Aug 11	Rachel, d of Thomas & Mary NASH	bap
Aug 11	Francis, s of David & Hannah WHITEHOUSE	bap
Aug 11	Ann, d of William & Elizabeth CONSTABLE	bap
Aug 11	John, s of James & Hannah DALE	bap
Aug 13	Elizabeth GORTON	bur
Aug 15	Mary GRIFFITHS	bur
Aug 18	John ROUND & Hannah JEWKES by Banns	mar
Aug 18	John, s of John & Selvia TART	bap
Aug 18	Phebe, d of John & Mary SMITH	bap
Aug 18	Susannah, d of William & Mary DOWNING	bap
Aug 18	Sophia, d of Edward & Sarah DUDLEY	bap
Aug 18	Joseph, s of James & Sarah CHATER	bap
Aug 18	Mary, d of Richard & Ann THOMPSON	bap
Aug 21	William ROBERTS	bur
Aug 25	William, s of John & Mary HILTON	bap
Aug 25	Maryann, d of James & Sarah SKELTON	bap
Aug 26	Abraham WHITEHOUSE	bur
Aug 30	Ann GEORGE	bur
Aug 31	Ann MILWARD	bur
Sep 1	Sarah, d of Thomas & Sarah EADES	bap
Sep 1	Thomas, s of Thomas & Elizabeth HOLIHEAD	bap
Sep 1	Ann, d of Samuel & Mary WHITEHOUSE	bap
Sep 1	Stephen, s of Isaac & Ann MILLS	bap
Sep 3	Thomas RICHARDS & Hannah WITHERS, by Banns	mar
Sep 4	Robert LAWTON	bur
Sep 8	Jeremiah, s of Ambrose & Ann STANTON	mar
Sep 8	James, s of James & Mary AMOSS	bap
Sep 8	Mary, d of James & Rebecca BRADSHAW	bap
Sep 8	Joseph, s of Joseph & Mary SMITH	bap
Sep 8	Mary, d of Stephen & Sarah FISHER	bap
Sep 15	William HILL & Maryann FLETCHER, by Banns	mar
Sep 15	William, s of James & Susanna STEPHENS	bap
Sep 15	Mary, d of James & Elizabeth HOLLIES	bap
Sep 15	Hannah, d of Joseph & Hannah JONES	bap
Sep 15	William, s of John & Sarah BANISTER	bap

Sep 15	Andrew STEWARD	bur
Sep 15	William WOODALL	bur
Sep 17	Ann MILLS	bur
Sep 18	Mary Ann HEWLEY	bur
Sep 19	Jeremiah STANTON	bur
Sep 20	Thomas HICKIN	bur
Sep 22	Joseph, s of Francis & Sarah GRIFFITHS	bap
Sep 22	Maryann, d of James & Elizabeth PICKARILL	bap
Sep 22	Elias, s of James & Ann PLANT	bap
Sep 27	James JONES	bur
Sep 29	Samuel RUDGE & Phebe BOUGH by Banns	mar
Sep 29	Roseanna, d of Joseph & Ann WHITEHOUSE	bap
Sep 29	Joseph, s of Edward & Sarah BROOKS	bap
Sep 29	Thomas, s of Thomas & Ann DUDLEY	bap
Sep 29	Eliza, d of Edward & Margarett FISHER	bap
Sep 29	Isaac, s of Isaiah & Hannah GRINSELL	bap
Sep 29	Joseph, s of Thomas & Sophia PARKES	bap
Sep 30	Richard STEWARD & Isabella SMITH by Banns	mar
Oct 6	Joseph, s of Richard & Elizabeth WHITEHOUSE	bap
Oct 6	Samuel, s of William & Maria HICKABOTTOM	bap
Oct 6	Thomas, s of Thomas & Elizabeth VAUGHAN	bap
Oct 6	William, s of John & Sarah DOWLEY	bap
Oct 6	Nancy, d of Joseph & Sarah HICKABOTTOM	bap
Oct 11	Martha INGRAM	bur
Oct 13	Josiah SMITH & Elizabeth ROBERTS by Banns	mar
Oct 13	Hannah, d of John & Phebe COTTERILL	bap
Oct 13	Emela, d of John & Cretia KIRKHAM	bap
Oct 13	Sarah, d of John & Prissilla SOUTHALL	bap
Oct 17	Joseph WHITEHOUSE	bur
Oct 20	Eliza, d of David & Hannah HORTON, from Birmingham, Born Oct 23 1810	bap
Oct 20	John, s of John & Elizabeth HORTON, Born May 31	bap
Oct 20	John, s of Thomas & Ann HICKMANS	bap
Oct 20	Sarah, d of John & Ann WALL	bap
Oct 20	Benjamin, s of Peter & Elizabeth SALT	bap
Oct 20	Ann, d of John & Mary HIGGINS	bap
Oct 20	Ann, d of William & Ann THOMAS	bap
Oct 20	Sarah, d of John & Ann WHITEHOUSE, Born Nov 10 1800	bap
Oct 20	David TIMMINS	bur
Oct 22	William DARBY	bur
Oct 23	Elizabeth HOWELLS	bur
Oct 24	William UNDERHILL (Church Warden)	bur
Oct 24	James WHITEHOUSE	bur
Oct 27	Benjamin, s of George & Sarah SHELDON	bap
Oct 27	Hannah, d of William & Sarah HAMMONDS	bap
Oct 28	Hugh EVANS & Elizabeth BROWN, by Banns	mar
Oct 29	James HEELEY	bur
Oct 30	Hannah WHEALE	bur
Nov 1	Sarah MORRIS	bur

Nov 3	Joseph COX & Catharine WOODWARD by Banns		mar
Nov 3	Sarah, d of William & Catharine SMITH		bap
Nov 3	Samuel, s of Samuel & Sarah HODGKINS, Born April 13		bap
Nov 3	Mary, d of William & Judith BROCKHOUSE		bap
Nov 3	Joseph, s of Henry & Sarah PUGH		bap
Nov 3	Harriott, d of William & Elizabeth DAVIS		bap
Nov 3	Ann, d of Joseph & Ann FEREDAY		bap
Nov 3	Hannah, d of Joseph & Elizabeth WHITEHOUSE		bap
Nov 3	John FISHER		bur
Nov 3	James DALE		bur
Nov 4	Henry BIBB & Sophia ONIONS by Banns		mar
Nov 10	William HICKIN		bur
Nov 10	Hannah GORTON		bur
Nov 10	Thomas, s of John & Elizabeth OCROFT		bap
Nov 10	William, s of William & Fanny WEBB		bap
Nov 10	Margarett, d of James & Scissa PROBERT		bap
Nov 10	William, s of James & Scissa PROBERT, Born June 25 1809		bap
Nov 15	Tobiatha BAKER		bur
Nov 15	James MILLS		bur
Nov 17	Joseph, s of Joseph & Lette EADES		bap
Nov 17	Hannah, d of William & Ann JONES		bap
Nov 17	John, s of John & Eleanor CLARK		bap
Nov 17	John FELLOWS		bur
Nov 23	William John GWINNETT		bur
Nov 24	Thomas, s of Joseph & Ann INGRAM		bap
Nov 24	Job, s of Job & Hannah SMITH		bap
Nov 24	John, s of John & Maria TAYLOR		bap
Nov 24	Joseph, s of John & Sarah EVANS		bap
Nov 24	Mary, d of Benjamin & Sarah PIERCE		bap
Nov 24	Mary, d of Joseph & Joyce TURNER		bap
Nov 24	Eliza, d of Joseph & Jane ASHTON		bap
Nov 24	Maryann, d of Joseph & Ann HICKMANS		bap
Nov 24	Abraham, s of John & Elizabeth LESTER		bap
Nov 24	John, s of Benjamin & Ann HOLLOWAY		bap
Nov 24	John, s of William & Rebecca ROUND		bap
Nov 24	Sarah FISHER		bur
Nov 24	Daniel BATE		bur
Nov 25	Thomas WHEALE & Mary DOVEY by Banns		mar
Nov 26	Joseph MILLARD		bur
Nov 28	Ann SMITH		bur
Nov 28	Richard THOMPSON		bur
Dec 1	John, s of John & Sarah HART		bap
Dec 1	Rebecca, d of Joseph & Ann LAMBETH		bap
Dec 1	Richard, s of Richard & Ann JONES		bap
Dec 1	Jeremiah, s of Jeremiah & Ann FIRKIN		bap
Dec 1	Joseph, s of James & Elizabeth PITT, Born Mar 6		bap
Dec 1	Mary, d of James & Mary SPARROW		bap
Dec 1	George, s of Charles & Ann SMITH		bap
Dec 1	Sarah HOLT		bur

1811

Dec 2	Hannah GREEN	bur
Dec 4	William NIBB & Elizabeth CORBET, by Banns	mar
Dec 4	John GALLOP	bur
Dec 4	Eliza RYLEY	bur
Dec 5	Charles MORGAN	bur
Dec 5	Catharine RYLEY	bur
Dec 8	Charles, s of Thomas & Elizabeth DANKS	bap
Dec 8	John LANGHORN	bur
Dec 9	Thomas MAREGOLD & Mary GILBIRTT, by Banns	mar
Dec 10	Hannah BAKER	bur
Dec 10	Karia BLACKHAM	bur
Dec 13	Sarah HARRIS	bur
Dec 15	Walter, s of John & Hannah DRYDEN	bap
Dec 15	Ann, d of Dudley & Sarah PLATT	bap
Dec 22	Ann, d of William & Zebra FORD	bap
Dec 22	Thomas, s of Joseph & Susanna WISE	bap
Dec 22	Richard, s of Elijah & Ann WILCOX	bap
Dec 22	Sarah, d of Joseph & Martha MILLINGTON	bap
Dec 22	Joseph GREEN	bur
Dec 22	Thomas WILLIS	bur
Dec 22	John BAKER	bur
Dec 24	Ann EVANS	bur
Dec 25	William, s of Samuel & Sarah THORNEYCROFT	bap
Dec 26	Daniel GORTON	bur
Dec 29	Jonas PEACOCK & Ann COOPER by Banns	mar
Dec 29	Elizabeth, d of John & Ann EDWARDS, Born June 23	bap
Dec 29	Sarah, d of John & Ann BALL	bap
Dec 29	Mary, d of Samuel & Rebecca HIPKISS	bap
Dec 29	Mary, d of Thomas & Ann DAVIS	bap
Dec 29	Joseph FISHER	bur
Dec 29	Pemilar KIRKHAM	bur
Dec 31	Joseph HANCOX	bur

1812

Jan 1	Sarah CHAMBERS	bur
Jan 2	Elizabeth FISHER	bur
Jan 2	Sarah DUDLEY	bur
Jan 5	Thomas, s of William & Ann PODMORE	bap
Jan 5	Rachael, d of John & Elizabeth ROUND	bap
Jan 5	Ruth, d of John & Elizabeth ROUND	bap
Jan 5	William, s of William & Ann GEORGE	bap
Jan 5	Hannah, d of Edward & Charlotte JAY	bap
Jan 5	Ann, d of James & Sarah COOKSEY	bap
Jan 5	Maryann, d of Thomas & Mary BENNETT	bap
Jan 5	Esther, d of James & Rebecca WHITEHOUSE	bap
Jan 5	James, s of William & Hannah WHITEHOUSE	bap
Jan 5	John, s of John & Hannah HODGKISS	bap
Jan 6	Samuel WRIGHT & Mary BANNISTER by Licence	mar
Jan 19	Thomas TONKS & Mary ADAMS by Banns	mar

	Jan 19	Mary, d of William & Jane WHITEHOUSE	bap
	Jan 19	Joseph, s of John & Elizabeth HYDE	bap
	Jan 19	Ann, d of Isaac & Hannah DARBY	bap
	Jan 19	William, s of William & Margarett NIGHTINGALE	bap
	Jan 23	Daniel MINCHER	bur
	Jan 26	Caroline, d of John & Mary HOLLAND	bap
	Jan 26	Isaiah, s of John & Mary HORTON	bap
	Jan 26	Joseph, s of Joseph & Sophia HOLT	bap
	Jan 26	Sarah, d of Samuel & Sarah SUTTON	bap
	Jan 26	Elizabeth, d of Joseph & Mary WRIGHT	bap
	Jan 26	William, s of James & Elizabeth HAWLEY	bap
	Jan 26	Ann, d of Valentine & Ann HARRISON	bap
	Jan 26	Diana, d of Samuel & Mary GOUGH	bap
	Jan 26	Mary SPARROW	bur
	Jan 28	Mary WILKES	bur
	Jan 28	Edward GRIFFITHS	bur
	Jan 31	Esther WHITEHOUSE	bur
	Jan 31	George HADEN	bur
	Feb 2	William WALKER & Sarah DODD by Banns	mar
	Feb 2	Mary, d of Samuel & Ann SKELDIN	bap
	Feb 2	James, s of James & Mary LANKSON	bap
	Feb 2	Hannah, d of Amos & Francis HODGSKINS	bap
	Feb 2	Phebe, d of Joseph & Sarah BAGGOTT	bap
	Feb 2	Joseph, s of Joseph & Ellen HOLT	bap
	Feb 2	George, s of George & Lois ALLEN	bap
	Feb 2	Joseph BROOKS	bur
	Feb 2	Joseph HOLT	bur
	Feb 4	Daniel PARTRIDGE	bur
	Feb 6	Mary Ann PERSEHOUSE	bur
	Feb 7	William PARTRIDGE	bur
	Feb 7	Mary GRIFFITHS	bur
	Feb 9	Mary, d of Abraham & Sarah WHITEHOUSE	bap
	Feb 9	Sarah, d of Richard & Lucy LANKFORD	bap
	Feb 9	Ann, d of John & Margarett HEELEY	bap
	Feb 9	Daniel, s of Joseph & Hannah WHITEHOUSE	bap
	Feb 9	Elizabeth, d of Thomas & Ann FEREDAY	bap
	Feb 9	Maryann, d of John & Mary SMITH	bap
	Feb 9	Edward, s of Edward & Phebe WHITEHOUSE	bap
	Feb 9	Catharine, d of Richard & Sophia PRICE	bap
	Feb 9	Edward, s of John & Rhoda SMITH	bap
	Feb 9	Phebe, d of Joseph & Ruth WORTON	bap
	Feb 9	Robert GOLDIN	bur
	Feb 10	Elizabeth DAINTY	bur
	Feb 12	William LAW	bur
	Feb 15	Richard TURNER	bur
	Feb 16	Leah, d of William & Sarah PHAYSEY	bap
	Feb 16	Thomas, s of William & Elizabeth STANTON	bap
	Feb 16	Robert, s of Robert & Sarah PUGH	bap
	Feb 16	Benjamin, s of John & Clare STANLEY	bap

1812

Feb 16	Daniel, s of Richard & Mary JEWKS	bap
Feb 16	Ann, d of Thomas & Ann RUSTON	bap
Feb 16	Hannah, d of Nicholas & Sarah WOOD	bap
Feb 16	William SHELDON	bur
Feb 18	Jane NICHOLLS	bur
Feb 20	Edward WHITEHOUSE	bur
Feb 20	Hannah ONIONS	bur
Feb 23	Maryann SKELDON	bur
Feb 23	William, s of Joseph & Ann WHITEHOUSE	bap
Feb 23	Ann, d of Abraham & Ann LAW	bap
Feb 23	Maria, d of John & Mary DAVIS	bap
Feb 23	John, base s of Ann HUGHES	bap
Feb 23	John, s of William & Elizabeth ROGERS	bap
Feb 28	William BARKER	bur
Mar 1	Sarah, d of John & Elizabeth FISHER	bap
Mar 1	Joseph, s of Francis & Esther NICHOLLS	bap
Mar 1	Elijah, s of John & Patience WILLIAMS	bap
Mar 1	Prisilla, d of Joseph & Elizabeth MARTIN	bap
Mar 1	Eliza, d of William & Maria WHITMORE	bap
Mar 1	Mary, d of John & Sarah JONES	bap
Mar 1	Mary, d of William & Naomi HIGGS	bap
Mar 1	Thomas LEE	bur
Mar 3	Joseph TIMMINS	bur
Mar 8	David SANDERS & Mary NOCK by Banns	mar
Mar 8	John, s of Thomas & Ann COTTERILL	bap
Mar 8	William, s of William & Sarah LEECH, Born Dec 8, 1811	bap
Mar 8	William, s of John & Sarah BEDDOE	bap
Mar 8	Hannah, d of William & Sophia BATE	bap
Mar 8	John, s of John & Hannah TIBITTS	bap
Mar 8	Thomas, s of John & Elizabeth JESSON	bap
Mar 8	Phebe, d of James & Hannah GRIFFITHS	bap
Mar 8	Antony, s of Benjamin & Rachael WHITEHOUSE	bap
Mar 8	John PERESHOUSE	bur
Mar 8	Elizabeth HOLLAND	bur
Mar 9	William NIGHTINGALE	bur
Mar 10	Rebecca MILLS	bur
Mar 10	Daniel WHITEHOUSE	bur
Mar 13	Maria WHITEHOUSE	bur
Mar 15	Tamor, d of William & Ellis GRIFFITHS	bap
Mar 15	John, s of John & Ann ROUPER	bap
Mar 15	Sarah, d of Joseph & Mary WARR	bap
Mar 15	Ann, d of William & Sarah HILL	bap
Mar 15	Edward, s of Joseph & Sophia RALPH	bap
Mar 15	Esther, d of William & Betty SANSOM, Born Novr 22, 1810	bap
Mar 15	James ROUND	bur
Mar 15	Mary WARR	bur
Mar 15	William DARBY	bur
Mar 16	Thomas POSTINGS & Martha DOWNING by Banns	mar
Mar 17	William GEORGE	bur

Mar 18	Hannah DAVIS	bur
Mar 19	Joseph NICHOLLS	bur
Mar 19	Mary WHITEHOUSE	bur
Mar 19	John LLOYD	bur
Mar 19	William LLOYD	bap
Mar 22	Henry, s of David & Mary DICKEN	bap
Mar 22	Samuel, s of William & Hannah LAWRANCE	bap
— Mar 22	Noah, d of Benjamin & Maria FELLOWS	bap
Mar 22	Susanna & Martha, Twin d of Francis & Sarah OWEN	bap
⌐ Mar 22	Hannah, d of William & Hannah HOPKINS	bap
Mar 22	Hannah SMITH	bur
Mar 24	Isaac ASTON	bur
Mar 25	Elizabeth WILLIAMS	bur
_ Mar 29	Ann, d of Joseph & Marable GUTTRIDGE	bap
Mar 29	Charlotte, d of Jesse & Mary STOTT	bap
Mar 29	James, s of James & Mary WHITEHOUSE	bap
Mar 29	Abraham, s of Abraham & Aylce WALTERS	bap
Mar 29	Isaiah, s of Joseph & Elizabeth SHEREWOOD	bap
Mar 29	Jesse, s of William & Sarah ROUND	bap
Mar 29	Hannah, d of Daniel & Sarah SCRIVEN	bap
Mar 29	Phebe, d of Joseph & Rebecca SMITH, Born Feby 26	bap
Mar 29	Samuel, s of John & Hannah ASTON, Born Nov 5, 1811	bap
Mar 29	Elizabeth, d of James & Maria FISHER	bap
Mar 29	Zacharias, s of James & Prisilla SHELDON	bap
— Mar 29	Nancy WEBB	bur
Mar 30	Benjamin GAUNT & Elizabeth STEWARD by Banns	mar
Mar 30	Thomas STOKES & Nancy EVANS by Banns	mar
Mar 30	Joseph WHITEHOUSE	bur
Mar 31	Samuel KIMBERLEY	bur
Mar 31	Catharine HORTON	bur
Apr 2	Nancy FISHER	bur
Apr 3	Harriott FEREDAY	bur
Apr 5	Sarah, d of Jeremiah & Sarah BUFFEY	bap
⌐ Apr 5	Elizabeth, d of Richard &Sarah NIBB	bap
Apr 5	John, s of Oliver Brown VALE by his wife Isabella	bap
Apr 5	Ann, d of Oliver Brown VALE by his wife Isabella	bap
Apr 5	John, s of John & Alse SHEERWOOD	bap
Apr 5	James, s of James & Mary STANTON	bap
Apr 5	William, s of William & Rebecca HATTON	bap
Apr 5	Sarah Nightingale, d of Daniel & Elizabeth GORTON	bap
— Apr 5	Isaiah EADES	bur
Apr 6	Daniel John Ridgley, s of Daniel & Mary Ann M^{c}NAUGHTON, Born Mar 6	bap
Apt 7	Joseph FISHER	bur
Apr 12	Maryann, d of Thomas & Sarah GUEST	bap
Apr 12	Samuel, s of Samuel & Sarah FEREDAY	bap
Apr 12	Martha, d of John & Sarah BAGLEY	bap
Apr 12	Robert, s of Robert & Ann MORRIS	bap
Apr 12	Mary, d of Thomas & Mary HEATHCOCK, Born Mar 7	bap

Apr 12	Isaac, d of Samuel & Mary LAW	bap
Apr 12	Betty, d of Joseph & Ann SANDERS	bap
Apr 12	Mary Ann, d of William & Hannah HARRINGTON	bap
Apr 12	Sarah, d of Elisha & Phebe GRIFFITHS	bap
Apr 12	Jesse ROUND	bur
Apr 15	Lettice WHITEHOUSE	bur
Apr 19	Hannah, d of William & Maria DANKS	bap
Apr 19	John, s of John & Mary BADGER	bap
Apr 19	Maryann, d of Simon & Elizabeth BLEWET	bap
Apr 19	Elizabeth, d of John & Hannah BUNCH	bap
Apr 19	Samuel HARTSHORN	bur
Apr 19	Sarah BELCHER	bur
Apr 20	Edward BULLOCK & Elizabeth BEARD by Banns	mar
Apr 20	James WRIGHT & Sarah FREGDLEY by Banns	mar
Apr 21	John LARAM	bur
Apr 22	Mary DAVIS	bur
Apr 26	Sophia, d of Joseph & Martha SMITH	bap
Apr 26	Ann, d of James & Mary JAMES	bap
Apr 26	Annmaria, d of Edward & Mary JONES	bap
Apr 26	Sarah, d of John & Catharine LATHAM	bap
Apr 26	Thomas, s of Thomas & Esther JONES	bap
Apr 26	Mary, d of Richard & Catharine HOLMES	bap
Apr 26	John, s of Nathan & Mary HILL	bap
Apr 26	Isaac, s of Isaac & Jane PERRINS of Dudley, Born Mar 25	bap
Apr 26	Sarah MILLARD	bur
Apr 30	Thomas GREEN	bur
May 3	Thomas Holland, s of Samuel & Elizabeth CLARKE	bap
May 3	Mary, d of Henry & Sarah LEWIS	bap
May 3	Joseph, s of Joseph & Sarah MILLS	bap
May 3	Benjamin Simeon, s of James & Nancy HORTON	bap
May 3	Mary, d of Edward & Sarah WALLERS	bap
May 3	John, s of William & Maria GRIFFITHS	bap
May 3	Richard FISHER	bur
May 3	Joseph PRESTON	bur
May 5	Roseanna MORRIS	bur
May 10	William, s of William & Sarah HANCOX	bap
May 10	Joseph, s of Joseph & Sarah MILS	bap
May 10	Robert ALLEN	bur
May 10	Benjamin BAYLEY	bur
May 13	James HENSHAW	bur
May 13	Zilliah HARTSHORN	bur
May 14	Francis SCADMAN & Ann DITHERIDGE, by Banns	mar
May 15	Daniel John Redgley M^c NAUGHTON	bur
May 17	William HARPER & Elizabeth DEAKIN, by Banns	mar
May 17	Phebe, d of James & Deborah NOCK	bap
May 17	Joseph, d of Daniel & Mary JEAVONS	bap
May 17	Eliza, d of Thomas & Ellen PARTON	bap
May 17	Sarah, d of John & Mary WRIGHT	bap
May 17	Mary, d of Simon & Elizabeth MILLS	bap

<u>1812</u>

May 17	John, s of Edward & Elizabeth MARTIN	bap
May 17	Mary, d of Samuel & Rhoda JONES	bap
May 17	Abraham, s of Richard & Sarah MILLS	bap
May 17	Sarah, d of Joseph & Mary RUBERY	bap
May 17	Samuel, s of Isaac & Sarah ASTON	bap
May 17	Joseph ALLCOCK	bur
May 17	James WHITEHOUSE	bur
May 18	Thomas EASTOPE & Sophia Hesper DARBY by Banns	bap
May 18	John FALKNER & Maria BAGNALL by Banns	mar
May 24	Samuel Wheeley, s of Thomas & Maria CANTRILL	bap
May 24	Ann, d of William & Hannah EDGE	bap
May 24	John, s of Benjamin & Sarah BATE	bap
May 24	James, s of Richard & Sarah ROWE	bap
May 24	James, s of Isaac & Elizabeth WHITEHOUSE	bap
May 24	Richard WHITEHOUSE	bur
May 24	Mary MILLS	bur
May 25	Hannah EVANS	bur
May 28	Daniel WHITEHOUSE	bur
— May 31	Thomas, s of Thomas & Cary HOPKINS	bap
May 31	Casiah, d of Thomas & Hannah KENNEDAY	bap
— May 31	Hannah, d of Paul & Mary COX	bap
May 31	Betsey, d of William & Ann LONGSTON	bap
⨭ May 31	Sarah, d of Samuel & Mary HICKMANS	bap
May 31	Jabes Joseph, s of Samson & Catharine AUSTIN	bap
May 31	Henry, s of Thomas & Sarah WILLIAMS	bap
May 31	Mary, d of Joseph & Mary PASKIN	bap
May 31	James, s of James & Nancy WOLFEINDALE	bap
May 31	Elizabeth, d of Abraham & Sarah FISHER	bap
— May 31	William, s of William & Martha LEA	bap
Jun 2	Samuel DUDLEY	bur
Jun 3	George DAVIS	bur
Jun 3	Elizabeth JONES	bur
— Jun 4	Eder TIMMINS	bur
Jun 6	Edward WILLIAMS & Mary JEAVONS by Licence	mar
Jun 7	Thomas, s of Charles & Mary RICHARDSON	bap
Jun 7	Nancy, d of Joseph & Mary SMITH	bap
Jun 7	William, s of James & Mary CADDICK	bap
Jun 7	Sarah, d of James & Rosehannah WALLEY	bap
Jun 7	Hannah, a base d of Ann GRIFFITHS	bap
Jun 7	Thomas, s of Robert & Mary COLES	bap
Jun 7	Benjamin YATES	bap
Jun 9	Benjamin, s of Daniel & Sarah STEALEY	bap
Jun 9	William, s of Daniel & Sarah STEALEY, Born July 18, 1808	bap
Jun 14	James, s of John & Peggy HEELEY	bap
Jun 14	Maryann, d of Thomas & Eleanor DUFFIN	bap
Jun 14	Phebe, d of Joseph & Maria LAW	bap
Jun 14	William, s of William & Phebe EDWARDS	bap
Jun 14	Maria, d of Thomas & Ann PASKIN	bap
Jun 14	Edward, s of Edward & Ann DUDLEY	bap

1812

Jun 14	Thomas, s of William & Sarah WHITEHOUSE	bap
Jun 14	Sarah, d of Thomas & Ann INGRAM	bap
Jun 14	William, s of John & Mary BLACKHAM	bap
Jun 14	David, s of Joseph & Mary GRIFFITHS	bap
Jun 14	Mary & Joseph, twin d & s of Richard & Ann MORGAN	bap
Jun 15	Joseph ROSE & Ann GREEN by Banns	mar
Jun 21	George Barnett, s of Thomas & Maria SMITH	bap
Jun 21	Charlotte, d of Thomas & Mary STANLEY	bap
Jun 21	Richard, s of Richard & Mary PASKIN	bap
Jun 21	Ann Maria, d of Charles & Susanna PERRY	bap
Jun 21	Martha, d of Edward & Elizabeth REED	bap
Jun 21	Nancy, d of John & Mary INGRAM	bap
Jun 21	Ann, d of Joseph & Ann HARTWELL	bap
Jun 21	Henry, s of Edward & Ann HARRIS	bap
Jun 21	Edward, s of Edward & Mary FISHER	bap
Jun 21	John FLETCHER	bur
Jun 22	Joseph DARBY & Sarah VILLERS by Banns	mar
Jun 22	Isaac PHILLIPS	bur
Jun 28	Samuel, s of James & Abigal PRICE	bap
Jun 28	Samuel, s of James & Elizabeth GOUGH	bap
Jun 28	Francis, s of Abraham & Maria HICKMANS	bap
Jun 28	Mary, d of Thomas & Margarett COOPER	bap
Jun 28	Thomas, s of William & Elizabeth MOORE	bap
Jun 28	Solomon, s of Robert & Mary CALLEAR	bap
Jun 30	William MINCHER	bur
Jul 2	Joseph HOYLE	bur
Jul 3	William Moore FISHER	bur
Jul 5	James, s of William & Roseanna SHEERWOOD	bap
Jul 5	William, s of William & Jemima ROWETT	bap
Jul 5	Charlotte, d of Joseph & Susanna TRANTER	bap
Jul 5	Maria, d of Thomas & Elizabeth PLIMMER	bap
Jul 5	Maryann, d of Isaac & Judith CLARK	bap
Jul 5	Ann, d of Richard & Ann JERVIS	bap
Jul 12	John BRACE & Sarah GOULD by Banns	mar
Jul 12	James, s of James & Mary ASTON, Born June 12	bap
Jul 12	John, s of Edward & Phebe SMITH, Born May 12	bap
Jul 12	Elizabeth, d of Samuel & Elizabeth GROVES	bap
Jul 12	Lydia, d of William & Sebra CADDICK	bap
Jul 12	Mary, d of Francis & Mary POTTS	bap
Jul 13	William SOUTHALL	bur
Jul 15	Thomas INGRAM	bur
Jul 19	John LOUCH & Sarah UNDERHILL by Banns	mar
Jul 19	Ann, d of Edward & Hannah HARRIS	bap
Jul 19	Jane, d of David & Mary SANDERS	bap
Jul 19	John, s of Edward & Martha WESTWOOD	bap
Jul 19	John, s of John & Elizabeth WALLEYS	bap
Jul 19	Samuel, s of George & Hannah CALLOWAY	bap
Jul 19	Sarah, d of Francis & Ann AMOSS	bap
Jul 19	Jane, d of James & Mary RUEBOTTOM	bap

<u>1812</u>

Jul 19	Samuel, s of William & Lucy BAGNALL	bap
Jul 19	Susanna, d of Charles & Ann WARRICK	bap
Jul 19	George BAYLISS	bur
Jul 22	Michael WILKES	bur
Jul 26	Ann, d of Joseph & Mary FLEET	bap
Jul 26	Mary, d of John & Sarah JONES	bap
Jul 26	Mary, d of Joseph & Sarah WARD	bap
Jul 26	William, s of William & Ann HARRIS	bap
Jul 26	Stephen, s of Stephen & Sarah FISHER	bap
Jul 26	Thomas, s of Thomas & Mary PUGH	bap
Jul 26	Hannah, d of William & Ann HIPKINS	bap
Jul 26	Sarah TIMMINS	bur
Jul 28	Sarah CADDICK	bur
Aug 2	Benjamin ALLEN & Sarah HADLEY by Banns	mar
Aug 2	Mary Elizabeth, d of Joseph & Mary HILL	bur
Aug 2	Henry, s of James & Martha BARTLOM	bap
Aug 2	Deborah, d of Henry & Violette HUGHES	bap
Aug 2	Joseph, s of William & Sarah SHEERWOOD	bap
Aug 2	Lydia, d of Samuel & Mary TAYLOR	bap
Aug 3	Edward SADLER & Sarah WHITTAKER by Banns	mar
Aug 3	Randoll CLARK	bur
Aug 6	Elizabeth MARKLEW	bur
Aug 7	Joseph BAYLIS & Sarah RICHARDS by Banns	mar
Aug 9	Joseph, s of Thomas & Hannah MOTTRAM	bap
Aug 12	William BARNETT & Sarah HALL, by Banns	mar
Aug 13	Elizabeth WHITEHOUSE	bur
Aug 14	John SHELDON	bur
Aug 16	Louisa Lloyd, d of Nathaniel & Sarah LEADBETTER	bap
Aug 16	Joseph & Mary, Twin s & d of Stephen & Nancy HIPKINS, Born June 16	bap
Aug 16	Esther, d of Thomas & Phebe WHITEHOUSE	bap
Aug 16	Maryann, d of Joseph & Mary GRIFFITHS	bap
Aug 16	Fanny, d of James & Eleanor WATSON	bap
Aug 17	William WYNN	bur
Aug 23	Elizabeth, d of Samuel & Ann DUDLEY	bap
Aug 23	William, s of Abraham & Leah JEAVONS	bap
Aug 23	John, s of William & Mary ELLERTON	bap
Aug 23	Sarah, d of Richard & Mary FISHER, Born July 2, 1811	bap
Aug 23	Noah, s of Richard & Mary FISHER, Born March 11, 1809	bap
Aug 23	Jacob INGRAM	bur
Aug 30	John, s of Francis & Mary TAYLOR	bap
Aug 30	John, s of Richard & Ann JEWKS	bap
Aug 30	Elizabeth, d of John & Hannah WARD	bap
Aug 30	Richard, s of Robert & Mary PATE	bap
Aug 30	Sarah TIMMINS	bur
Sep 3	John MILLARD & Sarah Sophia HUGHES by Licence	mar
Sep 6	John Powell, s of John & Mary JOHNSON	bap
Sep 6	Samuel Cox, s of Titus & Casiah SMITH	bap
Sep 6	William, s of William & Sarah BLACKHAM	bap

Sep 6	John WHEALE	bur
Sep 6	John JAMES	bur
Sep 8	Nancy BATE	bur
Sep 13	John, s of William & Sophia EVANS	bap
Sep 13	William, s of Daniel & Sarah MINCHER	bap
Sep 13	Mary, d of Robert & Ellen SKELTON	bap
Sep 13	Emma, d of Edward & Mary GREEN	bap
Sep 13	Mary, d of Samuel & Sarah TILSLEY	bap
Sep 13	Abraham, s of Thomas & Rachael HANCOX	bap
Sep 13	William, s of Silas & Hannah STONES	bap
Sep 13	Charlotte, d of John & Ann WARD	bap
Sep 13	Edward WORMWOOD	bur
Sep 14	Richard GREEN	bur
Sep 15	Isaiah SHEERWOOD	bur
Sep 16	John BATE	bur
Sep 20	Edward REYNOLDS & Mary HARRISON by Banns	mar
Sep 20	William, s of Thomas & Elizabeth COLLINS	bap
Sep 20	Martha, d of Daniel & Martha WHITEHOUSE	bap
Sep 20	Edward, s of John & Prudence JEAVONS	bap
Sep 20	Benjamin, s of Joseph & Mary HOOD	bap
Sep 20	John, s of Samuel & Charlotte CUTLER	bap
Sep 21	John JEWKES & Martha MALPAS by Banns	mar
Sep 21	Russell FISHER	bur
Sep 22	Harriott MILLS	bur
Sep 22	Henry WHITEHOUSE	bur
Sep 22	John EVANS	bur
Sep 25	Joseph SMITH	bur
Sep 25	Mary DICKEN	bur
Sep 27	Ann, d of George & Mary HUGHES	bap
Sep 28	Edward SMITH	bur
Sep 29	Thomas WHITEHOUSE	bur
Oct 1	Joseph TIMMINS	bur
Oct 4	Daniel PARKES & Joyce STEPHENTON by Banns	mar
Oct 4	Mary, d of Joseph & Eleanor HOLT	bap
Oct 4	Joseph, s of James & Mary FERNEVALL	bap
Oct 4	Sarah, d of John & Elizabeth DENT	bap
Oct 11	Sarah, d of John & Mary CADDICK	bap
Oct 11	Hannah, d of Richard & Sarah STEVENTON	bap
Oct 11	John, s of Job & Elizabeth SHELDON	bap
Oct 11	Maria, d of John & Mary CROFTS	bap
Oct 11	Hannah, d of Edward & Ann WHITEHOUSE	bap
Oct 11	William, s of Thomas & Sarah MORRALL	bap
Oct 11	Maria, a base d of Sarah HODGETTS	bap
Oct 11	Sarah, d of Josiah & Ann TURNER	bap
Oct 13	Maryann WARNER	bur
Oct 15	John MORRISS	bur
Oct 18	William HOLLIES & Rebecca PINNOCK, by Banns	mar
Oct 18	Hannah, d of James & Sarah ROBERTS	bap
Oct 18	William, s of William & Sarah WARNER	bap

<u>1812</u>

Oct 18	Philip, s of Philip & Charlotte MARTIN	bap
Oct 18	Isaiah, s of George & Nancy YORK	bap
Oct 18	Sarah HANCOX	bur
Oct 18	Phebe SMITH	bur
Oct 19	Henry LORTON & Hannah GAUNT by Banns	mar
Oct 25	Richard, s of Richard & Sarah PERRY	bap
Oct 25	Samuel, s of Samuel & Mary BOTT	bap
Oct 25	Emma, d of Benjamin & Mary MANWARING	bap
Oct 25	Susanna, d of Thomas & Susanna STEVENS	bap
Oct 25	Harriott, d of David & Frances HIPKINS	bap
Oct 25	James HILL	bur
Oct 27[?]	Ann ATTWOOD	bur
Oct 29	Thomas NOCK	bur
Oct 29	Ephraim DARBY	bur
Oct 30	William WARNER	bap
Oct 30	Phebe LITTLE	bur
Nov 1	Jabes SMITH	bur
Nov 1	John, s of James & Mary BOTT	bap
Nov 1	Sarah, d of Benjamin & Sarah WALTERS	bap
Nov 1	Richard, s of William & Susanna HOLLINS	bap
Nov 1	Rachael, d of James & Hannah DOWNES	bap
Nov 1	Edward, s of William & Mary REECE	bap
Nov 1	Delilah, d of Edward & Mary WHITEHOUSE	bap
Nov 1	Naomi, d of Thomas & Dinah ROBINS	bap
Nov 8	Henry HARPER & Susanna LEGGE by Banns	mar
Nov 8	Eliza, d of Thomas & Sarah PERRINS	bap
Nov 8	Richard, s of Richard & Elizabeth OWEN	bap
Nov 8	John, s of Francis & Ann CHAMBERS	bap
Nov 8	Maryann, d of Samuel Ann MORRIS	bap
Nov 8	Joseph, s of William & Ann COOPER	bap
Nov 10	Ann BATE	bur
Nov 15	John JONES	bur
Nov 15	Richard GRIFFITHS	bur
Nov 15	Jacob, s of James & Mary MILLS	bap
Nov 15	Margarett, d of William & Susanna GRIFFITHS	bap
Nov 16	Richard PRICE & Ann EVANS by Banns	mar
Nov 16	Dinah ALEXANDER	bur
Nov 16	Joseph NICKLISS	bur
Nov 17	William ROBINSON	bur
Nov 19	Honor JONES	bur
Nov 22	Mary, d of John & Hannah POTTS	bap
Nov 22	William, s of Joseph & Elizabeth WALTON	bap
Nov 22	Ann LAW	bur
Nov 23	Elizabeth TAYLOR	bur
Nov 25	David REEVES & Phillis FRANKS by Banns	mar
Nov 25	Margarett MORRISS	bur
Nov 29	William, s of William & Rachael SIMCOX	bap
Nov 29	Phebe Gorton, d of William & Phebe LITTLE	bap
Nov 29	Eleanor, d of John & Elizabeth SOUTHERN	bap

1812

Nov 29	William, s of Henry & Sarah HARRIS	bap
Nov 29	Sarah, d of William & Mary SMITH	bap
Nov 30	Joseph TINGLE & Phebe JONES, by Banns	mar
Nov 30	Lewis JONES & Margarett JONES, by Banns	mar
Nov 30	George & Elizabeth WHITEHOUSE, twins	bur
Dec 1	William MORRIS	bur
Dec 2	Thomas HOLLIOAKE	bur
Dec 2	Isaiah HACKETT	bur
Dec 3	George Samuel Fereday, s of Richard & Elizabeth SMITH, Born May 7	bap
Dec 6	William, s of William & Elizabeth HANCOX	bap
Dec 6	Isaiah, s of William & Eleanor PRATT	bap
Dec 6	James NICKLIN	bur
Dec 7	John MARSH & Amelia THOMAS by Banns	mar
Dec 7	Josiah CLEWLEY & Mary ARCH by Banns	mar
Dec 7	James JEWKES	bur
Dec 7	William FEREDAY	bur
Dec 8	William SHAW & Lydia WILLIAMS by Banns	mar
Dec 9	Elizabeth ROUND	bur
Dec 13	William HAWLEY	bur
Dec 13	Stephen TIMMINS	bur
Dec 13	Ann, d of John & Catharine LATHAM	bap
Dec 13	Samuel, s of John & Sarah DIGGORY	bap
Dec 13	James, s of George & Ann LAVENDER	bap
Dec 13	Thomas, s of Thomas & Hannah PATCHETT	bap
Dec 14	John BEARDSMORE & Susannah WILLIAMS, by Banns	mar
Dec 16	Sarah SMITH	bur
Dec 17	James PLANT	bur
Dec 20	Elizabeth MARSHALL	bur
Dec 20	Rebecca PRICE	bur
Dec 20	Francis SADLER	bur
Dec 20	Richard GRIFFITHS	bur
Dec 20	Daniel, s of Samuel Thomas & Mary WRIGHT	bap
Dec 20	Sarah, d of Thomas & Grace SMITH	bap
Dec 20	William, s of Richard & Mary PHILLIPS	bap
Dec 20	Jefferey, s of Edward & Amelia DUDLEY	bap
Dec 25	Daniel, s of George & Ann BRINDLEY	bap
Dec 25	Thomas, s of Thomas & Maria MAYBUREY	bap
Dec 25	Benjamin, s of Benjamin & Sarah MILLARD	bap
Dec 25	James WHITEHOUSE	bur
Dec 27	Elizabeth HAWTHORN	bur
Dec 27	Martha & Mary NIGHTINGALE	bur
Dec 27	Edward, s of John & Cretia KIRKHAM	bap
Dec 27	Thomas, s of Joseph & Mary ROUND	bap
Dec 27	James, s of John & Eleanor ROBERTS	bap
Dec 27	Edward, s of William & Phebe EDWARDS	bap
Dec 27	Phebe, d of Isaac & Mary BISSELL	bap
Dec 27	Timothy, s of Timothy & Juliet LEWIS	bap
Dec 28	Hannah EVANS	bur

<u>1812</u>
Dec 30   John PARTRIDGE   bur
Dec 30   John WILSON   bur
    [The remainder of this volume (about ¾) is blank]

OFFICIATING MINISTERS

The following ministers officiated at marriages at Tipton.   They are noted by the abbreviation of their name against each marriage listed in Part 2.

SA	Spencer ARDEN – Clerk
TB	Thos BAGNALL
GB	Geo. BARRS
TBe	T. BEST – Officiating Minister
CBi	Charles BILLINGE
CB	Charles BLACKHAM – Minister
BB	Ben BRISCOE – Clerk
EB	Edward BURN
RC	Richard CADDICK – Minister
JCa	J. CARTWRIGHT – Minister
JCl	John CLERRITT[?]
LC	L. CONIFORD
JC	James COPE – Curate
RCo	Robert COTTAM
WC	William COWLEY
GD	George DALLOWAY – Minister
TD	Thomas DAVENPORT – Minister
JD	James DOWNING
JG	John GAUNT – Clerk, Curate
JGr	J. GRIFFITHS
TSH	Thomas SHAW HOLLIER – formerly Thomas SHAW
JH	J. HODGETTS
JHo	John HOWELLS - Clerk
JK	John KAYE Clerk, Minster
WK	William KAYE – Minister
JL	J. LLOYD – Curate of Wednesbury
EM	Edward MEYRULE – Clerk, Curate
HN	Hugh NANNEY
CN	Charles NEVE
TN	Titus NEVE – Clerk
JP	J. PARKS
JWP	J.W. PHILLIPS – Minister
SP	Samuel PHILLIPS – Curate
WP	William POTTS – Minister of Colton
JR	Joseph REED
PR	Proctor ROBINSON
JSR	John Simpson RUTTER
JS	J. SEVERNE
JSl	J. SLANEY
JSn	J. SNAPE – Clerk
TS	Thomas SHAW – Later changed name to Thomas Shaw HOLLIER
RT	Richard THURSFIELD – Clerk
TW	Thomas WALKER
GW	George WATKIN
W	WELLAND – Minister
JW	J. WILMOT – Minister
MW	Matthew WILMOTT – Clerk
WW	Wm WRIGHT – Vicar of Dudley

Surname Index

ABEL...11,21
ACKERS...180
ADAMS...95,103,106,111,119,
136,137,141,157,173*,182,
188,199
ADAMSON...95
ADCOCK...86,176
ADDENBROOKE...132,141
ADLINGTON...168,192
AKER...133
ALCOCK...See ALLCOCK
ALDRETT...See ALLDRETT
ALDRIDGE...129
ALDWRIGHT...140
ALEXANDER...40,42,47,50*,57,
59,60,62,63,66,111,114,148,
157*,190,193,208
AL(L)COCK...133,204
ALLDEN, ALLDIN ...43*,87
AL(L)DRETT, ALLDRITT...54,71,
82,89,110
ALLEN, ALLIN...17,41,49,83,85,
90,95,96,98,104,106,112,117,
137,144,164,180,191,200,
203,206
ALLENDER...105,140,155
ALLINDER...106
ALLPORT...68
ALLWRITT...63
ALSOP...77,89*
AMASS...51
AMOSS...142,158,196,205
ANDERSON...181
ANDREWS...187
ANGSLEY...149
ARCH(E)...149,163,167,169,175,
193,209
ARCOT...134
ARCUT...162
ARNOLD...101,113
ARTIL(L)...39,44,50,53,67
ASH...175
ASHFORTH...179
ASHLEY...43,49
ASHTON...27,128,192,198
ASPLEY...74
ASPLIN...46,59

ASSON...160
ASTLEY...102,133,147
ASTON, AS(S)TON(S)...9,15,
19*,20,25*,26,27,28*,32,34,
36*,40,42,46*,49,52,55,56,
59,62*,64,69,76,79,81,83,86*,
89*,90,94,103,106,108,109,
114,118,122,127,133,135,
138,139*,143,145,150,151,
153,156,157*,163,164,166,
167,168,172,173,174,177,
179,187,189,192,195,202*,
204,205
ATKISS...104,112,116
ATTWOOD...19,21,24,33,38,50,
52,55,58,60,62*,63,66,67,70,
72,74,82,86,88,90,101,102,
104,116,121,142,146,208
AUSTIN...111,133,141*,159,180,
204
AUTHORN...110

BACHE...143
BADGER...9,23,77,157,203
BAGER...14
BAGGETT...121
BAGGIT...158
BAGGOT(T)...141,176,181,200
BAGLEY...70,105,117,136,149,
165,202
BAGNALL...158,165,171,176,
177,183*,193,195,204,206
BAGNOLL...91
BAILEY(S)...36,46,98,113,115,
117,144
BAKER...11,21,29,48,49,65,70,
72,73,76,79,80*,82,84,89,90,
93,98,99*,102*,113,114,116,
124,127,131,132,135*,138,
140,144,145,147,152,153*,
154,159,166,168,177,181,
182,188,198,199*
BALL...64,69,77,93,103,115,
123*,131,141,154,172*,173,
174,181,182,199
BANBURY...78,191
BANISTER...See BANNISTER

BANISTON...174
BANKING...131
BANKS...152
BANNER...163
BAN(N)ISTER...151,196,199
BARBER, BARBOR...31,45
BARKEBY...172
BARKER...201
BARN(E)S...29,92,101,134,172
BARNET(T)...11,14,25,27,33,51,
  60,105,114,143,175,177,190,
  206
BARNEY...28*,44
BARNS...See BARNES
BARNSLEY...117,126
BARNWELL...187
BARRAT...165,189
BARRETT...96
BARRS...121
BARTLAM...125,137,154,178
BARTLEY...12
BARTLOM...206
BATE(S)...8,9,11,13,16*,18,20,
  27,31,32,35,38,42,70,77*,81,
  82,85,87,88,89,92*,93,96,97,
  99,100,104,105,106,107,110,
  111,112,116,118,120*,124,
  128,132*,133*,135,136,137*,
  138*,142,149,151,155,163,
  166*,168,171,173,175,176,
  179,182,183*,188,189,194,
  198,201,204,207*,208
BATTY...162
BAXTER...158
BAYLEY(S)...62,65*,69*,76,79,
  83,93,103,110,114,115,119,
  127,130,137,140,142,189,203
BAYLIS(S)...194,206*
BAYNES...171
BEADLEY...121
BEAL...80
BEARD(S)...126,161,203
BEARDSMORE...209
BEARNS...20
BECK(S)...16,18,19,24,25,26*,
  28,29,30,36*,39,44,45,52,53,
  54,58,63,64*,68,71,73,76,78,
  88,121
BEDDOE...170,178,193,201

BEDDOW...75,83
BEDFORD...165
BEDWORTH...110,157
BELCHER...119,130,147,151,
  154,172,191,193,203
BELL...171,182
BENNET(T)...18,38,48,57,59,68,
  82,90,98,111,116,120,121,
  123,129,136,195,199
BENNITT...131,135,148,154,159,
  170,171,194
BENTON...129,141,152,164
BERBRIDGE...147
BERRY...97
BETREDGE...141
BETTS...160
BETTY...59,70,85
BIBB...198
BIDEL...162
BILL...111,137,164,166,193
BILLINGHAM...124
BILLINSLEY...161
BINGLEY...18
BINKS...130
BINTT...165
BIRCH...120
BIRD...7,9,28,106,140,157,160,
  187
BIRTON...12,48,50,53,58
BISSEL(L)...8,9,80,82,87,89,94,
  99,103,105,111,113,118*,
  126,128,131,137,138,139*,
  153,166,183,209
BLACKHAM...8*,9,10,15,16*,20,
  23,24*,29*,36,37,38,39,47,55,
  59,67,69,75,85,96,118,130,
  136,139,141,152,154,158,
  161,168*,170,184,186,190,
  192,196,199,205,206
BLAKEMORE...65
BLAKESLEY...63
BLANKLEY...112,118*
BLARE...51,56
BLASE...136,137*,151
BLAZE...140,183
BLEWET(T)...107,203
BLEWITT...118,129,134,150,151,
  165,179
BLINKHORN...17

BLISSET(T)...15,24
BLODWELL...112,144
BLOOMFIELD...41
BLOXWICH...12,13,27,37,83,112
BLOXWICHES...20
BLUNT...132,158,166,193
BOAD...93,94
BODEN...166,171
BODY...97,102,114,127,128,164
BOLT...29,85
BOLTON...53
BOND...20
BOOTH...104
BOTT...11,17,28,37,51,52,53,65,
80,83,87,91,93*,99,100,101,
105*,115,116,117*,118,125,
126,128,129*,141,142,144,
145,160*,162,170,172,176,
177,178,180,181*,182,190,
191,194,208*
BOUGH...191,197
BOURNE...122
BOWEN, BOWIN...39,56,63,68,
105,132,142,155,160,182
BOWING...24
BOWKLEY...106,119
BOWYER...104
BOYLE...133,151
BRACE...205
BRADBURY...111,120
BRADLEY...16,75,167
BRADNEY...86
BRADSHAW...186,196
BRAIN(E)...131,145,154,161,173
BRANT...160
BRASSINGTON...32
BRATT...58*,107,114,118,124,
128,135,148,152,170,174,
182,194
BRAWN...135
BRETT...98
BRETTEL(L)...147,177
BREVETT...51
BRIANN...94
BRIERLEY...112,122
BRINDLEY...88,116,117,124,142,
147,157,179,181,209
BRINLEY...27,58,61*,73,80,85,
88,97

BRINTON...16*,21,24,25
BRION...147
BRITTIN...131
BRITTLE...164
BROACHER...162
BROAD...71
BROCKHOUSE...187,198
BROCKHURST...40
BROFON...191
BROOKHOUSE...93
BROOK(E)(S)...21,28*,58,70,92,
93,106,118,120,121,126,128,
134,143,146,149,152,160,
162,166*,184,189,196,197,
200
BROWN...12,37,41*,45,47,74,84,
87,98,99,102*,115,156,169,
171,176,192*,197
BRUKES...117
BUFF...12,91,114,163
BUFFEY...202
BULLOCK...203
BULLOWS...153
BUMFORD...131,164
BUNCE...37,40,44,48,52,56,61,
67,76
BUNCH...101,119,133,153,161,
178,203
BUNN...14,15,112,177
BUNTING...46
BURN...176
BURROWS...66*
BURTON...133,138,181
BUSBAY...159
BUSHEL...21
BUT(T)LER...79,89,96*,98*,103,
106,107,112,120,123,128,
129,139,143*,157,165,170,
176,180,188,192
BUXTON...129
BYRCH...143,184

CADDICK...21,87,103,109,122,
129,134,135*,140,141,157,
160,161,167,175*,180*,184*,
186,188,190*,192,193*,204,
205,206,207
CAD(D)RACK...23,29,37,46,52,
60,67

CAD(D)ROCK...21,41
CALLAWAY...101,103
CALLEAR...119,205
CALLER...183
CALLEY...165
CALLIER...130
CALLINGTON...11,15,41*
CALLOP...137
CALLOW...8*,10,12,15,16,17,18,
21
CALLOWAY...17,19,21,22,24*,
27,30,32,34,36,39,49,51,54,
55,56,58,59,62,66,72*,74,78,
84,85*,94,95,98,103,104,112,
129,131,132,148,149,152,
173,175,179,205
CAMM...18,42,46
CANDLING...141,146
CANNADY...98
CANTRILL...204
CARTER...35,102
CARTWRIGHT...8,10,17,24,25*,
32,33,41,46,47,52,64,72,79,
80,81,91,100,103,106,112,
120,131,138,144,148*,149,
156,162,165,166,167,177,
179,186,187,190,192,195,
196
CASE...43
CASHMORE...59,67,75,90,97,
124,129,155,165,180
CASTRAY...190
CAUSER...135
CHALLENDER...195
CHAMBERS...114,129,148,152,
162,173,176,177*,192,199,
208
CHANNEY...110
CHARLOTON...91
CHARTER...102,167
CHATER...121,130,150,172,196
CHATTERTON...108
CHATTIN...150,159,188
CHATTINGTON...109
CHILD(E)S...89,93,102
CHINTON...101
CIVATER, CIVETER...57,60
CIVILL...47
CLARE...145

CLARK(E)...24,29,50,60,61,90,
113,149,151,154,155,159,
170,171,174,184,188,194,
198,203,205,206
CLARKSON...149
CLEAMENS...149
CLEATON...89,93,119,138
CLEMSON...140
CLERK...168*
CLEWLEY...168,209
CLIFFON...98
CLIFFORD...104
CLIFT...60,65,142,188
CLUET...183
CLULO...195
COAL...13,18
COALBOWIN...27
COCKERIN...57,78
COCKRAL...104
COCKRAM...142
COCKRAN...122,136,162,181
COLE...27,29,51,69,70,131
COLEMAN...142
COLES...204
COLEY...164
COLLINS...11,14,22*,28,30,33,
35,37,41,75,78,90,102,107,
108,126,128*,132,134,136,
144,147,161,166,172,207
COLTRILL...17
COMLEY...80
COMPSTON(E)...154,155,196
CONNOP...157,160,178
CONSTABLE...33,78,153,157,
172,174,196
COOK(E)...7,56,74,98,108,132,
153,160
COOKSEY...87,147,165,182,186,
187,199
COOPER...29,40,41,42,46,48,
53,54,55*,132,146,154,160,
163,168,183*,185,192,199,
205,208
COPE...122,135
CORBET(T)...107,134,199
CORBITT...148
CORFIELD...40,57,181
CORNFIELD...125,128,139,144,
159,187

CORNSFORTH...68
COTTAM...105
COTTERELL...100
COTTERILL...164,168,197,201
COTTOM...71,86,93*,97,107
COTTON...79,107,119,125,127,
194
COTTRELL...74,81,83,89,103,
114,118,119
COTTRIL(L)...12,48,90*,97,136,
137,142,144,152
COURT(S)...116*
COWDERELL...125
COWDRELL...109
COWLEY...19,37
− COX...27,34,36,57,98,106,108,
110,121,122,123,128,130,
135,138,140,145,149,157,
163,168,176,177,188,189,
192,198,204
CRANAGE...127
CRESSALL...56,84
CRES(S)WELL...32,39,46,52,68,
76,92,171,173,191
CRISTIAN...46
CROFTS...55,63,70,77,87,98,
194*,207
CROMPTON...120
CROSS...104
CRUMP...153
CRUMPT...129
CRUMPTON...28,152
CUMPSTON...162
CUMSTON(E)...117,123,124,139,
183*
CUNDLEY...117
CUNLEY...61,69,82
CUT(T)LER...139,188,207
DAINTY...104,121,171,172,200
− DALE...139,172,186,196,198
DANDLEY...115
DANGERFIELD...34,107,112,
120,122,131,134,154,157,
175,176,188,193
DANK(E)S......8,81,84,90,96,108,
121,131,140,148,149,156,
166,170,173,179,180,191,
199,203

DARB(E)Y...7*,10*,12,15*,23,24,
26*,27*,30,31,32*,36*,38*,40,
42,45*,48,52,53,59,60,61,62,
63*,65*,67,69,70,73,75,76*,
77,78,80,83,85,86*,87,88,89*,
91,98*,99,105,110,114,115,
117,118,123*,125,137,147,
149,150,156*,158*,162,163,
164,175,176,181,184,188,
192,197,200,201,204,205,208
DAVENALL...11
DAVI(E)S...39,43,50,56,68,70,78,
87,98,101,102,118,122*,125,
126*,131,132*,137,141,142,
148,150,152,153,157,159*,
160,162,165,173*,176,180*,
181,182,183*,185*,190,191,
193,194,195*,198,199,201,
202,203,204
DAWES...105
DAWLEY...187
DEAKIN...171,203
DEALEA...151*
DEBBS...189
DEEL(E)Y...122,129,131,160,
178*,191
DELEHAY...188
DENIEL...123
DENT...207
DERBY...100,110*,114,120,126,
133,134,135,139,143,154
DEVEY...126
DEWSON...55
DICKEN(S)...165,184,202,207
DICKENSON...176
DIGGERY...195
DIG(G)ORY...177,209
DIKE...88
DINESDALE...67
DITHERIDGE...203
DIXON...64,106
DODD...200
DOMINGO...23
DORRALL...27,44,51,127,140
DORRELL...158,178
DOUBTY...38
DOUGHTY...103,132,136,150,
174*,186,188

DOUTY...57,69
DOVASON...126
DOVEY...18,198
DOWERTY...125
DOWLEY...166,171,197
DOWN(E)S...122,142,164,181, 208
DOWNING...170,179,196,201
DOWNS...142,164,181
DOYNEY...124
DREW...9,15,22,23*,30,35,59*, 69,70,78*,86,100,121,125, 139,162,194
DRYDEN...190,199
DUDLEY...8,9,11*,14*,15,19,21*, 22,23,25,31,33*,35,40,46,48, 51,61,63,70,85,95,104,106, 109*,110,111*,113,115,117, 118,119,125,126,129,132, 139,140,148*,150,153,158*, 167*,168,170,175*,183*,185, 188,190,195*,196,197,199, 204*,206,209
DUFFEL(L)...106,115,119*,121
DUFFIELD...15,18,36,38,43,50, 53,55,58,62*,66,69*,72,73,78, 80,85,94,101,104,110,126, 129,134*,139,163,164,168, 182,183,184,189,196
DUFFIL(L)...100,105,106,114, 128
DUFFIN...165,166,195,204
DUKES...103
DUNN...13,84,90,171,176,195
DUTTON...25,32,39,54,60,193
DYSON...111

EADES...128,145,148,158,171, 182,192,196,198,202
EARP...171
EASTOPE...204
EASTTON...194
EBB ...145
ECCLES...109
EDGE...13*,23,24,30*,35,48,57, 58*,67,70,71,75,78,82,88,95, 101*,112*,113,123,124,134, 153,163,182,204
EDMONDS...120

EDMUNDS...160
EDWARDS...15,20,25,30,31,32, 35,36,41,42,44,45,48*,50,51*, 55,57,58,62,64,65,66*,69*, 72*,78,80,90,92,95,101,116*, 121,122,123,125,126,128, 133,134,136,137,143,153, 161,165*,174,179,187,190, 193,196,199,204,209
EGGINTON...167,194
ELLERTON...206
ELLET...167
ELLIS...172,191
ELLMES...183
EL(L)WELL...7*,8,10,11*,12,14, 17,20,22,25,26*,32*,37,41,44, 45,49,50,59,67,71,74,87,99, 104,106,119,122,123,128, 130,137,142,146,164,165, 167*,177,188,189,191*,192, 193,194
EMERY...93
ETHERWAY...121
EVANS...22,44,97,104,112,120, 121*,124,130,133*,136,139, 143,147,149,151*,152,153*, 155,156,160,161,163,168, 172,173*,179*,182,184,186*, 187,188*,189,191,194,197, 198,199,202,204,207*,208, 209
EVINS...17,46,52,65,70,79,88,90, 91,93,95,97
EYARE...139

FAIRFIELD...188
FALKNALL...172
FALKNER...129,204
FARMER...14
FAWKES...188
FELICITY...134
FELLOW(S)...9,20*,21,22,26,31, 32,37,39,46,49,51,66,71,74, 75,85,88,104,113,135,161, 163*,172,181,188,198,202
FERED(A)Y...7,9,11*,13,15,18, 21*,24,25,26,27*,28,30*,31*, 34,35*,37,40,42*43*,50,51*, 53,64,75,77,78,94,95,110*,

GARNER...156,166
GARRAT...152
GARROTT...13
GARVIS...123
GAUNT...31,39,46,59,202,208
GAYLEY...101
GEALEY...21,24,96,104
GEARY...155
GEATHAM...15,17
GEATHANE...25
GEATHEM...31
GELEA...154
GEORGE...7,18,31,43,44,61,69,
74,76,77*,82,85,86,88*,93,
94,96,105,108,114,120,140,
159,163,168,190,195,196,
199,201
GIBBANS...59,68*
GIBBENS...46
GIBBINS...13*,98,109,159
GIBBONS...19,75,76,85,109,111,
112
GIDDENS...108
GIDDINS...151
GILBERT, GILBIRTT...196,199
GILES...101,103,110,168,174
GILL...92
GILLAM...135
GLASSHARD...16
GLAZE...142
GLOVER...118
GOLD...146*
GOLDIN...200
GOODBY...23,112
GOODHALL...181*
GOODMAN...136
GOODWIN...184
GOODYER...170
GORTON...15,18,32,34,35,41,
48*,54,59,61,65*,71,76*,82,
85,87,88,89,105,121,137,
143,157,173,178,191,195,
196,198,199,202
GOUGH...149,190,200,205
GOULD...104,159,193,205
GOWER...113,133,145
GRAINGER...124
GRANDFIELD...126

GRANGER...12*,16,17,19,24,25,
32,49,55,61,64,66,90,185,186
GRANT...119,127,152,162*,177
GRATELY...106
GRATTON...62,114,159,189
GRAY...60
GREAER...120
GREATRER...130
GREEN...30,34,40,48,53,60,67,
74,83,84,91,99,100,111,114,
124,138,141,145,150,159*,
162,165*,170,173,182,184,
188,199*,203,205,207*
GREENAWAY, GREENEWAY
15,17,21,22,25,54,60,73,86,
91,101,112,116,120,128,135,
157,161,180,181,190,
GREENWOOD...158
GREGORY...68,77,83,90,93,96,
104,106,120,124,142,149,
156,157,167*,171,174
GRET(T)ON...70,77
GREYER...7,10,18,25,39,71
GREYOR...70,75,79
GRICE...43,51,76,94,102,127,
141*,142,144,149,154,164,
185
GRIFFIN...106,165
GRIFFIS(S)...25*,27,29*,31,33,
34*,35*,36,37,39*,40*,43,44*,
45,46,49,50*,51,52,54*,56,
57,58,61*,63*,67*,68*,70,71,
72,75,76,77*,78,80,81,83,87,
91*,95,105,108
GRIFFITH(E)(S)...8*,9,11,14,15,
16,17,18*,19,21*,22,24,25,
105,110,112,115,116*,117,
119,123,125,130,132,134,
137*,139,140,143,144*,147,
148,149,150,152*,155*,156*,
158,161*,162*,164*,165,167*,
168,170*,172,175*,176,177,
183*,184*,187*,188*,189,
192,196,197,200*,201*,203*,
204,205,206,208*,209
GRIGG...164,188
GRINSELL...197
GRINSILL...147,164

GRISE...8,11,13,17,19,51,63,64,
   67,71,81*,86
GRISNSILL...134
GROOM...160
GROUTAGE...173
GROVES...137,158,183,205
GROVSNOR...145
GUEST...46,53,73,83,88*,94*,
   102,104,108*,111,149,152*,
   159,170,177,188,191,202
GUTT(E)RIDGE(S)...7,9*,11,16,
   19*,20*,21*,24,26,27*,30,31,
   32,33,34,38*,40*,42,44,45*,
   46,47,50,53,55,58,59,60,61,
   64,69,74,76,79,84,85*,87,90,
   95,100,105,110*,111,116*,
   117,120,121*,123,125,130,
   138,143,148,151,154,155,
   166,175*,179,182,185,188,
   189*,190,195,202
GWIMMETT...129
GWINNETT...133,135,147,152,
   161,176,184,198

HACKET(T)...160,177,209
HACKWOOD...179
HADEN...200
HADINSON...100
HADLENTON...145
HADLEY...104,132,149,150,175,
   177,191,206
HADLINGTON...165
HADNEY...162
HALDEN...36
HALE...16,120,189
HALL...9,36,91,124,132,139,148,
   156,166,180,186,206
HAMBLETT...48
HAMER...116
HAMLET...192
HAMLINTON...182
HAMMERSLEY...182
HAMMONDS...197
HAMPTON...82,88,125,142
HANBURY...188
HANCOCK(S)...139,149
HANCOX...101,102,111,147,151,
   161,162,171,175,182,184,
   188,199,203,207,208,209

HAND(S)...28,127,129,134,136,
   143,180
HARCOT(T)...111,147,181,192
HARDEN...156
HARDY...195
HARGRIFF...105
HARGROVE...159
HARPER...64,99,140,156,164,
   166,177,184,188,203,208
HARPIN...12
HARRINGTON...187,203
HARRIS(S)...8,23,65,70,78,79,
   80,85,93,94,102,103,119,122,
   131,136,148,156,157,162,
   166*,174,178,180,190,191,
   192,199,205*,206,209
HARRISON...38,42,45,75,78,89,
   111,135,141,146,162,165,
   167,170,171,172,173,183,
   200,207
HART...54,55,58,66,122,167,181,
   198
HARTELL...164*
HARTER...129
HARTILL...32,137,178,195
HARTLAND...94,107,125,135,
   144,147,156,161,164,190
HARTLEY...114
HARTS(H)ORN(E)...139,151,156,
   159,185,186,203*
HARTWELL...146,152,172,205
HASLEHURST...165
HATTON...149,172,173,180,184,
   202
HATTWOOD...9,13
HAUGHTON...49,59,82*
HAWKINS...102,181
HAWLEY...179,200,209
HAWTHO(R)N...57,116,152,209
HAYES...156
HAYNES...156
HAYWOOD...159
HAZELHURST...159,186
HAZELDINE...130
HAZLEHURST...122,137,154
HEADES...51,55
HEATH...64,106
HEATHCOCK...181,187,202
HEDGE...17

HEEDS...35,41,48
HEELEY...13,35,46,51,52,58,60,
66*,73,75,77,81,85,90,92,97,
140,150,166,168,184*,188,
197,200,204
HEELIN...32*
HEELY...163
HEMMIN(G)S...50,196
HENLEY...143,157
HENSHALL...188
HENSHAW...203
HERRING...20,32,53,119
HERVY...117
HEWITT...124
HEWLEY...197
HEYLIR...38
HEYNES...124
HEYWARD...156
HEYWOOD...130
HICHENNER...168
HICK...69
HICKABOTTOM...127*,135,136,
138,149,157,163,173,180*,
186,197*
HICKENBOTTOM...113,117
HICKIN...96,139,197,198
HICKINBOTTOM...143
HICKMAN(S)...10*,11,12,13*,18,
20,23,27,33,37*,38,42,45*,52,
53*,57,60,64,68*,69,71,76*,
78,79*,82,85*,89*,90,91,97,
98,110,115*,119,125,130,
131,134*,136,138,141,146,
149,162,164*,173,176,184,
190,194*,197,198,204,205
HIDE...9,149,162
HIGGINS...120,172,197
HIGGINSON...26,44
HIGGS...33,176,201
HILL...7,8*,11,12,13*,14,15,17*,
19,20*,21*,23*,26,28*,30*,31,
34*,36*,38*,43,44*,45,46,49*,
50*,51,53*,54,55,56,57*,58,
59,61*,62*,63,65,66,67,69,
70,71,75,80,81,82,83,86*,88,
95,97,105,111,116,122,123,
126,127*,128,138,139,145,
149,160,161,163,164,165,
170,174,177*,185,194,201,

203,206,208
HILTON...129,150,174,196
HINTON...12,119,151
HIPKINS...115,138*,154,168,170,
186,188,189,206*,208
HIPKISS...7,8,14,17*,18,19,20,
21,22,24*,28*,33,34,35,36,
42,43,48,51,53,57,62,63,65,
69,73*,76,77,81,82,84,87*,
92,93,94,95,97,99,100,103,
106,107,108,144,156,158,
160,171,178,199
HIPPING...185
HITCHEN...192
HOBSON...106,158,168,192
HODGATTS...100
HODGET(T)S...25,45,56,105,
118*,158,171,207   (See also
HODGYETTS)
HOD(G)(S)KINS...12,14,15,27,
33,38,39,42,48,52*,58,60,62,
64,66,69*,72*,75,76,77*,79,
80,81,83*,84,88*,93,99,101,
102,104,106,108*,109,110*,
111,113,114,115,118,125,
131,134,135,136,140*,141,
143,145,148,152,155,157,
164,172,173,179,182*,183,
186,190,198,200
HODGSKIS(S)...74,84,117,118,
128,137,140,157,178,182,
191,199 (see also HOGKISS)
HO(D)GYET(T)S...10,61,65,72,
78*,98 (See also HODGETS)
HODSON...178
HOGKISS...124
HOGSKINS...68
HOLDEN...67,115,166,189
HOLDING...98
HOLEYOAK...72
HOLIHEAD...172,196
HOLIHOCK...123
HOLIOKE...145
HOLLAND...16,37,69,76*,77,83,
86,91,122,147,148,170,194,
200,201
HOLLEHEAD...159
HOLLIES...127,141,142,153,196,
207

HOLLIHEAD...143,161
HOLLINGS...180
HOLLINGTON...18
HOLLINS...208
HOLLIOAK(E)...57,209
HOLLOWAY...150,166,175,183,
190,195,198
HOLMES...116,120,189,203
HOLT...160,164,182,198,200*,
207
HOLTON...109
HOLWEYHEAD...103
HOLYHEAD...113,127,128,181
HOLYOAK...64
HOMER...90,182
HOMES...94
HONE(S)...26,30,34,93,188
HOOD...195,207
HOOLDRIDGE...60
HOOLEY...40,98
HOPKINS...104,125,143,166,
186,187,194,202,204
HORDEN...116,118,125
HORDERN...102
HORTHAN...101
HORTHON...145
HORTON...7,8,9,10*,11,12,14*,
16*,17,18*,20*,23*,25*,27,
28*,31,33*,34*,36,38,39*,40,
41*,42,44,46,48*,49,50*,53*,
54,55*,57,58,59,60*,63,65,
66,68*,69,71,72,74,75,76,79,
80,81*,82,83,85,86,87*,88*,
89,90,92,95*,97*,98*,101,
103,104,108,109*,111*,113,
114,116*,120,121,122,123,
124*,130,131,135,140,142,
143*,146*,148,153*,154,159,
174*,175,179,184,189,195,
197*,200,202,203
HOSBAND...68
HOSBORN(E)...140,161,176
HOSBOURN...96
HOSBOWIN...112
HOTLEY...73
HOUGH...56
HOUGHTON...52,81
HOWELL(S)...50,116,134,187,
188,197

HOWEN...9,51
HOWES...123
HOWL...23
HOXLEY...122,150
HOYLE...143,144,154,168,182,
194,205
HUBBARD...103,192
HUBBEL...13
HUBBILL...14
HUDSON...135
HUGH(E)S...10,11,14,17,18*,19,
20,23,29,39,44,47,50,51,55,
56,57,60,62,66,69,76,81,82,
86,90,91,92,93,99*,111,113,
117,118*,119,126,127,136,
139,140,142,144,149,151,
154,155,159,161,162,176,
187,193,201,206*,207
HUMPHREY(S)...80,90,92,107,
179
HUMPHRIES...147
HUNSTONE...142
HUNT(S)...9,140,150,175
HURLEY...107,108,120
HUSEY...153
HUTTON...188
HYDE...109,156*,177,186,187,
200

IKIN...191
ILLINGSLEY...72
INCHER...12,35,40,50,195
INCKER...47
INGLEY...63
INGRAM...7,11,12,13,14,20,21,
22,24*,25*,30,31,32,35*,37,
40,41,42*,45,46,47,49,53,54,
55,58,60,62,66,70,72,76,82,
83,84*,87*,92,97,101,115,
126,127*,128,129,130,131,
135,136,140,143,144,146,
150,151,155,159,170*,172,
173,174,175,180,185*,188,
189,190*,193,195,197,198,
205*,206
IRONS...182
IVINS...22,44

JACKSON...96,148,157,161,170,
180
JAMES...26,39,46,49,50,91,106,
141,153,165,166,183,203,207
JASPER...143,177
JAY...176*,199
JEAVONS...159,203,204,206,207
JEFFRIES...193
JENKIN...177
JENKS...122,179
JERVIS...100,111,126,205
JESSON...153,201
JEVON(S)...9,10*,11,12,14,16*,
20,23*,27,28*,29,32,34,37,38,
42*,44*,45*,49,53*,56,61*,65,
72,85,86,95,96,99,100,112*,
119,120,121,127,129,133,
138,140,145,150,153,158,
161,162,165,168,174,187,192
JEWIS...156
JEWK(E)S...7,14,21,32,36,43,47,
60,106,109,137,139,159*,
161,163,164,170,171,177*,
180*,181,192,195,196,201,
206,207,209
JINKS...142,156
JOHNSON...12,14,15,18,25,34,
35,37,38,41,44,51,56,65,95*,
103,117,118,126*,131,134,
145,149,152,156,169,172,
174,206
JOINER...158
JONES...7,20*,22,26,27*,29,33,
34*,51,52,55,56,57,64,65,66,
72,74*,75,76,80,81,82,87,88,
90,92,95,96,101,103,107,108,
109*,113,119*,120,121,122*,
130,131,133,134*,135,136,
139*,141,142,148,149*,150,
152*,153,156*,159,162,163,
165,167*,168*,171*,173*,174,
178*,179,181*,182*,185,186*,
187*,189,190,191*,193,195,
196,197,198*,201,203*,204*,
206,208*,209*,
JORDEN...118*
JUKES...19,25,28,29,71*,85,86*,
90,92,94,103,109,119,122,
130,134,155,174,180,186

KEAN...15
KEELING...176
KELSELL...191
KELSON...171
KEMP...168*
KEMSTOR...133
KENDALL...86,172
KENDRICK...32,33,38,44*,49,53,
54,61,63,71,79,80,88,135,
143,174
KENNEDAY...129,204
KENNEDY...88,115,173
KENT...161,178
KERRY...41,44,45,49,91
KEY...176,183
KIDIAR...95
KIDSON...69,84
KIMBERLEY...114,171,202
KINDON...125
KING...124,130,164,174,192
KIRK...80
KIRK(H)AM...89,122,131,132,
143,146,159,177,197,199,209
KIRKIM...99
KIRKOM...79
KIRKUM...98
KITSON...160
KNOWLE(S)...98,149

LAMBETH...189,198
LANCASTER...106
LANDER...174
LANE...156
LANGDON...149,166,189
LANGFORD...105*,106,182
LANGHORN...199
LANKFORD...96,132,144,146,
147,158*,200
LANKSON...24,200
LAPPAGE...120,140,154,173,193
LARAM...203
LARNGLEAN...121
LATHAM...116,139,142,143,150,
203,209
LAUD...27,132
LAUGHTON...175
LAVENDER...125,209

LAW(E)...31,38,40,41,42,43,45*,
47*,48,50*,51,54,59,60,61,63,
65,66,67,69,71*,73,77*,79*,
80*,82,87*,92*,93,94,96*,98,
100,101,104,108*,109*,113*,
114,116,117,118,120*,121,
122,123,124,125,126*,132,
136,137,138*,139*,140,143*,
144*,146,147*,148,149,151,
152*,154*,155,158,159,160,
161,162,163,164,167,168,
172,177*,178,179,180,184,
185,186,188,190,191,193,
194*,200,201,203,204,208
LAWD(S)...7,8,11,12,20,21,23,
35,41
LAWLEY...133,147,187
LAWRANCE...186,202
LAWRENCE...134,144,151
LAWTON...42,44,190,196
— LEA...42,151,204
LEACH...35,157
LEADBETTER...170,180,184,206
LEAGG...90
LEAKIN...133
— LEE...151,181,195,201
LEECH...27,40,48,55,111,123,
131,179,188,201
LEEK...121
— LEES...87,165,167
LEGER...109
— LEGGE...208
LEISTER...139,194
LEMM...125
LEONARD...135
LESTER...40,52,56*,60,67,72,74,
75,78,88,93,172,198
LEWIS(S)...20,30,148,151*,171,
183,190,203,209
LIESTER...121,124*,133,143,
148,152
LINES...195
LINFORD...140
LION...28,124,146
LISMORE...188
LITTLE...37,42,50,56,65,74,78,
94,208*
LLOID...92

LLOYD...82,85,110,115*,126,
133,143,148,152*,155,182,
202*
LOCK...34
LONES...156,192
LONGSTON...204
LORD...7,78,108
LORTON...208
LOUCH...174,205
— LOW(E)...27,34,35*,38,56*,69,
79*,87*,88,92,95,101,107,
116,131,150*,156*,160*,166,
172,174,182,187
LOWNDES...111
LUNN...123,125,131,135,143,
159,177
LYON...16,115

MACCLAUNE...192
MAC(K)MULLIN...64,71
MAIPAS...145
MALE...145
MALLEN...107
MALLIN...7,9,13,19,23,25,30
MALLORS...102
MALPAS...207
MANNING(S)...111,154*,183
MANSLEY...148,161
MANWARING...208
MAREGOLD...199
MARKLEW...206
→ MARSH...118,137,151,209
MARSHALL...55,65,69,77,78,83,
88,97,98,106,116,132,209
⌐ MARSON...14,18,29,31,39*,44,
48,145
MARTIN...10,28.51*,55,64,77,87,
115,119,125,132,134,148,
153,162,168,175,179,187,
189,192,201,204,207
MARYGOLD...116
MASH...8,20,42
— MASON...14,88,96,103,120,
134,157,176
MATHERS...132*,159,192
MATHIAS...149
MAT(T)HEWS...71,73,78,87,97,
102,110,126,139,148,167*,
171,176

MAULIN...42,52,78
MAUPASS...183
MAURICE...174
MAWPAS...101,107,154
MAWPER...129
MAYBUREY...159,165,209
M^{c}NAUGHTON...202,203
MEACHEL...177
MEEK...119
MEER(S)...50,170
MERCY...173
MEREDITH...193
MERREY...192
MIDDLETON...187
MIDLEMORE...21
MILICHIP...155
MILLARD...15*,19,20,41,45,55*,
63,66,71,73*,77*,86,91,96,
97,102,124,128,142,153,158,
174,176,185,191*,198,203,
206,209
MILLER...133
MILLINGTON...48,52,62,70,79,
80,86,143,165,166,168,174,
199
MIL(L)S...7*,12*,13*,15,17*,20*,
21,22,24*,26,27,28*,29*,30,
31*,32*,34*,35*,37*,39*,41*,
42,43*,44,45*,46,48*,49*,50*,
52*,53,54*,55*,56*,58*,59,
60*,61,62,63*,64*,65,67*,69*,
70*,72*,74*,75,77,78,79,80*,
81,82*,83,85,87*,88*,89,90,
91,92*,93*,96*,97*,99*,100,
101,102*,104,105,107*,109,
111*,112*,113*,114*,115,
116*,117*,118,119*,121*,122,
124*,125*,126,127,129*,130,
131*,133,134*,136,137,140*,
142,143*,144,146*,147,149,
150,151,152,155,159,160*,
161*,162*,163*,166,167,168,
170,173,174,175*,176,177*,
178*,179,183,187*,189,191,
193*,196,197,198,201,203*,
204*,207,208
MIL(L)WARD...28*,194,196
MILLYARD...145

MINCHER...84,89,94,109,125,
134,138,140,152,155,157,
160,173,183,184,193,200,
205,207
MITCHEL(L)...166,167,170,176,
179
MOESLEY...138
MOODY...196
MOOR(E)...59,60,64*,97,141,
150,160,161,180,205
MORFIELD...92
MORGAN...67,72,79,88,94,108,
166,199,205
MORLEY...152
MORRALL...183,207
MORRIS(S)...39,42,46,47*,51,55,
56,61,62,68,74,82,84,90,91,
92,96*,98,100,105*,106*,107,
109*,118,127,128,133,140,
142,143,150,151,152*,158,
160,162*,163*,165,168,169,
172*,175,178,179,180,182*,
183,184,185,189,192,194*,
195,197,202,203,207,208*,
209
MORTON...151
MOSLEY...8,36
MOSS...164*
MOTTRAM...171,189,206
MOUNTFORD...108,114,116
MULLEY...142
MULLINER...164
MUMFORD...159

NAILER, NAILOR...10,26,119
NASH...125,154,171,196
NEATH...103
NEEDAM...174
NEWAY...126,146
NEWBY...151
NEWELL...100,153,167,168
NEWEY...117,119,132,139
NEWIN...108
NEWTON...140,143,146,172
NIBB...185,199,202
NICHOLAS...114,159   204*,207,208
NICHOLDS...35,58*,60,75,84,
116,136

NICHOLIS...36,41,58,85
NICHOLLS...104,109,126,128,
129,159,181,192*,201*,202
NICKLIN...9,18,21,22,30,31*,33*,
39,41,43*,45,47*,52,54,55,58,
68*,71,72,79,83,85,96,97,99,
101,102,109,112,118,130,
140,147,171,174,180*,186,
190,196,209
NICKLISS...103*,104,110,113,
120,160,190,208
NICKOLAS...193
NIC(K)OLDS...8*,10,16,22,29,
31*,45,50,52,62*,63*,64,66,
70,75,80,84,90,91,93,102
NICKOLIS...34,90,99
NICOLD(S)...8,20,56
NIGHTINGALE...8,17,19,20,26,
28,29,30,31,34,39,40,41,44,
46,49,55,62,71,77,78,81,93,
95*,107,108*,113*,123,133,
135,139,160,168,174,186,
192,193*,195,200,201,209
NIMMS...81
— NOCK(E)...10,11,14*,15,16*,19,
21*,22,23*,26,29,31,35*,42,
43,44,49,50,51,55,57,59*,61,
65,67,68,71,74*,75,76,78*,79,
82,83,84*,85,94*,95*,96,102,
114,115,116,117,121,123*,
125,126,127,131,133,135,
140,141,146,147,148,154,
162,164,167,173,176,178,
179,180,184,186*,201,203,
208
NOONS...87
NORRIS...34,36,89
NORTON...94,119,127,160,182*,
195

— OAKES...100
OAKLEY...168,177,181,192
OCROFT...170,198
ONION(S)...19,22,24,34*,44,51,
52,55*,56,59,63,65,71,76,81,
89,111,117,149,198,201
ORTON...50
OSBOND...106

OSBORN(E)...104,118*,123,125,
128,133,135,151,153,157,
165,166,170,171,174,179,188
OSBOURN...84
OSBOWIN...103
OSELAND...125
OTTLEY...121
OWELL...43
OWEN...32,44*,57,64*,69,73*,
75,92,99,127*,135,136,138,
141,147,154,165,167,186,
188,191,202,208
OZBOURN...86

PACKETT...195
PADDOCK...151
PADMORE...182
PAGE...13,165*
PAINE...137,141
PAINTER...184,191
PALMER...102,176
PANE...8,105,157
PARISH...See PARRISH
PARKERS...113
← PARK(E)S...7*,8,9,11,15,17*,19,
23,26*,27,28,32,35*,38,39,43,
45,47,51,62,64,67,71,72,76,
77,78,81,82,83*,85,88,89,
92,94*,98,99,100,104*,105,
109,113,115,116,122,127,
136,137,138,139*,145,150,
151,155*,158,167,168,170,
172,174,175,180,192,197,207
PARRISH...10,109,128
↙ PARR(E)Y...66,105
PARSONS...53,194
PARTON...191,203
↖ PARTRI(D)GE...8*,10*,13,14*,
16,18*,24,28,30,31,33,36,
44,51,52,57,58,64*,68,69,74,
76,80,89,99,100*,106,115,
120*,121,124,130,131,133,
137,142,145,146*,148,155,
161,165,167,172,176,185*,
189,192,200*,210
PASE...33
PASKEN...15

PASKIN...9,10,15,19,22*,25,26,
28,29,34,50,52,57,61,71,85,
100,107,111,112,122,130,
134,136,140,141,142,145,
154,155,156*,159,166,168,
173,177,181,182,192,193*,
204*,205
PASMOR...175
PASSFIELD...173,195
PATCHETT...209
PATE...194,206
PAUMER, PAUMOR...63,64
PEACOCK...199
PEARCE...187
PEARSELL...8
PEARSHALL...16
PEARSON...133,142,145
PEASE...157
PEASEFALL...13
PEASOLL...8
PEAT...107,117
PEMBERTON...184
PENDENTON...99
PENN...84,93,125,153
PENNING(S)...27,28
PEPLAR...16,23
PERCALL...40,63,81
PERCIVAL...23,31
PERCON...45
PERRENS...12
PERKES...141*
PERRINGS...33
PERRINS...27,33,34,38,162,167,
203,208
PERRY...38,48,59,86,101,102,
104,107,117,120*,124,132,
135,136,141*,151,156,157*,
160,164,172,176,194,205,208
PERSALL...118
PER(E)SHOUSE...8,9,13,17,34,
35,40,47,53,54,67,73,74,78,
81,82,86,94,100,101,102,
108,129,147,153,154,157,
178,200,201
PERSIVALL...23
PERSMORE...132
PETERS...147,155,163,176,192
PEW...54
PHASELY...161

PHA(Y)SEY...147,176,200
PHILIP(P)S... 56,58,63,69,72,
73*,77,84,101,105,125,139,
148,161,181,186,205,209
PHIPPS...168,194
PICKARD...137
PICKARILL...197
PICKIN...67
PICKING...120
PIERCE...74,91,98,107,109,131,
186*,192,194,198
PIERSELL...176
PIGGOT...177
PINCHER...91,133
PINFIELD...97
PINNOCK...131,207
PINSON...183,188
PITCHFORK...40,81,87,90
PITEWAY...10,15,30,43,61,62
PITT...89*,99,105,110,135,151,
152,164,198
PLANT...127,136,149,150,151,
163,170,197,209
PLATT...168,173,187,194,199
PLIMMER...205
PODMORE...199
POOL...135,173,174
PORTER...92,109,140
POSTINGS...201
POTTER...141
POTTS...136,155,180,205,208
POWELL...126,134,136,143,150,
156,165,171*,175,190,194
POWERS...43
POWESS...138
PRATT...11,209
PRESSON...39,48,183
PRESTON...113,130,139,142,
164,171,194,203
PRICE...25,27,32,36,66,76,78,
85*,97,102,118,124,134,138,
150,154,156,158,160,161,
168,171,172,176,178,179,
186,190*,200,205,208,209
PRI(T)CHARD...26,146
PRI(T)CHET(T)...29,40,113,116,
128
PRISSEN...60
PROBERT...198*

PUGH...146,157,165,172,184,
   188,195,198,200,206
- PYATT...126

RABEL...7
RABONE...130,158,170,191
RADNELL...193
RALLEY...170
RALPH...96,201
RAMSDEN...124
RATHBONE...26,31,43,63
RAVENSCROFT...87
- RAY...174
RAYBONE...138
- RAYBOULD...105
- REA...142
- REDGEWAY...176
REECE...189,208
REED...41,43,48,53,60,64,68,71,
   76,123,126,130,135,144,150,
   151,171*,181,193,205
- REEVES...161,181,208
REUBERY...149
REWB(E)RY...113,122*,123*
RE(Y)NOLDS...92,103,106,110,
   111,120,136,207
RHOADS...79
RHODEN...81,91,92,138,181
RHODES...162
RHUBERY...156
RICHARD(S)...7,8,9,10,12,15,21,
   22,25,26,27,33,36,41,42,44,
   46,50,52,54,57,61,64,67,73,
   78,83*,84,86,91,95,96,104,
   106,110*,113,114,119,123,
   157,166,195,196,206
RICHARDSON...140,204
RIDDING...26,142
RIDER...62,68
ROBERTS...38,40,42,46,47,52*,
   58,59,60,61,65,71,73,74*,80,
   83,101,106,113,124,125,128,
   140*,146,147,149*,152,163,
   164,166,176,184,185,186,
   187,188,190,196,197,207,
   209
ROBINS...208
ROBINSON...67,123,124*,134,
   147,160,161,162,164,167,

183,184,188,189*,208
ROBISON...17,109*,110*,111*,
   121
ROCK...177
RODEN...166
ROGERS...103,147,148,166*,
   172,187,195,201
ROL(L)INSON...20,29,32,33,39,
   46,48,63,80
ROLLASON...154
ROSE...143,144,160,167,184,
   205
ROSS...39,55,188
ROTTON...112,126
ROUGHTON...146
ROUND...8,1011,13,14,15,19,20,
   21,22,24*,26,27,30,33,34*,
   36*,41*,45,46*,49,50,51,52,
   53*,58,59,61,62,65,67*,68*,
   72,73,74,75*,77,78,80*,84*,
   86,90*,91,93,97*,98*,99,100,
   104,105*,107,108,111,112*,
   115,117*,126,127*,131,133,
   134,139,140,142*,145,147,
   149,151,152,153,154,157,
   158,161,165,166,167,172,
   175,176,177*,186,189,190,
   193,194,196*,198,199*,201,
   202,203,209*
ROUPER...173,186,201
ROUVIER...184
ROW(E)...166,204
ROWETT...182,205
ROWLASON...9,16
- ROWLEY...11,32,37,45,46,51,
   54*,58,60,61,62,68,69,70,72,
   73,81,84,89,94,99,100,102,
   106*,112,119*,132*,133,134,
   138,145,150,153,170,174,188
ROWLINGSON...17
ROYLANDS...79
RUBBOTTOM...114
RUBERY...147,148,189,204
RUBOOTOM...89
RU(E)BOTTOM...98,118,155,
   156,205
- RUDGE(S)...7,11,26,32,37,43,45,
   51,69,76,83,110,127,159*,
   197

RUSSELL...183
RUSSON...19
RUSTON...168,177,191,201
RYLEY...131,144,168,169,180,
184,191,195,199*

SADLER...206,209
SAINT...118
SALLMAN...85
SAL(L)MON...54,61,83,89,105,
115,117
⌐ SALT...28,115,121,197
SAMBRIDGE...86*
SAMBROOK...176
SAMSON...114
SANDBIGE...112
SANDERS...15,16,19,26,28,29,
107,114,115,120,127,129*,
133,136,142,145*,152,176,
178,179,187,193*,195,201,
203,205
SANKEY...122,143
SANSOM(E)...149,201
SARGENT...88,97
SARVIER...55
SATCHEL(L)...14,24,109,121,
126,141,149,152,164,180,
194
SATCHILL...10
SATCHWELL...30,33,39
⌐ SAULT...44,72
SAUNDERS...10,12,13,23,28,32,
33,34,36,40,43,47*,50,52,54*,
56,57*,59,60,61,65,66*,67,68,
70*,73,74,79,80,81,82,83,84*,
86,88,91,92*,94*,101,102,107
SAXON...77
SAYES...181
SCADMAN...203
SCHOLEFIELD...164,172,180
SCRIBENS...10
SCRIVEN...202
SHAREWOOD...118
SHARP...189*
SHARRATT...94,150
⌐ SHARROD...32,69
⌐ SHARROT(T)...47,52,61,70,73,
82,91,92

SHAW...14,33,111,119,120,129,
137,151,162,166,178,209
SHEAR(E)WOOD...36,118,146,
181,186,188
SHEDDEN...192
SHEERWOOD...145*,202,205,
206,207   (See also
SHEREWOOD)
SHELDON(S)...7,8,9,11*,13,14*,
16,17,18,19,21,22*,26,27,28*,
29,30,32*,33,35,36,37,38,40,
41,42*,45*,47,48*,50*,53,54,
58*,59*,62,65,66,70*,71,72*,
73,76,77*,78,79*,81,82*,83,
84*,85*,86,89,93,95,96,98,99,
100,101*,103*,105*,108,109*,
113*,114*,116*,117*,119*,
124*,125,126*,127,129*,130*,
131*,132*,133,134*,135*,136,
137,138*,139,140,141,142*,
143,145*,146,147,148*,149,
152,154,155,156,165*,166,
167,168,170,174,178,182,
184,185,186,187,189,191*,
192,197,201,202,206,207
SHENSTON...133
SHENTON...147,178*
SHER(E)WOOD...36,99,103,113,
115,118,121,122,125,130*,
131,132,140,155,157,160,
162,173,176,177,178,185,
191,194,202   (See also
SHEERWOOD)
SHEW...189
SHINGLETON...89*,95,108,129,
138,139,158,176,182
SHORT...15,29,30,35,47,58,102,
106,114,115,125,126,130,
142,159,174*,184
SHORTHOUSE...11,16,28,40,48,
78,82,90,97*,101,106,120,
122,130,133,142,153
SHRED...180
SILK...103
⌐ SILVESTER...105,129
SIMCOX...73,128,135,157,170,
185,189,208
SIMES...175

SIMKIN(S)...129,179
SIMMETER...158
SIMMONS...152,153
SIM(M)S...109,119,143
SIMSON...102,163
SINCOX...66
SITCH...116
SIVATOR...65
SIVITER...74,83,85
SKELDIN...195,200
SKELDING...127,165,175
SKELDON...147,201
SKELETON...137
SKELTON...111,196,207
SKIDMORE...19,20,96,103,105,
    122,123,126,138,145,146*,
    154,155,159,164,166,173
SKITHERT...47
SLATER...176
SLOIN...92
SMALLMAN...84,105
SMITH...8*,9*,10*,11*,12*,13*,
    14*,15*,16*,17*,19*,20*,21,
    22,23*,24*,26*,27*,28*,29*,
    30*,31*,32*,33*,34*,36*,37*,
    38,39*,40*,42*,43*,45,46*,
    48*,49*,51,52,53,54*,55*,56*,
    57*,58*,59*,60*,62,63*,64,65,
    66*,67*,68*,69,71*,72,73*,
    74*,75,76*,78,79,80,81*,82*,
    83*,85*,87*,88*,89*,90*,92*,
    93*,94*,95*,96,97*,98,99*,
    100,101,102*,103*,104*,105*,
    106*,107*,108*,109*,110*,
    111*,113*,114*,115*,116,117,
    118*,121,122,123*,124*,125*,
    126*,127*,129,131*,132,135*,
    136,137*,138*,139,141*,142,
    143*,144*,145,146*,147*,149,
    150*,151,153,154*,155,156*,
    157*,158,159*,160,161*,162,
    163*,164,165,166*,167*,170,
    172,173,174,175*,176*,178*,
    179*,180,181*,182*,183,185,
    187*,189*,190,191,192,193*,
    194,195*,196*,197,198*,200*,
    202*,203,204,205*,206,207*,
    208*,209*
SNELSON...18

SOCKET...155
SOUTHALL...112,129,131,166,
    181,197,205
SOUTHERN...208
SOWER...63
SPARROW...198,200
SPINK...55,64
SPITTLE...88,133,164,167
SROPSHIRE...80
STAFFORD...60
STANDLEY...15,189
STANFIELD...184
STANHOPE...155,163
STANL(E)Y...8*,25,36,39,83,150,
    152,171,200,205
STANSFIELD...111,115
STANTON...38,40*,47,52,72,80,
    88,98,101*,107,124*,128*,
    132*,133,140,145,148,156,
    157,159,166,168,173,180,
    184,185,190,196,197,200,202
STATCHELL...96
STEACEY...193
STEALEY...204*
STEPHENS...14*,72,142,144,196
STEPHENSON...141,145,170,
    184
STEPHENTON...188,207
STEVENS...161,171,184,208
STEVENSON...138,158,176
STEVENTON...132,149,152,171,
    172,180,207
STEWARD...197*,202
STILLARD...90,97,115,127,144,
    156,179
STINSON...171
STOCKTON...156
STOCKWIN...9,16,22,29,39,45,
    54,65,133,180,183
STOKES...12,13,14,30,32,40,76,
    80,82,86,92,96,100,106,107,
    118,122*,128,133,145*,152,
    162,164,202
STONE(S)...93,162,184,192,207
STORY...114
STOTT...202
STREET...174
STRETTON...184
STRINGER...38

SULTCH...144
SUMMERFIELD...143
SUTTON...9,37,49,56,62,69,76,
84,168,190,200
SWADLE...175
SWIFT...130*

TAILOR...See TAYLOR
TALBOTT...8,37,46,60
TANGE...181
TART...11,196
TATE...10,19,27,34,79,91*,98,
100,118,137,143
TAYLER, TAYLOR...8,27,30,36,
40,46,52,58*,60,69,73,74,75*,
81*,82,84,88,90*,91,93,95*,
98*,99,100,104*,105,108,112,
114,117,119,121,126,128*,
132,133*,136*,137,142,152,
153*,154,155*,156*,158,161,
163,165,168,172*,174,176*,
178,179*,181*,183,184*,189,
190,198,206*,208
TEATOM...139
THOMAS...28,34*,92,99,128,
139,146,153,163,168,184,
187,197,209
THOMASON...106
THOMEY...99
THOMMINSON...154
THOMPSON...31,106,120,138,
143,162,177,192,196,198
THORNEY...109
THORNE(Y)CROFT...137,139*,
146,176,191,199
THROPP...179
TIBBET(T)S...129,188
TIBBIT(T)S...126,136,150*,161,
180,191,201
TILL...104
TILL(E)Y, TILEY...51,69,78,85,
94 ,98,99,104,121,134,136,
152,157,172,178,179,181,
191,194
TILSLEY...191,207
TILTINGTON...141
TIMMING...177

TIMMIN(S)...8,11,14,15,17,19*,
20,22,26*,30,32,37*,38*,39,
40,41,42,43,45,51*,53,54*,
57,59*,60,62,65,67,68,70*,
71,77,78,79,81,83,87*,88,92,
93,96*,99,107,110*,111,113,
114,122*,124,125,126,129,
131,135,137,139,148,150*,
154,157,159*,161,163,164,
165,166*,167,172*,175,178*,
181*,185,187,188,189,190*,
191*,192,196,197,201,204,
206*,207,209
TINGLE...209
TINKER...29,49
TINSLEY...87,114,117,179
TISDALL...29,32
TITLEY...11,19,127,185
TITTERTON...182
TITTLEY...100
TOLLEY...187
TOMASON...125
TOMBLINSON...45,47
TOMLINSON...134
TOMPSON...55,63
TOMSON...171
TONER...28
TONK(E)S...29,35,37,39,42,45,
47,52,107,131,145,150,170,
171,173,194*,199
TOOKEY...189
TOOKLEY...167,191
TOY...88
TRAN(N)TER...41,119,130,144,
157*,176,205
TROWMAN...147,150,168
TRUEMAN...107,130,160
TRUMAN...7,16,24,43
TRUSTON...61
TUADAL...144
TUBBS...7,12*,18
TUCKL(E)Y...91,98,104*,108,
120,123,128,137,147,163
TUDAR...77
TUDER...162,177
TUDOR...86,95,108,166
TUNKS...17,27,99

TURLEY...23,27,33,37,44,52
TURNBULL...103,127
TURNER(S)...8,12,14,17,18,23*,
  25,28*,30,32,34,37*,38,44*,
  48,51,52,61,62,63*,65*,68*,
  71*,74,75*,77,79,82*,83,84*,
  88,93,94,95,99,108,109,116,
  119,123*,129,130*,131,134,
  138*,139,143,146,149,153*,
  157,158,159,161,162,165,
  166,167*,169,174,175,177,
  179,185,189*,198,200,207
TURNEYFOOT...48
TURTON...53,158
TURVEY...41
TWIGG...96,105,117,127,146,
  160,175
TWIST...167

UNDERHILL...99,148*,197,205
UNIT...117,163
UNITE...39,61*
Unknown...10,15,16,19,20,22,
  113,178

VALE...202*
VAUGHAN...189,197
VERNON...165,194
VERNUM...183
VILLERS...205
VINSIM...178
VIPOMD...105

WACKLAM...10
WAGSTAFF...123
WAIN...89
WAIN(W)RIGHT...23,29,36,45,
  52,61,65*,68,69,79
WAKEFIELD...195
WAKELAM...106
WALDRON...150
WALKER...64,105,112,122,126,
  140,147,156,159,168*,200
WALL...50,57,67,72,73,77,86,
  118,141,180,197
WALLERS...55,203
WALLEY(S)...183,204,205
WALLIS...139

WALLORS...49
WALTERHOUSE...45,61,75,90,
  98
WALTERS...9,14,20,24,28,30,31,
  39,49*,52,53,55,57,59,68*,75,
  107,110,129,135,149,156,
  157,167,170,177,180,181,
  183,187,196,202,208
WALTON...9,16,26,29,31,38,43,
  60,99,159,170,173,177,193,
  208
WANDWRIGHT...10,11,15
WARD...33,46,51,53,54,55,61,
  65,72,74,79,84,90,95,97,
  103*,110,115,116,119,121,
  123,126,127,137,143,145,
  150*,151,158,162,163,165*,
  168,175,176,180,183,185*,
  186,190,206*,207
WARNER...207*,208
WARR...8,9,12,13,14,15*,16,17,
  22*,23,26*,29,32,35,37,39,41,
  43,49*,50,54,55*,58,60,63,66,
  70,79,81,94,96,100,102,107,
  109,117*,121*,123,150,155*,
  160,161,173,184,189,193,
  194,201*
WARREN...10
WARRICK...206
WARRINGTON...179,191
WARRS...20
WARTON(S)...18*,20,21*,22,24,
  37,42,44,51*,54,55,67,73*,
  147,150,151,157,158,162,
  166,185,193,196
WARWICK...180
WASSALL...109,144
WASSEL(L)...97,124,157,172*,
  192
WATERFIELD...190
WATERHOUSE...101,144,172,
  175,182
WATERS...103,122
WATSON...206
WATTON...134
WEAL...19
WEATL(E)Y...7,22,24,25,39,91
WEAVER...67,156

WEBB...15,22,29,38,84,91,93,
99,104,114,116,119,126,
134*,140,144,155,158,161,
174,185,191,194,198,202
WEBSTER...98,170
WELCH...106,114,121,133,155
WELLS...62
WESSON...19,31,43,70
WEST...115
WESTWOOD...44,77,86,99,115,
143,147,153,172,177,178,
193,205
WETHAM...139
WHALE...101,115
WHEAL(E)...7,9,10,11,12,13,14,
17*,21,25*,27*,29,35*,38,
39*,40,41,43,44,47,49,56*,
59,60,61,62,64,70,71*,73,75,
81*,88,108,119,121,128,134,
137,138,146*,151,157*,160*,
164,165,166,178,184,185,
195,197,198,207
WHEATLEY...8,101
WHEEL...82
WHESSON(S)...8,12,15,18,36,
47,68,73,75,79,82,88,89*,93,
94,95,109,147,165,191
WHESTON...7
WHIELD...166
WHILD...125
WHILE...122,151,158
WHITAKER...174,183,184,185
WHITE...126*,134,142,174,176
WHITEHEAD...121,130,150,169,
185
WHITEHOUSE...7*,8*,9*,10*,11*,
12*,13*,14*,15*,16*,17*,18*,
19*,20*,21*,22*,23*,24*,25*,
26*,27*,28*,29*,30*,31*,32*,
33*,34*,35,36*,37*,38*,39*,
40*,41*,42*,43*,44*,45*,46*,
47*,48*,49*,50*,51*,53*,54*,
55,56*,57*,58,59*,60*,61*,
62*,63*,64*,65*,66*,67*,68*,
70*,71*,72*,73*,74*,75*,76*,
77*,78*,79*,80*,81*,82*,83*,
84*,86*,88*,89*,90*,91*,92*,
93*,94*,95*,96*,97*,98*,99*,
101*,102*,103*,104*,105*,
106,107*,108*,109,110*,111*,
112*,113,114*,115*,116*,
117*,118*,119*,120*,121*,
122*,123,124*,125*,126*,
127*,128*,129*,130*,131*,
132*,133,134*,135*,136*,
137*,138*,139*,140*,141*,
143*,144*,145*,146*,147*,
148*,149*,150,151*,152*,
153*,154*,155*,156*,157,
158*,159,160,161*,162*,163*,
164*,165*,166*,167*,168*,
170*,171*,172*,173*,174*,
175*,176*,177*,178*,179*,
180,181*,182*,183,184*,185*,
186*,187*,188*,189,190*,191,
192*,193*,194,195*,196*,
197*,198,199*,200*,201*,
202*,203,204*,205,206*,207*,
208,209*
WHITMORE...106,116,144,155,
201
WHITTAKER...206
WHITTALL...122
WHITTEN...131
WHITTINGHAM...22
WHOLLEY...75*,76
WILCOX...129,154,170,199
WILDAY...93,195*
WILDE...136
WILK(E)S...78,88,100,110,116,
121,141,179,200,206
WILKINSON...13*,16,23,35,42,
87,90,116,173,177,193,194
WILLDAY...107*,108
WILLDEY...7,91
WILLET(T)S...71,91,97,108,111,
135,173,194
WILLEY(S)...12,25,30*,34,35*,
44,45,53,60,79
WILLIAM(S)...7*,13,16,22,30*,34,
36,48*,62,70,76,83,92,98,
101,108,117,123,126,128,
134*,137,138,142,144*,146,
150*,152,153,159,160,164,
165*,167,168,170,172,175,
185*,188,190*,191,192,194,
201,202,204*,209*
WILLIES...162

WILLIM...43
WILLINGTON...42,118,120,139,
162
WILLIS...29,108,134,151,160,
177,186,199
WILLMORE...91,96
WILLOCK...76
WIL(L)SON...11,87,120,128,132,
152,161,191,210
WINCHURCH...7
WINDSOR...103
WINN...135
WINNINGTON...13,17,25,42,47,
54,60,63,64,71,72*,78,92,
101,102,140,193
WINSER...99
WISE...142,166,199
WITHERS...151,196
WITMORE...62,83
WITTALL...24,25,28,35,44,52,
58,67,76
WITTLE...15
WITTMORE...75,90
WOLFEINDALE...204
WOLLERS...44
WOLLEY...188
WOLLOWS...63
WOOD...58,87,89,98,102,118,
128,136,137,144,160,163,
177,179,190,201
WOODALL...89,97,101,102,108,
109,120,130,144,197
WOODBURN...162
WOODCROFT...87
WOODERTS...133
WOODHALL...145,165,167,177
WOODHOUSE...9,12,14,18
WOODMAN...180
WOODWARD...25,64,178,195,
198
WOOL(L)EY...10,90,174
WORLEY...163,193
WORMWOOD...207
WORSEY...50,72*,83
WORTEN...127,128
WORTON...51,65,69,74,75,86,
90,94,100*,106,111,115,116,
117*,120,132*,141,142,160,
167,176,200

WOTHEIT...12
WOTHERT...16,18,25
WRIDER...73
WRIGHT...9,20,21,27,51,64,70,
82,88,95,96,103,110,114,116,
120,123,128,131,133,149,
159,169,175,181,199,200,
203*,209
WYNN...206

YALSE...23
YARDLEY...8,14
YATES...126,147,148,178,194,
204
YORK...98,112,151,156,159,180,
185,208